Quality of Life

Quality of life is one of the most important issues facing the world today and is central to the development of social policy. Very little, however, has been written on this crucial topic.

This innovative book discusses criteria for judging attempts to raise the quality of life, including the satisfaction of basic and social needs, autonomy to enjoy life and social connectivity. It considers topics such as:

- individual well-being and health-related quality of life
- human needs – living fulfilling and flourishing lives
- poverty and social exclusion
- social solidarity, altruism and trust within communities.

Quality of Life is the first systematic presentation of this subject from both individual and collective perspectives. It provides a powerful overview of a concept which is becoming increasingly prominent in the social sciences and is essential reading for students of social policy, sociology and health studies.

David Phillips is Senior Lecturer in Social Policy in the Department of Sociological Studies, University of Sheffield. He has undertaken research on a wide range of topics in the health and social services, on community solidarity within minority communities, and on quality of life. At present he is studying the contribution of trust, reciprocity and altruism to social cohesion.

Quality of Life

Concept, policy and practice

David Phillips

Routledge
Taylor & Francis Group

LONDON AND NEW YORK

First published 2006
by Routledge
2 Park Square, Milton Park, Abingdon, Oxon OX14 4RN

Simultaneously published in the USA and Canada
by Routledge
270 Madison Ave, New York, NY 10016

Routledge is an imprint of the Taylor & Francis Group

© 2006 David Phillips

Typeset in Times New Roman by
Keystroke, Jacaranda Lodge, Wolverhampton
Printed and bound in Great Britain by
MPG Books Ltd, Bodmin

British Library Cataloguing in Publication Data
A catalogue record for this book is available from the British Library

Library of Congress Cataloging in Publication Data
Phillips, David, 1949–
Quality of life : concept, policy and practice / David Phillips.
p. cm.
Includes bibliographical referenes.
1. Quality of life. 2. Basic needs. 3. Social policy. I. Title.
HN25.P55 2006
306′.01–dc22
2005020589

ISBN10: 0–415–32354–1 (hbk)
ISBN10: 0–415–32355–x (pbk)

ISBN13: 9–78–0–415–32354–3 (hbk)
ISBN13: 9–78–0–415–32355–0 (pbk)

Dedicated to the familial bastions of my quality of life: Jane, Ruth, Alison, Sarah (and in memory of Jaffa)

Contents

Illustrations

Figures

Tables

Acknowledgements

Over a long period three people in particular have had an enormous influence on the development of my academic interest in quality of life. In the early 1970s, Kathleen Jones, then Professor of Social Administration at the University of York where I was a postgraduate student, continually advocated the normative role of social policy in creating the 'good society' which nurtures the welfare and well-being of all its members. Eric Sainsbury, Professor of Social Administration at Sheffield, and my mentor as a newly appointed lecturer in the mid-1970s and guide thereafter, always emphasised the importance of the quality of life of each person with their individual and uniquely personal needs. John Westergaard, Professor of Sociology during my early years at Sheffield, and tireless protagonist for a fair, just and equal society, constantly stressed the social structural determinants of divisions and inequalities in society. Their combined influence has ensured that this book is interdisciplinary and addresses both individual and collective aspects of quality of life.

The idea for this book emerged from my introduction to *Social Quality* by Alan Walker in the late 1990s. Subsequently, Alan and Laurent van der Maesen, Chair and Director respectively of the European Foundation on Social Quality (EFSQ) kindly invited me to join an EU Fifth Framework Thematic Network developing indicators for social quality. This was an immensely stimulating and challenging endeavour where a group of around twenty academics debated issues central to social quality across the differing cultural, social and political characters of the EU Member States. I learned a great deal from these discussions, thanks in particular to contributions from Peter Herrmann, Chiara Saraceno, Seamus O'Cinneide and Chris de Neubourg. Thanks are also due to the EFSQ staff for their support, particularly to Margo Keizer.

The person to whom I am most indebted in the writing of this book is Yitzhak Berman, with whom I have co-authored several articles and chapters on social quality over the past few years (as well as a book and many other articles on unrelated subjects). Because we have worked so closely on a topic which forms a part of a chapter of this book, it is inevitable that many of his ideas inform its writing. I hope I have acknowledged them in the text but it is likely that some remain unacknowledged and for this I ask his forbearance. Yitzhak's conscientiousness, acumen and sharply focused skills of critical appraisal have all been highly beneficial to the development of my thoughts, and Yitzhak has generously brought all of these attributes to bear in diligently and insightfully critiquing the manuscript.

Several other people read and commented on either all or part of the manuscript: Angharad Beckett, Joe d'Angelo, Sue Thompson, Sarah Huntley, Christina Prell, Louise Warwick, Andy Gibson. I owe them all thanks, plus apologies when I have not dealt effectively with their criticisms. Special thanks to John Rogers and Ollie Barton-Jones who carefully proofread the manuscript.

Others have kindly corrected my misrepresentations of their work in the text, given detailed advice and/or steered me to relevant literature: Ian Gough, Martha Nussbaum, Cathy Campbell, Heinz-Herbert Noll, Steven Vertovec, Èd Guiton, and Mark Rapley.

I wish formally to acknowledge permission to reproduce text and illustrations as follows: Guardian Newspapers for Emma Brocks, 'View from the chair' *Guardian*, 4 March 2004; Ed Guiton for 'Would I trade my life now for the old me? I'd be surprisingly reluctant', *Guardian*, 24 March 2004; BMJ Publishing Group for Figure 7.2 from *British Medical Journal*, 316, 382–5, 1998; Kluwer Law International for Figure 6.2 from *Social Quality: A Vision for Europe*, 2001; Paul Bernard for Figure 6.1 from *Social Cohesion: A Critique*, 1999; Laurent van der Maesen for Figure 6.3 from the forthcoming book on social quality.

Introduction

A first view of quality of life

'Quality of life' is one of those popular phrases we see and hear with increasing frequency. For example, at the individual level it is a commonplace in professional discussions about disability and serious illness, and at the collective level it is given serious attention in social policy debates, and is a stock-in-trade for EU policy-makers (Noll, 2002). Unfortunately, though, it is used so often, and in so many different contexts for so many different purposes, that it is difficult to pin down an agreed meaning. The problem is exacerbated by its use by different academic disciplines, each with differing traditions.

At first sight, quality of life is a simple, straightforward construct. Most of us have a reasonably clear idea of what sorts of things would enhance our own individual quality of life (and probably the quality of life of other individuals too), for example, higher pay; longer holidays; more satisfaction in our working lives; time to pursue enjoyable and satisfying leisure pursuits; emotional fulfilment in our relationships; and having a long healthy and happy life – all lived within a safe, caring and supportive local community. Similarly, there is little dispute about some of the factors which enhance *collective* quality of life – of communities, societies, and indeed, globally. On most people's lists these would include: a peaceful, non-coercive and congenial social environment; social norms of interpersonal respect; a sustainable and pollution-free physical environment; and, perhaps slightly more controversially, collectively resourced provision of education of children up to a reasonable level of literacy and numeracy; and adequate physical, economic and nutritional resources for everyone.

But the problems, disagreements and even contradictions start to emerge as we move from the general, rather vague, warm and fuzzy vision of quality of life through to more specific definitions. To give some simple examples, just three different aspects are introduced to start with: two at the individual and one at the collective level. At the individual level, first, are the objective aspects of quality of life, including income and longevity, more important than its subjective elements, such as happiness and emotional fulfilment? And, second, at the subjective level, how do we measure the difference in quality of life between, on the one hand, someone who is happy but leads a pleasure-seeking life, making less of themselves than they could do and, on the other, a person who fulfils their human capabilities, seeks enlightenment rather than pleasure, has a satisfying life but is perhaps less happy than their more hedonistic counterpart? Does the happier or the more enlightened person have a higher level of subjective well-being and how does this translate into comparing the quality of their lives? These questions are as old as intellectual thought itself.

At the collective level the problems are perhaps more intense. The blueprint for a society which maximises its members' quality of life – the vision of a 'perfect society' – has also been the centre of debates by philosophers, political scientists and sociologists since the time of the ancient Greeks. For example, there have been huge ideological disagreements about the values that might underpin a non-coercive and congenial social environment and the mechanisms for providing and distributing adequate resources. Put rather crudely, one set of these arguments boils down to the relative merits of, and the balance to be struck between, liberty and equality.

No-one with a balanced interest in collective quality of life would want all of one and none of the other. Unbridled liberty with no checks and balances is inherently unstable in that the exercise of liberty by the strong could enslave the weak and therefore deprive them of their liberty. So even the most ardent libertarian must accept some constraints in order to maintain liberty for all: in other words, equal access to liberty. Similarly, complete equality is almost inconceivable: equality of income is imaginable, and some societies have striven to achieve this, but total equality – equality of *condition* – would require such draconian interventions in citizens' daily lives as to deny their individuality. This vision of total equality has been wickedly satirised in Kurt Vonnegut's fictional figure of the Handicapper General who forces fit people to wear heavy weights, highly intelligent people to wear headphones permanently emanating distracting noises, and beautiful people to wear disfiguring masks (Vonnegut, 1994). A chilling example of a non-fictional – but unrealistic – attempt to impose absolute equality can be seen in Ceauşescu's Romania where his ultimate aim was to ensure that everyone was thinking the same thoughts (Deletant, 1995).

So in the world of realistic ideological debates, no libertarian would deny the importance of *equal access* to liberty and, indeed, many would support equality of opportunity, aimed at enabling everyone to live their lives to the full. Similarly, no realistic egalitarian would deny individuals the right to a range of individual liberties, so long as they do not adversely affect the lives or life chances of other people. The fundamental difference between these two perspectives is that libertarians, while supporting some sorts of procedural equality, do not believe that *substantive* inequality in itself is a bad thing; indeed, they welcome and embrace it as a defining characteristic of a vibrant and thriving society. For them, *coercion* is the main enemy, whereas egalitarians are willing to constrain the liberty of some people by redistributing income from the rich to the poor in order to reduce substantive inequalities.

Both sides have to make compromises. Libertarians have to endure some level of coercion by the state in the form of paying taxes and therefore reducing their freedom, in order to pay for policing, national defence, and the relief of destitution or avoidance of starvation. Taking this qualification into account, though, libertarians believe in an unequal society where people are responsible for their own quality of life and are free to pursue it in accordance with their own wishes. The situation for egalitarians is less clear-cut: most egalitarians would claim that they value freedom almost as highly, if not as highly, as equality. But freedom for the egalitarian has a different emphasis from that of liberty for the libertarian. For egalitarians it is *positive* freedom that is important, in other words, the freedom *to* do things, such as to be nourished, or educated, rather than the freedom *from* coercion or constraint that is so central to libertarianism. Maximising this freedom, by distributing it as equally as possible, will lead to some coercion, reducing some people's liberty by requiring them to give up some resources to be redistributed to the less well-off, but this is a price the egalitarian is willing to pay. From an egalitarian perspective, quality of life is important at both an individual and a collective level whereas for a libertarian it is situated firmly at the individual level.

Underpinning these differences are different views on human nature: for the libertarian, human beings are essentially *individualists*, seeking their own quality of life as discrete, independent, free-thinking beings, whereas for the egalitarian, humans are essentially *social*, at the centre of interlocking rights, duties, obligations and collective identities. So the foundational criteria for quality of life are completely different in these two ideological perspectives.

There are similar ontological differences separating proponents of objective versus subjective approaches to individual well-being. Subjectivists focus on pleasure as the basic building block of human happiness or quality of life, following the work of Jeremy Bentham, who invented the 'pleasure principle' and the notion of an 'hedonic calculus' where the aim is to maximise pleasure. John Stuart Mill built on this precept by developing a theory of 'utility' which ultimately leads t o the prescription for maximising quality of life of the *greatest happiness of the greatest number*. Objectivists, on the other hand, have a radically different perspective: for them the important questions to ask are whether people are healthy, well fed, appropriately housed, economically secure and well educated rather than whether they feel happy; their central concern is to do with meeting *needs*. So, again, there are two completely different criteria for quality of life: subjectivists promote happiness whereas objectivists want to meet needs.

These examples of different approaches at each end of the social spectrum give a flavour of some of the many debates and discussions about quality of life. Their purpose is to indicate the challenges in drawing together the often contradictory strands of the debates about quality of life and to be a prelude to stating the major purposes of this book, which are twofold: to demonstrate the importance of quality of life, and to try to give a coherent account of it – the latter task being more difficult than might appear at first.

Overview of the book

The first aim of this book is to demonstrate the centrality of quality of life to the social sciences in general and to sociology and social policy, in particular. In doing so, it gives an overview of contemporary social science coverage of formulations of quality of life and explores conceptual, theoretical, empirical and policy-related aspects of different notions of quality of life. It addresses the contested nature of what it is, how it can be understood, and what steps can be taken to optimise it. Because the term has only come into common use in the past forty years or so, it might be assumed that quality of life might not be such an important construct as is being claimed here. However, this is partly to do with changes in fashion in common usage. In ancient Greek times the construct was often labelled 'the good life'; and more recently the term 'welfare' was its most common label until this took on the excess baggage from the 'welfare state', 'being on welfare' and other specific and sometimes derogatory connotations. Not only are there different labels for quality of life, but it also takes on different meanings in the different academic disciplines. For example, most economists account for quality of life through money values whereas in some areas of health sciences it is linked to levels of functional ability in undertaking daily activities.

The second aim is to compare and critically appraise these different approaches with a view to paving the way for the development of a conceptualisation of quality of life which, among other things, incorporates the individual and collective and the subjective and objective and which can be applied in relation to conflicting macro-ideological frameworks. In order to be fully effective, such a conceptualisation needs to be theoretically robust and intuitively comprehensible and must be capable of being operationalised and applied in practice. Because of the wide breadth of ideological and social science disciplinary approaches to the subject, this is no easy task, particularly in relation to potential contradictions and incompatibilities between the two ends of the ideological spectrum. The disciplinary differences, though great, are less intractable and it is hoped that progress can be made in bringing these together.

In order to try to effect cross-disciplinary accommodation and synthesis, the nature of quality of life is addressed from a perspective which is both multi-disciplinary and holistic. This is done by incorporating and integrating the insights from each relevant discipline rather than treating them as separate entities. In substantive terms the book deals with quality of life as incorporating subjective and objective individual well-being and quality of family, community and societal life, the latter mostly with reference to constructs of social capital, social inclusion, social exclusion and social cohesion. In disciplinary terms, in addition to social policy and sociology, the book also draws upon philosophy, political theory, economics, psychology, development studies, health and disability studies, public health and epidemiology, and, to a very limited extent, socio-biology.

Here it is worth pointing out what this book is *not* aiming to achieve. It does not draw on the extensive empiricist discussion of the 'social indicators' literature; it does not address methodological or technical issues in measuring quality of life; and does not describe in detail any specific quality of life research instruments, particularly those in clinical psychology and medicine – all these have been covered in great depth elsewhere (see Hagerty *et al.*, 2001; Rapley, 2003; Bowling, 1991, 1995a; and Fayers and Machin, 2000 respectively).

The starting point of analysis here is the self-perceived quality of life, the subjective well-being (SWB) of the individual. Chapter 1 begins with the most elemental building block of an individual's SWB, with the sensation of pleasure which is the actual experience of happiness. Then the two other major elements of SWB, pain and satisfaction, are introduced prior to an overview of empirical findings on which groups have the highest levels of SWB. The analytical task of the book then begins in earnest with an inquiry into why people at some stages of their lives, in some demographic groups, and living in some countries, tend to have higher levels of SWB than others. Three different sets of possible explanations – related to genetics, to politics and national identity, and finally to money and access to resources more generally – are investigated in some depth.

At this point a foray is made into philosophical theories of quality of life with a critical appraisal of the appropriateness of SWB as an operationalisation of quality of life in the light of its avowedly hedonic nature. An alternative, 'eudaimonic' interpretation of individual quality of life is presented which is based less on the arguably shallow foundation of pleasure and more on the profounder attribute of self-realisation or 'flourishing'. This interpretation is the basis for a set of theories of individual quality of life based on notions of self-determination and psychological well-being. These introduce the concept of autonomy which is central to major theories of quality of life in a social setting that are predicated on enabling people to fully exercise their human capabilities. In other words, these eudaimonic approaches stress people's essential *humanity*.

Two further sets of individual approaches to quality of life are introduced here. The first, and crucially important, of these refers to people's self-defined verdicts – what they themselves think are the most important elements of their quality of life. Four factors emerge as the most important: (1) their relationships with family and friends; (2) their own health; (3) the health of their family and friends; and then (4) their finances and standard of living. It is noteworthy that finances only came fourth; this has significant consequences for utilitarian approaches to quality of life discussed in Chapter 3. Finally, objective approaches to quality of life, such as income and living conditions, are introduced. These do not necessarily have any causal relationship with SWB at all and indeed a section of the chapter is devoted to the, at first sight, puzzling phenomenon of the 'happy poor'. The chapter concludes with two short case studies of individual quality of life constructs: Veenhoven's *happy life expectancy*; and Raphael's *being, belonging and becoming*.

Following on from the importance attributed by people to their own and their relatives' health, Chapter 2 is entirely devoted to health-related quality of life (HRQOL). This topic is highly interdisciplinary in nature and draws heavily upon specialist areas such as medical ethics, palliative care, health economics and medical sociology. It is, of course, also of immense practical importance in the fields of social policy, health policy and medical and health care practice. Many of the issues discussed in this chapter are of profound existential significance – in other words, literally matters of life and death – and are centrally concerned with the *value* of life as well as its quality. The scope of the chapter is informed by the very wide-ranging definition of health adopted by the World Health Organization (WHO) as a state of complete physical mental and social well-being, hence the importance of wider social policy as well as health policy because the causes of health and sickness reside more in the society at large than in the health care and medical treatment systems.

The early part of the chapter is taken up with a discussion of the striking differences between two apparently equally valid approaches to HRQOL: personal and experiential verdicts given by people actually suffering from the medical conditions under discussion versus what are called consensus and normative verdicts made by panels comprising healthy members of the general public faced with the hypothetical prospect of suffering from such a condition. Surprisingly, people actually suffering from debilitating conditions normally report that these result in relatively small negative effects on their quality of life whereas members of the general public attribute much higher detrimental effects. Among people with long-term disabilities, the findings are even more paradoxical: this phenomenon is explored via a case study. The upshot of these studies is that the resources allocated to medical care would be under threat if the views of patients were taken as seriously as those of the general public or indeed of the medical profession.

Even more difficult issues are addressed when assessing the role of quality of life instruments in deciding who gets which treatment and when making 'end-of-life' decisions such as when to turn off life-support machines or withhold life-saving treatment. The normative and consensual approaches are used in assessing the relative values of different medical procedures, particularly through measures such as *Quality Adjusted Life Years* (QALYs) in a form of cost-benefit analysis. But as well as being used to choose between medical procedures, they can be used to choose between *people* so that faced with two people with the same needs, the procedure might be offered to the person with the highest potential QALY outcome, for example, the younger or the more intellectually able of the two. Such a use of HRQOL in effect puts different values on different people's lives and can be seen to be particularly detrimental to people with learning disabilities who can thus be attributed with having lower *quality* and perhaps thus lower *value* lives. Some evidence is presented that, in countries where end-of-life decisions are relatively common, there is a higher incidence of such decisions being made in respect of people with learning disabilities than other members of the general public (Rapley, 2003).

The final part of the chapter returns to the WHO definition of health and situates it firmly in its social context via an ecological model of health, comprising the concentric spheres of the individual and their family and kinship network (the micro-system), their local community (together forming the meso-system) and through to the nation, including national identity and government services and then on to international and global factors (the macro-system). This is linked in with Berkman and Glass's (2000) 'upstream–downstream' social epidemiology model based on social network theories. There are four pathways in their model: (1) social support; (2) social engagement and attachment; (3) social influence; and (4) access to resources and goods.

The ecological and social epidemiological models place quality of life in its social context, moving inexorably away from an individualistic and arguably atomistic

SWB-oriented perspective that could be claimed to be based upon seeing each person as 'an island'. Chapter 3 places the debate on quality of life firmly within this social perspective. It begins with a critique of the philosophical basis of utilitarianism and its operationalisation in the field of positivistic economics through achieving 'experienced utility' by the satisfaction of desires, normally through purchases in the marketplace. This critique leads to a move from hedonic to eudaimonic approaches by replacing the 'actual desires' basis of utilitarianism with a philosophical edifice based on 'informed desires', that is on what a person would desire if they had full access to all relevant knowledge and information. This leads into the world of normative philosophy with the notion of *prudential values* as the basis for ascertaining what such informed desires might look like. Prudential values concern what makes people's lives valuable to themselves, how good human life can be and how it can be made better.

In terms of theory of knowledge, prudential values are predicated upon what is taken to constitute a *characteristically human life* and this is based on our mutual intelligibility as human beings, and ultimately on notions of intersubjectivity derived from Ludwig Wittgenstein's proposition that humans are unable to make sense of each other unless they share certain basic values. The most central of these values – that is, the core prudential values – are held in common with utilitarianism (and thus SWB) and are enjoyment and avoidance of pain. Other non-core but nonetheless 'heavyweight' prudential values include: accomplishment, freedom, autonomy, aspiration, understanding and significant relationships. The remaining prudential values are less intellectually heavyweight but are closer to the core in that they are essential for survival: minimum levels of nutrition, health, sanitation, shelter, rest and security; and basic intellectual and physical capacities and literacy.

These latter, survival-based, values also form the basis of another perspective on quality of life: the needs-based approach. While the heavyweight prudential values may be intellectually worthwhile and eudaimonic in nature, they are not essential for survival, unlike needs which – by definition – are. The most foundational and indeed minimalist need-based approach is *basic needs*: enough nutrition, health provision and basic education to enable a person to have a minimally decent life. Such an approach says absolutely nothing about quality of life above this 'decency' threshold: its only purpose is to try to ensure that everyone reaches the threshold.

Another approach with affinities to basic needs but having a much wider coverage is the United Nations human development index (HDI). This has three elements: (1) a country's per capita gross national product (GNP); (2) its average life expectancy; and (3) its literacy level (augmented by years of schooling). The HDI is rather problematic in that GNP gives no indication about levels of inequality and thus cannot indicate what proportion of the population is below the needs threshold. An advantage of including GNP is that it can thus provide a ranking of all countries in the world whereas basic needs focuses only on those with some citizens below the threshold. Therefore, the HDI provides a link between the income-oriented utilitarian perspective and the subsistence-oriented basic needs approach.

The most well-developed and theoretically important needs-based approach is Doyal and Gough's (1991) theory of human need (THN). In addition to its rigorous theoretical and conceptual logic, the THN has the most thoroughgoing and elegant justification for a society's obligation to meet needs as a necessary precondition to enable individuals to fulfil their obligation to perform the social duties required by membership of that society. Thus, unambiguous needs, according to the THN, necessarily entail social rights – but these needs have to be unambiguous and therefore have to be rigorously defined and parsimonious in nature. The THN edifice is based upon two universal needs-based goals – avoiding serious harm and the ability to participate – which in turn lead to two primary needs: physical health and autonomy of agency. Further, a series of intermediate needs have to be met in order to ensure the meeting of the primary needs. There is another major element to the THN outside the main lines derived from avoidance of pain and participation. This is a 'liberation facet' which has a universal goal of *critical participation* with an associated primary need of critical autonomy.

The main lines of the THN encapsulate a tightly argued, obligatory, hierarchical conceptual framework resulting in a highly specific list of requirements. One of the other internationally influential models of quality of life has almost an exactly opposite starting point. Amatrya Sen's (1993) *capabilities* approach is wide-ranging, freedom-oriented, non-hierarchical and in it he emphatically and deliberately refuses to specify any comprehensive list. Sen's basis is in terms of freedoms to choose between various alternatives in order to do valuable acts or to reach valuable states of well-being. According to Sen, we flourish as human beings by having the ability and the freedom to choose between different 'capability sets', in other words, between different collections of these 'doings' and 'beings'. So whereas meeting specified needs is central to all needs-based approaches, having the freedom to choose to exercise one's capabilities is central to Sen's approach.

There is one facet of the capabilities approach, that of *basic capabilities*, which results in a similar outcome to that of basic needs in relation to the most deprived groups who are living at the subsistence level. But beyond that, Sen refuses to be specific or to produce a capability list precisely because for him freedom to choose is so central to the notion of capabilities. This is a controversial position, though, and one other proponent of a capabilities approach, Martha Nussbaum (1995, 2000, 2006), takes a radically different perspective and produces a list of capabilities not dissimilar to the prudential values or THN lists.

Her perspective, like the THN, has a strong basis in social justice and she demands equal opportunities for all to live a flourishing life. Nussbaum, unlike Sen, argues that there are universal norms of human capability and, more pertinently here, she is explicit about the functionings which make up the good life which, for her are based on Aristotelian notions of practical reason and on other-regarding affiliations. Indeed, these notions are the starting point for the two most significant capabilities on her list, with practical reason incorporating critical reflection and conscience, and affiliation including friendship, love and compassion.

Apart from utilitarianism, all the constructs discussed in Chapter 3 are centrally concerned with meeting needs and avoiding bodily and material deprivation. Similarly, the social affiliation aspect of human lives plays a large role in these constructs. These two themes are the major subject matter of Chapter 4 which deals with poverty and social exclusion. A central feature in this chapter is people's quality of life in relation to the communities and societies in which they live and it concerns both relative and relational issues. Thus, the discussion of poverty deals not only with absolute subsistence-oriented approaches but also, and more centrally, with the different sorts of relative approaches to the definition and amelioration of poverty, including the citizenship, social needs and income-threshold-based definitions. The focus in the discussion of poverty is not so much on the political debates about its existence and extent but on the implication for quality of life of the relationship between access to disposable resources and both 'objective' (needs-based) and 'subjective' (desires-based) conceptualisations of well-being.

The discussion of social exclusion or, more accurately, social inclusion and social exclusion, is more extensive and is concerned with both social processes and outcomes. The breadth of the construct, covering social, cultural, political and moral discourses as well as dealing with material issues, makes it especially relevant to the notion of quality of life which is similarly holistic in nature. Indeed, social exclusion and inclusion are major themes in subsequent chapters dealing with macro and societal quality of life constructs. However, social exclusion is by no means a straightforward construct and is not easy to pin down. Some commentators have even gone so far as to say that it is unusable in practical terms because there is so much imprecision and confusion about what it means. A considerable part of Chapter 4 is devoted to an attempt to disentangle its various meanings and to give a coherent account of its different facets.

Three different manifestations of social exclusion are identified: (1) as an *outcome*, affecting individuals, groups and communities; (2) as a *process* whereby social institutions influence and determine who is and is not able to belong to a society; and (3), following Wessels and Miedema (2002), in *causal* terms in relation to societal norms and values associated with trust. Broadly speaking, outcome-oriented manifestations can be seen as inhabiting the same territory as the broader definitions of poverty whereby social exclusion is seen as multiple deprivation with an extreme form representing what Room (1999) has called 'catastrophic rupture'. It has to be noted, though, that this multiple deprivation does not *necessarily* include material deprivation (though it nearly always does): some of the most infamous cases of extreme social exclusion in the twentieth century, for example, the Holocaust, have been associated with socio-cultural rather than material factors.

Social exclusionary processes can be seen as the triggers that control entry into and exit from this multiple deprivation, often emanating from the labour market, the legal system and state education and welfare services. These processes can operate at the macro-, meso- and micro-levels, as in the ecological model of quality of life. The causes of social exclusion are linked to normative value systems particularly in relation to constructs such as social capital and social cohesion which are the subject of Chapter 5.

It is in Chapter 5 that collective aspects of quality of life take centre stage. According to most commentators, the constructs of social capital and social cohesion operate entirely at a collective level and cannot be disaggregated or owned by individuals. In general, social capital can be seen as comprising the composition and distribution of the social resources available in society, and social cohesion refers to the norms and institutions that keep society together. These social resources reside in networks, both horizontal, between people and groups at the same level in society and often face-to-face, or vertical between groups at different levels such as those linking community groups and local government representatives and officials. Perhaps the most important of these resources are trust and reciprocity.

A continuum can be seen from social capital through to social cohesion where elements of social structure become included in the vertical networks, along with norms of civic responsibility and generalised as well as specific trust – what Fukuyama (1999) calls a 'wide radius of trust'. Social cohesion itself can be seen as comprising collective values giving a society social and cultural coherence and a binding normative framework along with integrative social institutions with high levels of efficiency and integrity. When social cohesion is at its most highly integrative, these collective values will incorporate high levels of reciprocity and mutual dependence and may be predicated on egalitarian theories of social justice.

Without social capital and social cohesion, there is no society and therefore their existence is essential. However, it is not always the case that 'more is better' with these constructs. Unlike poverty and social exclusion, which are, in general, negative and counter-productive and therefore should be minimised or eliminated, both social capital and social cohesion are attributes which need to be optimised rather than maximised in order to ensure the most beneficial consequences for collective quality of life. For example, organisations such as criminal gangs and the Mafia have high levels of trust and reciprocity or what can be called strong 'bonding' social capital, whereas social capital is perhaps at its most beneficial where there are loose networks of weaker linkages both between as well as within groups – in other words, 'bridging' social capital. Similarly, high levels of homogeneity in relation to social cohesion, while resulting in a tightly knit and highly cohesive society, can lead to intolerance of, and discrimination against, non-conformists and anyone else who is 'different'. Here a society with a less intense but more heterogeneous or pluralistic form of social cohesion would be more likely to promote higher levels of collective quality of life even though it is less overtly 'cohesive'.

This issue of the *nature* as well as the strength of social cohesion is discussed in the final section of the chapter where the relationship between social exclusion and social cohesion is explored in depth. It is concluded that there can be a tension between social cohesion, on the one hand, and the interaction between social exclusion and social inclusion on the other. Societies with high levels of social cohesion tend to have a high *quality* of social inclusion, for example, via the provision of extensive welfare and social security provision. But this is expensive, and a price of such cohesion is often a high *quantity* of social exclusion: it is not easy to join such a homogeneously cohesive society. On the other hand, a society with more pluralistic social cohesion and which encourages diversity, may have less social exclusion along with a lower threshold of social inclusion – in other words, it is easier to enter and be included in a society which is less homogeneous and places less emphasis on 'togetherness', belonging, reciprocal obligations and shared identity.

Chapter 6 brings together themes from all the preceding chapters in addressing macro or overarching quality of life constructs. The three major constructs discussed – Bernard's *democratic dialectic*; Berger-Schmitt and Noll's *overarching quality of life*; and Beck, van der Maesen and Walker's *social quality* – all address issues relating to social exclusion, social cohesion and social justice, and the latter two also incorporate both individual and collective and subjective and objective perspectives on quality of life.

The first of these, Bernard's democratic dialectic, interposes social cohesion, or solidarity, between the two polar political goals of liberty and equality in a conscious revisiting of the watchwords of the French Revolution, with solidarity replacing fraternity. Part of his aim is to tighten up what he sees as the 'quasi concept' of social cohesion. He does this by constructing a typology, classifying social cohesion into three spheres of activity – economic, political and socio-cultural – each having both a formal and substantive identity, giving a total of six dimensions. He presents liberty, equality and solidarity as a triangle where there are tensions between the three points, both overall and as three pairs. For Bernard, the optimum balance between liberty and equality is struck by achieving maximum levels of inclusion, social justice, legitimacy, participation, recognition and belonging. His analysis is at the collective level only, so it does not incorporate insights in relation to individuals' quality of life per se but his formulation has the great merit of being overtly applicable to the issues of social cohesion in multicultural societies as it is specifically oriented to the situation in Canada.

Social cohesion is also central in Berger-Schmitt and Noll's (2000) overarching quality of life construct which has been developed with the aim of tracking changes in welfare in Europe resulting from EU policy initiatives. Unlike Bernard, they consciously address individual quality of life and they do this in relation to both subjective (cognitive and affective) and objective (material and environmental) dimensions in one of the three components of their model. A second component is at the other end of the spectrum and deals with macro issues of sustainability encompassing human, physical, social and natural capital. Sustainability has two dimensions: first, in relation to current and future generations; and, second, *within* generations in contemporary society. Social cohesion is their third component, which again is split into two dimensions: first, reduction in disparities, inequalities and social exclusion; and second, strengthening of relations, interactions and ties – or, in other words, social capital.

The strengths of this construct lie in its well-developed operationalisation in terms of components, dimensions, domains and indicators in relation to its explicit goal of evaluating the impact of specific EU legislation and policy. It is worth noting that its formulation of social cohesion is both innovative in its juxtaposition of social exclusion and social capital as two discrete sub-categories and also politically radical in its espousal of egalitarian ideological ends.

The final construct discussed in Chapter 6, social quality, is similarly radical. It is defined as: 'the extent to which citizens are able to participate in the social and economic life of their communities under conditions which enhance their well-being and individual potential' (Beck *et al.*, 1997a: 3). The social quality of a society is not just the accumulation of the quality of life of each of its individual members: it incorporates collective as well as individual attributes and is holistic and overtly egalitarian in its orientation. It has many similarities to the overarching quality of life construct but its major difference is that social quality is explicitly theoretical in its aim of both encapsulating and explaining societal quality of life.

Social quality theory is predicated on the proposition that the subject matter of 'the social' refers to the outcomes of the dialectic between the processes of self-realisation of individuals as social beings and the processes resulting in the formation of social identities. According to social quality proponents, the resulting 'constitutive interdependency' is then determined by interaction between four conditional factors: (1) socio-economic security, defined as the extent to which people have sufficient resources over time; (2) social inclusion, the extent to which people have access to institutions and social relations; (3) social cohesion, the nature of social relations based on shared identities, values and norms; and (4) social empowerment, the extent to which the personal capabilities of individual people and their ability to act are enhanced by social relations.

Chapter 7 commences with another overarching quality of life construct, Hancock's (2001) public health model, which again takes a social justice perspective. He combines three systems – an adequately prosperous economy, a viable environment and a convivial community – to produce the overarching constructs of *liveability, sustainability* and *equitability*. Together, these are the ingredients of what Hancock conceives as a 'healthy society'. As with the constructs in Chapter 6, this is a radical model which is predicated on the notion that meeting human needs is not just a worthwhile goal but is also a societal requirement and the unalienable right of all citizens. A particularly noteworthy aspect of Hancock's approach is the notion of a convivial community which depends upon high stocks of what he calls 'community capital', that is a community's resources maximised and augmented by harmonious participation.

The theme of community social capital is also paramount in the second part of Chapter 7 where a detailed study of two communities with similar low income levels but different health profiles provides the basis for the development of Campbell's (1999) health pathways model. Here, the healthier community had high levels of civic engagement but it did not have strong face-to-face local networks. The less healthy community, on the other hand, had strong, face-to-face bonding networks, often in public spaces, which gave emotional support, but were only horizontal in nature and were not civically engaged. In her model, macro-social relations interact with community social relations, which are themselves dependent upon interactions between various aspects of social capital including trust, reciprocity, civic engagement, local identity and density of local networks. Together these influence psycho-social mediators (including social support and relative deprivation) and behavioural and physiological pathways to determine health outcomes including levels of well-being, mortality and morbidity.

Hancock's and Campbell's constructs set the scene for the culmination of all the themes developed in the book: a discussion of what factors lead to some societies having higher quality of life than others. The discussion is based on Richard

Wilkinson's (1996, 2005) thesis that, for developed societies at least, it is not material factors but psycho-social factors that determine quality of life, healthiness and life expectancy. According to Wilkinson, other things being equal, the most egalitarian societies are healthier than the wealthier societies.

He argues that this is because egalitarian societies have a better and more nurturing social fabric than unequal societies and it is their social cohesion that is the crucial factor. These societies are more trusting; they have a stronger sense of social morality and community life; they have high quality, health-promoting social networks and are highly supportive of their members. All this leads to higher levels of subjective well-being (SWB) and self-esteem and to reductions in levels of stress and thus in morbidity and mortality rates.

On the other hand, in unequal societies, according to Wilkinson, it is not the level of absolute income and material circumstances of the poorest citizens that increase their death rates but their relative deprivation and psycho-social characteristics. So it is not poor nutrition, lack of money or inadequate housing, etc. which disadvantage them but the psychological burdens associated with stress and poor self-esteem resulting from their low social status:

> To feel depressed, cheated, bitter, desperate, vulnerable, frightened, angry, worried about debts or job and housing insecurity; to feel devalued, useless, helpless, uncared for, hopeless, isolated, anxious and a failure . . . It is the chronic stress arising from feelings like these which does the damage.
>
> (Wilkinson, 1996: 215)

Wilkinson's thesis is highly controversial and has sparked off a major debate. Three alternative theories are explored: individual SWB-related, psychological pathways (excluding social cohesion); neo-materialist explanations, relating to poor health services and systematic under-investment in social infrastructure in poor areas; and an absolute income explanation which claims that egalitarian societies *do* have lower death rates but this is all due to a statistical artefact, that absolute, not relative, death rates are the main causal factor. There is considerable evidence to support all these alternative accounts. Whereas the jury is still out in relation to social cohesion, locally based studies support the individual psycho-social pathways account, and the detrimental effects of poor health services and infra-structure are incontrovertible. Perhaps most importantly, the absolute income approach, while having different causal mechanisms to Wilkinson's thesis, leads to the same policy conclusions: that the best way to increase the health of a society is to make it more equal by redistributing resources from the richest to providing health-related resources to the poorest.

Chapter 8 brings together the threads from all these chapters but before doing this it identifies cross-cutting themes. The first of these are three sets of pathways which permeate quality of life from the individual to the collective settings. Pathway one links subjective well-being and health in terms of both the proximate and ultimate causes of stress in the context of the roles of perceived injustice in society as an alternative to perceptions of inequality. In these circumstances it is possible to conceive of a just but unequal society with high levels of social cohesion, thus providing an explanation for the 'happy poor' phenomenon discussed in Chapter 1. Pathway two provides a link – albeit tenuous and indirect – between Doyal and Gough's theory of human need, on the one hand, and utilitarianism and subjective well-being, on the other, via Sen's capabilities approach. Pathway three deals with material well-being, poverty and quality of life through consensual and normative socially defined requirements for fulfilling the duties of citizenship. Insights derived from each of the pathways inform the conceptual development of quality of life discussed at the end of the chapter.

Issues related to thresholds and measuring the different quality of life constructs are then discussed, not from a methodological perspective but in relation to the nature of the constructs themselves. Core values permeating the different approaches are then identified along with tensions and conflicts underlying them. The biggest is the one used to introduce the book: individualism and libertarianism versus collectivism and egalitarianism, along with middle-range and interconnecting approaches. Another relates to hedonism and whether or not it can be construed as a collective as well as an individual attribute. Then the potential tensions between individual freedom and autonomy and social cohesion are explored. The last topic, avoidance of pain, is the only one on which there is universal agreement, and this is used as the basis for the delineation of core attributes of quality of life and as a foundation for the definition of quality of life at the end of the chapter.

This sets the scene for a discussion of the major themes from the individual, social, collective and the overarching and holistic approaches discussed in Chapters 1 to 7. Particular attention is paid here to the implications for quality of life theoretical development of the complexities and ambiguities surrounding the conceptualisation and operationalisation of social capital and social cohesion and their relationship with social inclusion and social exclusion.

The conclusion of the book is in the section on the principles of quality of life. This begins with pen portraits of the characteristics of quality of life and is followed by the exposition of core attributes of quality of life, five at the individual level and five at the collective level. These are then used in the construction of a definition of quality of life, both in a discursive and shorter version. The book ends with a brief discussion of unfinished business, including the operationalisation of the definition, conceptual developments and, finally, a prescription for immediate, practical steps to increase contemporary quality of life.

1 Quality of life and the individual

This chapter starts with the basic building blocks of quality of life, with the actual sensations of pleasure and pain that are the foundations of feelings of happiness. Then the important notion of subjective well-being (SWB) is introduced and explored in relation to two big questions: 'What makes us happy?' and 'Why are some people happier than others?' The search for answers to these questions moves from individual, genetic and biological explanations related to personality, through to economic perspectives – is it all down to money? – on to large-scale social and political aspects of the culture and politics in different societies. Along the way, these questions are explored from two different perspectives, incorporating people's own verdicts on what affects their quality of life as well as the views of social science academics.

The second part of the chapter builds on these insights in moving from notions of SWB towards a wider view of 'quality of life', bringing in other aspects in addition to people's subjective appraisals. The chapter concludes with some case studies of visions of what a good quality of life looks like.

Happiness, life satisfaction, subjective well-being

Happiness, life satisfaction and subjective well-being are mutually interrelated – and indeed they are all closely connected with the notion of quality of life – but they are also highly contested constructs. 'Happiness' is perhaps the most contested; indeed, the disagreement about happiness is at an absolutely basic level. One of the leading figures in the study of quality of life and a Nobel Laureate, Daniel Kahneman does not trust people's own statements and beliefs on this topic. Indeed, he goes further than this and claims: 'they do not generally know how happy they are, and they must construct an answer to that question whenever it is raised' (Kahneman, 1999). He claims that the starting point should not be people's subjective views about how happy they are but instead objective measures of those sensations that are associated with the real-time *feeling* of happiness – in other words, *objective happiness*.

Objective happiness and pleasure

The idea of objective happiness is at first sight fanciful and bizarre in that it can lead to a person being happy when not actually thinking they are happy and – potentially much more problematically – can at least in principle lead to a person thinking they are happy when they are not happy in this objective sense. The first of these alternatives is not really too problematic so long as the person is not actively believing that they are unhappy. This is because it is not necessary for a person to be articulating a sensation, feeling or mood at the moment they are experiencing it. Indeed, people's happiest moments are often when they are too deeply engrossed in an activity to be self-conscious about their state of mind. The second alternative is much more problematic because if a person is believing that they have a certain mental state at a time when an objective measurement is demonstrating that this is not the case, then the person, again within this formulation, is either deceiving themselves or else is attaching a different and, from Kahneman's perspective, incorrect meaning to the word.

It is instructive to look at each of these alternatives in some more detail but first it is necessary to be rather more specific about what objective happiness is. For Warburton (1996: 2) it is a pleasant physiological sensation caused by a neurochemical response of the dopamine system of the brain to external stimuli. He notes that drugs used to treat depression act on these brain systems, as do a range of drugs which produce 'anhedonia' (a loss of pleasure). He claims that people strive to achieve objective happiness by maximising their contact with pleasurable stimuli. This is good for individuals and, he claims, good for the species in that the sensations associated with sexual interactions and consuming food are in general pleasurable: 'it would seem of evolutionary importance that these biological experiences should be associated with a feeling of well-being which results in the repetition of the experience' (ibid.: 3).

The important aspect of this proposition for the purposes of this book is not the role of pleasurable experience in the propagation of the species but in relation to theories of quality of life. Warburton explicitly links this seeking of pleasurable sensations to a utilitarian rational choice economic theory: 'This is an attractive theory of rational choice because it proposes a single metric by which individuals choose among competing alternatives' (ibid.: 2). This 'single metric' is the basis for utilitarian theory, in at least some of its manifestations. This is discussed at length in Chapter 3.

Kahneman (1999) has a similar starting point to Warburton's but he develops the utilitarian perspective even further. For Kahneman, it is of primary importance to maximise *good experiences* rather than maximising 'satisfaction' or SWB: according to Kahneman, true well-being is not necessarily related to a person's judgement of how happy they are. Instead:

> Real-time measures of experience can be obtained, stored without error, and aggregated to yield a measure of objective well-being that is anchored in the reality of present experience, not in fallible reconstructions and evaluations of the past.
>
> (Kahneman, 1999: 22)

These real-time measures are of what Kahneman calls *instant utility*, that is, being pleased as an attribute of experience at a particular moment. The term *utility* is crucial here because the datum of instant utility is the absolute indivisible basis for a bottom-up utilitarian approach: here the greatest happiness of the greatest number is the maximised aggregation of each datum of instant utility. So Kahneman's theory of objective happiness is an extraordinarily rigorous utilitarian vision of quality of life. Indeed, it is perhaps the ultimate presentation of utilitarianism because it is impossible to imagine a more stringent foundation that that of instant utility.

It is important to note here that there is no place whatsoever for an assessment of either subjective well-being or even *objective good fortune* in what Kahneman calls his 'objective and normatively justified definition of true well-being'. This is because, as noted above, for him, true *objective* well-being is anchored in 'the reality of present experience' (ibid.: 22).

Therefore, to return to the two questions asked above, according to Kahneman, it is indeed possible for a person to *think* they are happy, and to be in circumstances of great objective good fortune while not being objectively happy and, conversely, for a person to be objectively happy while having low levels of both subjective happiness and of objective good fortune: 'All combinations of levels of good or bad fortune, objective happiness or misery are possible, *and are all probably quite common*' (ibid.: 5; italics in original).

It was noted above that the idea of objective happiness appears rather bizarre, and the quote above from Kahneman perhaps underlines this. On a practical level, it is possible to think of the most paradoxical examples where the pursuit of pleasurable stimuli leads to extreme situations, such as an early death for a person addicted to pleasurable but dangerous drugs.

Also there is another potential problem with the link which Kahneman makes between 'objective happiness' and 'good experience'. This is that different people may well have – and as seen later in this chapter, indeed *do* have – different levels of dopamine and related chemicals in their bodies because of genetic factors rather than in response to external stimulus, that is, some people have happier personalities or dispositions than other people. These 'happy people' will have greater 'instant utility', irrespective of external experiences. So objective happiness may comprise two parts, one genetic and the other experiential.

This opens the unnerving possibility of a further way to increase instant utility and objective happiness: that is by genetic engineering via manipulating the chemicals in people's bodies. There are less sophisticated ways of achieving this aim by use of anti-depressant-type drugs, for example, through a nation's drinking-water supply system. This science-fiction possibility was foreshadowed in Aldous Huxley's (1932) *Brave New World* in the use of the recreational drug 'soma'.

There is, in fact, another and, fortunately, far less dangerous way of enhancing objective happiness – by taking aerobic exercise. Argyle (1996: 24), for example, reports that: 'brisk walks of ten minutes produced a positive mood, together with more energy, less anxiety, depression and tiredness, for two hours'. Two questions arise from this. The first relates to the use of 'happiness' or 'instant utility' here. There is no doubt that moderate exercise is a good thing and that it has a beneficial physiological effect and indeed that a part of that effect can be a feeling of well-being. But is it reasonable to call this *objective happiness*? In this context,

Veenhoven (2003) makes the useful distinction between *hedonism* as being open to pleasurable experience and *happiness* as being more holistic and related to life satisfaction.

The second question is to do with issues of importance as opposed to intensity: the objective measurement for this physiological event might be able to differentiate on the basis of physiological intensity but does not necessarily indicate its *meaning* or its *importance* to its recipient. Thus it is entirely possible that two events may score the same 'instant utility' even if one has very little meaning and the other is of massive significance in a person's life.

Thus, there are serious conceptual problems in the use of instant utility as the foundation for a utilitarian vision of quality of life. Nevertheless, there are lessons to be drawn from this exposition, the most important of which is the centrality of the *experience* of pleasure to well-being. This perhaps appears to be too obvious to be worth stating yet, as can be seen in Chapter 3, whole edifices of quality of life have been constructed and implemented – and some are extensively used by international agencies – which have no place at all for the experience of pleasure or even happiness. So it is clear that this message has still not been fully received.

Definitions of subjective well-being (SWB)

In practical terms, subjective happiness and subjective well-being are much more easy to deal with than their objective counterparts. Also, according to Diener and Oishi (2000), subjective well-being (SWB) is very democratic because it allows people to judge their own lives instead of focusing on judgements made on the quality of their lives by 'experts'. Basically, a person's level of subjective happiness can be ascertained from the reply given when asked how happy they are (Kahneman, 1999). So it can only be measured indirectly and it cannot be verified or validated objectively, as can objective happiness. Similarly it cannot be measured with precision and, as noted above, many people will not have a response ready to hand and will have to think about their circumstances in order to construct an answer.

SWB is rather more complex than happiness and comprises three or four elements. For Diener and Lucas (1999), SWB has three components: (1) pleasant affect; (2) unpleasant affect; and (3) satisfaction. It is interesting to note that they identify pleasant and unpleasant affect as two separate items rather than as two sides of the same coin. They do this because it is possible to have high levels of both or indeed low levels of both. Thus Diener and Lucas identify four different classifications of affect, as follows:

1   High levels of pleasant affect plus low levels of unpleasant affect = happy.
2   Low levels of pleasant affect plus high levels of unpleasant affect = unhappy.
3   High levels of both pleasant and unpleasant affect = emotional.
4   Low levels of both pleasant and unpleasant affect = unemotional.

The first two are intuitively unproblematic but the last two might appear a little contrived at first sight. However, Diener and Suh (1999) show that they are substantively important in a comparison between the 'hedonistic balance scores' of different countries. They found that Japan and Turkey had identical average scores, taking pleasant and unpleasant affect together, but that Turkey had higher levels on both than did Japan, so Turkey had higher levels of emotional response than Japan.

Some other interesting aspects emerge when satisfaction is included in the equations. Leaving aside the 'emotional' and unemotional responses for the moment, we can construct the following four classifications:

1   happy and satisfied
2   unhappy and dissatisfied
3   happy and dissatisfied
4   unhappy and satisfied.

The first two instances are straightforward. The satisfied, happy person with high pleasant and low unpleasant affect has very high SWB and the dissatisfied, unhappy person with low pleasant and high unpleasant affect has very low SWB. But what of the other two classifications? There seem to be three plausible answers. The first is that they are self-contradictory and in fact impossible, on the grounds that a satisfied person must be happy, a happy person must be satisfied and the opposites must also be true with regard to dissatisfaction and unhappiness. The second is that, yes they are self-contradictory but that people may well be ambivalent and simultaneously hold contradictory views (as stated by Kahneman in the quote above on objective and subjective happiness and objective good fortune).

The third and most interesting answer, is that they are not necessarily contradictory but can tap into different *dimensions* of SWB. To some extent the answer selected depends upon definitional issues but rather than trying to define these terms minutely, instead an attempt is made here to identify some real-life situations where the third and fourth categories have substantive meanings. If this attempt succeeds, then the distinction between happiness and satisfaction can be seen to be meaningful, in at least some circumstances. It can be noted in passing that this debate is not entirely abstract and esoteric: it does have some important significance when operationalising the SWB construct, and it might even throw some light upon recent research results which show an unexpected divergence between trends in SWB between Britain and the USA, discussed later in this chapter.

Happy and dissatisfied: critics of the notion of objective happiness can have considerable impact if they can demonstrate that this is a valid and substantive classification. There are several possible avenues here, perhaps the most popular one is the 'poor little rich boy/girl' of contemporary fiction and music. An example would be a person who has full and unfettered access to all life's hedonistic pleasures but eventually finds them unrewarding and shallow and who is looking for deeper and perhaps more spiritual meaning in life. This issue is dealt with in more detail in Chapter 3 when exploring 'heavyweight' value and capabilities. Another, and rather disconcerting example at the national level is the high level of suicide in countries with both high material standards of living and reported levels of happiness (Diener and Suh, 1999).

Unhappy and satisfied: such a person would have low levels of pleasant affect, high levels of unpleasant affect and yet be satisfied with their lives. Perhaps the most obvious candidates for this classification would be people doing extremely distressing and unpleasant jobs who perform an essential and highly valuable service to humanity. Regrettably there are very many examples which can be given here, including those international aid workers who are uncovering and identifying the bodies of genocide victims in former Yugoslavia and investigators and prosecutors in war crime tribunals.

Returning to the 'emotional' and 'unemotional' categories, it is clear that there are no conceptual difficulties in identifying 'emotional and satisfied', 'emotional and dissatisfied', 'unemotional and satisfied', and 'unemotional and dissatisfied' combinations. Indeed, with a little imagination it is possible to think of a wide range of examples, including at one extreme, a colourful and perhaps torrid life led by a person with high levels of pleasant and unpleasant affect and a satisfied life and at the other extreme a perhaps drab and dull life for a dissatisfied person with low levels of any sort of affect.

Argyle (1996) has a slightly different perspective to Diener and Lucas on SWB. One component in his formulation is the same as theirs: satisfaction with life. Another two components cover the same overall ground as the Diener and Lucas coverage of pleasant/unpleasant affect but from a different perspective. These are: a state of joy or positive emotion; and absence of positive emotion. Again Argyle demonstrates that these latter two are not the obverse of each other. He did not fund a correlation of -1.0 but only of -0.5 between them. Interestingly, he also found only a 0.5 correlation between satisfaction and positive emotion, thus adding empirical substance to the claim made above about the potential practical meaningfulness of happy dissatisfaction and unhappy satisfaction.

One strength of Argyle's approach is that he allows for a possible fourth dimension relating to issues such as: purpose in life, personal growth and positive relations with others; 'feeling really alive' and 'knowing who I really am'; and he even introduces the concept of 'serious leisure' (Argyle, 1996: 19). This idea is revisited in Chapter 3 when discussing 'heavyweight' prudential values.

For the present, though, these deeper aspects of SWB are assumed to be a facet of overall life satisfaction, so that the ensuing discussion does not become overly complicated. The final word here on the nature of SWB and on the sort of society where SWB can flourish, is left to Diener and Suh:

> In this tradition, the individual with a desirable life is satisfied and experiences frequent pleasant emotions and infrequent unpleasant emotions. The ideal society is defined as one where all people are happy and satisfied and experience an abundance of pleasure.
>
> (1999: 434)

Methodology

Conceptually SWB is relatively straightforward: it comprises satisfaction with life in general coupled with happiness or pleasant/unpleasant affect and possibly also includes a dimension relating to meaning of life, spirituality or self-knowledge. Methodologically, it is a bit more challenging to study because, unlike objective happiness, it is not directly accessible to external measures. By definition, SWB is the respondent's own judgement on their well-being, not any one else's, and has to be taken at face value, so long as there are no obvious clues that the respondent is dishonestly reporting their judgement.

This has led to the perplexing problem of conflict with the judgement of an external commentator. The 'happy poor', the 'happy slave' and the 'happy oppressed woman' are all examples of this phenomenon and are discussed in Chapter 3. For the present, though, given that subjective rather than objective quality of life is being discussed here, this ideological and normative problem will be left to one side. These happy but deprived people may well have 'false consciousness' of their situation from the perspective of experts who claim they know better than the respondent what their SWB *should be*. However, so long as they are reporting their 'false consciousness' accurately, then they are giving a valid report of their actual SWB and therefore do not induce any *methodological* problems, irrespective of any moral, normative and ideological problems their responses may raise.

In addition to issues of validity of self-reported measures of SWB, there are problems associated with reliability and salience. Such self-reports might be subject to volatility and can be a reflection of transient circumstances and be particularly sensitive to comparisons with other times in a person's life. In this context, Blanchflower and Oswald (2004a) agree that there are serious limitations to well-being statistics as a measure of genuine happiness, however that may be defined. But they make the telling point that it is unlikely that human happiness can be understood without, in part, listening to what human beings themselves say. They also provide some reassuring methodological evidence for the reliability of self-reported SWB via strong correlations between reported SWB and assessments of people's happiness by their spouses and by friends and family members (Blanchflower and Oswald, 2004a: 1,361).

There has been a debate in the quality of life literature about whether people's subjective well-being should be assessed as a holistic entity or as a multi-dimensional construct: in other words, should people be asked to give an overall appraisal of their SWB or should they be asked questions about, e.g. their life satisfaction, pleasant affect and unpleasant affect, or indeed whether these components should be further decomposed into different life-areas (Cummins, 1996)? An advantage of the latter approach is that it enables researchers to undertake a wide range of multivariate analyses and to investigate different facets of SWB and their inter-relationship with each other. It is particularly useful when trying to ascertain the composition of a person's overall SWB in terms of aggregating their relationship-SWB, their money-SWB, their employment-SWB, etc. Empirical research results from meta-analyses demonstrate a very close relationship between scores on single-item measures of SWB and the aggregate scores on multiple-domain measures. As a result, Cummins (1996) raised the question about whether the multiple domain measures are redundant as summary indicators. Given this, only the summary measures are discussed here.

There is a final issue which has both methodological and conceptual connotations: this is whether SWB is finitely bound or whether it has boundless possibilities for expansion. People are richer than they were and it is difficult to imagine a time when it would be impossible for the wealth of the world to expand, but can people's *happiness* keep on increasing or are there only limited possibilities for increasing human happiness? Alternatively, are increments in happiness harder and harder to achieve once one reaches higher levels of SWB? In other words, is subjective well-being much more inelastic than financial well-being? An alternative way of conceptualising this issue is to ask two questions: first, 'Are you as happy as you could possibly be?' and the second, is 'Are you as rich as you could possibly be?' If it is appropriate ever to give an affirmative answer to the first question but never to the second, then they are indeed examples of two different *kinds* of entity. If this is the case, then SWB cannot be measured in the same way as income or wealth.

Overview of findings on subjective well-being

This section gives a short summary of some of the major findings on SWB: what impact it has on people's lives; what sort of people have high and low levels of SWB; what aspects of people's lives affect their SWB; and, finally, on the causes of SWB. Then in the following sections, these potential causes are explored in more detail.

The impact of SWB

It is not easy to quantify the intangible impact of SWB on an individual's life course in terms of achievements and accomplishments but it is relatively straightforward to measure the different physiological conditions of people with high and low SWB. Blanchflower and Oswald (2004a) cite evidence that recorded happiness levels have been demonstrated to be correlated with:

1   duration of 'authentic smiles';
2   heart rate and blood pressure, measures of stress, and psychosomatic illnesses;
3   skin resistance measures of responses to stress;
4   electroencephelogram measures of prefrontal brain activity.

Of course, there are issues of cause and effect here: it is not completely clear, for example, whether happiness leads to changes in prefrontal brain activity and skin resistance stress levels or whether these physiological conditions predispose a person to be happy. And it is certainly the case that there is a complex relationship between SWB, psychosomatic illness and high blood pressure. However, it is clear that people smile because they are happy rather than are happy because they smile.

Argyle (1996: 28) produces strong evidence for SWB having beneficial effects upon physical and mental health. He identifies a relationship between being happy and having a strong immune system, even to the extent of happy people having fewer colds and other diseases than less happy people. Perhaps the most important effect of high SWB is increased longevity. Argyle (ibid.: 37) reports that happy people tend to live about a year longer than unhappy people (even after controlling for health).

Who has high SWB?

It has to be admitted that some of these positive circumstances associated with high levels of SWB might not merely be straightforward effects; the causality might be more complicated that this. Nevertheless, a high level of subjective well-being is good in itself and it is heartening to know that it is associated with other life-enhancing attributes: happy people are more altruistic and generous and are more sociable; they might also be more productive in their work; and they do seem to be better at problem solving (ibid.: 37–8).

Demographics and money (summarised from Argyle, 1999; Blanchflower and Oswald, 2004a; and Willitts *et al.*, 2004). The one overriding finding about who is and who is not happy is that people in long-term, loving relationships are more happy than people who are not. Married people, particularly people who have never remarried, are substantially happier than unmarried people. In general, at least in the USA and Britain, women are happier than men and there is a dip in SWB at around the age of 40: both older and younger people are happier. In the UK SWB also decreases above the age of 70 (Gabriel and Bowling, 2004) It also appears though that, after the age of 40, men's SWB increases faster than women's, although not fast enough to enable them to catch up.

Reported well-being is higher than average among the highly educated, and those whose parents did not divorce and it is lower than average among the unemployed. There is no statistical difference in SWB between homosexuals and heterosexuals (Blanchflower and Oswald, 2004b). Unsurprisingly, people with sufficient money to live comfortably are happier than people with less money, and people care about relative income as well as absolute income. However, perhaps less predictably, those who enjoy money a lot are less happy than we might expect: 'People do enjoy having possessions, but those who score high on materialism scales are found to be less happy than others' (Argyle, 1999: 358).

National differences (summarised from Argyle, 1996; Diener and Suh, 1999; Inglehart and Klingermann, 2000; Donovan and Halpern, 2002: Blanchflower and Oswald, 2004a). Scandinavian countries are the happiest, followed by Britain, the USA, Canada and Australia. The least happy are the Asian countries. There are some oddities: Italy, France and Japan have much lower than expected levels of SWB. In general, SWB remains very stable over time within countries but there have been some dramatic exceptions. These include Russia, Hungary and Belgium which have suffered major reductions in SWB. SWB has remained about the same in Britain over the past quarter of a century but during this time it appears that SWB has declined in the USA.

At the national level there appears to be a correlation between SWB and political freedom and economic prosperity. In Europe there is an inverse correlation between SWB and economic inequality, but this is not the case in the USA (Donovan and Halpern, 2002). Perhaps surprisingly, nations which are homogeneous in ethnicity, religion and language do not have higher levels of SWB than heterogeneous nations. It seems instead that nations with the highest levels of sociability, trust, interpersonal warmth and lack of excessive worry have the highest levels of SWB (Diener and Suh, 1999). This is an extraordinarily important finding which has major implications for societal perspectives on quality of life and indeed on the quantity of life – longevity – in societies. This topic is revisited in Chapter 7.

Reasons for SWB

It is clear that people in long-term, deep, loving relationships are, in general, far happier than those who are emotionally unattached. Now, it is highly likely that unattached people with high levels of SWB will find it easier to strike up and maintain a loving relationship than unattached people who are unhappy. So to some extent there may well be an interactive causal effect here. However, it has also been demonstrated from longitudinal studies that people become more happy after marriage than before, so it is likely that these relationships in themselves do enhance SWB. Similarly, employment normally raises and unemployment normally lowers SWB (Argyle, 1999). Argyle (1996) adds the following as causes of SWB: success and achievement; sex; eating and drinking; music, reading and other cultural experiences; religion and other spiritual and aesthetic experiences. Donovan and Halpern (2002) include regular walking, swimming, sports activities, gardening and community participation. Argyle (1999) also states that assertiveness and social skills and high levels of social support have been shown to be strong sources of happiness.

Access to the resources necessary to live a comfortable life is also an important factor in achieving high levels of SWB. However, as hinted at above, the role that money plays in SWB is in fact highly complex and is discussed in detail below. But first the pressing issue of genetics needs to be dealt with: is SWB – are happiness and satisfaction – all down to our personalities? Are some people born happier than others and do people retain more or less the same level of SWB throughout their lives, irrespective of what happens to them?

Genetics

At first sight genetics appears to be of overriding importance in relation to happiness and SWB. Some people are born with a cheerful or a miserable disposition and in general it looks like their personalities remain remarkably stable throughout their lives. This does not mean that they keep exactly the same level of SWB whatever happens to them but that their SWB will return to its 'normal' position relatively soon after e.g. rising after falling in love or falling after being made redundant or becoming disabled. There are two strands of evidence for this proposition. The first is from twin studies and other genetically based research and the second is from a range of studies of responses to dramatic life events such as winning a major lottery prize or becoming disabled in an accident.

Several authorities make a strong case that people's levels of happiness, life satisfaction and overall SWB are stable, related to their personalities and, to a large extent, determined by their genetic make-up (Diener and Lucas, 1999; Kahneman, 1999; Cummins *et al.*, 2002). Inglehart and Klingermann (2000) have undertaken an extensive study of international levels of SWB in relation to a range of biological, cultural and political factors and conclude that 'differences in income, education, occupation, gender, marital status and other demographic characteristics explain surprisingly little of people's levels of subjective well-being' (ibid.: 166). They start their analysis with neuroscientific findings about the close linkage between reported happiness and seratonin and dopamine levels in the brain – and the apparent strong influence that genetics has on this. They cite evidence which indicates that, although people with higher incomes have in general higher levels of SWB than those on lower incomes, socio-economic factors explain less than 4 per cent of variance in SWB and that other demographic variables such as education, occupation, age, religiosity and gender explain even less. On the other hand, their evidence indicates that genetic variation explains between 44 per cent and 52 per cent of variance in SWB. Diener and Lucas (1999: 215) support this and, overall, they claim that personality and genetics account for about 50 per cent of short-term SWB and up to 80 per cent of long-term SWB.

Research undertaken by Cummins *et al.* (2002) supports the higher figure of up to 80 per cent put forward rather than the lower figure of around 50 per cent proposed by Inglehart and Klingermann. Cummins *et al.* postulate the notion of 'homeostasis': that everyone has a natural 'in-built set point' which is hard-wired or genetically determined, that it normally ranges (on a scale where 0 = no satisfaction and 100 = fully satisfied) between 50 per cent and 100 per cent and that this leads to national norms being between 70 per cent and 80 per cent (reported in Rapley, 2003: 195).

Empirically, this proposition can be tested by a longitudinal study of people's responses to dramatic life events. One such study was undertaken by Brickman *et al.* (1978) who investigated the long-term SWB of lottery winners and spinal injury sufferers. He found that the SWB of the former initially went up, the latter went down and a control group stayed the same. But 18 months later only minor differences could be found between these groups (cited in Rapley, 2003: 208). Further similar evidence is cited by Kahneman (1999) that people who go through life-altering experiences often return eventually to a level of SWB that is characteristic of their personality. Inglehart and Klingermann (2000) refer to this phenomenon as 'aspiration adjustment'.

So, on the basis of the above arguments, it looks as if deep and loving relationships, major financial windfalls and even catastrophically disabling injuries have only temporary effects on the self-assessed well-being of most people. Instead, our SWB is largely determined – at the very least over half of it – by our genetic make-up and is 'hard wired', that is, impervious in the long run at least, to external events. It is certainly the case that genetics must play a major part in our personality make-up and it looks likely from the empirical research noted above that our personalities have a major effect on our SWB judgements. But if this were the whole story, then there would be some rather alarming consequences. One would be that national differences in SWB would be largely genetically determined and that any major changes in national SWB levels, other than those at the margin, would have to be caused by changes in the genetic stock of the nation. Fortunately, this is not entirely the case, as can now be seen.

National differences: politics, history, culture

Inglehart and Klingermann (2000) find the evidence of genetic effects convincing but claim that cultural and historical factors are important too, and are extremely important for variation *between* societies (ibid.: 166).

Using the results from the European Union Eurobarometer surveys of public opinion from the EU's inception in 1975, Inglehart and Klingermann show that nearly all the EU countries have highly stable SWB life satisfaction scores. It is noteworthy that there are wide and again mostly stable differences between the countries. Denmark has always had the highest national average level of SWB with around two-thirds of its population self-reporting as 'very satisfied'. At the other extreme, Portugal has always been at the bottom with consistently less than 5 per cent of its population self-reporting as 'very satisfied'. These findings prompt Inglehart and Klingermann (2000: 169) to comment: 'It seems that cultures, as well as individuals, have a normal baseline level of well-being that varies only moderately in response to current events.'

However, they do not think that these long-term stable patterns reflect genetic differences. They give two examples where there have been dramatic changes in national SWB levels. the first, again using the Eurobarometer statistics, is of Belgium where the proportion of the population self-reporting as 'very satisfied' more than halved from about 45 per cent in 1975 to 20 per cent in 1998. In order for this to be the result of genetic changes, there would have had to have been a dramatic change in the genetic make-up of the Belgian populace within the space of one generation – which is impossible. Inglehart and Klingermann claim that this change is to do with interethnic tension between the French-speaking and Flemish-speaking communities which have led to the virtual splitting of Belgium into two (Leibfried, 1998).

Their second example is of the nations which previously comprised the USSR, particularly Russia, which have undergone dramatic changes in their SWB from the 1980s to the present. Here they used the World Values Survey results which show a dramatic fall in SWB in these nations with the proportion reporting themselves as either happy or satisfied falling from over 70 per cent in 1981 to less than 40 per cent in 1995. This leads them to comment: 'The sharp decline in subjective well-being experienced by the Russian people since 1981 is impossible to reconcile with a genetic interpretation of the cross-national differences: it must reflect historical events' (Inglehart and Klingermann, 2000: 177). Donovan and Halpern (2002) show a similar effect for Hungary using data up to 2000. They identify rapid social and constitutional change over the period as being the most important factor and showed that economic factors were not relevant as Hungary achieved modest economic growth over this period.

One cultural factor that appears to have a major impact on national levels of SWB – and which is discussed at length in Chapter 5 – is the central social value of trust. For example, the French and Italians have lower levels of both SWB and interpersonal trust than countries at a similar level of economic and social development. In this context Inglehart *et al.* (1998: 41) conclude that: 'Life satisfaction, political satisfaction, interpersonal trust, high rates of political discussion, and support for the existing order all tend to go together.' They also say that democratic institutions seem to depend on life satisfaction and trust.

Does money make people happier?

In one sense, this is such an obvious question that there is no choice but to answer with a resounding 'Yes, of course, money makes people happier!' This is particularly and manifestly the case if the person concerned has none or only a little to start with: in situations such as this, having more money can make the difference between life and death. So there should be a simple equation: more money = more SWB. But the situation is much more complicated than this. It will be remembered that Inglehart and Klingermann (2000) and Diener and Lucas (1999) all claim that money accounts for less than 4 per cent in variance in SWB in developed countries. So this topic requires careful investigation. The situation is further complicated by the sheer number of studies in this area and by their often apparently contradictory findings.

Broadly, the findings from these studies fall into two categories; first, those where the unit of analysis is the relationship between SWB and income for each individual person in a country: and, second, where the unit of analysis is the relationship between the average SWB of all people in a country and the country's national income.

Overall, Diener and Oishi (2000) find there are small relationships between income and SWB for individuals within nations. These relationships are statistically significant but not very strong: the average correlation is 0.13 on World Values Survey data, ranging from 0.02 in Finland and through to 0.38 in South Africa. On average there is about an 11 per cent difference in SWB between the richest and poorest groups within nations – equivalent to around one point on a satisfaction measure scaled from 1–10. Diener and Oishi (ibid.: 194) cautiously summarise these findings as follows: 'Thus it would be an error to claim that income had no relation to SWB but also a mistake to suppose that the relation is immense.' Argyle (1999: 353) comes to similar conclusions, that income has complex and generally weak effects on happiness. He found a small positive effect but only at the lower end of the income scale. Diener and Lucas (1999: 215) conclude from their review of empirical studies that SWB stays relatively stable over long periods of time, even when income goes up and down. They state that wealth 'barely correlated with SWB'.

Blanchflower and Oswald, in their study of the USA and Britain, come to a more assertively positive conclusion about the relationship between income and SWB: 'Money buys happiness' and 'richer people are systematically more satisfied with their lives' (2004a: 1359). But they also note that 'The amount of happiness bought by extra income is not as large as some might expect. To put this differently, the non-economic variables in happiness equations enter with large coefficients, relative to that of income' (ibid.: 1371–2).

Their last point is well taken: in other words, money matters but not as much as we might expect and not as much as many other non-financial factors. All in all, at an individual level, it seems to be the case that there is a relationship between money and SWB, that it is strong at low income levels but weakens as people get richer.

Moving from the individual to the international level, Diener and Oishi (2000) identify a much stronger relationship between average national income and average national SWB (ranging from 0.59 to 0.69 over several surveys). Using the same data, Inglehart and Klingermann (2000) come to different conclusions. They agree with Diener and Oishi that there is an effect on human happiness as nations move from extreme poverty to prosperity, but that the effect is non-linear. It is very strong among poor nations, with incomes below $13,000 at 1995 levels, but fades away as national income increases: 'above the level of Portugal or Spain, economic growth no longer makes a difference' (Inglehart and Klingermann, 2000: 171).

All commentators agree, however, that changes *within* countries over time, particularly developed countries, show on average very little, if any, growth in SWB in spite of massive growth in national income since the 1940s. In the USA, Japan and France, SWB has been virtually flat since the Second World War (Diener and Oishi, 2000: 202). Argyle (1999: 353) even goes as far as to say that 'increased prosperity for all during recent years has had no effect'.

There have been several attempts to explain this lack of advance in human happiness during a period of growth in material and financial resources. One is that expectations and desires increase in line with income so that only a dramatic increase in income will lead to a marked increase in SWB. Another related possible explanation lies in the perils of materialism. Several commentators have noted that people who put a high value on materialism tend to be less happy than would be expected from their income level. Diener and Oishi (2000: 208) found that respondents who rated money as less important were more satisfied than those who rated it as more important.

Kahneman (1999: 13) gives a possible insight into these processes in what he identifies as the 'deeply troubling' concepts of the *hedonic treadmill* and *satisfaction treadmill*. The treadmill metaphor here is very telling in that it gives a picture of people exerting energy going round in circles getting nowhere and achieving nothing of benefit to themselves thus: 'improved circumstances could cause people to require even more frequent and more intense pleasure to maintain the same level of satisfaction . . . the satisfaction treadmill causes subjective happiness to remain constant even when objective happiness improves' (ibid.: 14).

Perhaps a simpler explanation can be summarised by the following equation: 'increased economic growth = more expensive desirable goods'. Thus, in the 1950s a black and white television was the height of affluence; to be replaced by colour TVs; surround sound, video recorders; DVDs; plasma screens; and doubtless three-dimensional images in the foreseeable future – all initially affordable by the very rich but swiftly available to all, thus negating their status and rarity value.

In bringing these findings together, Ryan and Deci (2001) and Diener and Biswas-Diener (2002) helpfully summarise the relevant literature. The following list incorporates their findings plus further relevant insights gained from subsequent studies, starting with the least disputed findings:

1   Increases in national wealth in developed countries over the past 50 years have not led to any discernible increases in SWB.
2   It is probable, though, that SWB in poorer nations has increased as they have got richer.
3   People who strongly desire wealth and money are more unhappy than people who do not.
4   Within-nation differences in wealth show a positive correlation with happiness (Diener and Oishi, 2000) but only a small one (Diener and Biswas-Diener, 2002).

There is perhaps one further finding that can be added to the list:

5   People's SWB will not necessarily increase if they get richer at the same rate as their peers but may well do so if they get richer faster than their peers. They will certainly be likely to suffer a reduction in their SWB if their peers get richer and they do not.

This ties in with suggestions of Argyle (1996) and Layard (2004, 2005) that, given the relatively low correlation with income, the explanation may lie in either: social comparison in terms of expectations and reference groups (that is, relative rather than absolute levels of income); or adaptation or habituation, that is, getting used to or coming to terms with one's situation.

Ryan and Deci summarise recent studies as pointing to the following recipe for happiness: avoiding poverty, living in a rich country, and focusing on goals other than material wealth:

> Several studies have supported this overall model, showing that the more people focus on financial and materialistic gains, the lower their well-being . . . further, both cross-sectional . . . and longitudinal . . . studies suggest that, whereas progress towards intrinsic goals enhance well-being, progress towards extrinsic goals such as money either does not enhance well-being or does so to a lesser extent . . . In sum, . . . money does not appear to be a reliable route to either happiness or well-being.
>
> (2001: 153–4)

Perhaps it is appropriate to give the final word here to Diener and Oishi (2000: 211): 'a more prosperous material world will not inevitably increase life satisfaction. If people's desires outstrip reality, it is likely that people will be more dissatisfied even in a very affluent world.' It may be people's desires that determine whether they are psychologically rich or poor.

SWB: summary and policy implications

The more information that becomes available on SWB, the more perplexing this construct appears to be. First, it is clear that genetics, personality and 'homeostasis' are extremely important to SWB. It seems very likely that some people are born cheerful and others are born miserable and that they will mostly stay that way throughout their lives: certainly they may have major ups and downs, particularly if they have a financial windfall or suffer a serious disability, but in the long run their SWB will probably revert to their personal norm. On the other hand, though, people's SWB – and indeed the SWB of *peoples*, that is, whole nations – is vulnerable to dramatic decline if there is a long-term downturn in national fortunes, through political disintegration or national financial collapse.

Second, it is clear that money is – under differing circumstances – both completely irrelevant and extremely important. At the national level it seems to be irrelevant in relation to economic growth (and even doubling or more of national income) in nations that are already rich. People's expectations seem to rise in line with economic growth so that, as national income rises, the population expects more and more in order merely to remain as happy as it was before. Thus, the objective benefits of increased national wealth, in terms of longevity, reduced infant mortality, better infrastructure, etc., do not translate into higher national levels of subjective well-being. At individual level, it looks like materialists, in other words, people with an excessive love for money or rather for the things that money can buy, find themselves still wanting more, no matter how much they have and thus never increasing their long-term SWB, even though they will get short-term increases. Here the hedonic treadmill is in operation at both the macro and micro levels.

On the other hand, for poor countries and more generally, for poor people whose basic needs have not yet been fully met, then an increase in income will almost certainly translate into a substantive enhancement of SWB. There is a clear relationship here between an increase in absolute income and an increase in SWB. The other circumstance where it is likely that there will be an increase in SWB consequent to an increase in income at above basic needs level, is where the increase in income is relative. If one group gets an increase in money and their peers do not, then the former will feel, and will be, relatively as well as absolutely, better off. This largely explains the small but significant correlations between income and SWB within developed nations.

Third, it seems clear that the best way for a person to enhance their SWB is to enter – and stay in – a long-term emotionally satisfying relationship. If they are also employed and well educated, this will be a bonus.

What, then, are the policy implications for enhancing people's subjective well-being? In relation to people as individuals, and leaving aside the spectre of genetic engineering, it seems that it is important for governments to provide opportunities for education and employment and to facilitate and nurture long-term emotional relationships through family and tax laws. In this context Argyle (1999) comments that governments should place less emphasis on raising incomes, except among the very poor, and more emphasis should be placed on employment. Similarly, Diener and Lucas (1999) say that if they want to enhance people's quality of life, then governments need to focus less on people's subjective well-being and more on their objective well-being.

Therefore, it is clear that in policy terms there is not a lot that governments can do directly to enhance SWB. It looks like their best policy option, ironically, is to strive instead to enhance objective well-being irrespective of any direct impact on SWB. Ironically, though, perhaps the most direct government policy impact on SWB is at a very abstract level through nurturing the fabric of society itself through actively promoting national trust, social inclusion and social cohesion. This theme forms a *leitmotif* for the rest of this book. The next task now is to move from happiness, satisfaction and subjective well-being towards a more holistic approach to quality of life.

From subjective well-being to quality of life

SWB has been seen to have it strengths and its limitations. Perhaps the greatest strength of any approach to subjective well-being is that it pays serious attention to people's happiness and life satisfaction. Happiness may not be enough as a measure of quality of life as can be seen from the case of the 'happy poor'. But even though SWB cannot be a sufficient criterion of quality of life, any measure of quality of life that took no account at all of whether a person was miserable or dissatisfied would surely be lacking an important dimension. It is clear, though, that there is more to quality of life than just subjective attributes such as happiness or satisfaction. There are objective qualities too, and some of these, such as sufficient nutrition, a non-hazardous environment, and a long and healthy life are universally, or virtually universally uncontroversial as components of quality of life. This section starts where the previous section left off, with subjective notions of quality of life, and broadens them, first, from the hedonic to the eudaimonic within an essentially subjectivist framework and then from subjective to objective, but always with a view to people's own conceptions of what is good for their quality of life, as well as incorporating the views of academics and other 'experts'.

Hedonic and eudaimonic approaches to SWB

Two broadly differing traditions in subjective approaches to quality of life have been identified in the literature: hedonic and eudaimonic (Diener and Suh, 1999; Ryan and Deci, 2001). The hedonic tradition stresses the nobility of the individual, with an emphasis upon personal freedom, self-preservation and self-enhancement, and is derived from a philosophical tradition encompassing Hobbes, Locke and Rousseau. This tradition relates specifically to subjective well-being and is the starting point for hedonistic psychology with its emphasis on the integrity of individuals' personal judgements about the good and bad elements of their lives, the attainment of pleasure and the avoidance of pain.

The eudaimonic tradition stretches even further back, to the Aristotelian conception of 'the good life', of moderation, reason and justice, and it focuses on meaning, self-realisation and the actualisation of human potential. Here well-being is defined in terms of the degree to which a person is 'flourishing' or 'fully functioning'. Diener and Suh (1999) include in this tradition teachings of St Thomas Aquinas on the importance of virtue and personal salvation and they trace the pedigree of this school of thought back as far as Confucianism with its emphasis on scholarship and duty in relationships.

Ryan and Deci (2001) claim that the philosophical basis for the eudaimonic approach is derived from Aristotle's dismissal of hedonism as vulgar and from his search for higher values. They make the point that pleasure and happiness are not always the same as, or even necessarily related to, well-being. They cite Waterman (1993) as saying that eudaimonia occurs when people's life activities are most congruent or meshing with deeply held values and are holistically or fully engaged, a state Waterman called *personal expressiveness*. Unlike hedonic measures (which are intrinsically linked to desire fulfilment), personal expressiveness is strongly related to personal growth and development and to the realisation of one's true potential. This approach has considerable similarities with both Griffin's prudential values theory, which emphasises 'heavyweight values' and Nussbaum's 'thick' and extensive version of capability theory which also follows an Aristotelian tradition of the good life, both of which are discussed in detail in Chapter 3.

Following on from Waterman's initiative, Ryff and Keyes (1995) introduce the construct of *psychological well-being* which taps into six aspects of human actualisation: autonomy; personal growth; self-acceptance; life purpose; mastery; and positive relatedness. Within the same tradition, Ryan and Deci (2001) have developed *self-determination theory* which attempts to specify both what it means to 'actualise the self' and how that can be accomplished. Self-determination theory posits three basic psychological needs: autonomy; competence; and relatedness.

According to self-determination theory, satisfaction of basic psychological needs normally promotes hedonic as well as eudaimonic well-being. Therefore, it uses measures of SWB along with assessments of self-actualisation, vitality and mental health 'in an effort to assess well-being conceived of as healthy, congruent and vital functioning' (Ryan and Deci, 2001: 147). Ryan and Deci conclude from an extensive literature review that it is most appropriate to conceive of well-being as a multidimensional phenomenon including aspects of both hedonic and eudaimonic well-being, while taking into account that there are tensions and divergences between these two features.

Self-defined quality of life

A major empirical study undertaken by Anne Bowling (1995b) supports Ryan and Deci's self-determination theory and casts light on the potential balance between its hedonic and eudaimonic components. She ascertained the views of the most important experts of all: members of the general public – the people who make judgements about their own quality of life. Bowling undertook a study of the factors that people think are central to their own quality of life by asking open-ended questions about what was important in their lives. Given the overall findings noted above, it is perhaps not surprising that people ranked their relationship with family or relatives most highly. This was followed by their own health, then health of other significant person(s) in their lives. The item that came fourth in importance covered finances and standard of living. It is perhaps surprising that this item came so low in the list but it is interesting to note that it was the one most often cited in the first five choices overall, even though it was not cited as the most important.

It is significant that health, both their own and of their loved ones, came so high in this list, and this is discussed in detail in Chapter 2. It is also interesting that money, which is central to utilitarian, hedonic approaches to quality of life, was ranked as less important not only than close relationships but also than the well-being of family and friends – both of these probably having more affinity with eudaimonic aspects of quality of life, and the latter definitely being 'other-regarding' rather than (or as well as) self-centred in nature.

Staying with the subjective perspective on quality of life, Rapley (2003: 50) summarises the key characteristics of what he refers to as several widely accepted definitions of quality of life: 'All specify that QOL is an *individual psychological perception of the material reality of aspects of the world*' (italics in original). So this perspective is firmly embedded in individuals' psychological perceptions rather than in the independent objective reality of their existence. The perspective he starts from is the definition given by the influential World Health Organization Quality of Life (WHOQOL) Group:

> [Quality of life] is an individual's perception of their position in life in the context of the culture and value systems in which they live and in relation to their goals, expectations, values and concerns . . . incorporating . . . physical health, psychological state, level of independence, social relations, personal beliefs and their relationship to salient features of the environment . . . quality of life refers to a subjective evaluation which is embedded in a cultural, social and environmental context.
>
> (1995: 1403)

Relevant to both Rapley's overview and the WHO definition is another British empirical study complementary to Bowling's, but focusing on perceptions of this environmental context. Rogerson *et al.* (1996) undertook a nationwide survey of public opinion about environmental issues having a major impact on people's quality of life. The researchers again here did not rely on their own definitions but asked respondents to select and rank the important elements. According to Rogerson *et al.* (1996: 38), they are as follows:

- crime, both violent and non-violent;
- health services;
- the environment, including pollution, access to scenic areas and the climate;
- housing (cost of owner-occupied and private rented housing and quality of public rented housing);
- racial harmony;
- educational facilities;
- employment prospects, including wage levels and time spent travelling to work;
- unemployment levels;
- cost of living;
- shopping, sports and leisure facilities.

Their results echo Bowling's in the sense that financial issues are not at the top of the list and health provision is seen as of very high importance. It is not surprising that concern about crime comes first but it is perhaps less predictable that the environment comes higher than housing or education. In passing, it is probably an idiosyncrasy of British culture rather than any extremes of weather in the UK that led to the climate being in the list at all. In geographical terms Rogerson *et al.* report that London and the Midlands (particularly around Birmingham) do not score very high on these quality of life indicators, whereas the locations with the highest quality of life seem mostly to be in the north and the west (including Aberdeen, Dundee, Edinburgh, Exeter, Plymouth, York, Halifax) along with Cambridge, and Southend.

The approach taken by Bowling and Rogerson *et al.*, in consulting people about what they see as being most important to their quality of life, is an important development away from the internal world of subjective well-being itself while still keeping individuals' agency, integrity and autonomy in a central position. Rapley (2003) takes this a stage further. Whereas Rogerson *et al.* asked people nationally for their views and then produced locally based results using these national criteria, Rapley (2003: 42) contends that it is more valid and meaningful to undertake studies using local rather than national criteria. In other words, the Rogerson *et al.* study compared, for example, Plymouth and London on the basis of a nationally aggregated ranking of quality of life indicators. Rapley would have wanted Plymouth to be assessed on the rankings of those items that Plymouth people thought were most important to their quality of life, and similarly London to be assessed on the basis of what Londoners thought were the most important items.

This way of classifying quality of life is not entirely uncontroversial. As can be seen in Chapter 3, some commentators have no place at all for subjective well-being in their conceptualisations of quality of life (let alone, locality-based formulations of SWB) and it is noted in the following section that there can be tensions and even contradictions between a person's subjective and objective well-being.

Introducing an objective dimension

Although Rapley (2003) espouses an overtly locally-oriented subjectively defined approach to quality of life, he accepts too that quality of life usually also refers to normative expectations of what citizens should reasonably be able to expect from their lives. In this context he refers to Cummins' (1997) contention that subjective and objective approaches to quality of life are both essential but that they are often poorly related to each other (Rapley, 2003: 30). To demonstrate this, he constructs a taxonomy that contrasts subjective well-being and objective living conditions. This is presented in Table 1.1, along with labels added here in italics.

Two of the cells are uncontroversial, intuitively obvious and straightforward: well-being and deprivation, or the happy rich and the unhappy poor. Within this straightforward view of the world the aim of policy for maximising the good life is to move people from the latter to the former cell. At first sight, the other two cells look like oddities, possibly self-contradictory but at this juncture it is worth recalling the discussion earlier in this chapter of the similar issue of the relationship between happiness and satisfaction which introduced the 'poor little rich boy/girl' syndrome of the happy but dissatisfied person and the 'satisfied but unhappy' situation perhaps epitomised by international aid workers. The relationship between objective circumstances and SWB adds an extra dimension of complexity to this issue.

The judgement of Argyle (1999: 357) on the happy poor is forceful: 'their apparent satisfaction with their lot has been interpreted as a state of adaptation and learned helplessness produced by long experience of being unable to do anything about it'. It is certainly the case that Argyle's judgement is correct for very large numbers of people in the most utmost and indefensible states of deprivation for whom it is imperative that steps be taken to ameliorate their objective circumstances.

However, above the level of meeting basic, or perhaps intermediate, needs it is important not to throw out the quality of life baby along with the 'adaptation' bathwater. There is a real danger of privileging objective, material conditions at the expense of the 'heavyweight', though nonetheless subjective, values of eudaimonic quality of life and thus fighting an inappropriate battle against the circumstances of an at present deeply satisfied group among the 'happy poor' which might lead inexorably to them falling into the worse quality of life situation of being among

Table 1.1 Subjective well-being and objective living conditions

Objective living conditions	*Subjective well-being*	
	Good	Bad
Good	Well-being *The happy rich*	Dissonance *The unhappy rich*
Bad	Adaptation *The happy poor*	Deprivation *The unhappy poor*

Source: Adapted from Rapley (2003: 31)

the 'unhappy rich'. Here the essential thing is to ensure that no-one falls beneath the threshold of an unacceptable objective standard of living.

It is at this point in the discussion that it becomes clear that the straightforward taxonomy which dichotomises SWB versus objective living conditions is only of limited usefulness and that it is necessary to move to a more sophisticated model. This process has already commenced with the expanding of SWB from its hedonic base through to a eudaimonic perspective that in one sense remains at the subjective level because it still entirely concerns features internal to people's minds. In other words, it does not include external objective and material features that affect their lives. On the other hand, though, it goes beyond their actual affect and satisfaction and desires and moves towards what their desires would be if they fully conformed to self-realisation and the actualisation of human potential. So, from a eudaimonic perspective, the subjective part of the taxonomy can be seen as including autonomy, competence and relatedness as well as the hedonic features of positive affect, negative affect and life satisfaction.

Models of quality of life

This final section of this chapter consists of two short case studies of different approaches to what quality of life actually looks like or actually *is*. The first is radical, simple and straightforward: Veenhoven's *happy life expectancy* model, which enables average levels of quality of life to be measured at national levels in countries across the world. It also combines a 'soft' subjective hedonic measure (happiness), with the most rigorous and 'hard' objective indicator (life expectancy). The second, Raphael's *being, belonging and becoming* model is at a more micro-level and is based on the notion of quality of life being universal, holistic and unitary; in other words, there are no differences in the needs of people who are healthy or chronically ill, with or without learning disabilities. It does not utilise highly sophisticated statistical devices but has the major advantage of having been operationalised in relation to widely different groups in the community, including those with a range of disadvantages and disabilities.

Veenhoven's **happy life** *expectancy*

Veenhoven (1996) complains that most quality of life instruments are either too complicated, having indices and scales that are not intuitively understandable, or else they measure the wrong things. The latter charge is a serious one and he levels it against many measures extensively used by agencies such as the UN and World Bank that include, for example, income or years of schooling or health services. He claims that these items are only indirectly relevant to quality of life: they are inputs to quality of life and he asserts that the only valid indicators are direct measures of outputs of quality of life. In other words he claims that the measures he criticises only measure *presumed* rather than *actual* quality of life, or what he calls 'live-ability'. His solution to the problem of measuring liveability is disarmingly simple: '[It] can be measured by the degree to which its citizens live long and happily. The longer and happier the citizens live, the better the provision and requirements of society apparently fit in with their needs and capabilities' (Veenhoven, 1996: 28). Thus, his measure of quality of life combines estimates of life expectancy in years with survey data on subjective well-being measured on a scale from 0 to 1. The former is multiplied by the latter to produce a figure of 'happy life expectancy' (HLE) in years. It can be interpreted as the number of years the average citizen in a country lives happily at a certain time.

It has to be said that HLE is rather a blunt instrument. It is clear that a high HLE means that, on average, citizens live both long and happy lives and that, conversely, a low HLE means that, on average, citizens live short and miserable lives. However, it is not immediately clear whether a middling HLE means, on average, that people live lives of middling length and happiness, long and unhappy lives, short and happy lives or whether the society comprises a mixture of all of these.

Nevertheless the empirical findings are of considerable interest. HLE is highest in the countries of north-western Europe where the average citizen has an HLE of around 60 years (the equivalent of a life expectancy of approximately 80 years and a SWB rating of 0.75) and lowest in Africa where the HLE is only just over half as high at around 35 years. Happy life expectancy is higher in nations where people live most securely, where the material standard of living is highest, in the most free and individualistic nations and the most equal in terms of gender equality and educational homogeneity. Interestingly, HLE is not correlated with unemployment, state welfare, income inequality, religiousness, trust in institutions, military dominance or population pressure.

Raphael's 'being, belonging and becoming' model

Raphael's model uses a rather vaguer definition of quality of life than Veenhoven's HLE: the degree to which a person enjoys the important possibilities of his/her life. This definition at first view seems uncontroversial but its implications are seriously radical. Here *enjoyment* has both the subjective, hedonistic meaning and a more objective meaning encompassing 'enjoying a high standard of living'. This definition is highly individualistic in that *possibilities* 'reflect the opportunities and limitations each person has' (Raphael *et al.*, 1996: 80). Quality of life here is the degree of enjoyment that results from possibilities that have taken on importance to the person; that is, quality of life is uniquely identified for each individual.

This approach has four defining characteristics. The first and second can be taken together: first, it focuses on the individual and, second, it is universal in that, as a matter of basic principle, it includes everyone, no matter how disabled or restricted in their physical life possibilities. Here the definition's lack of specificity and its individualised orientation enable a realistic comparison to be made between two people with widely differing objective life chances. The model does not necessarily aim for equality of outcomes, but it does aim for an equal level of fulfilment in relation to the important possibilities in each person's life. Third, it is both multi-dimensional and holistic. In comparison, Veenhoven's happy life expectancy is holistic but has only two dimensions, whereas the list put forward by the respondents in Rogerson *et al.*'s. (1996) research was multidimensional but had no holistic singular identity.

Fourth, it maximises personal control over life consistent with principles of minimising danger to self and others. This, of course, is central to issues of independence, autonomy and agency, but it is by no means straightforward. Its positive characteristic of refuting paternalism, of someone else 'knowing best' has a potential negative consequence too, of potential underachievement, adaptability and a syndrome similar to the happy poor. There does seem to be a danger here that someone with low expectations and horizons may be deemed to have a high quality of life. Having said that, it has to be recognised that even Veenhoven's pared-down, output-oriented approach has exactly the same problem in using 'happiness'. The only quality of life instruments that do not suffer from this problem are those which do not take subjective well-being or life satisfaction into account at all.

With regard to its multidimensionality, the model has three domains, *being*, *belonging* and *becoming*, each with three dimensions. They are as follows:

- *Being* – who one is:
  - physical – physical health, exercise, etc.;
  - psychological – mental health, adjustment, feelings, cognition, etc.;
  - spiritual – personal values, standards of conduct and beliefs.
- *Belonging* – a person's fit with their environment:
  - physical – home, workplace, neighbourhood, school and community;
  - social – family, friends, neighbours, etc.;
  - community – income, health, social services, employment, education, community events, etc.
- *Becoming* – purposeful activities to express oneself and achieve personal goals, hopes and aspirations:
  - practical – day-to-day activities: domestic work; paid work; school, etc.;
  - leisure – activities that promote relaxation and reduce stress;
  - growth – maintenance and improvement of knowledge and skills and adaptation to change.

As can be seen from these nine areas of functioning, this approach is very wide-ranging indeed. It is particularly strong on the interaction between the personal, interpersonal and environmental aspects of people's lives, and the emphasis on growth in the 'becoming' domain, which itself focuses on an individual's goals, hopes and aspirations, and puts down a marker about the importance of the stress on 'possibilities' in the definition of quality of life that is used here.

Conclusion

A fundamental theme of this chapter is that quality of life must start with the individual, her or his own feelings, thoughts and emotions. It is a tenet of this book that any rounded and comprehensive theory or conceptualisation of quality of life, whether at individual, community or societal level, must take account of individuals' own judgements about their own lives. Omitting or devaluing such a perspective denies the importance of human autonomy, which is arguably central to the notion of humanity itself.

Such an approach, highly principled and person-centred though it is, is not without its problems. It is clear that there is no necessary relationship between subjective and objective well-being, for example, the massive increases in income accruing to developed countries over the past half-century have not led to corresponding increases in subjective well-being. In addition, there are strong genetic causes for differences in SWB between people. Perhaps most important from a moral perspective is the issue of adaptation or false consciousness among individuals and groups who suffer high levels of deprivation but also report high levels of SWB – the 'happy poor'. It is another tenet of this book that the quality of life of people in such circumstances must encompass more than the success of their adaptive responses to adversity – it is that adversity itself which needs to be ameliorated.

This then leads on to another essential requirement for a person's quality of life: the pursuit of *objective* as well as subjective well-being. Kahneman (1999) summarises this well by making a plea for policies that increase *good experiences* irrespective of whether they increase SWB, in other words, that enhance objective well-being. These good experiences are in general universally enhanced by the provision of sufficient nutrition and a non-hazardous environment and are epitomised in the living of a long and healthy life.

So far, this summary has been on safe ground: it is difficult for all but the most nihilistic or misanthropic to deny the value of subjective well-being or of a long and healthy life. However, one other feature of an individual's well-being which is a theme throughout this book, is somewhat more controversial. This is of living a 'flourishing' life in the Aristotelian sense of self-realisation and personal growth: in other words a eudaimonic approach to well-being which incorporates but transcends the hedonism of pleasure. This facet of quality of life is presented in detail in Chapter 3 and is developed within the prudential values and capabilities frameworks. It is also central to some of the macro-level quality of life constructs discussed in Chapter 6.

In the next chapter the spotlight is placed on the aspect of quality of life that has attracted the most attention and controversy – health-related quality of life. It is in this field that the greatest steps have been taken in operationalising quality of life constructs and in using these operationalisations in policy and practice to take decisions on patient treatment priorities: and these decisions can relate to matters of life and death.

2 Health-related quality of life

In 1942, when Britain was in the depths of the Second World War the Beveridge Report was published. Its full title, *A Report on Social Insurance and Allied Services*, seems uninspiring yet it was the best-selling British book of the war years and it provided the foundations for the post-war welfare state. In his report, Lord Beveridge identified five 'giants' which had to be defeated in order to create a welfare state. In his now rather quaint Edwardian language, perhaps deliberately reminiscent of Bunyan's *Pilgrim's Progress*, he called these evil giants: *Want*; *Disease*; *Ignorance*; *Squalor*; and *Idleness* (Beveridge, 1942). We would now probably call them: poverty; ill-health; educational disadvantage; environmental degradation; and unemployment. Want, or poverty, is central to quality of life and is discussed in detail in Chapter 4. Indeed, all the five giants are integrally related to issues of quality of life and all are central to the societal quality of life constructs discussed in Chapter 6.

However, it is health and ill-health that have taken centre stage in relations to academic debates on, and real-world operationalisations of, quality of life. There are now literally hundreds of health-related quality of life (HRQOL) measures, ranging from the broad and general *Short Form 36* (*SF36*) which has spawned over 4,000 articles in scholarly journals, through to highly specialised HRQOL instruments designed specifically for administering to patients suffering from rare medical conditions. No other area of life, and none of the other 'five giants' have attracted such attention in relation to measures of quality of life.

It is partly for these reasons that a whole chapter is being devoted here to the specific issue of health-related quality of life. However, there is another reason too: this is to do with the what might be seen as the empire building – in an entirely benign sense – of the World Health Organization (WHO) in its definition of *health* and in its extraordinarily successful campaign to get this definition universally accepted. The WHO has defined health not just as absence of illness but in wide-ranging quality of life terms as a 'state of complete physical, mental and social well-being'. This in itself fits in many broad-ranging definitions of quality of life (including the WHO's own highly expansive definition, as seen in Chapter 1) but the WHO has subsequently gone even further and augmented the definition, rather more controversially and without such complete universal acceptance, to include 'autonomy' as well (WHOQOL Group, 1995: 1404). The issue of autonomy is highly contested in debates about a wide range of quality of life conceptualisations and is revisited throughout the rest of this book.

The WHO definition lends itself well to a sociometric or social indicators-based approach to assessing the success of medical intervention in treating the whole gamut of illness and medical conditions because here health is not just the absence of symptoms but affects the whole person.

The first part of this chapter deals with these individually-oriented quality of life instruments and discusses the passionate debate surrounding their use in literally life and death situations. The second section moves beyond the individual to ecological perspectives on collective quality of life and the 'healthy communities' movement.

The health-related quality of life of individuals

There are two major and distinct strands in health-related quality of life as applied to individuals (Morreim, 1992; Fitzpatrick, 1996). The first follows on from the subjective well-being and life satisfaction approach towards quality of life discussed in Chapter 1. This is known as the *personal* or *experiential* approach to HRQOL and it relates specifically to people's judgements about their own health-related quality of life. The second is much more impersonal, 'scientific' and objective in nature and relies on statistical models derived from responses to hypothetical questions by samples of the general public. This is known as the 'consensus' or 'normative' approach and is the one which raises the most problematic and controversial issues about matters of life and death. These two approaches are dealt with separately below and then are exemplified in a case study on what has been called 'the disability paradox'.

Personal and experiential approaches

Anne Bowling, one of the pioneers of HRQOL in the UK, gave the following definition in her influential book, *Measuring Disease: A Review of Disease-Specific Quality of Life Measurement Scales*:

> Health-related quality of life is defined here as optimum levels of physical role (e.g. work, carer, parent etc.) and social functioning, including relationships and perceptions of health, fitness, life satisfaction and well-being. It should also include some assessment of the patient's level of satisfaction with treatment, outcome and health status and with future prospects.
>
> (Bowling, 1995a: 2)

It can be seen immediately that this definition fully incorporates the components of subjective well-being plus both subjective and objective 'physical well-being': that is, feeling healthy and fit and having the actual physical competence to perform one's social roles. This is *in addition* to the 'medical' components of the second part of the definition which, it should be noted, are defined in terms of *satisfaction* rather than in terms of objective medical outcomes. So this commonly accepted HRQOL definition goes much further than standard hedonic SWB, although it does not incorporate the normative standards of eudaimonic quality of life. Bowling claims that this definition is narrower than what she calls 'quality of life as a whole', which incorporates, among other things, a person's housing, income and immediate environment. Thus, for her, the theoretical framework for HRQOL is based on a multi-dimensional perspective of health along the lines of the WHO definition given above and incorporating SWB and psychological, physical and social functioning.

Other commentators have given an even wider range of definitions of HRQOL. For example, Fitzpatrick (1996: 141) notes that it can cover any of the following: emotional well-being; spirituality; sexuality; social functioning; family life; occupational functioning; communication; eating; functional ability; physical status; treatment satisfaction; self-esteem; stigma; body image; future orientation; global ratings of health or life satisfaction. He concludes that most HRQOL definitions include: emotional status; physical functioning; social functioning; and medical symptoms.

Thus far, HRQOL does not appear to be very controversial in its aims. In general, HRQOL instruments seem to be aimed at identifying people's non-material quality of life in a multidimensional way, with an emphasis upon physical well-being and specifically in relation to the outcome of medical or other treatment. Indeed, put this way, it looks like most HRQOL instruments, particularly the wide-ranging and multidimensional ones, should actually be classified in terms of quality of life generally rather than just HRQOL because they measure overall quality of life, including health. On this basis, several commentators make a strong principled case along these lines that there should in effect be no *specific* health-related quality of life construct because it should be covered by quality of life in general (Fitzpatrick, 1996; Albrecht and Devlieger, 1998). This is a sensible, coherent and, at face value, practical approach and is feasible for instruments dealing with health in general. Indeed, such an approach has been used to good effect by Grundy and Bowling (1999) in their ground-breaking longitudinal study of quality of life among the 'oldest old', that is people over the age of 85. However, issues of practicality become problematic when specific medical or symptom-related issues need to be included so it does make practical sense to have instruments tailored to specific medical interventions.

But what is the *purpose* of all these HRQOL measures? Apart from an academic interest in how health impacts on other aspects of our quality of life it appears at first sight that HRQOL might not be relevant to doctors or medical planners at all. Given that there are only finite resources that can be spent on medical care and that as people live longer and at increasing levels of frailty and as more sophisticated and expensive life-prolonging treatments are discovered, then it can be argued that the purpose of medicine and of health services is to treat disease according to criteria of clinical need and cost-effectiveness, not in relation to how people are feeling about themselves.

In other words, if medical services are about saving lives, curing illness and treating the sick, then the criteria of success should be survival and 'cure' (or, less ambitiously in chronic illness, amelioration of symptoms). In order to meet these criteria, then the necessary outcome indicators are mortality and morbidity statistics and not HRQOL indicators. It can be argued too that a similar calculus emerges in allocating resources between medical treatment and disease prevention services. From this perspective it is the effectiveness of, for example, immunisation, in terms of the number of lives saved that is crucial here rather than levels of experiential HRQOL among the population.

Part of the rationale behind this argument is that its goals are specific and precise whereas the wide-ranging, multi-dimensional, holistic and amorphous nature of the notion of HRQOL and even of the WHO definition of health itself are so broad and vague as to be of little practical use in planning medical services. There is also a potential paradox here between notions of, on the one hand, *health* and, on the other, *medical treatment*. It can be argued with considerable force that what we call 'health services' are in fact, *sickness* services and that health and ill-health are not opposites of each other, that health is far more than just the absence of ill-health and lies far beyond the remit of medicine. In other words, medical care only addresses a part of health, and an even smaller part of HRQOL so its aims and effectiveness should be judged on much narrower criteria than these.

This argument against the use of HRQOL also has an important moral element which relates to the whole area of elective treatment or treatment that is not essential in medical terms. An elective medical procedure may well be of major importance to an individual's well-being and life satisfaction and therefore their HRQOL and on this basis therefore should be accorded priority, but might have no 'clinical' medical significance at all and thus can be seen from a medical perspective as being a waste of time. More importantly, it can be seen as depriving someone else from having clinically significant and 'essential' medical treatment that would cure an illness or ameliorate a chronic medical condition but which perhaps might have less impact on that person's HRQOL.

Now, the magnitude of this dissonance between a 'medical' versus a 'health' approach or a needs/effectiveness-based clinical approach versus a HRQOL approach to health and medical services depends upon the size of the gap between these two perspectives. The problem would be very small if there was near-complete agreement between what for the sake of brevity will be called the 'clinical' and 'HRQOL' perspectives. Unfortunately, however, the gap is rather large. Bowling (1995a: 17), for example, reports that 'research suggests that there are wide discrepancies between patients' and doctors' ratings of outcome after specific therapies' with doctors being unable to measure adequately patients' quality of life. These discrepancies have a strong bias towards professional pessimism, with doctors regularly and routinely rating many health states more negatively than patients (Bowling, 1991). This leads Bowling (1995a: 10) to conclude: 'What matters is what the patient feels, rather than what the doctor thinks the patient ought to feel.'

Rosenberg (1995: 1413), taking an hermeneutical approach, stresses the importance of subjective HRQOL aspects of disease not just in terms of the immediacy of any emotional response but also in the context of what he calls the 'horizon of understanding' of a patient and his or her relatives, and he insists that here the medical decision to be made should be 'an *existential* decision based on the individual's values, norms, morals, attitudes and knowledge' rather than just about the doctor's judgement of the clinical efficacy of the decision.

Under these circumstances it is important that patients' views are taken fully into account. For many conditions a balance often has to be struck between the positive and negative aspects of alternative treatments, where sometimes therapeutic benefits may be outweighed by quality of life considerations, particularly in relation to the patient's emotional and physical functioning and lifestyle.

In moral and existential terms, then, it is important for patients to be involved in medical decisions about their treatment, taking their personal health-related quality of life fully into account. But what are the consequences of this strategy? Fitzpatrick's (1996) review of the findings of experiential studies came to the following conclusions. First, and mirroring the findings of Bowling (1991, 1995a), Rosenberg (1995) and Rapley (2003) noted above, health professionals' and patients' HRQOL ratings agree only moderately overall and less in relation to psychological and social than physiological dimensions. Second, it is these social and psychological dimensions that patients prioritise in contrast to doctors who prioritise physical functioning.

Fitzpatrick reports three other sets of interrelated findings which, taken together, have major and disconcerting policy implications These are: (1) the majority of patients with significant illnesses report their quality of life in positive terms; (2) there are only modest differences in psychological well-being between healthy individuals and those with significant illness; and (3) disease severity is weakly related to quality of life – 'very little of the variance in QOL is explained by disease' (Fitzpatrick, 1996: 148). In one sense this is very positive news: people in general do not let serious illness get too much in the way of their quality of life in general and their health-related quality of life in particular. In other words, patients tend to rise above their health problems. Perhaps this helps explain the comparative negativity of doctors compared to their patients about the implications of the patients' medical conditions, as noted above by Rapley.

The policy implications of this laudable and heartening resilience and stoicism of patients are discussed below. For the present it is worth recalling that there are three inter-related sets of constructs under discussion: (1) clinical success – will the treatment do what it is supposed to do?; (2) personal or existential HRQOL – is the outcome consistent with the patient's views, values and desires?; and (3) normative or consensus HRQOL – providing an impersonal, 'scientific' and objective approach. It is this latter approach which is now explored.

Consensus and normative approaches

Given that personal HRQOL, no matter how useful it is in identifying the patient's own, self-perceived best interest, would not necessarily lead to a better provision of medical services, should we not return to the clinical judgement of doctors in decision-making and just ignore the views of patients? Bowling (1995a: 10) is emphatic that this should not be done: 'Clinical indicators of outcome are no longer sufficient, particularly in view of the debate about whether to survive in a vegetative state is better or worse than death.' Her example here is a very stark one indeed; classic medical ethics and responsibility require that a patient be kept alive at all costs but this can be at odds with either the patient's informed wishes or their 'best interests' as defined by law. In this context, Fayers and Machin (2000) comment that quality of life may be the major, or in some cases even the *only*, consideration in circumstances such as these. The central quality of life question here is whether treatment, or continuation of life support, leads to a *life worth living*.

But how can 'a life worth living' be ascertained if the person concerned is unable to communicate their own view? Also, in a much less dramatic but equally important context, decisions have to be made between different clinical procedures. Clinical judgement cannot decide between the value of a heart transplant and kidney dialysis; other criteria have to be used. Cost-benefit analysis seems an appropriate way forward and the cost side is relatively straightforward but it is not easy to ascertain the comparative benefit of different clinical outcomes. Here is where the consensus or normative HRQOL approaches come into play.

Morreim (1992) identifies consensus quality of life research in terms of asking healthy people to answer hypothetical 'time trade-off' questions or to assign relative (quality of life) utility values to different sorts of health statuses and impairments. The importance of the label 'consensus' here is that these judgements are based not on moral or theoretical principles or by reference to wisdom or deep philosophical values (such as, for example, prudential values or Nussbaum's 'thick' version of the capabilities approach, both discussed in Chapter 3). Instead they gain their legitimacy from their reflection of the views of ordinary people; in other words they reflect 'common sense' or a 'democratic' perception rather than something that is necessarily *right*: hence their other label of *normative* – they reflect societal norms.

It is interesting to note that the results obtained from these normative hypothetical studies are sometimes different from those obtained from real-life personal and experiential HRQOL studies. Findings from normative studies have been variable but can be summarised as follows: (1) individuals imagine that different health states vary very considerably in terms of quality of life; and (2) individuals regard physical, social and psychological functions to be equally important to quality of life (Fitzpatrick, 1996). It will be recalled that, on the contrary, the findings of experiential studies were that, in general, differences in health statuses resulted in very small differences in personal quality of life and that social and psychological functioning were in practice considered to be much more important that physical functioning. This, of course raises serious problems over the applicability of normative approaches. Controversially, Fitzpatrick overrides these objections:

> The objective of most utility studies is to achieve various pragmatic goals, particularly the most appropriate allocation of scarce health care resources. For that purpose the social consensus of the desirability of various imagined health states is a better basis for decision-making than the reported quality of life of the sick.

(1996: 156)

His grounds for riding in such a roughshod manner over people's actual real-life sensibilities is that the normative consensual approach derived from the views of healthy people about hypothetical situations puts a much higher value on medical treatment and positive physiological health statuses than sick people in real life do. Thus, for Fitzpatrick, experiential appraisals should be given relatively low weighting in medical policy-making, otherwise spending on health services might actually *decrease*. He summarises this situation cuttingly as follows: 'To be simplistic the sick would be their own worst enemies in such an approach, given their tendencies to view severe health states favourably' (ibid.: 156).

There are a wide range of normative HRQOL approaches but the one in most common use can be divided into two types: 'life years'; and 'time trade-offs' or 'standard gamble'. Both types, in effect, use the same currency, that is years of good health. These years can then be costed so two different medical procedures having completely different effects can be compared in terms of cost-effectiveness, or utility. The procedure with the best cost effectiveness or utility is the one for which a healthy life year costs less.

The best-known among the 'life year' approaches are 'quality-adjusted life years', commonly known as *QALYs*. Another version, more relevant to disability than ill-health, relates to disability-adjusted life years, or *DALYs*. A QALY or, more precisely, a QALY of 1.0, is one year of good health in a patient's life. A person with reasonably good health will in an average year have a QALY of around 0.9, whereas a person with poor health may be judged to have a QALY of only 0.5. Bowling (1995a) gives some thought-provoking examples of the uses to which QALYs can be put; for example, it has been estimated that in the mid-1990s the cost per QALY of GPs advising patients to stop smoking was £170 compared to £14,000 per QALY for kidney dialysis. This means that – in the currency of quality-adjusted life years – smoking-related health promotion is 82 times more effective than dialysis, or put more bluntly, will – pound for pound – save 82 years of life for each year of life saved by dialysis.

The second set of approaches deals with perhaps more complex issues than QALYs. This moves beyond the notion of *currency* towards choosing between alternative levels of pain and disability or between different life expectances at different levels of disability. The basis of a 'time trade-off' is a choice between full-health for x years and different disability states for y years, where x and y are variables. These choices are normally made on the basis of a vignette where a respondent has to decide in relation to a hypothetical situation. An alternative is the *standard gamble* approach where a condition reduces life by x years whereas an operation provides a y per cent chance of extending life by z years by curing the condition. These examples are all used in health-care planning: e.g. how many hip replacements are worth the same as one liver transplant?

The potential usefulness of these normative approaches can be seen instantly in comparing the relative costs and outcomes of different procedures and in deciding whether and when to undertake high risk surgery. But these approaches have serious potential dangers too. The first problem, already alluded to, is whether these artificial and rather stilted constructs bear any relationship to *real* quality of life judgements that people make. It has already been seen that there are some major empirical differences between the two types of approaches.

Methodologically and theoretically there are problems too. QALYs and time trade-offs are predicated on the assumption that we are all able to predict now the evaluation we would give in the future to any state of disability we may incur. As the following case study demonstrates, this methodological assumption is by no means universally tenable. Cummins (1997: 126) is highly critical. He claims that QALYs have no relationship at all with subjective quality of life and that no-one can validly respond to such hypothetical situations. Woodrow (2001: 205) goes even further and maintains that quality of life in health terms cannot be measured either reliably or with validity and therefore should not be used at all in health services. Rapley too is extremely critical about these normative HRQOL measures. He has no arguments against policy-makers and professionals using the notion of quality of life as a sensitising notion but states: 'in the case of using QOL as a formally operationalised and measurable construct, it seems clear that the problems involved probably outweigh the putative benefits' (2003: 223).

However, it is not just empirical, methodological and theoretical problems that are raised by normative approaches to health-related quality of life. Perhaps the most pressing problem of all is about the value of individual human lives and human life in general. Returning to the example of QALYs, a severely disabled person will have a much lower QALY ranking than a person in full health and therefore each year they live will have a lower (normative) quality of life ranking. But does this means that the former person's life is less worth living than the latter's; is it thus *worth less*? This goes against a profound belief, both spiritual and secular, that all lives are equally valuable. From one perspective this looks like a paradox but from another it does not. On the one hand, if two people have the same life expectancy and one has an average QALY of 0.4 and the other has 0.8, then the latter has twice the 'quality life years' of the former. Would the latter then be the automatic choice for medical treatment in a rational QALY-oriented health service if both had the same life-threatening disease? On the other hand, if all lives are equally valuable, it makes sense to save as many as possible for each pound spent, and it is QALYs that tells us that smoking-reducing health promotion saves more lives than renal dialysis, so should a person with kidney failure be left to die and the money instead be spent on stopping people from smoking who at present are not ill?

There is no way that an easy or necessarily consensual answer can be found to these questions but some basic principles can be enumerated that will help clarify their meanings. To start with, it is necessary to explore the relationship between the *value* of life and the *quality* of life. Broadly speaking, there are two schools of thought here, The first is an absolutist or egalitarian perspective starting from the basic principled propositions that human life is absolutely precious and that all human lives are equal in value (and that none are more equal than any others). This is fixed and non-negotiable: therefore, a reduction in the quality of a person's life, as a matter of principle, has no effect at all on the *value* of that life. This position seems entirely consistent and indeed irrefutable if one holds to the basic principled assumption. Rapley (2003: 76) sums this position up as follows: 'Respecting persons *as such* means adhering to the *equality principle* that each individual is valued as an individual . . . whatever their life expectancy or present or predicted quality of life' (italics in original). This is a clear-cut and unambiguous position and appears to be the last word on the topic. Indeed it *is* the last word on the topic in the sense that it means a person's quality of life must not be used in making any life-or-death decisions about them and particularly that a *change* in a person's quality of life must not be used in making such decisions (though this does not stop HRQOL from being used in non-life-threatening medical decisions).

However, this perspective flatly contradicts the positions, noted above, taken by Bowling on patients in a persistent vegetative state and by Fayers and Machin on continuation of life support: both make the strong case that quality of life assessments are essential in these instances and therefore have an important effect on the *value* of a human's life. Thus, a person after succumbing to a persistent vegetative state has a less valuable life than previously precisely because their quality of life has dramatically reduced. Thus, the second school of thought links quality of life to value of life in that a dramatic reduction in a person's quality of life affects its value. This can be labelled as a *relativist* position in comparison to the absolutist egalitarian, non-negotiable position outlined above. This, like all relativist positions, can be portrayed as a slippery slope, and it has been so portrayed, as can be seen below. But it is possible to correlate quality and value of life while retaining the moral and ethical high ground. This is done by placing an absolute respect on the value of the person – that is, their personhood – rather than on the value of their life *per se*.

Arguments for the value of personhood rather than the value of life itself are arguably best initially expressed in relation to the issue of palliative care for a person who is articulate and fully in control of their senses rather than in the extreme case of persistent vegetative state. Someone, for example, in the terminal stages of cancer may have to make a decision between, on the one hand, prolonging life through chemotherapy or radiation therapy, both with painful and distressing side effects and a subsequent dramatic reduction in quality of life or, on the other hand, accepting an earlier death by not undergoing this treatment but having less pain and distress and having more comfort and peace of mind. Many people opt for the latter course of action in practice. Such a decision enhances experiential or personal quality of life but shortens the life and raises questions about the 'value' of that life itself – or at least the value of prolonging it. However, it is also contrary to both the anticipated clinical priority of prolonging life and the egalitarian absolutist position on the value of human life. But a decision of this nature values that *person* and is also respectful of that person's wishes and judgement on the quality of their life. So, here quality of life can be seen as an important and morally and ethically valuable element in the decision the person makes about the timing and nature of the ending of their life.

The question that the 'absolutists' have to answer here is whether they would deny the person the right to make this decision based on their own judgement of the quality of that person's life. This is perhaps the most fundamental and important question addressed in this chapter. And *any* answer here is problematic. A denial of this right, although justifiable from an absolute perspective of protecting, and upholding the value of, human life, can be seen as paternalistic and as disrespectful of that person's autonomy, agency and control over their life (all very heavyweight values) and as condemning them to cruel and unnecessary suffering. Upholding this right, though, is the beginning of a slippery slope and exposes people to pressure from, for example, family members with a financial interest in inheritance.

Once the sanctity of life is breached, in this instance through not providing life-prolonging treatment to a fully sentient person close to death, then the door is opened to doing the same for a person for whom informed consent is problematic, for example, with severe learning disabilities. It does not take much of a moral leap to move from here to discontinuing life support for a person in a persistent vegetative state who has previously made a 'living will' to end their life in these circumstances, or to move to doing the same for a person who has not made a living will. This is the point at which Bowling (1995a) came in and insisted that quality of life considerations should be taken into account. Somewhere a bit further down the slope the issue of mercy killing or euthanasia is introduced for people in great pain and distress and who want their lives to end. And so it goes on down the slope.

Once the relativist position is taken, then the crucial question is over where to draw the line, and this is probably one of the most difficult and important question that faces us all as individuals. It informs our moral views on abortion, euthanasia, capital punishment and war, among other issues. In this context, Rapley (2003: 81) makes an impassioned case against such relativism. He reminds us that quality of life judgements are now frequently the basis for life or death decisions in what he calls 'ethically problematic practices in medicine', including selective abortions and 'end-of-life decisions', in which he includes 'withholding or withdrawing of treatment, giving lethal doses of analgesic or active killing'.

He cites a study by van der Mass *et al.* (1996) in The Netherlands, where 43 per cent of all deaths involve 'end-of-life' decisions. They found higher rates for people with learning disabilities, including cases where patients were unable to give consent:

> That Dutch psychiatrists kill people they describe as 'mentally disordered' or 'incompetent' raises serious ethical questions about the criteria against which the quality of these lives were judged and found wanting, and the evidence base upon which these judgements were made.
>
> (Rapley, 2003: 142)

Now, it needs to be made clear that end-of-life decisions were not being made about these people because they had learning disabilities; end-of-life decisions were being made about a range of people with terminal illnesses, some of whom had learning disabilities and for whom therefore there were more complex and serious issues of informed consent than among patients without learning disabilities. However, the spectre of the slippery slope rises again because end-of-life decisions are taken about people in persistent vegetative states, *because* they show no signs of conscious life or sentient brain activity and there appears to be no prospect of them ever returning to consciousness. No brain activity is at the bottom of the slippery slope but what about the value of a life with very low brain activity? Is this person's personhood to be equally valued with that of a fully sentient person? Rapley (2003) has deep-felt concerns on this issue. He concludes that if the quality of some people's lives is conceded to be so appalling that their life is hardly worth living (therefore justifying end-of-life decisions), then the quality of some other people's lives might be seen as permanently diminished by learning disabilities. Thus we get to the problematic proposition that what makes this life less worth living is its low 'quality of life'.

Thus, he counsels policy-makers against using HRQOL instruments, particularly QALYs, for decisions which are not *technical* but are *ethical* in nature. In other words, QALYs and similar measures might be useful for allocating resources in the most effective way between different value-neutral medical provision decisions but there is a real danger that, again sliding down that slippery slope, the difference in QALY-status between people with learning disabilities and other people might lead policy-makers to make value-laden decisions detrimental to the former group's life chances without even considering the ethical consequences of their decisions. The crucial issue here is that a QALY is an abstract unit of 'quality of life currency' about the positive or negative value of medical interventions to people of certain statuses, not about the positive or negative value of *people* with these statuses: 'when we are discussing the quality of people's lives we are engaged in the weighing of moral questions, not simply the dry dissection of putative biological mechanisms of hypothetical statistical abstractions' (Rapley, 2003: 225).

Disability and quality of life – a paradox?

It is clear from the above discussion that there are serious ethical dilemmas in the utilisation of quality of life judgements in relation to life and death decisions and that these dilemmas are particularly stark when dealing with issues relating to people with learning disabilities whose level of intellectual understanding is, by definition, lower than average and who therefore may be more susceptible than other people to pressures to make a decision against their own interests.

There is another range of less traumatic but extremely important issues relating to the quality of life of people with physical disabilities, both congenital and acquired. These considerations strike at the heart of the notion of health-related quality of life *per se* and at what appear to be not just differences but contradictions between experiential and normative approaches. These issues can be lumped together into what has been called 'the disability paradox' and are broadly manifested by the higher than expected levels of self-reported quality of life among people either disabled from birth or with recently acquired disabilities, and more specifically by the *increase* in self-reported quality of life by a proportion of the latter group after, in comparison with before, they incurred their disability. Rapley (2003: 165) also includes some terminally ill people in this phenomenon: 'Many people with conditions that doctors regard as so near death as not to be worth arguing about regularly report that the quality of their life *after* diagnosis or disablement is higher than previously.'

In effect, there appear to be two different issues emerging here. The first is a 'disability contradiction' which is not entirely unexpected given the generally high reports of experiential quality of life among people with long-standing illnesses and disabilities: in many instances there is a flat contradiction between experiential or personal judgements on quality of life and normative or 'scientific' quality of life judgements or 'objective' clinical judgements. Albrecht and Devlieger (1998: 982) express the disability contradiction thus: 'people with disabilities report that they have serious limitations in activities of daily living, problems in performing their social roles and experience persistent discrimination yet they say they have an excellent or good quality of life'.

This phenomenon can be situated within the 'salutogenic' tradition of studying well-being (as opposed to a 'pathogenesis' tradition which places an emphasis upon negative aspects of health) which was developed by Antonovsky (1987) in order to try to explain how people manage well despite adverse health experiences. For Antonovsky, a strong sense of coherence and meaningfulness and a rational understanding of their situation are required for a disabled person to maintain a deep sense of well-being. Albrecht and Devlieger (1998) further develop this salutogenic orientation to include a balance between 'body, mind and spirit' along with maintaining a harmonious set of relationships within the person's social context and external environment.

Over half (54 per cent) of people with serious disabilities in Albrecht and Devlieger's study of 153 disabled people living in the community in the Chicago area in the mid-1990s report an excellent or good quality of life compared with around 80 per cent to 85 per cent of members of the general public without disabilities from a range of national US studies in the 1990s (Albrecht and Devlieger, 1998: 981). For Albrecht and Devlieger, the core factors in achieving high levels of life satisfaction relate to having control over their bodies, minds and lives and having a 'can do' approach to life. Furthermore, for many respondents, the experience of disability serves to clarify and reorient their views on their lives. They do not deny the negative consequences of disability but rather

> respondents explain their well-being in terms of acknowledging their impairment, being in control of their minds and bodies, . . . finding a purpose, meaning and harmony in life . . . and feeling satisfied when comparing one's self to one's capabilities and the conditions of others in similar situations.
>
> (Albrecht and Devlieger, 1998: 984)

On the other hand, pain, fatigue and loss of control over bodily functions are all important contributory factors to the 46 per cent of respondents in this study who report a poor quality of life.

Albrecht and Devlieger's formulation of the disability contradiction is controversial at two levels. First, and less problematically, there is disagreement about the explanation of high quality of life among people with severe disabilities. Instead of, or perhaps in addition to, a body, mind and spirit balance some commentators have identified high and consistent levels of practical and social support from family and social networks (Rapley, 2003: 164). Second, the construct itself has been robustly attacked, particularly by Koch, (2000, 2001) – see also Albrecht and Devlieger (2000) – and its epistemological basis does not sit easily with the 'difference' perspective on disability taken by the Disability Movement (Barnes and Mercer, 2004). There are important issues at stake here; the first of which is whether 'disability' more properly equates with 'difference' or with 'deficit' in relation to quality of life. For example, Koch pointedly asserts that

> While congenital deafness means a lifeworld without audible stimuli, the resulting social and perceptual reality is potentially as rich as any other. Deafness requires a different means of communication, sign language and lip reading rather than audible speech and hearing. This does not create of itself a context of either social or interpersonal impoverishment. The resulting life quality while by definition different is not necessarily lessened.
>
> (2000: 758)

This point is well taken and perhaps Albrecht and Devlieger could have presented a more cautious exposition of their thesis particularly in relation to congenital disabilities resulting in stable and non-degenerative conditions. Nevertheless, their position does have considerable merit particularly in relation to acquired disabilities leading to life situations which could be appropriately classified as falling into the category of 'deficit', such as multiple sclerosis:

> I don't like the way my disease is going but I can't complain. I have good days and bad days but all in all I have a good life.

or cerebral palsy:

> When I realised I had CP I was crushed. But you know what? I don't care what others think when they see me. I live my own life and can do about anything.

or AIDS:

> I found meaning, values and the spiritual aspects of life.

or chronic heart conditions:

> People look at me with my chronic obstructive pulmonary disease and think what a poor bastard . . . They don't understand. Visually you see an oxygen bottle, impairments and limits, but the spirit is boundless.

and

> [without] my faith, I would never have been able to deal with my congestive heart failure. I felt like a time bomb waiting to explode but I deepened my

belief . . . My faith gave me the strength to accept my condition and live each day to its fullest.

(all quotes from Albrecht and Devlieger, 1998: 982–3)

These examples give strong support to those commentators who say that there should not be any distinct HRQOL but that health and disability issues should be incorporated within multi-dimensional and holistic models leading with the quality of all aspects of people's lives. This would convert an apparent logical contradiction into an explainable discrepancy. And the discrepancy can be explained simply by the common phenomenon of adaptation: instead of the 'happy poor' we have the 'happy poorly' or 'happy disabled' where one aspect of a person's overall quality of life specifically related to physical functioning has reduced in value and in compensation other specific aspects have increased in value.

The second manifestation – the 'disability paradox' in its strongest form – is at first sight a completely baffling phenomenon: this is where a person's quality of life actually *increases* after the onset of a major and irreversible disability. This, of course, does not happen in all – or even most – cases, in many, the person concerned reports a dramatic decrease in quality of life. However, it certainly does in some: the quotes given above give an indication of the discovery of new facets of psychological strength or spirituality or focus on meaningfulness in life brought about by the onset of the disability itself. In order to explore this phenomenon in more detail one person's experience is discussed in depth here. Much of the material below appeared in fortnightly columns in the *Guardian* newspaper and further material is available from the *Guardian Unlimited* website.

Ed's story

Ed Guiton broke his neck in a freak accident then spent a year in a spinal unit. He has no feeling below his neck. He can read an electronic book on his computer, thanks to an electronic gadget in the bridge of his spectacles that moves a cursor on the screen and he can send voice-activated emails. To read a 'real' book he needs someone to turn the pages and has two carers to undertake everyday routine body-maintenance tasks. Emma Brockes, interviewing him for *The Guardian*, reports:

> In some ways, he says, he actually prefers himself since the accident. He plays a bigger role in the lives of his three children. He has become calmer and more reflective. 'I used to be quite aggressive, at least verbally, and have become less so. There are definite gains in terms of one's own mental life. I suppose I would trade off a degree of disability for that.' He grins painfully, 'Not quite this amount.'

(Brockes, 2004)

In March 2004, in a landmark case 'Miss B', a woman with the same level of disability to Ed was given the legal right to end her life. Ed's *Guardian* column on 24 March deals at length with this issue and how it affects him:

The major difference between Miss B and me is that I have a loving partner and three children to enrich my life. It was the thought of my family that kept me alive when I almost died of pneumonia after my accident. I couldn't bear the thought of leaving them and not see my children grow and have children of their own . . . On another occasion, when I was trying to spit the ventilator tube out of my mouth because it was hurting, my wife . . . grabbed me firmly by the shoulder and shouted: 'Don't you dare die, you have a young son.'

Miss B admits that children would probably make her see things differently. I can fully understand the difference that makes. Even so, I have discovered new reasons for living: not only have my relationships become deeper and more open, but my passion for reading has reawakened and I find I want to write, about my inner life and what's going on in the world.

I had an odd thought recently – would I trade the improvements in my life since my accident for the 'me' prior to my accident? I found I had a surprising reluctance, to the outrage of my children, though not entirely of my wife, who finds me more accessible and, dare I say it, gentler. My relationships with my wife and children have become more intense. If I could wind the clock back to before the accident and alter the subsequent course of events, all of this would be lost.

(Guiton, 2004)

The health-related quality of life of communities

Moving from the individual to the community level of health-related quality of life, we enter the territory of the discipline of social epidemiology that studies the collective characteristics that determine the health status of communities and societies (Kawachi and Berkman, 2000). In other words, social epidemiologists ask the question: why are some communities and societies healthier than others? In doing so, their aim is to uncover the foundations of good health – salutogenisis – rather than just identifying the causes of illness (Kawachi, 2000).

Broadly, there are two sorts of context for discussing 'healthy communities'. The first relates, obviously enough, to communities populated by healthy *people*. Here, health-related quality of life in communities focuses on prevention of communicable diseases, through activities such as immunisation and vaccination, environmental health measures, such as pest control (particularly disease carriers such as rats and mosquitoes), food hygiene, health education and health promotion. In this context it can be seen that 'community health' reaches into many environ-mental areas of life that go beyond the individual. It also raises the issue of paternalism and potential compulsion, particularly in the area of vaccination and immunisation.

But this context is the narrower of the two and is oriented specifically to individuals, either singly or in collectivities. The second is much broader and relates, not just to communities with healthy people but to *healthy communities*. Some commentators have argued that a healthy community, or a healthy nation even, is one characterised by social cohesion and egalitarianism (Wilkinson, 1996; Kawachi *et al.*, 1997; Kennedy *et al.*, 2003). These macro features of a community or a society deal entirely with collective and holistic constructs and are discussed in detail in Chapter 7 in the context of macro societal quality of life models which are presented in Chapter 6.

This chapter concentrates on the first, narrower approach which focuses on collective activities designed to enhance the health status of individual community members. But even this narrow approach has a strong community orientation. Returning to Beveridge's five giants, there has always been a strong link between squalor and disease. Poor housing, rudimentary sewage disposal and lack of clean drinking water were breeding grounds for the major epidemics of the nineteenth century. The high cost of disease and its assault on rich and poor alike meant that communities had to act collectively. The great public health works, particularly mass civil engineering to provide adequate sewers and drinking water (incurring the construction of massive reservoirs often many miles away from urban communities) was a collective and collectivist activity.

This link between public health and collectivism has led to public health being an intensely political activity. An individualistic, *laissez-faire* or economic liberal political philosophy would wish to restrict collectivism as far as possible as a matter of principle, viewing it as creeping socialism. There are also major issues of liberty and coercion concerning vaccination and immunisation, in relation to moral and religious beliefs, as well as with regard to possible health dangers.

A further issue that needs to be kept in mind in this context in addition to the debate over liberty versus coercion, relates to health inequalities: are these caused by structured inequalities and thus require redistribution of resources for their amelioration or are they due to the personal habits and lifestyles of the least healthy individuals, requiring health education and health promotion? Within the UK there have been lively debates over inequalities and health, with influential government-sponsored inquiries into the causes of health inequalities being disowned by the government for putting forward explanations based on structured inequalities rather than providing individualistic behavioural explanations (Whitehead, 1992). This politicisation of explanations for health differences needs to be kept in mind when interpreting the substantive debates on public health. The burning question of what proportion of the problem is structural and what proportion behavioural is not discussed here.

It is of course true that health differences have both structural and behavioural causes, whatever their proportional causality, and that both need to be dealt with. This has led to two major strands in public health policy: one individualistic strand comprising health education and health promotion aimed at enabling people to choose healthier lifestyles for themselves and their children; and the other more collective strand, often referred to as 'ecological' comprising both collective intervention (through e.g. water supply, sanitation, food hygiene) and the coercion of individuals through isolation of infectious diseases, vaccination and immunisation, etc. in addition to health promotion and education.

The difference between these two approaches can be seen in relation to, for example, campaigns to encourage people to lead healthier lifestyles by stopping smoking and drinking less. An individualistic approach would use health education and consciousness-raising techniques whereas an ecological approach would ban smoking and drinking in public places and would enable sufferers from smoking-related diseases to prosecute tobacco companies.

In the remainder of this section the emphasis is upon the structure rather than the substance of public health which is presented from an ecological perspective in the form of a concentric model. The main thrust of this approach concerns *vertical* links between different systems. Following Bulbolz *et al.* (1980), this ecological perspective is presented diagrammatically in Figure 2.1.

The innermost of these circles concerns individuals; their subjective well-being, both hedonic and eudaimonic, and their objective well-being, including their health and material circumstances. It is worth noting here that there is a strong interaction, indeed permeability, between the first two ovals, between the individual and their family, kinship and associational networks (along with associated norms and obligations). This is particularly true in relation to material circumstances and the important facet of our subjective well-being that is influenced by family and other close relationships. It was noted in Chapter 1 that close relationships influence perhaps the most important aspect of our SWB that is within individuals' control. It is also worth recalling Bowling's findings from her large-scale British study that relationships with family were ranked the most important aspect of people's self-assessed quality of life.

These two ovals, taken together, represent the *microsystem* within which people negotiate their day-to-day quality of life. The third oval, including the neighbour-hood and community, taken with the first two, comprises the *mesosystem*. For most people. it is these three areas that are the most central for their quality of life and it is within the ambit of the micro and mesosystems that the more individualistic, health promotion-oriented approach to public health is focused.

The fourth oval is of central importance to ecological perspectives on public health. It denotes the macrosystem, including national identity, culture, wealth, politics, citizenship and, crucially, central government health policy. Its content can be further expanded to include what Bulbolz *et al.* (1980) call the *exosystem* including international aspects of sustainability, global governance, global environmental conditions among others. This area is a major feature of the large-scale quality of life constructs such as the notion of *social quality* developed by Beck *et al.* and Berger-Schmitt and Noll's *overarching quality of life* construct, the latter of which has an explicit sustainability component. These constructs are discussed in detail in Chapter 6.

The details of Figure 2.1 can be argued over, particularly the interaction between the meso and macrosystems, and indeed other somewhat different concentric approaches have been used, such as Gillies' 'onion model', cited in Campbell (1999). Nonetheless, the principle is robust and it can be used as a framework for presenting and exploring the theoretical dimensions of quality of life. The strength of this approach is that it shows the potential impact of both the meso and macroenvironments upon individuals' quality of life.

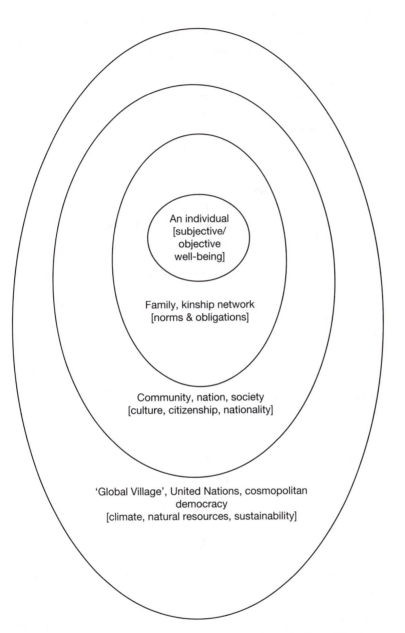

An individual
[subjective/
objective
well-being]

Family, kinship network
[norms & obligations]

Community, nation, society
[culture, citizenship, nationality]

'Global Village', United Nations, cosmopolitan
democracy
[climate, natural resources, sustainability]

Figure 2.1 An ecological perspective of the health-related quality of life of communities

Lindstrom (1992), cited in Raphael *et al.* (1996), developed an influential quality of life model which highlights the importance of societal and structural determinants of health using these four spheres. He labels them as follows:

- personal – physical, mental and spiritual;
- interpersonal – family structure and function, intimate friends and extended social networks;
- external – work, income, housing;
- global – societal macro-environment, specific cultural aspects, human rights and social welfare.

One advantage of Lindstrom's model is that it is one of the few approaches that is both psychologically and system-oriented. He analyses the first two areas through large-scale surveys and the last two through analysis of policy and of resource distribution. His work has been particularly influential in relation to children's health in Scandinavia (Raphael *et al.*, 1996). Rogerson takes a similar perspective when comparing environmental and health-related quality of life. He expresses the relationship between the psychological and system orientations as follows: 'an internal psychological-physiological mechanism producing a sense of satisfaction or gratification with life either at an individual level or collectively for communities or other social groups: and those external conditions which trigger the internal mechanisms' (1995: 1373).

Berkman and Glass (2000) add considerable substance to this approach by creating an *upstream* and *downstream* model involving cascading causal processes between the different levels. Social network theory is central to their model, and this emphasis on networks is a conceptual precursor to Wilkinson's thesis on the relationship between social cohesion, inequality and health, discussed in Chapter 7. In their view, the strength of social network theory 'rests on the testable assumption that the social structure of the network itself is largely responsible for determining individual behaviour and attitudes by shaping the flow of resources which determine access to opportunities and constraints on behaviour' (Berkman and Glass, 2000: 140). They insist that support from *within* the network is not enough to ensure positive health outcomes, as evidenced by poor outcomes in some highly supportive networks such as those of some drug users. Instead it is the 'upstream' context of the network's structure in relation to the larger, macro, social and cultural factors that shape both the structure of the networks and the salutogenic resources available to them.

The upstream factors at the macro-level influencing networks' impacts on health can be classified into four areas: (1) culture, including norms and values associated with co-operation and conflict; (2) socio-economic, including poverty, inequality and other aspects of political economy; (3) politics, including public policy, political culture and opportunities for political participation; and (4) social change, including urbanisation and cycles of economic activity. Taken together, these provide the upstream parameters and constraints on the ability of networks to enhance the health of their members.

In this context, networks are mediating agents at the meso-level between the macro-level of societal factors and the micro-level of interpersonal behaviour and individuals' health status. Berkman and Glass claim that networks operate at the interpersonal level through four primary pathways: (1) provision of social support; (2) social engagement and attachment; (3) social influence; and (4) access to resources and material goods.

Social support is at its most powerful when it is *transactional*, involving both giving and receiving within a normative framework based on interdependence, solidarity and reciprocity. This is entirely consistent with Bowling's (1995a) findings, noted above and with Wilkinson's (1996) discussion of the detrimental effects of social isolation which are discussed in Chapter 7. Berkman and Glass (2000) stress that many network studies focus exclusively on support received – or one-way support – rather than upon the much stronger and salutogenic reciprocal type of support.

Their second pathway, social engagement and attachment, relates to participation in a meaningful social context as an end in itself. This has strong resonance with the notion of social inclusion, discussed in Chapter 4. Here the emphasis is on *meaning*:

> We hypothesise that part of the reason measures of social integration or 'connectedness' have been such powerful predictors of mortality for long periods of follow up is that these ties give meaning to an individual's life by virtue of enabling him or her to participate in it fully, to be obligated (in fact, often to be the provider of support), and to feel attached to one's community.
>
> (Berkman and Glass, 2000: 147)

This attachment is strengthened by the third pathway, social influence, in its interactive effect with both social support and social engagement particularly in the context of role models, shared norms and reference groups. This formulation has many similarities to Kelly's personal construct theory where individuals construct their self-identity inter-subjectively in relation to their peers (Bannister and Fransella, 1986). Finally, access to resources and material goods links very strongly to Bourdieu's (1986) formulation of cultural and social capital, discussed in Chapter 5. These resources range from the intangible intra-personal such as self-esteem through to employment opportunities and access to financial capital (Putnam, 1993a, 2000).

Hancock and Perkins (1985) have developed this concentric circle approach even further in their 'Mandala of Health' model by identifying links and cross-overs between the individual, family and community in relation to work, lifestyle and the health-care system (or what they more properly call the 'sick-care' system). Each of these domains is linked to two cross-over realms: the sick-care system to human biology and personal behaviour; lifestyle to personal behaviour and the psycho-socio-economic environment; and work to the psycho-socio-economic environment and the physical environment.

This is an attractive formulation in that it emphasises the role of mind and spirit as well as body in relation to an individual's health (as do Albrecht and Devlieger

(1998) in a somewhat different context) and also starts to sketch in some of the interactions between the different systems and the ways in which they influence each other. However, this 'model of the human ecosystem' can be constraining as well as liberating, for example, the schema does not fully identify the extent to which these spheres interact. In addition, Hancock himself has subsequently identified a key substantive and normative omission: 'in particular it fails to explicitly address two key determinants of health, namely equity and sustainability' (Hancock, 1993: 43). Both of these term are, at face value, non-controversial but as seen in Chapter 8, their normative nature can lead to them being interpreted in a ideologically contested manner. Moreover, these constructs, along with social inclusion/exclusion and social capital, are all holistic, macro-level constructs which are dealt with in the second half of this book.

Conclusion

It can be seen that health-related quality of life is extremely important in policy terms, both at an individual level in relation to the treatment of illnesses and the provision of services to disabled people, and at a collective level in terms of providing public services to safeguard the health of community members. In both of these areas, though, HRQOL is controversial and perhaps even paradoxical.

The first issue to be resolved is whether doctors' judgements or patients' self-assessments of their HRQOL should prevail, given the serious problem of consistent and significant differences between them. Here it is, of course, in principle, vital to take the patients' views seriously in terms of respecting their dignity and autonomy. However, in the light of Fitzpatrick's (1996) conclusion that the sick are their own worst enemies, given that they often take a favourable view of even very severe health statuses, then acting on patients' assessments would result in them not getting the most beneficial treatment.

The situation is no better in relation to disability. In many cases, again, there would be a strong disadvantage to the objective life chances of disabled people if their self-assessed quality of life were used in policy-making and service provision because of their consistently positive quality of life assessments in general and the 'disability paradox' in particular.

If it can be seen to be contrary to the interests of sick and disabled people to take fully into account their own assessments of their HRQOL, then is there a better way of making decisions without ceding power to the medical profession? Some commentators say 'yes', that perspectives of members of the general public – i.e. people who are not sick or disabled but one day might become so – should be substituted for the views of the actually sick or disabled. These consensus or normative perspectives are operationalised by asking hypothetical questions about the 'cost' in quality of life of, for example, certain levels of disability into a currency such as 'quality adjusted life years' (QALYs) which can then be used as the 'benefit' side of a cost-benefit analysis.

From one perspective this can be seen as enhancing quality of life in comparison with sick and disabled people's own self-assessments in that they – or most of them – would normally get a better deal from this approach. However, many commentators perceive such normative approaches to be dangerous and part of a slippery slope leading to the devaluation of the lives of many groups in society, particularly of people with learning disabilities whose lives would automatically have a lower QALY status than that of non-disabled people. Would this then reduce their value as humans, and more practically would it put them lower on the waiting list for medical treatment than someone with an identical medical need but a higher 'QALY status'?

These are the troubling implications of some approaches to HRQOL at individual level. There are other, perhaps less existentially disquieting, but nonetheless fundamental ideologically divisive issues in relation to HRQOL at community level. These relate to different visions of society, whether it in essence comprises a group of free individuals coming together in a liberal, non-coercive setting where people are free to make their own decisions, even if in consequence their health and quality of life are damaged, or whether it is a collectivity with interlocking rights, duties and obligations where individual freedoms are constrained so that individuals' health-related needs can be more fully met. This fundamental ideological difference is one of the themes running through the next chapter which addresses quality of life within a social context.

3　The social context
Utility, needs, prudential values and capabilities

This chapter starts with pleasure and pain, then moves on to prudence. In other words, it commences with an exploration of utilitarianism, based on pleasure, happiness and people's actual desires and then explores the notion of informed desires with the prudential values framework. This is followed by an exploration of needs-based approaches, from the simplest basic needs model, via the hybrid and ubiquitous human development index, through to the theoretically sophisticated and highly influential theory of human need developed by Doyal and Gough. Finally, two versions of the 'capabilities' approach are presented: first, Amatrya Sen's initial 'thin' formulation which has influenced so much of the work of the United Nations Development Programme; and then Martha Nussbaum's radical and 'thick' reformulation with its list of central human functional capabilities for providing a decent social minimum for human flourishing.

Happiness and utilitarianism

Subjective well-being is an important aspect of quality of life or well-being in general. Indeed, one of its main components – happiness – is the foundation for the philosophical school of thought of utilitarianism which was initially propounded in the nineteenth century by Jeremy Bentham and James Mill, then developed by J. S. Mill (Collard, 2003). Utilitarianism gave a vision of the goal of the ideal society: one where utility is maximised. Utility in its most basic form is defined as the mental state of pleasure or happiness and its opposite, disutility, is pain or suffering. Thus a utilitarian society is one which strives to achieve the greatest happiness of the greatest number of its citizens. Two aspects of utilitarianism are central to discussions of quality of life. The first is at a theoretical level and is related to notions of values and desires. The second is at a practical level and relates to measuring utility in the material world.

Its theoretical approach has the merit of being easy to understand and intuitively unproblematic. For example, other things being equal, it is clearly better for each individual to be more rather than less happy and similarly better for a society to have a greater rather than a smaller number of happy people. It also has to be said that the centrality given by utilitarianism to the self-assessment by each person of their own well-being – to their own happiness – places great respect on the integrity, dignity and liberty of people as autonomous individuals. This is an important moral stance which must not be forgotten.

In its practical manifestation, utility is certainly the most commonly used and perhaps the most straightforward of all quality of life constructs to grasp: basically we do what makes us happy. In relation to the material world of goods and services, the following formula for achieving utility can be presented:

> happiness = getting what you want = choosing to purchase and consume certain goods and services.

In other words, our happiness can be measured by our purchases. The huge advantage that utilitarianism has over most other quality of life constructs is that these purchases are easily measurable – in money. Even more importantly, from a utilitarian perspective it can be seen that utility increases along with opportunity to consume. In other words, high levels of income lead to high levels of utility. So income can be used a *measure* or an *indicator* of utility, at least for all aspects of the material world that have a price on them. Therefore, rich people have more utility than poor people and it is the countries with the highest levels of GNP that have the most utility.

Given all this, it would seem apparent that utilitarianism is the ideal approach to the study of well-being and that we need look no further in trying to find a scientific approach to quality of life. However, this is not the case. This analysis begins with some of the conceptual and theoretical problems associated with equating quality of life with happiness.

Theoretical problems: desires and values

Utilitarianism might well be the epitome of a 'hedonic science' but there is considerable debate about whether hedonism – happiness – can always be equated with quality of life. For this to be the case, our best interests must always be met by doing the things that make us happy, or in other words, by fulfilling our desires rather than by doing things which can be seen as meaningful, valuable or worthwhile. Similarly, in this happiness-based utilitarian world it will always be 'better' to do things that are not worthwhile but which do make us happy than to do things that are worthwhile but do not make us happy. So to take a trivial example, in this simplistic version of the utilitarian world it will always be better (or will maximise utility) to eat sweets than to brush one's teeth. Similarly, some people's utility will be enhanced more by watching violent pornographic videos rather than engaging in more edifying pastimes. As can be seen later, even in less simplistic versions of utilitarianism, this sort of hedonistic problem is not easy to overcome.

It is clear therefore that there is an intrinsic tension in utilitarian positions. On the one hand, respect for the integrity and freedom of choice of the individual is paramount, along with a corresponding distrust of paternalism and interference in the lives of individuals. On the other hand, the inherent subjectivity of the approach, centred as it is on the individual's *happiness*, sets criteria for quality of life that can be met at a very low level of accomplishment or achievement or indeed of any objective assessment of what is a high quality existence for a human being.

This final criticism is the most difficult one for utilitarianism to deal with as a fully rounded theory of quality of life. Its most telling exemplification is in the problem of the 'happy slave': it makes sense for a slave – or a woman in a society that restricts women's rights – to adapt to their situation and to make the best of it rather than to rail against an inevitable servitude. Indeed, a very well-adapted slave or disempowered woman might even be *happier* than someone in an objectively better situation in the same society, so would thus be assigned a higher level of utility. This is perverse in any measure of comparative well-being which purports to give a rounded perspective on quality of life. Therefore utilitarianism, in order to be effective as a coherent theory of well-being, has to move away from an emphasis on happiness *per se*. This can be done, with a consequent increase in sophistication and applicability but also with a reduction in precision and intuitive clarity.

But there is an even more basic problem with utilitarianism which relates to the link between its theoretical foundation of mental states and its measurement in the real world, normally in terms of money. Utilitarianism makes this link in terms of experiences of the real world and desires which are motivations for gaining these experiences. Thus people achieve utility, the mental state of happiness, by meeting their desires via real-world experiences. Thus, moving from SWB to a more holistic perspective on well-being can be undertaken via a desires-based approach to utilitarianism. Here the meeting of desires is the key rather than maximising 'happy' mental states. Moreover, the desire-based utilitarian approach augments and complements 'happiness-based' approaches to utility: taken together, these two approaches can provide insights into both internal and external aspects of well-being.

Nevertheless, the notion of individual choice – consumer sovereignty and autonomy – remains central to the success of a utilitarian perspective. In this account, people maximise their utility by getting what they *actually* want rather than what they *ought* to want or what they would want if they were fully informed. This, according to Griffin (1986, 1996) is a fatal conceptual flaw – in effect the same flaw as the 'happy slave' problem, with experiences replacing mental states. The perils of consumer sovereignty can be seen at their starkest in the example of undiagnosed diabetics whose revealed preference, actual desire and – according to utilitarianism – experienced utility is to consume sugar when their best interests are to take insulin instead. On this basis, Griffin (1986: 10) concludes that 'the objection to the actual-desire account is overwhelming'. His response is to develop a theory of well-being based not on *actual* desires but on informed desires or rational choices or more prosaically, on our interests. This theory – prudential values – is discussed after looking at some of the practical problems with utilitarianism.

Ultimately, the debate about the appropriateness or otherwise of utilitarianism is based upon normative and ideological perspectives: either accepting it on the basis of autonomy and consumer sovereignty, or rejecting it because of the perils of basing the whole edifice on people's fallible desires. It would be easy, and appropriate, also to criticise the materialist emphasis of utilitarianism as operationalised in terms of money values because this misses out many non-material aspects of quality of life that are central to our human existence. These criticisms are not addressed here because some of the main practical alternatives to the utilitarian approach to measuring quality of life in the real world – including, for example, the basic needs approach and the human development index – are also based on a materialist perspective and therefore can be judged on the same, rather narrowly focused, criteria. The problems of a total reliance on materialism are, however, dealt with below in the section discussing the prudential values and capabilities approaches, which encompass non-material as well as material aspects of quality of life.

Practical problems: price, consumption and income

Within this practical, materialist, level there are two sets of criticisms that can be addressed to the operationalisation of utilitarianism in its own terms of consumption of goods and services, one from within a utilitarian theoretical perspective and the other from a perspective critical of utilitarianism. Before embarking on these critiques, though, it is worthwhile spending a little time outlining 'utilitarianism in practice'.

Utilitarianism, or at least a 'vulgar materialist' version of utilitarianism can be characterised with disarming simplicity though the operation of *expressed desires*. In the material sphere people usually express their desires by choosing to purchase and consume material goods and services. Going even further down this road, it is clear that resources are required to purchase material goods so income and purchase can be seen as two indicators, if not precise measures, of those aspects of utility that relate to the material world. Thus, from a vulgar materialist perspective, other things being equal, increased income leads to increased utility by providing the wherewithal for increased consumption of chosen goods and services.

Where utilitarianism is of considerable importance here is that it gives a (largely) coherent theoretical justification for arriving at this position by making connections between internal mental states of happiness, through expressing and meeting desires by the purchase and consumption of material goods and services. Thus, central to this materialist form of utilitarianism is the notion of *revealed preferences*: what we want as measured by what we choose to buy and to do. Such a definition is highly consonant with consumerism: we are what we consume or, more precisely in this context, our quality of life is largely derived from – and possibly even measurable by – our consumption. Kahneman *et al.* (1997: 375) express this view thus: 'Choice provides all necessary information about the utility of outcomes because rational agents who wish to do so will optimise their hedonistic experiences.'

As noted above, purchase is commonly used as a surrogate measure or indicator of the material manifestation of actual desires, known to economists as 'decision utility', and purchase depends upon income so, therefore, income can be seen as an indicator of utility or quality of life. Put briefly from an economics perspective, people, when given free choice, behave in rational ways to enhance their utility by doing things that make them happy. Many of these things involve consumption of material goods which have to be purchased with money. The more money a person has, then the wider their choice of consumption and the greater their opportunity of exercising decision utility. Therefore, at least in material terms, the purchasing power of money can be seen as a useful indicator of utility. In neo-classical economics this perspective led to the goal of maximising national per capita income, and in contemporary economics national income, as measured through Gross National Product (GNP) is seen as a *necessary*, although not a sufficient, proxy of well-being (Alkire, 2002a).

Problems of price and consumption within utilitarianism

The first, and most fundamental criticism from a utilitarian perspective of this vulgar materialist view of utility, is about whether we can actually infer utility from purchase and consumption. Kahneman *et al*. (1997: 375) question whether observed choices of purchase of goods and services, or *decision utility*, actually do represent real utility. In order for this to be the case, then this decision utility must always result in *experienced utility*, which in basic utilitarian terms is what utilitarianism is all about – pleasurable mental states. Kahneman *et al*. say that experienced utility is governed by a distinctive normative logic, is measurable, and is empirically distinct from decision utility. More importantly from a quality of life perspective, they claim to have found important empirical differences between experienced utility and decision utility which raise serious doubts as to whether we can in fact always infer utility from consumption.

Kahneman *et al*. (ibid.: 392) claim that this finding is relevant to an important debate between Scitovsky and Gary Becker. Scitovsky (1976) claimed that in general people are not effectively able to maximise their experienced utility because of their limited understanding and ability to predict their own enjoyment of goods and activities. Scitovsky also pointed to cultural differences whereby, for example, Americans seem to overinvest in comforts and are less successful than some other cultures in achieving success in the pursuit of happiness. (echoing the findings of Inglehart and Klingermann, (2000) discussed in Chapter 1). Becker (1996), on the other hand, assumes that people correctly anticipate the effects of consumption on future preferences and correctly incorporate these preferences in their choices. The importance of Kahneman *et al*.'s (1997) study is that it lends weight to Scitovsky's position and undermines Becker's contention. What is crucial here is not that money or purchase of goods and services have been denigrated from an *economic* point of view. They have not. The point is that purchases, and therefore income, have been shown to be less clearly connected with *utility*, with happiness, pleasure and with quality of life, than is conventionally assumed. Therefore, an increase in purchases or an increase in income does not necessarily mean an increase in quality of life, even within a rigorous utilitarian perspective.

The Kahneman *et al*. (1997) study also has implications for the debate on autonomy, paternalism and consumer sovereignty. It is noted above that one of the potential strengths of utilitarianism is that it respects the autonomy and choice of the individual and that alternative non-subjective approaches could be accused of a paternalism. Kahneman *et al*. conclude their analysis as follows:

The point of these observations is not to support paternalism, but to reject one of the arguments commonly raised against it. The claim that agents should be left alone because they generally know what is good for them is less secure than is generally assumed in economic discourse.

(1997: 397)

The importance of this critique of using purchasing and income as indicators of experienced utility is that it comes from within a utilitarian perspective. It starts off from a pure Benthamite pleasure-principle utilitarianism, reiterates that experienced utility is the utilitarian 'gold standard', then demonstrates that experienced utility is conceptually distinct from, and in practice not the same as, decision utility and therefore that decision utility is suspect as a surrogate for utility *per se*. Therefore, actual choice, consumption, and thus income are less adequate measures of utility than previously assumed. Similarly, from a utilitarian perspective, doubt has been cast on whether people's actual choices in fact maximise their experienced utility.

Stewart (1996) reiterates and develops the critique expressed by Kahneman *et al*. She states that people's actual consumption choices are constrained and mediated by inter-personal expectations and social norms as much as by utility and logic or rationality. She quotes here Sen's famous quip that 'the perfectly rational man is close to being a social moron' (Stewart, 1996: 47). Similarly, Svendsen and Svendsen (2004: 25) cite both observational and experimental research showing the domination of social norms over economic rationality in a wide range of settings.

Stewart also notes that a price-based approach assumes that all types of purchases are equally valuable because they are all measured in the same units. Here money spent on the basic necessities of life is presumed to have the same utility as money spent on luxuries. This odd conclusion necessarily flows from treating price as a proxy for value of goods and then using money, and thus income, as a general measure of value. It is interesting to note that this approach ignores the law of diminishing returns; a law which in itself is not incompatible with utilitarianism. It is entirely reasonable within utilitarian theory to posit that the resources spent on ensuring survival and basic physical comfort have higher utility value than those spent on an afterthought or a whim.

However, it is not only what the money is spent on but who it is spent by that is important. Often the person who holds and spends the money does so on behalf not only of themselves but of their families too. In a decision utility-based approach it is assumed that the head of household spends the money in the most efficient and equitable way in maximising the household's utility (Becker, 1996). This is a manifestly wishful assumption because poverty studies the world over (e.g. Gordon and Pantazis, 1997; Gordon and Townsend, 2000; Townsend and Gordon, 2002) demonstrate that a great deal of poverty exists within families and households where the total household income is more than enough to keep all its members above the poverty line. This sorry state of affairs occurs because the head of household is either selfish or inefficient or both in controlling expenditure. Here it becomes clear that there is a large gap between levels of assumed and actual utility, that is between the decision utility of the purchaser and the experienced utility of everyone on whose behalf the purchase is made.

Problems with using income as a measure of utility

All these above problems relate to flaws in measuring utility through purchasing goods or services: decision utility or expressed desire does not necessarily equate with experienced utility. Similarly, an absolute necessity does not have the same utility value, pound for pound, as a luxury purchased on a whim; and purchase by one person for a whole household does not necessarily represent utility for other household members. However, there is a second stage of distancing from utility in this approach – by substituting *income* for purchases. This causes additional problems.

This can be seen clearly in the above 'head of household' example because in many societies the majority of the population (i.e. children and very often adult females) do not have direct access to income at all but only to the goods and services provided for them by the, male, head of household. Alternatively, they may be given access to a proportion of the household income with which to purchase goods and services. Here, it is not the household income, but the goods and services that each member of the household has access to that is central to their quality of life.

This household example can be see as a microcosm of the issues involved in using income as a measure of utility at national level. there are two strands here: that of *distribution* and *aggregation*. At a national level, per capita GNP is virtually universally used as a measure of national income. Leaving aside whether income is or can be an effective measure of utility or quality of life, the use of per capita income implies or assumes that income distribution is either irrelevant or in principle satisfactory. However, two countries with exactly the same GNP can have dramatically different 'utility distributions' if one has a more equal distribution than the other. Assume, for instance, that this average GNP is relatively high and can provide a comfortable material living. In this case all members of the relatively equal society will have an acceptable quality of life or utility. In the more unequal society, however, a considerable minority of the population may be living in extreme deprivation and a similar proportion may be living very comfortable lives indeed (as is the case in the USA, see Wilkinson, 1996). Irrespective of any moral issues here, it is absolutely clear that the identical per capita GNP in these two societies hides huge differences in patterns of utility or quality of life. Thus average income alone is hopelessly inadequate as an indicator of levels of utility in a society.

Therefore, if use is to be made of per capita GNP, it is necessary to make corrections for income distribution. Inequalities in income distribution can be effectively measured by the Gini coefficient but this does not give any indication of the proportion of the population living below the level of adequate subsistence or any indication of where this measure may lie. This latter problem is an important weakness in any approach to quality of life based on per capita income and, as can be seen below, is immensely problematic for any utilitarian account.

Utilitarians can in principle deal with some aspects of income distribution, but the problem of aggregating from individual to national income strikes at the heart of the rationale for utilitarianism as an effective way of operationalising quality of life at societal level. The central issue is whether the maximisation of utility for each individual leads to the maximisation of social utility. In other words, is the greatest happiness of the greatest number simply a matter of adding the utility of all individuals without taking any social factors into account?

An example of the difficulties encountered in providing a practical metric of social utility relates to the issues of externalities and public goods. Where is the place of public goods such as civic gardens and national parks or of externalities such as pollution in such a utilitarian accounting system? To be fair to utilitarians, most do accept that, in principle, public goods need to be factored in to their national income accounts – although they need to find an alternative measure to decision utility here. Externalities are not easy to account for and this problem is an important principle put forward by proponents of collectivist, anti-utilitarian, approaches to well-being or welfare, especially by the 'father of British social policy and administration' Richard Titmuss in the 1960s who was a very persuasive advocate of this position (Titmuss, 1963, 1968).

Over-riding all this is the knowledge that the massive increases in GNP in developed nations in the past half-century have not led to similar increases in levels of SWB or 'happiness'. Given that SWB is an indicator for the happiness which is central to utilitarianism, the lack of a relationship over time between the two variables must cast doubts on the efficacy of income as a proxy for utility.

These different strands can be brought together in a two-stage approach. The first stage is to appraise the use of income in general, and GNP in particular, as a measure of utility within a utilitarian perspective and the second stage is to appraise it from a perspective critical to utilitarianism. The logic of using per capita income as a proxy for utility is as follows. People maximise their experience of utility by doing things which give them pleasure, so they choose to purchase goods and services in such a way that their decision utility maximises their experienced utility. This costs them money: the more money they have, then the more opportunity they have to exercise choice. Therefore the more money there is collectively in a society then, other things being equal, the more opportunity there is for choosing to consume goods and services and therefore to maximise utility.

From a utilitarian perspective there are two crucial issues here. The first is whether purchases actually do maximise experienced utility. As has been seen, this is by no means straightforward. The second issue concerns the relationship between an individual's utility and utility at a societal level. In effect, this conundrum has opened up an area of complexity which is highly problematic for utilitarianism.

The second stage is from a perspective critical to utilitarianism. Here there are at least four strands of attack. The first concerns the problems and inconsistencies noted above within the utilitarian discourse itself: until these get sorted out, then utilitarianism cannot even stand on its own two feet. The second criticism concerns the majority of the population in many countries who do not purchase the goods and services consumed in their households: the utility connection between pleasure and purchase just does not exist for them so they are completely outside the utility equation. The third is lack of evidence that there has been any link over the past 50 years between the massive growth in national income in Western nations and any growth at all in any independent measures of utility: if happiness is central to utility then why has happiness, as measured in terms of subjective well-being, stayed stable in developed countries in a period when GNP has doubled? This seems to be strong empirical evidence that in the most developed countries, GNP bears no relationship to utility as measured in terms of pleasure, pain or happiness. Finally, returning to the conceptual and theoretical critique, there seems to be no evidence in the empirical exposition of utilitarianism which might counter the problem of adaptation – the happy slave or contented dispossessed woman.

It is for these reasons that alternative materialist approaches to utility have been established, which attempt to overcome the practical problems associated with income as a proxy for quality of life. The most straightforward of these is the basic needs approach, which deals not with desires but with needs, not with the proxy income but directly with goods and services, and not with averages or per capita aggregations but with the needs of the most deprived members of societies.

Basic needs and other needs-based and materialistic approaches to quality of life are discussed later in this chapter. Beforehand though, the vexed question of desires is revisited: is there an alternative to the problematic 'actual desires' approach and can this overcome the potential problems of paternalism?

Prudential values

Informed desires – the road to prudential values

If a person's actual desires are seen as at best a partial and potentially seriously flawed representation of their quality of life, then is it therefore necessary to put an objective needs-based formulation at centre stage in any meaningful quality of life framework? Given the above critique, then the answer to this is probably 'yes' in relation to *actual* desires but this does not necessarily have to lead to the banishment of all forms of desires to the quality of life sidelines. There is a strong argument that a less individualistic and hedonistic formulation of desires can overcome these problems: this formulation replaces actual desires by *informed* desires. One of the most important representations of informed desires is that of *prudential values*, initiated by James Griffin (Griffin, 1986, 1996) and developed by Mozaffar Qizilbash (Qizilbash, 1997a, 1997b, 1998). Prudential values are values which make any human life go better and are predicated on a notion of the good life based on our essential humanity.

People's actual SWB and the above variants of utilitarianism can be seen as having an essentially subjective and empirical basis in that their starting points are what people feel, want and do. The prudential values approach on the other hand, is based not on people's actual desires but on what their desires would be if people were fully informed. This, Griffin claims, overcomes the 'happy slave' problem, because informed desires appeal 'to what really would increase or decrease the quality of their lives. It does not matter if some people have modest expectations: their informed desires include what they would want if they raised their sights' (1986: 47). Similarly an informed desire can be the exact opposite of an actual desire if a person desires what is bad for them, because informed desires relate to *real* rather than *believed* benefit.

But this leaves one crucial question unanswered: what exactly would people desire if they were fully informed? Actual desires, in principle at least, can be ascertained by *asking* people and/or observing their behaviour, but informed desires are not so easily accessible. Indeed, in one sense, they are not empirically accessible at all because fully informed desires are a utopian goal: increases in knowledge and understanding ensure that becoming fully informed is a dynamic and ever changing objective. So a method needs to be chosen whereby a framework for identifying a set of informed desires can be constructed either by identifying empirical examples of well-informed desires from the real world within an inductive, positivistic theoretical framework or by constructing a set of rules for identifying such a set based on a normative theory of informed desires.

In principle, it looks as if it should be possible to construct an inductive approach to prudential values based upon the observed desires of the best-informed people throughout history. This is certainly an attractive procedure which would yield interesting outcomes. Many of these outcomes too would be non-controversial, for example, the wish to live a long, healthy and comfortable life appears to be an uncontentious desire held by a large number of well-informed people throughout history. But there is a problem here because exactly what is it that they are well informed about which has led to this action coming into the category of *informed* rather than any other kind of desires? Also this purported informed desire becomes problematic in the light of experience of other, admittedly fewer, well-informed people living comfortable lives in regimes that they consider to be unjust who take the opposite view and choose to sacrifice or risk losing their lives for beliefs they hold strongly. Regrettably, these sorts of events have not been uncommon in recent history, particularly in relation to religious and political freedoms.

At a less dramatic level, too, the appeal to actual desires of well-informed people is fraught with difficulties because they have a habit, again consistently through history, of systematically disagreeing with each other over what well-informed people *ought* to desire. It is at this stage that recourse to normative theory becomes unavoidable. At its most straightforward level, normative theory is an organised set of statements about what ought to happen and why. Many disagreements about what a well-informed desire would look like are not factual or practical (i.e. related to errors and what is true and what is false) but about what is appropriate or what is right.

Notions of what is right are firmly in the domain of ethics and moral theory and are highly relevant to discussions of quality of life. But these are exceedingly difficult and complex areas in which it is easy to get permanently lost. More to the point, they are essentially contested among well-informed commentators and are at the highest level of conceptual abstraction. Also there are important issues which need to be sorted out before addressing moral theory. So the present task is to address what it is appropriate for well-informed people to desire on the under-standing (or at least in the belief) that the set of appropriate desires is wider than the set of morally right desires and that the latter is contained within the former. Therefore, it is hoped that issues of morality can be dealt with effectively (if they can be dealt with at all) subsequent to dealing with issues of appropriateness.

From desires to values

So, then, what are the criteria for appropriate informed desires? Griffin (1986) starts from the position that it is appropriate for people to behave prudently and thus he proposes an approach based on prudential values. Prudential values concern what makes a person's life valuable to herself or himself whereas moral values concerns what makes it worthwhile more generally according to abstract principles of what is right or wrong. Griffin (ibid.: 119) summarises prudential values thus: 'Basic prudential values provide us with an important standard for judging many (ordinary) human lives. They let us say, though only roughly, how good the life is, how it could be better, and how it compares to other lives'. Griffin (ibid.: 19) states that the prudential values approach: 'has to do with everything that makes a life good simply for the person living it'. He sees a thing which is prudentially valuable 'as enhancing life in a general intelligible way, in a way that pertains to human life, not one particular person's life' and 'anything is prudentially valuable if it is generally intelligible as valuable and as valuable for any (normal) human' (ibid.: 27).

Even more simply, Qizilbash identifies prudential values as values which 'make any human life better' (1997a: 262). Qizilbash and Griffin both make links between actual desires, informed desires, values and interests, but also accept that that in many circumstances desires may not relate at all well to genuine prudential values: 'A more direct way to approaching prudential values may be to look at the nature of a characteristically human life, and the grounds of our mutual intelligibility as human beings' (ibid.: 263). This is an important conceptual point of departure in that a new criterion for quality of life has been introduced that is completely distinct from desires, whether actual or informed: an appeal to the notion of what it is that makes us distinctively members of humanity. In essence, according to this perspective, it is the nature of our humanity which provides the context and framework for assessing the criterion of desires being informed rather than a criterion of 'value-free' scientific knowledge as the basis for being informed. This perspective provides an important link with Sen's notion of capabilities which is discussed later in this chapter.

The notion of being characteristically human also moves away from an individual-centred to a more inter-subjective approach strongly linked to Wittgenstein's proposition that in order to make sense of each other's utterances and of language in general, we must share certain values:

> Indeed, we need to share some values to be able to see each other as human beings, as beings with certain sorts of aims, desires, needs and so on. So a shared realm of human values is necessary for our mutual intelligibility. That

seems right . . . So, at some basic level, our understanding of language implies a bedrock of shared values.

(Qizilbash, 1997a: 263)

These shared values necessary for mutual intelligibility and for seeing each other as humans are identified as core prudential values and are values which will make any human life go well. Core values are seen as essential to the definition of humanity: 'To see each other as humans is to see each other as people whose lives fare better with the elements of core value' (Qizilbash, 1998: 64).

Two central core prudential values, perhaps ironically, perhaps unsurprisingly, are shared with utilitarianism. These are: enjoyment and avoidance of pain. The absence of such core values impoverish a characteristically human life. Qizilbash identifies other prudential values as being non-core: these are values which give human life point and weight, which enhance life in a generally intelligible way, but which are not necessary for mutual intelligibility. An important non-core prudential value would be accomplishment. A life of accomplishment would – other things being equal – be better and more prudentially valuable than a life without accomplishment, but accomplishment is not a requirement for mutual intelligibility and so therefore, although important, is not seen as core.

The distinction between core and non-core prudential values is both potentially important and potentially confusing. It seems to be important in terms of providing a theoretical grounding for prudential values in linking core values to Wittgenstein's (1953) influential treatise on the essential inter-subjectivity of human identity. Yet it appears confusing – at least at first sight – that the more profound and 'heavy-weight' prudential values are seen as non-core whereas the ones which prudential value proponents are striving to escape from in their utilitarian guise, i.e. pleasure and pain, are seen as core.

On a more positive and fruitful note, the notion of prudential deliberation, that is deliberation about what makes a characteristically human life better, according to Qizilbash, leads to the identification of prudential values such as friendship and requited love, which even if they are not strictly necessary for mutual intelligibility, can certainly be seen as important for the preservation and continuation of the human species so perhaps might be placed closer to core than to non-core prudential values. Other non-core but heavyweight prudential value such as freedom and autonomy perhaps have a different status in that they are not essentially interactive in a positive sense, although they require freedom from coercion and are therefore relational in a negative sense. They also have a different status to friendship and requited love in that they need to be qualified by a 'golden rule' provision in that one person's freedom and agency must not be detrimental to the freedom and agency of others. In addition, freedom and autonomy can lead to non-prudent outcomes if they are exercised unwisely. Qizilbash defends the inclusion of these values thus: 'Mature human beings are typically given the choice of living their lives in various ways, of finding their own way. The exercise of that choice, even if it is abused, is part of what makes a human life valuable' (1998: 64). This freedom and autonomy includes, of course, the freedom to indulge our actual desires irrespective of our real interests, which brings prudential values, or one prudential value at least, perilously close to first-principles utilitarianism.

To be fair, freedom and autonomy are highly problematic for any non-hedonic approach to quality of life: a life without basic freedom is in principle a diminished life; whereas non-prudential activities, freely chosen, are damaging and are tautologically contrary to a prudential values approach to quality of life. There are at least three responses to this criticism. The first is that it is the lesser of two evils – the non-prudential use of autonomy is better in terms of well-being than slavery, no matter how adaptive and happy the slave is. This answer is common to all non-utilitarian approaches discussed here. Second, freedom, agency and autonomy are not seen as core prudential values (and in the account given above, can even be seen as less central than other non-core values such as friendship and requited love) and are certainly not given any priority over other values. Here prudential values differs from both Sen's (1993) capabilities approach and Rawls' (1998) fairness approach which *do* prioritise and privilege freedom and autonomy and therefore have even more problems on this topic. Third, *understanding* is seen as an important prudential value and understanding, of course, enables us to use our freedom more wisely. Thus according similar priority to understanding and freedom both enables freedom to be used more wisely and actual desires to become closer to informed desires. So in a well-ordered prudential values universe, high levels of understanding would lead to freedom being exercised in a positively prudential way.

An indication of the purpose and scope of the prudential values approach has now been given, along with examples of individual prudential values. The next step is to enumerate how many there are and what areas of human life they cover. Both Griffin and Qizilbash provide lists of prudential values. Indeed, several lists related to values, needs and capabilities are presented in this book. The prudential values lists, however, have a different status to most of the others in that they are seen as indicative rather than definitive. Griffin accepts that the list he provides is culturally defined and is open to amendment but he makes the point that prudential deliberation would lead everyone to a list of some kind, and that our shared human values would – or should – lead to all the lists having considerable similarities.

Griffin has presented his list in slightly different forms on different occasions. The following is based on Griffin (1996: 29–30 and 1986: 67).

(a) Accomplishment
(b) Components of a characteristically human existence:
    Agency
    Autonomy
    Liberty
    Basic capabilities that enable one to act:
        limbs and senses that work
        minimum material goods that keep body and soul together
        freedom from great pain and anxiety
(c) Understanding, including:
    self-knowledge

knowledge about the world

being in touch with reality

freedom from muddle, ignorance and mistake

(d) Enjoyment, including general pleasures, the day-to-day textures of life and appreciating beauty

(e) Deep personal relations: 'deep, authentic, reciprocal relations of friendship and love ... they in themselves go a long way towards filling and completing life'.

(Griffin, 1986: 67)

Most items on the above list have already been mentioned. However, some elements of item (b) 'components of a characteristically human existence' are new, and some have a different status to others. For example, 'limbs and senses that work' are certainly attributes that would make any human life go better but it is not clear in what sense these are *values* – and they are certainly not desires. Perhaps they can best be called prudential *attributes*. These attributes can then be seen as facilitating the prudential value of autonomy because impairment can diminish autonomy. 'Basic capabilities that enable one to act' similarly do not fit comfortably as values. The notion of capabilities opens up a whole new approach to quality of life, epitomised in the work of Amatrya Sen, which is discussed later in this chapter. All that needs to be said here is that capabilities are generally seen to be a different kind of characteristic than values and therefore the inclusion of a capability set within a set of values leads to some lack of precision and clarity – even though there are good pragmatic grounds for including capabilities among those things that make a characteristically human life go better.

Qizilbash raises a question too over the status of 'the minimum material goods that keep body and soul together' in that these material goods are instrumental rather than intrinsic in their nature. He recommends being more specific about what actually constitutes the intrinsic goal of keeping body and soul together and thus includes: minimum levels of nutrition, health, shelter, rest, security, sanitation, basic physical and mental capacities, and literacy,

There is one general aspect of item (b) that is rather odd too. It is labelled as 'components of a characteristically human existence' but surely all the other items also fall into this category? Also why are the extremely important values of autonomy, liberty, agency and life-choice bundled together with 'limbs and senses that work' and not each given independent status? Their core/non-core status cannot be the reason because enjoyment, seen as a core value, has independent status whereas avoidance of pain, another core value, is relegated to a subsection of item (b).

Qizilbash also contends that the list is incomplete because it does not include self-respect, dignity or aspiration – although the last of these is perhaps implicitly included in Griffin's category of accomplishment. The case Qizilbash makes for self-esteem is important in relation to a holistic notion of quality of life and is highly relevant to discussion of Doyal and Gough's theory of human need later in this chapter and of overarching quality of life theories in Chapter 6. In the context of the Wittgensteinian perspective used by Griffin it can be seen to lie at the heart of our conception of ourselves as human in that our self-identity is central to our inter-subjective way of seeing each other as human beings. A human being with a self-perceived spoiled or impaired identity through low or damaged self-esteem will certainly find it hard to sustain the prudential values of friendship and requited love that could be seen as close to being core prudential values. Qizilbash makes this case perhaps even more strongly:

> Without some notion of our own importance we would not aim to make something of our lives . . . Dignity is closely related to agency . . . self-respect may have its basis in complex social relationships. If I count as nothing, or close to nothing, in the society I live in, my self-esteem may be so poor that I cease to care about my own life or destiny, let alone pursue accomplishments or significant relations.
>
> (1998: 66)

This has strong resonances with Wilkinson's *healthy societies* thesis discussed in Chapter 7.

Obviously there is a balance to be struck between self-esteem and self-respect, on the one hand, and self-importance or hubris, on the other. It perhaps needs to be stated here that the notion of prudential values itself is related strongly to self-interest. To ensure that self-interest is not equated to selfishness in any prudential values account, it is necessary always to keep in mind the essential inter-subjectivity of its formulation, in making *any* human life go better there is a requirement not to make *any other* human life worse.

The list of prudential values that Qizilbash (1998: 67) arrives at is as follows:

1   minimum levels of nutrition, health, sanitation shelter, rest and security;
2   certain basic intellectual and physical capacities and literacy;
3   certain levels of self-respect and aspiration;
4   enjoyment;
5   autonomy or self-determination ('positive freedom');
6   liberty (negative freedom);
7   understanding;
8   significant relations with others and some participation in social life;
9   accomplishment.

This list is clearer, more consistent and more comprehensive than that given by Griffin and is used as a benchmark for comparing with lists derived from other approaches to quality of life.

Prudential values in action

A list of prudential values gives us an overview of the sorts of things that make up quality of life from a prudential values perspective but it does not give any indication of how to make an overall assessment of quality of life or of how choices might be made between different prudential values themselves. In this context it is important to be aware that the individual prudential values are entirely separate from one another and cannot be aggregated into a 'super value'. Qizilbash (1998) calls this 'component pluralism'. The situation is further compounded by two further forms of pluralism: 'good life pluralism' because individuals can have *conflicting*, not merely different conceptions of the good life; and 'weight pluralism' because different weights can be given to the different components of well-being. This multiple pluralism reflects a fundamental difference between prudential values and utilitarianism: that of pluralism versus monism. Utilitarianism is monistic in principle and its material measure – income – can be aggregated into GNP to give national comparisons.

The fundamental question arising from this pluralism is whether there is any possibility of creating an overall well-being ranking based on such disparate prudential values or: 'can we go from a set of plural value rankings to a ranking or index of overall well-being?' (Qizilbash, 1997b: 2013). Qizilbash sets about attempting to do just this, comparing indicators of prudential values at national level for developing countries. The indicators he uses are: per capita consumption (as a rough indicator for the prudential value of enjoyment); life expectancy at birth and infant mortality rate (both tapping into different aspects of minimum levels of nutrition, health, sanitation, shelter, rest and security and into basic intellectual and physical characteristics, albeit with some double counting); adult literacy rates (literacy); index of political rights and index of civil rights (both tapping into aspects of positive and negative freedom: see Berlin, 1969). Indicators for the other identified prudential values are not available for the developing countries, although he suggests that for developed countries, employment and unemployment data could be used as rough indicators of accomplishment.

The countries are then ranked on their scores for each of these indicators. These ranks are then added together so that each country is given an overall score (known in development studies as a *Borda score*). For example, a country that is ranked first on four of the six items and second on the other two would achieve a Borda score of $1 + 1 + 1 + 1 + 2 + 2 = 8$ whereas a country ranked tenth on all six would have a Borda score of 60. Then the Borda scores themselves are ranked from top to bottom.

This approach gives a rough and ready overall score which deals with the problem of *component* pluralism and enables all countries to be compared with each other so long as there is not too much missing data. However, it does not overcome the problems of good life and weight pluralism. Qizilbash utilises another statistical tool to address these issues. This is known as the *Pareto rule* and is as follows: a country is ranked higher than another overall if it does better in terms of at least one value and does no worse on any of the others. In our example above, the two countries with Borda scores of 8 and 60, the former is also ahead of the latter on the Pareto rule because it did better on *all* the individual indicators. The Pareto rule only gives a partial answer because there will be several pairs of countries where each is better than the other on at least one item. This is an important and interesting issue: for example, it leaves unresolved whether India is in advance of or behind

China because the former has higher freedom scores and the latter higher literacy scores.

Thus, it can be seen from inter-country comparisons that prudential values can be used in empirical international comparisons of the good life, even though these values are in essence irreducible and subject to different dimensions of plurality. It is worth at this point repeating Qizilbash's observation that more is needed than just a list of prudential values in order to compare well-being between two people. In particular we need to know the relative weightings and operationalisations for each person of each prudential value set. As will be seen below, this is a problem for all list-based approaches to quality of life.

Overview of prudential values – strengths and weaknesses

By substituting informed desires for actual desires the way is opened for a transformation from the essentially one-dimensional, individualistic and atomistic utilitarian approach to an essentially multidimensional, social and inter-subjective prudential values approach to conceptualising and measuring quality of life. A utilitarian calculus is – at least in relation to material desires – empirically straightforward in that utility is measured in money values which can be added together to give a total. The utilitarian calculus is undoubtedly seriously flawed but it has the advantage of being clear-cut and intuitively easy to grasp. The prudential values calculus is far more complex in its multiple plurality, but this is inevitable given that the reality it aims to represent is in itself plural and complex.

In addressing the desires that people would have if they were fully knowledgeable, rather than what people actually desire, and in addressing prudence rather than hedonism, prudential values tap into a deeper and more aspirational vision of human nature than that of utilitarianism. However, any move to replace what people actually choose to desire will reduce their independence and in at least one important sense, their autonomy. It also introduces the possibility – or from some perspectives, the certainty – of paternalism, of being told that what is best for you may not be what you want to do. Griffin perhaps wants to both keep his cake and eat it here because he accepts that autonomy is reduced by moving away from actual desires and yet it is an important facet of any enlightened person's conception of the 'good life'. He maintains, however, that autonomy is not a be-all or end-all and cannot be judged in isolation. In other words, although it is important, it should not be privileged over other important values. This is an central issue in operationalising non-utilitarian approaches to quality of life which is returned to later when discussing Sen's capabilities approach.

Weaknesses

So prudential values are more complex than utilitarianism and are open to charges of paternalism or at least to the diminution of autonomy. These can be seen as potential points of criticism but equally can be seen as positive attributes in that oversimplification is potentially dangerous, as is unbridled licence. It can be argued, however, that the prudential values approach is seriously flawed by internal inconsistency or incompleteness.

Two examples can be given of this. The first relates to the plurality of values and the apparent lack of clarity over whether there is *a priori* ranking among them. Griffin appears not to differentiate prudential values from each other in terms of intrinsic importance, and this seems to be consistent with the notion of weight pluralism. In Qizilbash's exposition, however, it looks as if there are two or possibly three potential intrinsic rankings of prudential values: with, first, core values of enjoyment and avoidance of pain; second, deep personal relationships of friendship and requited love (or, more prosaically, 'significant relations with others') being close to core values; and third, with the remaining values being somewhat more distant from the core. But does this mean that enjoyment must therefore be prudentially more important than deep personal relations which in turn are more important than liberty and accomplishment? Qizilbash's use of the Pareto rule sidesteps this and does not address what must in terms of any definition of prudence be the overriding issue of survival. His prudential value of 'minimum levels of nutrition, health, sanitation, shelter, rest and security' (matching Griffin's of 'minimum material goods that keep body and soul together') is of such overriding practical and existential importance to nations at subsistence level that it seems it must take priority here over, for example, enjoyment.

The second example is linked to the conceptualisation of prudential values as being concerned with what makes any human life go better. Both Griffin and Qizilbash accept that their prudential deliberation on this issue will lead to different lists being created and that there are dangers of cultural specificity affecting the outcome. Qizilbash claims, however, that this can be overcome:

> The point of prudential value theory is to list the things that make any *human* life go better, independent of cultural, social or class background . . . the fact that human beings live in different cultures does not deny the possibility of a distinctively human form of life which is independent of culture. So prudential values need not be culture bound.
>
> (1998: 70; italics in original)

Similarly, Griffin contends that shared human values would – or should – lead to the lists having considerable similarities on the basis that there are genuine objects of human value and that if list-makers were all informed and understanding enough then they would all produce relatively similar lists (Qizilbash, 1998: 65). The nomination of 'genuine objects of human value' hints at a strong element of objectivity in prudential values. Indeed, Griffin (1986: 72) goes as far as to claim that prudential values 'are not in any simple way subjective. They are not a matter of taste. They too, are in an important way, objective goods.' The assertion of objectivity is a bold claim but is not supported in terms of the criteria by which the purported objectivity of any or all of the listed prudential values can be judged.

The lack of a rigorous demonstration of objectivity, in effect, leaves the appeal to an ultimate outcome of 'relatively similar lists' as rather a vague and pious hope and leaves prudential values incomplete and dangling in a kind of limbo. This leaves prudential values open to criticism for lack of rigour in comparison with hierarchical needs-based approaches which start from a position very similar to one of the core prudential values, that of avoiding serious harm, and then rigorously derive all, or most, other elements of their theories from this position and furthermore provide a strong theoretical justification for a societal obligation for meeting these needs. One such approach, Doyal and Gough's theory of human need, is discussed below.

Strengths

The element of fuzziness surrounding the pluralism of prudential values and the lack of clarity about to what extent they are in any sense objective, seem to be serious weaknesses in prudential values. It is certainly true that prudential values cannot be used with the precision – albeit spurious – of 'decision utility' measured in money values and that any attempt to make international comparisons of prudential values will give only partial results. But the great strength of prudential values lies in their appropriate representation of the complexity of values relevant to quality of life, including the 'higher things in life' or what Griffin calls 'heavyweight values' – a representation that is entirely missing from utilitarianism. This representation takes place via the medium of prudential deliberation which fully faces up to issues such as the 'happy slave' problem which again utilitarianism has no way of dealing with.

The fundamental question about a prudential values approach relates to the security of its foundations: it is based on the twin pillars of informed desires and a shared realm of human values necessary for intelligibility. Both of these are at a rather cerebral level and lead to a centrality of core values associated with mental state and understanding rather than of survival, subsistence and physical thriving. These latter, more visceral, attributes are more closely related to a quality of life tradition based on addressing *needs* rather than to values.

Needs

The notion of a need is refreshingly simple and straightforward compared to that of informed desire and prudential values. A need is a necessity and, in the context of development studies and quality of life more generally, meeting needs provides the necessities for survival or, slightly more ambitiously, for a minimally decent life. At its most basic level, as will be seen below, a needs-based approach deals with food, shelter, and elementary health care and education services.

Even if needs are conceptually simple, however, their ideological ramifications are more controversial in that the notion of a *necessity* implies an imperative to action, unlike the notions of desires (actual or informed) and prudence. Enoch Powell, the right-wing British politician, who paved the way for Thatcherism, famously said that the 'translation of a want or a need into a right is one of the most widespread and dangerous of modern heresies' (George and Wilding, 1976: 27). This became a slogan for the emerging New Right in the 1950s and the 1960s against what they saw as the tyranny imposed on individual citizens by societies taxing them in order to meet the needs of other citizens worse off than themselves. This theme recurs throughout the book and is revisited in detail in Chapter 8.

The discussion of needs-based approaches starts with basic needs. Then a universally used international hybrid needs measure, the United Nations human development index, is introduced. This is followed by a discussion of the important and immensely influential theory of human need developed by Len Doyal and Ian Gough. Finally, the capabilities approach, as initiated by Amatrya Sen and modified by Sabina Alkire and Martha Nussbaum, is discussed. Capabilities are a fitting end to this chapter in that they encompass conceptual areas common to needs and prudential values and even to some extent, utility.

Basic needs

Unlike the prudential values approach, which deals with abstract heavyweight values, the basic needs approach deals with practicalities. It also differs fundamentally from utilitarianism both conceptually, in distinguishing between desires and needs, and in terms of measurement. Utility, or at least decision utility, is measured in terms of money; and a nation's utility is measured in terms of its national income. From a basic needs perspective, however, the absolute requirement for quality of life is not income at all, and average or per capita income in a nation is seen as an irrelevance, given that many people might not have their basic needs met even in a society with high average income if that society is highly unequal.

It has to be said that the basic needs approach is very modest, indeed minimalist in scope. It does not aim to provide a sophisticated theoretical framework for understanding all human aspirations, as does prudential values (with its characteristically human values that make any life better) and utilitarianism (with its pure mental states of experienced utility). But it does provide an absolutely firm foundation for acceptable minimum threshold standards for a decently acceptable life – and neither prudential values nor utilitarianism do that (Wiggins, 1998).

The central tenets of the basic needs approach are that everyone should be entitled to expect at the very least a minimally decent life and have access to food, water, shelter, and some medical services and education. The basic needs approach has nothing to say about quality of life above that level. The most minimalist basic needs approach is known as *basic goods* and comprises only nutrition, basic health services and some degree of educational attainment. The underlying rationale for the basic goods approach is that these three items are probably universally and uncontroversially accepted as meeting the most elementary human needs. They can also be seen as the preconditions for other aspects of a full life. They are also relatively easy to identify and there are widely available sets of international statistical indicators on life expectancy, malnutrition among children and on educational attainment that can be used as proxy measures. There is a problem, however, in amalgamating the three aspects of basic goods: should they be equally weighted or, for example, is life expectancy up to a certain age more important than literacy and, if so, then how is that age decided?

These accounting problems with the basic goods approach are similar to those encountered in the component pluralism of prudential values. Because there is no simple mechanism for comparing the relative values of these distinct needs, then their balance has to be worked out pragmatically through a process similar to that of prudential deliberation. There is no such problem in utilitarianism, of course, because all comparisons are in money terms and are resolved by the 'invisible hand' of the economic marketplace.

A basic needs approach does, however, overcome all the major substantive problems of a utilitarian calculus identified earlier in the chapter thus: the issue of income distribution at national level is taken into consideration up to the basic needs threshold point because, in a society meeting basic needs, no-one would be below this point (income distribution above this point is of no concern in a basic needs calculus); income distribution at household level is taken into account because the individual and not the household is the unit of basic needs assessment; externalities relevant to meeting basic needs are factored into the calculus – particularly those such as pollution that adversely affect health – because of the emphasis on health and life expectancy; and similarly public goods are catered for because of the emphasis on supply rather than consumption – this is particularly important in areas of public health and literacy. Indeed, public goods are the key to a basic needs strategy in that the provision, or at the very least the guaranteeing, of basic health and educational services for all has to be the responsibility of the state.

All of the preceding discussion of basic needs has been in the context of its relationship to utilitarianism. But it also has a complex and difficult interaction with prudential values. Griffin in his original exposition of prudential values, after discarding utilitarianism, tested his informed desires model against a basic needs model in the search for a theory of well-being. One of Griffin's main reasons for rejecting a needs-based approach was that it was not, and could not be, comprehensive. whereas prudential values in effect cover all aspects of human existence, from basic survival to 'heavyweight values'; the basic needs approach is positioned unambiguously only at the basic survival end of the spectrum and has nothing to say about the finer points of well-being. This is a valid criticism if one's standpoint towards well-being is all-encompassing, but it has less merit if one takes a 'threshold approach' which identifies a baseline of well-being and has no concern with what happens to people once they have achieved a decent minimum.

A more telling criticism which Griffin levels at basic needs concerns the issue of *importance*. Given that prudential values are about the things that make 'any human life go well', they deal at a very general level and do not have to take into account the specificities of, for example, resources needed to enable people with disabilities to reach a threshold of decent living. Arguably, because of the commitment to raise everyone to the decency threshold, basic needs does have to deal with these issues. Here, things get very complicated in relation to, for example, a baby born with multiple disabilities or the health needs of frail elderly people. Griffin presents the 'importance' problem very vividly in an example comparing the costs of road or rail safety versus those of a specialist university library: a basic needs approach would probably put road safety first even if only very few lives were saved (unless the library would make a substantial addition to that other basic need of literacy), whereas Griffin makes a case for providing a library service on the basis of 'heavyweight values' because adding to a society's culture may be seen as *more important* than spending hundreds of millions of pounds to save a relatively small number of lives in the case of, for example, proposed sophisticated infrastructural advances in rail safety.

From one perspective this criticism might seem unfair because it does not take account of the starting point of basic needs. From a basic needs perspective the university library would be put on hold until everyone's basic needs were met in terms of nutrition and basic health and education. Making a relatively safe road or rail system even safer might be seen as irrelevant to basic needs, in which case any form of basic needs calculus would be irrelevant to Griffin's example here.

A more vivid – and more valid – example would be performing an expensive operation on an elderly and frail patient versus buying a major work of art for a national gallery. A basic needs approach with a very high age threshold of needs fulfilment would prioritise the operation whereas prudential values would prioritise the work of art, but there would probably not be such a contradiction with a basic needs approach with a lower age threshold. Thus, there will be an age-related cut-off point at which the results of a basic needs and a prudential values approach will differ and this cut-off point will be contingent upon the results of a 'needs deliberation' process not dissimilar to the notion of prudential deliberation.

For Griffin, the bottom line is that informed desires can be more important than needs. This, he claims, is because the class of legitimate expectations in a needs-based account is smaller than in an informed desires account and that a needs-based account is too inflexible in (according to Griffin) always putting needs ahead of desires. However, Griffin does make an extremely important claim about the relationship between needs and informed desires which can be used as the basis for developing both prudential values and basic needs into a synthesised approach retaining the strengths of both approaches: 'All basic needs will have their place, and their importance marked, in the hierarchy of prudential values. Basic needs go deeper than desires but informed desires, as they figure in prudential values, go deeper than basic needs' (1986: 52).

He also states that basic needs require flexibility and the addition of *importance* 'which lead us to a form of judgement that could take place only in a full prudential value theory' (ibid.: 72). It is in the 'needs deliberation' procedure noted above that the issue of importance is weighed in setting the bounds of what are basic needs and what needs go beyond this threshold. For the present, the links between basic needs and the prudential values list are noted. It will be recalled that the first two items on Qizilbash's list of prudential values are: (1) minimum levels of nutrition, health, sanitation, shelter, rest and security; and (2) certain basic intellectual and physical capacities and literacy. These, of course encompass the primary basic goods aspects of basic needs. It is clear, therefore that, whatever the theoretical differences between the two approaches, the set of basic needs is entirely contained within the set of prudential values.

The basic needs model has often been criticised for 'commodity fetishism', in other words, for concentrating on goods and services rather than on the quality of human lives (Sen, 1982: 368). Alkire (2002b) also points out the dangers of coercion where the meeting of basic needs is imposed upon an unwilling population, for example, through enforced culturally inappropriate immunisation.

It is true that a basic needs approach does tend to neglect differences in personal characteristics and focuses very strongly on the public provision of goods. But the strength of basic needs lies in its simplicity, its clarity, its limited and completely unimpeachable objectives. These are summarised effectively by Stewart:

> The [basic needs] approach is based on a simple moral imperative – that everyone should have access to minimally decent condition of life and that this objective should be given priority over other objectives. It thus represents a quite robust political philosophy for poor societies, which has implications for income distribution and desirable patterns of consumption and suggests strong policy conclusions . . . In practice, something very close to a [basic needs] approach has to be adopted to yield policy conclusions in poor countries.
>
> (1996: 64)

This is not only important for poor countries, it also has profound implications for many developed countries – those with high levels of inequality and a significant proportion of their population living below the basic needs threshold (Wilkinson, 1996).

The human development index (HDI)

The arguments in favour of using the basic needs approach seem to be over-whelming, if for no other reason than for its incontrovertible moral imperative of ensuring the right to a basic minimum level of survival for all people. This does not mean, however, that basic needs is the only approach that needs to be used, particularly in relation to the world as a whole. While there is a strong case for using basic needs as the primary quality of life measure in countries with very high levels of deprivation, it becomes rather a blunt instrument for the less deprived developing nations and becomes virtually totally undiscriminating among the more egalitarian of the richer countries which share high levels of nutrition, life expectancy and educational attainment. Here there is an overriding case for introducing other aspects of quality of life as being (in Griffin's terms) more *important* than a small marginal addition to an already long life expectancy or high level of educational attainment.

These arguments have already been rehearsed in relation to the prudential values approach which adds several extra goals to the basic needs list. The human development approach starts from similar principles to prudential values, but instead of being based on 'what makes any human life go well' or being 'characteristically human' the human development approach is centred firmly on *well-being*. Human development was initiated by the United Nations Development Programme

(UNDP) and, like basic needs, is aimed primarily at developing countries. The central idea of the human development approach is that human well-being is central to the goal of development and that human beings form the major development resource:

> People are the real wealth of a nation. The basic objective of development is to create an enabling environment for people to live long, healthy and creative lives . . . human development is a process of enlarging people's choices. The most critical ones are to lead a long and healthy life, to be educated and to enjoy a decent standard of living. Additional choices include political freedom, guaranteed human rights and self-respect.
>
> (UNDP, 1990: 9–10)

The first two objectives, to lead a long and healthy life and to be educated, entirely match two of the three basic needs objectives. The third, to enjoy a decent standard of living, goes beyond the notion of needs and is capable of several interpretations. The most obvious, and the easiest to measure, relates to material standards of living rather than social, political or interpersonal standards. Indeed, those other aspects of standards of life, are included in the 'additional choices' listed by UNDP.

Now, the human development index (HDI) was designed to be a practical as well as a conceptual tool so it is imperative that it is measurable and that measures or indicators of the HDI can be ascertained for even the poorest countries with the most limited data sources. Therefore a simple and straightforward measure of standard of living needs to be found. Of course, the most common, indeed ubiquitous measure, is national income, i.e. GNP. The shortcomings of GNP have been discussed at length above, but this is the measure that the UNDP chose, partly for want of any better indicator of standard of living in developing countries and – presumably – partly because, after all, GNP is the major indicator used by international organisations such as the World Bank as a measure of national wealth. It also has to be admitted, that whatever the objections that can be legitimately levelled at the sensitivity of income as a measure of well-being, it is unarguable that increased income leads to increased material choice and that this, while not necessarily meeting needs, certainly can fulfil material desires. Again, GNP is a commonly accepted measure of standard of living so any potential criticism of this indicator needs really to be levelled at the attribute that it is measuring. It will be seen later that alternative approaches to needs and human development in fact do propose empirical measures of quality of life that do not include indicators of income. It is interesting to note that these measures do tend to correlate well with national income (Gough, 2000b: 122). So for all its conceptual weaknesses, its inclusion in the HDI can be defended on practical grounds as well as in terms of expediency.

In its initial formulation the HDI had three indicators: (1) life expectancy for the society as a whole; (2) literacy; and (3) the log of per capita GNP, adjusted for international differences in purchasing power. It has since been adjusted to take average years of schooling into account. There is no weighting of income within societies so no effect is taken of inequalities in income in this indicator. The indicators are aggregated in a complex but essentially arbitrary fashion (ibid.). The arbitrariness in the weighting of the indicators is because there is no formal rationale for comparing them. In effect, they are seen as three or four incommensurable factors, each of which is equally important. Therefore the most appropriate mensuration approach would be by the Borda or Pareto methods discussed above in relation to prudential values (Qizilbash, 1997b). These methods are not regularly used, probably because they do not yield a simple, one-figure result. Therefore, the resulting HDI gives results that are easy to compare but are not straightforwardly justifiable in terms of the relative merits of its components.

Conceptually, the human development approach can be placed between utility (as measured by average incomes) and basic needs. It draws on both of their empirical strengths but in so doing has a resulting hybrid and weak theoretical justification (Stewart, 1996: 59). Therefore, HDI is not an accurate indicator of either decision utility or the basic needs of societies: the literacy, years of schooling and life expectancy components are, in principle, non-problematic but the income variable is a societal average and therefore not sensitive to income distribution. So it therefore does not effectively measure people's ability to achieve their basic needs. It has also been criticised for being too economically dominated and not taking any account of social structures or institutions (Gasper, 2002: 445).

Its great merit though is at a practical level because it is comprehensive across nations and has become recognised as an alternative measure of well-being to GNP by itself. Perhaps most importantly, comparison of the elements of the HDI does place an emphasis on countries' achievements in meeting basic needs where these differ significantly from GNP per capita. So the HDI, by incorporating GNP, can highlight those countries with similar national incomes which have different levels of success in meeting the basic needs of their citizens. Also, because it is a universally accepted measure and has incorporated at least the most elementary level of basic needs, it has unambiguously placed basic needs on the international league tables – and this is a considerable step forward.

Doyal and Gough's *theory of human need* (THN)

As noted above, the foundational measure of quality of life is probably life expectancy, followed by basic needs and then the human development approach. Doyal and Gough's (1991) *theory of human need* (THN) is a logical continuation to a higher level of needs-fulfilment. Their approach has two particular merits. The first is ideological in that Doyal and Gough insist that there is a strong moral link between the existence of needs and an obligation by societies (including the nascent global society) to meet them. Their ultimate goal is to develop 'a genuinely universal argument for human emancipation' (Gough, 2003: 1). It is here that their theory has extremely radical consequences that fulfil the worst fears of Enoch Powell, noted above, in that these needs, according to Doyal and Gough then necessarily entail corresponding social rights:

If human needs are the universal precondition for participation in social life, we contend that all people have a strong right to need satisfaction. This follows because membership of all social groups entail corresponding duties, yet without adequate levels of need satisfaction a person will be unable to act in accordance with these duties. It is contradictory to ask of someone that they fulfil their social duties, yet to deny them the prerequisite need satisfaction which will enable them to do so. This is why the social rights of citizenship follow from an unambiguous concept of human need.

(Gough 1998: 52)

The THN's second merit is theoretical in that it creates a framework firmly grounded in objective needs which has a reach ultimately nearly as broad as that of prudential values. The THN's theoretical starting point is the notion of universal needs which are in everyone's interest to achieve. Doyal and Gough claim that everyone has an objective interest in avoiding serious harm (which would prevent them from pursuing their vision of the good life) which in turn entails an ability to participate socially (ibid.: 52). According to Doyal and Gough, there are two universal needs-based goals: avoiding serious harm; and an ability to participate. This latter goal is formally defined as 'minimally disabled social participation'. The objective nature of these needs is central to their approach which is not directly concerned with subjective feelings at all except incidentally in so far as they may be reflections of unmet objective needs. Similarly, a person's wants are not relevant in the THN unless they mirror needs.

These two objective needs-based goals are the foundation of a major edifice. According to Doyal and Gough, the whole theoretical structure of the THN is derived from this starting point (with one addition which is discussed below). The THN structure has two levels of needs: basic or primary needs and intermediate needs. The THN is seen as providing external and independent standards which can be used to compare across different societies with a wide range of social, political and economic systems, with the ultimate goal of enabling objective human welfare to be assessed independently of cultural values.

There are two primary needs which require to be met at what Doyal and Gough call an 'optimum level': physical health; and autonomy of agency. Optimum levels of physical health can be seen as congruent with the WHO definition of health as a state of complete physical, mental and social well-being, including autonomy (WHOQOL Group, 1995: 1404). But the bottom line here for Doyal and Gough is survival with associated complexities relating to reduction of functional ability associated with ageing or with optimum life expectancy. These are complex and difficult issues as seen in the discussion of basic needs, which have repercussions elsewhere in their approach in terms of the trade-off in resources required to meet different primary and intermediate needs.

Autonomy of agency is seen by Doyal and Gough as the defining characteristic of human beings. It is interesting to note that, in a prudential values approach, autonomy is a major but not a core value (these are enjoyment and the avoidance of pain). Autonomy of agency is defined as the capacity to make informed choices about what should be done and how to go about doing it. This insistence on *informed* choices is entirely consistent with prudential values. Autonomy requires self-confidence and is impaired when there is a deficit in three attributes: mental health; cognitive skills; and opportunities to engage in social participation (Doyal and Gough, 1991: 63).

This identification and the delineation of constraints on autonomy are extremely important and represent a theoretical advance upon prudential values both in the conceptual linking of autonomy to the universal needs-based goal of participation and in terms of a requirement for it being both minimally disabled in terms of capacity as well as being informed in terms of understanding. It also links in closely with Wilkinson's (1996) postulation of the central role of self-esteem in the maintenance of health and its complex relationship with perceptions of societal inequality.

In order to satisfy primary needs, Doyal and Gough identify eleven intermediate needs which require meeting at a 'minopt' level, which is the minimum quantity of any given intermediate need-satisfaction required to produce the optimum level of basic need satisfaction. These intermediate needs are:

1   nutritional food and clean water
2   protective housing
3   non-hazardous work environment
4   non hazardous physical environment
5   safe birth control and child bearing
6   appropriate health care
7   secure childhood
8   significant primary relationships
9   physical security
10   economic security
11   appropriate education.

Their rule for inclusion as an intermediate need is extremely rigorous and is as follows: 'The only criterion for inclusion in this list is whether or not any set of satisfier characteristics universally and positively contributes to physical health and autonomy. If it does then it is classified as an intermediate need' (Gough 2003: 11). The first six intermediate needs contribute to physical health and the last five to autonomy.

It is noted above that there is another element to the THN in addition to its main focus on participation with its universal goals of avoidance of serious harm and minimally disabled social participation. This is the 'liberation' facet with its universal goal of *critical* participation in one's chosen form of life and the associated primary need, at 'second-order level' (Gough, 2004a) of critical autonomy, but with no associated intermediate needs. The justification for the creation of this additional strand comes about through the realisation of the potential problem of successful participation in a cruel or exploitative system within the unaugmented THN model. It is interesting to note here that Geoff Wood, joint author of Gough's recent major monograph on welfare regimes, would promote personal and family-level security from an intermediate to a universal primary need, particularly in the context of 'insecure' welfare regimes in developing nations (Gough and Wood, 2004: 2n).

At this stage it is interesting to compare the THN list of primary and intermediate needs with the human development index and basic needs and with prudential values. The major omission in relation to the HDI, of course, is a measure of income, but this is to be expected, given the controversial rationale for its inclusion in the HDI and its lack of a necessary – as opposed to a ubiquitous – relationship with needs. The literacy and schooling component of the HDI is covered by the THN intermediate need of appropriate education and the life-expectancy HDI component is covered by the THN basic need of physical health. There is similar coverage for the health and education components of basic needs, while the nutrition basic needs component is covered by the first THN intermediate need.

The relationship between the THN and prudential values is rather more complex. First, with regard to the THN primary needs and the core values of prudential values, although avoidance of pain and physical health are central to both, the other primary THN need is autonomy (related to the goal of participation) whereas the other core prudential value is enjoyment. Now, the issue over autonomy is not too problematic because it is also included in prudential values as a major value. Enjoyment, however, has no explicit place whatsoever in Doyal and Gough's theory of human need and it is difficult to find even an implicit niche for it, unless it is understood to be embedded within the intermediate need for significant primary relationships. This makes the THN not only objective, but also austere in nature.

Second, there is rather more commonality between the list of intermediate needs and of prudential values. Intermediate needs, 1, 2, 4 and 6 are all contained in Qizilbash's first prudential value of minimum levels of nutrition, health, sanitation, shelter, rest and security. There also appears to be considerable overlap between needs 9 and 10 and the first prudential value, except that by implication of 'minopt' this are probably at a higher level than the minimum specified in the prudential values approach. Similarly, needs 5 and 7, related to childbearing and childhood, explicate what is left implicit in this prudential value. Need 3, for a non-hazardous work environment, is even more specific but again can be seen as consistent with the broad sweep of the first prudential value. Need 11, appropriate education covers similar ground to the prudential value associated with intellectual capacities and literacy. Also need 8, for significant primary relationships meshes in with the prudential value associated with significant relationships with others and participation in social life, which itself links in with the THN universal goal of minimally disabled social participation.

Thus, all the THN primary and intermediate needs have their counterparts within prudential values. On the other hand, at first sight there appear to be some prudential values in addition to enjoyment that seem to have no direct counterpart in the THN list. These are: self-respect and aspiration; understanding; accomplishment; and liberty. Liberty is the most straightforward in that it is both integral to autonomy of agency and is also a precondition for critical autonomy. The others can be seen to be at least implicitly subsumed under the primary need of autonomy of agency which includes informed choices, confidence and understanding – although it is not entirely clear whether these aspects of the primary need of autonomy are satisfied by any of the intermediate needs or whether these are, in effect, independent sub-basic needs.

Notwithstanding these similarities, one central difference remains between the prudential values and THN lists: the absence of enjoyment or any related construct from the latter. In addition, there is a dissonance here with utilitarianism, which shares a fundamental 'absence of pain' value with both prudential values and the THN and a fundamental enjoyment/pleasure value with prudential values. Thus, Doyal and Gough share with utilitarians and proponents of prudential values a strong belief in the importance of avoidance of pain as a universal goal but not in the importance of pleasure or enjoyment. This may appear somewhat shocking in the context of the approaches discussed in Chapter 1 which focus on subjective well-being and satisfaction but the omission of such subjective and 'non-need oriented' values is deliberate. Gough characterises THN as a 'thin', two-stage, neo-Kantian theory: 'When focusing on health and autonomy of agency it is explicitly designed to fit all human societies. It deliberately seeks, so to speak, the lowest common denominator of universalisable preconditions for human action and social participation' (2003: 16).

The THN approach has been operationalised at both international and local level. The international operationalisation faces similar problems over availability of data to those found by Qizilbash in trying to operationalise prudential values. Therefore, it is necessary to make compromises. For example, life expectancy at birth is used as an indicator of physical health and adult literacy is used for autonomy in place of their preferred indicators of mental disorder, cognitive deprivation and lack of opportunities to participate in socially significant activities (Gough and Thomas, 1994). After undertaking statistical analyses of the data, they conclude that the following factors contributed positively to need satisfaction and human welfare: level of economic development; low levels of national economic dependency; early political independence, state capacity, democracy and human rights, and relative gender equality (Gough, 2000b: 129). Perhaps ironically Gough and Thomas report that the most important factor in needs satisfaction is the level of economic development which, of course, is virtually synonymous with standard of living or GNP, that is, the 'rogue' non-needs-based element of the HDI.

Overall, the THN is undoubtedly the most important and powerful of the needs-based quality of life constructs. It is robust, clear, forceful and elegant in its formulation. Because of this, it is revisited in Chapter 8 as one of the foundations for the further development of quality of life conceptualisation. It has been subject to criticism, though, on three counts. First, the inclusion of the extra 'liberation' strand of critical autonomy does dilute the clear 'thin' lines of the original conception with its sparse, parsimonious and austerely logical progression from first principles to primary and intermediate needs. Second, as noted above, it can be characterised as a rather stark representation of the human condition in its lack of presentation of any fundamental need for enjoyment in life.

The most important potential criticism, though, is about its purported incipient paternalism. In this context, Gough accepts that the theory is couched in terms of people's *functionings* as delineated by the theory's authors rather than people's own choices among their *capabilities* for functioning. And it is capabilities that Gough accepts as being the appropriate currency for the THN, thus permitting 'universal goals to be identified yet individuals' rights not to pursue them to be given due weight . . . The functioning–capability distinction would help us to diminish lingering charges of paternalism' (Gough, 2003: 16).

Capabilities

Sen's approach

Nobel Laureate, Amatrya Sen first used the word 'capability' in its present meaning in 1979 to refer to an approach to well-being in terms of *freedoms*, particularly freedom to choose among various alternatives including: 'being happy; achieving self-respect; taking part in the life of the community' (Sen, 1993: 36). Capabilities are about a person's ability to do valuable acts or to reach valuable states of well-being – or 'doing' and 'being' – together referred to as *functionings*. So capabilities are to do with the freedom to pursue valuable 'doings' and 'beings' in order to flourish as a human being. Central to this approach is the notion of a *capability set* which refers to the alternative combinations of things a person is able to do or be.

Thus, a capabilities approach looks about as far removed from basic needs as it is possible to imagine. This is because basic needs start from a narrow and parsimonious perspective of what is minimally needed to ensure survival whereas capabilities start from an expansive and generous conception of what is valuable in human life.

However, one facet of the capabilities approach, that of *basic capabilities*, covers very similar ground to that covered by basic needs, and this is the aspect of capabilities to which Sen has devoted most of his attention in practice. Basic capabilities refer to the 'ability to satisfy certain crucially important functionings up to certain minimally adequate levels' (ibid.: 40). These include 'escaping morbidity and mortality, being adequately nourished, having mobility etc.' (ibid.: 36). A major similarity between basic needs and basic capabilities – and which differentiates them both from utilitarianism – is that they rely on resources/functionings rather than upon income, which is only relevant in so far as it enhances capabilities or can be used to meet needs. Indeed, Alkire (2002b: 163) links basic capabilities and basic needs very specifically: she defines a basic capability as a capability to meet a basic need.

Stewart (1996) has undertaken an extensive analysis of the differences and similarities between a basic needs and basic capabilities approach and concludes that they would come to broadly similar conclusions in the poorest countries. However, a basic needs approach would strongly emphasise public provision of goods, particularly in its most elemental basic goods incarnation, but would not privilege differences in personal characteristics, whereas the basic capabilities approach puts a strong emphasis on freedom of personal choice and therefore does not prioritise public sector provision. Moreover, there is a major theoretical difference between the two approaches: the ultimate objective of basic needs is to promulgate decent life characteristics (or in capabilities terms, basic functioning) whereas a basic capabilities approach goes beyond that and aims at enhancing *capabilities*.

Sen has reservations about specifically delineating what this means, but Alkire (2002b: 180–1) identifies the following four strategies for safeguarding the freedom and choice that are so central to the capabilities perspective: (1) to identify long-term valued capability goals and strategies; (2) to work in the short term to establish functionings relevant to these goals; (3) to implement a strategy which safeguards negative freedoms (for example, to avoid coerced culturally insensitive immunisation); and (4) to mitigate any reduction in wider capabilities that might occur as a result of expanding basic capabilities. At such a basic level, this is mostly only an academic difference and has little practical significance because the urgency of these most basic requirements leaves little room for choice.

However, moving even a little beyond this absolute basic level, the differences become significant, and at higher levels of capability they become profound. In order to make comparisons it is necessary to move beyond the basic needs approach and instead compare capabilities with a more wide-ranging needs-based approach, such as Doyal and Gough's THN. As noted, above the THN has a very specific, and rigorously derived, set of intermediate needs, all of which are logically derived from basic principles and which provide firm boundaries of appropriate needs-satisfaction. The capabilities approach, on the other hand, includes a wide range of 'higher level' capabilities and functionings based on what is perceived to be valuable and which form, for each individual, a capability set from which that person is free to choose. It is interesting to note that the capabilities approach is potentially even wider in scope than utilitarianism: for utilitarianism, happiness is the over-riding goal, whereas it is *only one* of the potential valuable functionings in a person's capability set. From this perspective, it can be seen that there are potential similarities between a capabilities and a prudential values approach, given that the latter relates to 'what makes any human life go well'.

Sen's presentation of the capabilities approach is highly sophisticated, is respectful of the breadth and depth of valued human actions and states of well-being and has potential relevance for the whole of humanity. Nevertheless, his formulation is immensely frustrating because he is impossible to pin down. Beyond the identification of functionings associated with basic capabilities (all closely related to basic needs) he *never* provides a list – or even an indication – of a range of appropriate functionings or of what an ideal or model or even a typical capability set might look like. In other words, he gives no substantive account whatsoever of the good life. In addition, he makes a strong case for accepting cultural relativity in relation to capability sets – that these may differ from culture to culture rather than being necessarily universal in nature (Sen, 1995).

In refusing to be specific about desired functionings he is not just being perverse, he is refusing to be pinned down because of his emphasis on the value of *freedom*.

Qizilbash (1998: 53) characterises this perspective as follows: 'Positive freedoms and valuable functions are, for Sen, amongst the chief objects of intrinsic importance. Resources are means to freedom' and 'Well-being is part of the idea of valuable functioning, and quality of life should be judged in terms of the ability to achieve well-being.' Even so, the open-endedness of Sen's list is, according to Qizilbash, his Achilles' heel in that he fails to give any specific account of the good life: for example, *how* is one capable of achieving functionings – for example, is it acceptable to avoid starvation by stealing food?

So Sen's formulation of the capabilities approach has the strength of sophistication and unimpeachable theoretical integrity in his 'thin' formulation. But it is empirically unsubstantial, only being operationalised at the most urgent extreme of absolute poverty and thus, according to Robeyns (2003: 371) is 'still far removed from a mature and well-established framework'. Gasper (2002: 437) puts forward a more ontologically substantive critique, claiming that Sen does not have a strong conception of 'personhood' which results in a thin and unduly individualistic analysis of well-being.

Alkire's impressive monograph *Valuing Freedoms* (2002b) attempts to deal with Robeyns' critique by evaluating three development case studies from an operationalised capabilities perspective. In so doing she follows Finnis in identifying 'basic human values' derived from 'reasons for acting which need no further reasons', based on what is self-evidently true (Alkire, 2002a: 185). These values emerge from an iterative process of continually asking, Why do I do what I do? Why do others do what they do? The resulting list is intended to give an account of all the basic purposes of human actions:

- life itself – health and safety
- knowledge and aesthetic experience
- (excellence in) work and play
- friendship
- self-integration (inner peace rather than inner conflict)
- self-expression or practical reasonableness (harmony among one's judgements, choices and performances)
- religion (peace with a 'more than human' source of meaning and value).

This list, although wide-ranging, is sparse and not overspecified, in order to retain choice (Alkire, 2002a: 186). For her the ultimate goal is 'equality in persons' capability to meet their basic needs that does not comprise their capability to enjoy non-basic valuable beings and doings' (Alkire, 2002b: 195). The above list, though, is not universally accepted. Gough (2004b: 294) reports from a review of participatory studies researching the priorities of members of poorer communities in developing countries that one of the above items, knowledge, is not in general considered as good *in itself* as a basic human value but only instrumentally so in relation to the impact the knowledge has upon life chances.

Nussbaum's approach

There is another formulation of the capabilities approach that is much 'thicker' than Sen's, addresses Gasper's (2004) critique and focused more strongly upon moral imperatives than on freedoms and choice. This is the universalistic capabilities approach, as expounded by Martha Nussbaum, which, according to Gasper (1997: 299) 'gives a rich picture of what is a full human life, and talks in terms of real people, real life, not thin abstractions'. Nussbaum' thinking on this area has developed over many years and incorporates and develops both Aristotelian traditions of 'practical reasoning' and a neo-Rawlesian approach to social justice.

There are four areas where Nussbaum develops Sen's capabilities approach. First, she argues for objective universal norms of human capability across cultural boundaries which therefore are not constrained by cultural relativism (Gough, 2003: 2). For her, the good life 'is "non-relative" – in that it is invariant across classes, societies and cultures' (Qizilbash, 1998: 56); this tenet puts her at odds with Alkire's approach outlined above (Gasper, 1997: 282). Second, her account of the good human life is singular: she demands an account that 'should preserve liberties and opportunities for each and every person, taken one by one, respecting each of them as an end' (Nussbaum, 2000: 55). Third, Nussbaum is explicit about the functionings that make up a distinctively good life which for her are based on Aristotelian foundations of being organised by practical reason and which takes shape around other-regarding affiliations: 'So, for Nussbaum, the good life is the life of correct choice of action' (Qizilbash, 1998: 55). Finally, Qizilbash states that she distinguishes 'those capabilities for functioning which are to do with the individual's personal constitution from the external conditions which facilitate the exercise of such capabilities' (ibid.). As will be seen below, though, Gough criticises her for not consistently maintaining this distinction.

Nussbaum's approach to capabilities is much more unequivocal than Sen's, even at the basic capabilities level. She takes a similar stance to basic needs in insisting that the central goal is to get *everyone* above the threshold – that is, to achieve an initial 'capability equality' – and that until this is done, those inequalities above the threshold can only be tolerated so long as they move more people across it. Once *all* are across the boundary then, from Nussbaum's perspective, societies should be free to choose other goals. But even these goals, according to her formulation, have to be consistent with all humans having an equal opportunity to achieve a 'good' human life, which, from her Aristotelian perspective, means 'to do well and live a flourishing life' (Nussbaum, 1995: 81).

> In certain core areas of human functioning a necessary condition of justice for a public political arrangement is that it delivers to citizens a certain basic level of capability. If people are systematically falling below the threshold in any of these core areas this should be seen as a situation both unjust and tragic.
>
> (Nussbaum, 2000: 5)

Her most tangible difference from Sen is that she provides an extensive list of central human functional capabilities as a basis for determining a decent social minimum in a variety of areas (ibid.: 75). The version of the list given below is derived from Nussbaum (ibid.: 78–80), with additional material in square brackets from an earlier list (Nussbaum, 1995: 81):

1 *Life*: being able to live to the end of a normal human life.
2 *Bodily health*: being able to have good health, including reproductive health; nourishment; shelter.
3 *Bodily integrity*: being able to move freely; having bodily boundaries (i.e. secure against assault); having opportunities for sexual satisfaction and choice in reproduction.
4 *Senses, imagination and thought*: freedom of use and expression of all three, including politics and religion [all informed and cultivated by education] – and pleasure and avoiding non-necessary pain.
5 *Emotions*: to be able to feel them and not for them to be blighted by fear, anxiety, abuse or neglect.
6 *Practical reason*: being able to form a conception of the good and to engage in critical reflection – including the use of conscience. [Being able to plan one's life, seek employment and participate in politics.]
7 *Affiliation*: to be able to interact, show compassion, etc., to have friendships. [Being able to live for and to others. Being able to have attachments to people and things; to love; to grieve.] Protection against discrimination and enabling of dignity, self-respect, etc.
8 *Other species*: being able to live with concern for and in relation to animals, plants and the world of nature.
9 *Play*: being able to laugh, play and enjoy recreation.
10 *Control over one's environment*: political – effective participation; material – being able to hold property on an equal basis with others and to have equal access to employment, etc. [Being able to live one's life in one's own surroundings and context, i.e. guaranteed freedom of association and freedom from unwarranted search and seizure. Freedom of assembly and speech.]
11 [*Being able to live one's life and nobody else's*: i.e. non-interference with choices over marriage, child-bearing, sexual expression, speech and employment.]

As with prudential values Nussbaum claims that there is component pluralism and irreducibility in her list: these are all separate and the scope for trade-offs between them is limited. Furthermore, a lack in any one of them leads to a shortfall in 'a good human life'.

Reason and affiliation (items 6 and 7) are of special significance to her – and possibly bodily integrity too. She is explicitly neo-Aristotelian in her approach, identifying 'spheres of human experience that figure in more or less any human life and in which more or less any human being will have to make some choices rather than others'. A human being is a 'dignified free being who shapes his or her life in co-operation and reciprocity with others . . . a life that is truly human is one that is shaped throughout by these human powers of practical reason and sociability'

(Nussbaum, 2000: 72). This provides a 'thick' Aristotelian rather than Sen's 'thin' neo-Kantian approach. Item 9, play, might seem a lightweight attribute but has proved to be important in empirical development studies, with Clarke (2003) stressing the importance of recreation in making the difference between a minimally decent life and a good life among both urban and rural poor communities in South Africa.

Many of the items on Nussbaum's list are similar to those enumerated by Alkire. Perhaps the main difference is that Nussbaum's list is far more highly specified, detailed and obligatory: there are none of the caveats about capabilities for meeting basic needs not compromising higher-level capabilities that are central to Alkire's formulation. It also addresses a higher level of generality, relating to national government policies whereas Alkire stresses the importance of epistemological decentralisation.

There are many similarities here too with the prudential values approach, in both orientation and detail. In relation to orientation, there are striking similarities between Nussbaum's notion of spheres of human existence that figure in any human life and the prudential values orientation towards a characteristically human life and values that make any life go better. In relation to the details of their respective lists, the most obvious is the stress that both give to enjoyment/play, significant relations with others/affiliation and opportunities for sexual satisfaction, self-respect and aspiration/being able to live one's own life.

There are divergences, as well as commonalties, between Nussbaum's approach to capabilities and Doyal and Gough's theory of human need. Gough (2003) has undertaken a minutely detailed comparison of the two. The first major difference, according to Gough, is that Nussbaum does not *theoretically* privilege her core elements as Doyal and Gough do – even though these elements are very similar. Gough also cites the THN distinction between human needs and the societal preconditions for their realisation as being more helpful than what he sees as Nussbaum's mixing together of internal capabilities and suitable external conditions for the exercise of the function within what he calls 'combined capabilities': 'The former are attributes of individuals, the latter of collectivities' (Gough, 2003: 14).

On a more detailed level, Gough is rather scathing about her 'other species' category: 'It is incredible to consider that this component ranks on a par with bodily integrity or practical reason' (ibid.: 14). For a spirited response to a similar critique, see Nussbaum (2004) and Nussbaum (2006: Chapter 6).

Gough concludes his analysis as follows:

> Nussbaum's thick approach to human capabilities embraces a wide range of human activities and extols a broad vision of human flourishing, but its foundations are shaky and its potential for securing cross-cultural consensus is unproven and probably weak. Sen's thin theory of capabilities has greater potential for identifying priority capacities and has a proven record of underpinning an international consensus on human development, but it provides little systematic or comprehensive guidance on components of human functioning or well-being. Our theory of human need [i.e. the THN], we would

claim, combines the merits of both, by expounding a thin derivation, and by carefully distinguishing autonomy of agency from critical autonomy, it recognises cultural differences within a universalistic framework, but by positing universal satisfier characteristics and recognising our collective understanding of these it provides a richer framework for conceiving, measuring and – conceivably – improving human well-being.

(Gough, 2003: 19)

Qizilbash is also critical of Nussbaum's approach: 'Nussbaum leaves her conception of the good "vague" so that it is open to "plural" specifications by different people and particular "local" specifications in different contexts.' He claims 'vagueness' just won't work: in an Aristotelian view there is only one good life and this just is not compatible with pluralism (Qizilbash, 1998: 56). At face value, however, it seems that prudential values are open to very similar criticisms to the ones Qizilbash directs at Nussbaum in terms of vagueness in its list and the perils of multiple pluralism. So, at a heavyweight, theoretical, level it may come down to the differences between the insights into human nature afforded by, on the one hand, Wittgenstein's notion of mutual intelligibility and shared values and, on the other, Aristotle's notions of practical reasoning and flourishing – and perhaps more importantly on the extent to which prudential values and Nussbaum's version of capabilities effectively and validly apply these insights in practice.

These debates on the integrity and provenance of the theoretical justification of both prudential values and capabilities and on their operationalisation are extremely important in furthering knowledge and understanding in order to construct stronger and better theories. However, they are rather esoteric and do not need to be explored in depth here. For the present it is time to draw together the discussion on the practical aspects of these models of quality of life, to note their many and important similarities, to identify areas of conflict and contradiction among them, and to try to build on their strengths.

Conclusion

Four main approaches to quality of life are presented in this chapter: utility; needs, prudential values and capabilities. Utility is the simplest, the most easily implemented and the most commonly used. It is the simplest in that it is monistic: it has a central overriding conceptual theme of the absolute importance of mental states of pleasure or happiness (or utility); it is operationalised through the expression and meeting of people's actual desires which reflect these mental states of happiness; and it is measured, at least in relation to desires for goods and services, by price. It can be summatively measured in terms of income. Utility is individual-istic in nature. All the other constructs discussed in this chapter are underpinned by social concerns, commencing with social notions of decency, moving through to prerequisites for participation and culminating with universal values and norms.

Needs are relatively straightforward too, at least in their most modest formulation. Because basic needs, by definition, are *necessities of life*, they can be identified in terms of the provision of resources to provide minimum threshold standards for a decently acceptable life, in terms of nutrition, shelter, basic health services and a modicum of education (normally taken as basic literacy). Doyal and Gough provide a wider, more complex and more sophisticated theory of human need. Their THN starts with the absolute necessities of avoiding serious harm and the ability to participate. From this they derive two primary needs of physical health and autonomy of agency. The latter is achieved when people can make informed choices in their lives. The THN goes much further than basic needs in its stipulation of eleven intermediate needs which have to be fulfilled to meet the two primary needs. The intermediate needs cover all areas related to basic needs but also include such wider-ranging items as significant primary relationships and safe birth control and child-bearing. Doyal and Gough insist that the THN, although wider than basic needs, is still parsimonious and rigorously derived from first principles in order to provide 'the lowest common denominator of universalisable preconditions for human action' (Gough, 2003: 16). The other needs-based formulation discussed here is the human development index which can be seen to some extent as a hybrid with utilitarianism in that it includes a national income measure, GNP, as well as life expectancy and literacy.

Prudential values are more complex and less clear-cut than either utilitarianism or needs. Their starting place, like utilitarianism, is with desires but not *actual* desires which are seen as being too fallible. Instead *informed* desires are the basis for a recipe for making 'any human life go better'. The epistemological foundations of prudential values lie in the nature of *a characteristically human life* which relates to the essential intersubjectivity and mutual intelligibility of human beings. Again, like utilitarianism, the core of prudential values lies in pleasure and in its opposite, pain. Some of the other prudential values cover the same areas as does the THN, while others deal with more 'heavyweight' aesthetic and aspirational values. Prudential values are not clear-cut because no definitive list has yet been provided but its proponents claim that this is not a major problem in that it encourages the construction of a range of lists via a process of prudential deliberation about what makes a characteristically human life go better. It is assumed that because of our shared human values, such deliberation would result in these lists having considerable similarities.

Thus, a major difference between prudential values and needs-based approaches is that the latter have closed and rigorously defined lists whereas in the former there is the opportunity for the exercise of freedom in compiling lists. Sen's capabilities approach shares this strong valuation of freedom. In fact, capabilities, according to Sen, are to do with the freedom to pursue valuable 'doings' and 'beings' in order to flourish as a human being. 'Flourishing' here includes pleasure and enjoyment so has resonances with both utilitarianism and prudential values. There is also a version of capabilities that is very similar to basic needs: the 'basic capabilities' approach covers the same substantive areas as basic needs but has more flexibility in its repertoire of delivery mechanisms and taking account of differences in personal characteristics.

Because of his insistence on freedom, Sen refuses to provide a list of capabilities beyond this basic level. So he gives no substantive account at all of the good life.

More pertinently, he accepts the likelihood of there being cultural differences in capability sets between cultures. Nussbaum's approach to capabilities takes on board Sen's structure of beings and doings but is predicated on a more tightly knit and 'thick' version of flourishing based on 'other-regarding' Aristotelian reasoning about the 'correct' choice of action. Her version of capabilities, then, does not allow for cultural relativity. It is both universal and singular and, unlike Sen's, does have a list – indeed an extensive list – of central human functional capabilities. Her list covers all the areas dealt with by prudential values and THN, but also stresses the value of play and of respect for other species. Gough (2004b: 293) states: 'Our theory of human need perhaps sits between the Sen and Nussbaum approaches' and Gough (2004a: 18) effectively summarises the similarities between these perspectives as follows: 'Despite differences between the work of Sen, Nussbaum, Doyal and Gough and others the upshot is a non-monetary and multi-dimensional concept of human needs, functions and well-being.'

Approaches to quality of life

There are many different ways of comparing and contrasting the approaches discussed in this chapter from a quality of life perspective. Four strands in particular are discussed here and will reappear throughout the rest of the book. These are: (1) their moral implications for social action; (2) their representations of human nature; (3) the extent to which they take account of factors such as enjoyment and other facets of subjective well-being; and (4) their relationship to income and wealth. One further strand which needs to be discussed here relates to their practical applicability.

Moral implications for social action

There are four levels of moral implications for social action embedded in these approaches. The first and by far the strongest is the clear-cut and rigorous normative requirement in Doyal and Gough's theory of human need for social action to ensure needs are met: membership of a society entails duties, but a person cannot fulfil these duties unless his or her needs are met, therefore the meeting of these needs is a social right. This is undoubtedly controversial but is entirely consistent with a strong republican perspective on citizenship (Oldfield, 1990) and is revisited in the next two chapters in the context of social inclusion and social cohesion. This purported theoretical link between needs and rights is one reason for Doyal and Gough's insistence on objectivity, parsimoniousness and even austerity (in terms of the exclusion of pleasure and enjoyment) from the account of human need. The needs have to be totally defensible in order to entail a corresponding social right

The second level is equally strong to the first in terms of moral imperative to meet needs but its justification is on the ethical basis of an appeal to social justice, fairness, egalitarianism and common humanity rather than normative theory. This stance is central to basic needs and to both Nussbaum's and Sen's versions of basic capabilities and is implicit in the HDI. In all these formulations minimum needs must be met in order to achieve a more just world, and in Nussbaum's formulation there is a stronger requirement of restricting inequalities *above* this level until it is reached by all.

At the third level there is no *explicit* discourse on meeting social needs. Sen's moral imperative with regard to capability rights is explicit in relation to the fulfilling of basic capabilities but does not reach beyond this level except in safeguarding freedoms. As seen above, Nussbaum's approach is more overtly egalitarian, at least in terms of opportunity, so her approach is less value-neutral than Sen's at high levels of capabilities. The prudential values approach is not easy to place. Its emphasis on heavyweight values seems to imply at best a limited scope for social action to meet needs but Griffin does explicitly state that all important basic needs lie within the realm of informed desires so there is an implicit moral imperative to social action here, particularly in the light of Qizilbash's use of prudential values in development studies.

At the fourth level there is no discourse at all. This is most obvious in utilitarianism where the moral implication for social action lies in striving to achieve the greatest happiness of the greatest number, which is normally interpreted as maximising per capita GNP rather than being to do with the distribution of incomes or the meeting of needs.

Representations of human nature

Explicit visions of human nature loom large in four of the approaches: utilitarianism; prudential values; capabilities (particularly Nussbaum's version); and in Doyal and Gough's THN. Human nature does not play a large part in basic needs or the human development index which are more concerned with the prerequisites for human survival and thriving than with what attributes are essentially human. The utilitarian perspective on human nature is individualistic rather than collectivist. People are hedonic beings, seeking pleasure, avoiding pain and thus maximising their utility. Personal liberty, freedom of choice and freedom from coercion and paternalism are central to enabling the utilitarian human to thrive.

Prudential values differ radically from utilitarianism in their perspective on human nature. The dominance of actual desires is seen as shallow and misguided. Instead the essence of human nature is seen as striving to achieve informed desires which would make any human life better, and within an intersubjective rather than an individualistic perspective. To be characteristically human is to have shared values of mutual intelligibility within an unambiguously societal setting. Such an interdependent view of human nature is shared by some of the macro-societal models of quality that are introduced in Chapter 6.

Sen's vision of human flourishing, comprising the freedom to choose between sets of valuable beings and doings, lies between a utilitarian and a prudential values approach in that it privileges individual freedom but within a societal context where all basic human capabilities are deemed to be met. Nussbaum's perspective on human nature is markedly similar to the prudential values perspective expressed by Qizilbash in that it is in essence other-regarding and thus social rather than individualistic, and it foregrounds heavyweight values informed by Aristotelian practical reason – for her the good life is the *correct* life.

For Doyal and Gough's THN, as noted above, human nature is in essence social and is bounded by sets of interlocking rights and associated responsibilities. It is also closely bound up with their primary need of autonomy. Autonomy of agency, the human capacity for making informed choices, is seen in the THN as a defining characteristic of being human in relation to the human need for social participation. Any impairment of autonomy, particularly in relation to mental health, cognitive and emotional capacity, is thus seen as a potential diminution of our humanity. This is an important characterisation in that it links the individual and the social within a needs-related conception of humanity and thus provides a bridge between needs, prudential values and capabilities. The stress on autonomy, and its consonance with notions of positive freedom, particularly within the capabilities framework, also reduce the potential import of any charges of paternalism in THN.

Enjoyment

One of the most striking differences among these approaches to quality of life is in the way they treat enjoyment and other subjective aspects of life. Basically there is a major divide between utilitarianism, prudential values and capabilities, on the one hand, and the needs-based approaches, on the other. Enjoyment, or pleasure, is absolutely central to utilitarianism; indeed, it is its essence. It has to be admitted that enjoyment is not deeply theorised in utilitarianism except to the extent that it is expressed as a hedonic mental state. Enjoyment is treated as a much more eudaimonic, multi-dimensional and complex attribute within prudential values, as being an important part of 'what makes any human life go well'. Here its hedonic aspects are given lower priority than its deeper, more heavyweight expression in terms of appreciating the day-to-day textures of life and consciousness of aesthetic beauty. Nussbaum takes a similar multidimensional perspective in relation to capabilities and a flourishing life but she also foregrounds expressive enjoyment: one item in her list includes being able to laugh, play, and enjoy recreation.

There is no place for enjoyment, however, in needs-based accounts. And there is a very good reason for this. The moral imperative related to meeting needs depends upon these needs being seen as unambiguously basic and absolute lowest common denominators for survival at a minimally decent level. Thus food, shelter, basic medical services and education up to functional literacy can be justified in this calculus but enjoyment cannot. This is not to say that proponents of needs-based approaches are against enjoyment or see it as irrelevant to a flourishing life. They do not. But they cannot defend the *social right* to enjoyment in the same way as they can defend the right to nutrition, so therefore it has to be excluded here. This rigour and austerity enhance the ideological strength of the requirement for these needs to be met *as of right*. People need enjoyment to lead a fully flourishing life but, so it is argued, do not need enjoyment to survive at a minimally decent level.

It has to be admitted that the THN has a more nuanced stance on this than the more basic needs-oriented approaches, in that its insistence upon liberty as integral to autonomy of agency and as a prerequisite for critical autonomy both encapsulates the right to *pursue* happiness (if not necessarily to achieve it) and raises THN above the lowest common denominator for survival at a minimally decent level.

Income and wealth

Two of the approaches explicitly include income: utilitarianism, for which money is the central measure, at least with regard to material utility; and the HDI, which combines GNP and aspects of basic needs. Income is not explicitly included in the basic needs approach, largely because of the problems discussed earlier in the chapter, particularly issues of distribution both nationally and within households. The same is true for the THN approach, but Gough (2000a) does point out that in empirical studies the level of economic development, measured in GNP, is the most important factor in needs satisfaction. It is undeniable also, that increased access to material resources, increased income in other words, will – other things being equal – enhance many capabilities and prudential values too. Therefore it is impossible to ignore income totally in any account which deals at least in part with material aspects of quality of life, but it is essential to bear in mind that it can lead to serious distortions, even within utilitarianism and needs to be used with extreme caution in any other approach where quality of life is not directly measured in terms of price.

Practicability

Finally, it is worth noting some issues related to practicality in applying these constructs in the real world. It has to be said that, in spite of all its theoretical, methodological and operational shortcomings, utilitarianism is the most straight-forward and practical of them all. This is for two reasons: first, it is monistic and not pluralistic: there is one unit of measurement, money. Second, the actual measuring is done by the invisible hand of the market: utility is measured in terms of the price a person is willing to pay for a good or service and a person's or a country's total potential utility is measured by how much money they have – their income or their wealth.

None of the other approaches have this dual advantage. The HDI is the closest because it can be expressed as a single figure, but this is only at the expense of an arbitrary bundling together of independent and incommensurate items. Pluralism, leading to the impossibility of unitary summation, bedevils the operationalisation of all the other approaches. Even for the simplest of the basic goods approaches, there are serious issues about cut-off points for levels of medical service provision in relation to age and disability. Pluralism is particularly problematic in relation to approaches such as prudential values and Sen's version of capabilities where there are no definitive lists. Nussbaum's list is very worthy and encapsulates much of what is important and worthwhile in human existence, but is, as Gough (2003) points out, extraordinarily difficult to operationalise. On the positive side, it has been shown with regard to prudential values that the use of Borda scores and the Pareto rule can give partial comparisons between countries. The THN too has been partially operationalised, using multivariate statistical techniques, which provide a fuller analysis, at the loss of intuitive comprehensibility. Both of these approaches provide fruitful avenues for further work.

4 Poverty and wealth, inclusion and exclusion
Social processes and social outcomes

In Chapters 1 and 2 the emphasis is set squarely on the subjective and objective well-being and quality of life of people as individuals. In Chapter 4 the emphasis shifts from individuals' internal desires and feelings towards the social context within which they are expressed. Two themes from Chapter 3, relating to utilitarian (desires-based) and needs-based approaches re-appear here, but in a broader societal context where the distribution of material resources and life chances are fore-grounded. A central feature emerging in this chapter is people's quality of life in relation to the communities and societies in which they live. The main foci in this chapter comprise *relative* and *relational* issues (Lister, 2004: 7).

The first section briefly introduces the perennially controversial issues of poverty and social inequality, looking at both national and international perspectives. The approach here does not just rehearse familiar political debates on the definition, existence and putative extent of poverty. Instead, attention is primarily focused on the relationship between disposable resources and both objective (needs-based) and subjective (desires-based) well-being – all within a social and societal context.

The second section discusses social inclusion and exclusion, both as social processes and outcomes. Social exclusion too is a hotly contested construct, ideologically and theoretically. Different approaches are discussed in relation to their interaction with quality of life and their implications for social policy. Here again, links are made with themes from Chapter 3, particularly to participation and affiliation common to prudential values, Doyal and Gough's theory of human needs and Sen's and Nussbaum's 'thin' and 'thick' versions of capabilities.

Then the relative merits of the two constructs of poverty and social exclusion/ inclusion are discussed in relation to both individual and societal perspectives on quality of life as a precursor to Chapters 5 and 6 which move away from individual perspectives and deal with the collective constructs of social capital, social cohesion, overarching quality of life and social quality.

Poverty and quality of life

From Chapter 3 it can be seen that utilitarianism is operationalised through the fulfilling of *actual desires*, mostly via the medium of money (at least in relation to material desires): the more money – or income – one has, then the more utility one also has. Similarly, basic needs, at least in their absolutely basic formulation, are realised through the provision of basic goods, again comprising material resources. Poverty too, in its worldly rather than its spiritual manifestation, is to do with money, goods and material resources. Poverty can be defined by direct reference to needs, both material and social, and it can also be defined in terms of income. Therefore a person who is poor is not having their material or social needs met and/or has an unacceptably low level of income.

It is, of course, taken for granted here that poverty is 'a bad thing' in terms of quality of life. Before going any further, though, it is necessary to mention a few caveats. The first is that in this context poverty refers *only* to deprivation in material resources, albeit in a social context. Any notions of spiritual or moral poverty, although both entirely valid in relation to theology or moral philosophy, are beyond the scope of this less ethereal discussion. A more complex issue, particularly in relation to operationalisations of poverty based on income levels is whether, and to what extent, the imposition of a 'poverty line' might be inappropriate for any who may deliberately choose to eschew material values and live a life of material simplicity. An obvious example here is people who choose to live in a monastic or other religious order, taking a *vow* of poverty. In principle, this is quite a tricky issue but in practice it can be circumvented by reference to volition and choice in operational definitions of poverty.

A more pressing practical problem concerns the issue of income versus expenditure or access versus use of resources. A person might have access to income or other resources but may face barriers in using them to meet their needs. These barriers might be entirely non-volitional, for example, during times of food shortages, or else volitional where, for example, a person uses money to purchase 'non-essential' items such as alcohol or other drugs. Perhaps most crucially, in practical terms, most countries have to measure income at *household* rather than individual level and many households that have enough aggregate income may well contain household members in extreme poverty because of inappropriate allocation of intra-household resources. Therefore, in subsequent discussions it is assumed that any mention of income is as a proxy for access to resources appropriate to meeting needs which are distributed equitably among household members.

More formally (following Room, 1995b; Abrahamson, 1997; da Costa, 1997) poverty can be generically defined as a lack of resources, measured in terms of either income or expenditure, at the disposal of an individual (or household, subject to the above qualification) at a specific point of time. Admittedly 'lack of resources' is an unsatisfyingly vague term which needs to be more tightly defined if it is to be of any use in assessing quality of life either for individuals or within societies. Before engaging in this endeavour, though, it might be helpful to mention the historical and political context of the use of 'poverty'. For reasons that will soon become clear, Britain – or more precisely, England – is the focus of attention here.

Extreme poverty, or destitution, was a perennial problem in pre-industrial England. It was an economic and political problem as well one relating to quality of life. The economic problem, starkly, was that in times of famine, and otherwise in economic slumps, there was a real danger of loss, through starvation, of labour which – as a major factor of production – would be needed when the famine ended or the economic cycle started to recover. The political problem was more immediate, particularly after the beginning of the agricultural revolution: here bands of destitute landless labourers moved from parish to parish seeking work or 'relief', that is, amelioration of their poverty. From the inception of the great Elizabethan Poor Laws in the early seventeenth century through to the epoch-making and notorious Victorian Poor Law Amendment Act of 1834 and finally up to the passage of the National Assistance Act in 1948, the 'Poor Law' was a central feature of English society.

Throughout this period, poverty was highly stigmatising and indeed a British Prime Minister, Disraeli, during the post-1834 'workhouse era', said that Britain was the only country where poverty was a 'crime' in that destitute families were treated like criminals. They had to enter the workhouse where husband and wife were separated from each other and from their children and all were made to work excessively long hours at tiring menial tasks, including working treadmills, in order to get fed.

The 1834 Poor Law Amendment Act enshrined the doctrine of 'less eligibility' for people in poverty (renamed *paupers* once they applied for 'relief'): the condition of the pauper shall be less eligible than that of the lowest paid labourer. 'Less eligibility' was introduced in order to dissuade the shiftless and work-shy from applying for poor relief. Unfortunately for several decades of the nineteenth century, the wages of the lowest paid labourers were too low to live on. This made less eligibility difficult to enforce unless the relief given was highly punitive, hence the horrors of the workhouse so graphically portrayed in novels such as *Oliver Twist*.

By a perverse stroke of administrative genius, the Poor Law policy of less eligibility was enforced by the simplest test possible. Instead of all the form-filling associated with contemporary means tests, Victorian paupers merely had to undertake the 'Workhouse Test': anyone who wanted relief only had to knock on the door of the workhouse – workhouses were so dreaded and feared that no-one would dream of entering one unless they were totally desperate. It has to be noted that the above description was of the Victorian Poor Law at its very worst. In some areas paupers, particularly old and infirm people 'of good character' were given 'out-relief' that is, food or money without having to enter the workhouse: but the Poor Law was on the statute book and was rigorously enforced in many areas, particularly in non-industrial counties in southern England.

The English Poor Law bequeathed two tangible policies to British social policy, both central to contemporary social security policy and to the quality of life of a substantial proportion of citizens. The first is the linking of 'poverty' with the notion of less eligibility; that a family is poor if their income is lower than that of the lowest paid worker. This, as can be seen below, provides a link to defining poverty as a proportion of average wages, nominally that proportion earned by the lowest paid workers. Incidentally, this issue is central to the debates on fixing the statutory minimum wage level. The second is the implementation of a 'needs test' to identify those 'genuinely' in poverty. The major challenge in implementing social security policy that enhances rather than demeans people's quality of life is to institute ways of identifying people's needs without at the same time stigmatising them and thereby dissuading people in poverty from claiming the benefits that will alleviate this poverty and enhance their quality of life.

Thus, the historic problems associated with poverty, and government responses to them, were centrally associated not just with issues of quality of life for the poor but also with important societal imperatives to do with economics and politics. It is not surprising, therefore, that poverty was of major interest to scholars and academics in the nascent social sciences, particularly in economics and political science. Indeed, towards the end of the nineteenth century, political scientists and social reformers, particularly Sidney and Beatrice Webb, founded the London School of Economics. The Webbs' studies of poverty and of the Poor Law were a central plank in the new academic discipline of sociology and laid the foundations for the study and teaching of 'administration for social workers', later gaining a more independent identity as social administration and now known as social policy.

The English Poor Law system was unique in Europe, as was the development of the interrelationships between politics, economics, sociology and social policy as academic subjects, all with a more or less central interest in 'the problem of poverty'. This has led to the study of poverty being a particularly English or Anglo-Saxon activity (given its export to the dominions and colonies of the British Empire).

Most constructs central to the study of sociology and social policy are sites for political contestation, and poverty is no exception. Poverty is seldom seen as a 'good thing' and no government wants to be seen as presiding over an increase in something so damaging as poverty. For the generation after the Second World War, successive governments supported, or at least paid lip service to, the welfare state and pledged that there would not be a return to the poverty and mass unemployment of the inter-war years. Even during this time of consensus, though, there were spirited debates about the extent to which poverty had been reduced. Much of the disagreement was about *definitions*, broadly split between left-wing and right-wing perspectives. The former, led by pioneering social scientists such as Peter Townsend and Brian Abel-Smith championed contemporary, socially-oriented relative inequality-based definitions, identifying poverty as being to do with not having the resources to participate effectively in everyday social life (see, for example, Abel-Smith, 1965; Townsend, 1967). The latter, including many New Right academics and even some mainstream British sociologists such as the venerable T. H. Marshall (1972) defended long-established physiological subsistence-based *absolute* definitions deriving from Booth's and Rowntree's classifications of minimum requirements for physical efficiency in their ground-breaking surveys of poverty at the end of the nineteenth century.

These arguments were at centre stage during the years of the Thatcher and Major governments from the 1970s to the 1990s with their espousal of market economics and the rolling back of the welfare state. The liberal market philosophy associated with the eras of Thatcher in Britain and Regan in the USA led inexorably to greater inequalities in societies throughout the developed Western world, with rewards for the enterprising and risk-taking entrepreneurs and lower social protection for those unwilling, or too unenterprising, to look after their own interests. The increase in inequality inevitably leads to a higher proportion of people with below-average incomes which in turn increases the likelihood of more people being defined as being poor in terms of a relative definition of poverty. Hence, the definition of poverty became an immensely important political issue during these times.

Politically, it is essential for economic liberals to make a clear distinction between poverty and inequality, the former being 'bad' and the latter being acceptable, or even 'good'. Broadly, then, poverty in this New Right context is seen in absolute terms whereas any relative definitions of poverty, more favoured by Social Democrats and the Left, are just seen as manifestations of an entirely acceptable inequality – so long, of course, as no-one is in a state of absolute want. The political importance of this distinction comes into clear focus in the context of the extent of the increase in inequality – and thus according to a relative definition, the increase in *poverty* – during the years of Conservative rule: between 1970 and 1997 the percentage of the population on less than half the average household income (perhaps the strictest measure of relative poverty in general use) increased threefold to 14 million people (Townsend and Gordon, 2000). This, of course, was a dramatic change in the distribution of income, and therefore, arguably, quality of life, in Britain.

In 1999 the New Labour Prime Minister, Tony Blair, who had been come to power in 1997, committed his government to halving child poverty by 2009 and eliminating it entirely by 2019. Some progress has been made here. By 2000/1 the number of children on 60 per cent of median income (the measure chosen by the Blair government) was 3.9 million, a fall of 0.5 million since 1996/7 but nevertheless this is still double the 1980 figure (Palmer *et al.*, 2002: 30).

Perhaps the tide has turned internationally on poverty too. At a World Summit on Social Development in 1995, 117 countries declared their intentions to prepare annual anti-poverty plans. Also in 1997 over seventy European social scientists signed the 'Brussels Declaration' (*An International Approach to the Measurement and Explanation of Poverty*) which reiterated that poverty is a concept based primarily on income or resources. Both the 1995 World Summit and the 1997 Brussels Declaration agreed to develop a two-level approach in all countries, covering both absolute *and* relative approaches.

Absolute poverty

In its most rigorous formulation this is, in principle, universally applicable and refers to situations where people have access to only enough resources for physiological efficiency, subsistence or avoidance of starvation: in other words the most very basic of the basic goods approaches identified in Chapter 3. It is usually defined without reference to social contexts, norms or needs. Everyone at the limit of absolute poverty will have an extremely low but marginally sustainable material quality of life. Sachs maintains that absolute – or in his terminology – *extreme* poverty specifically means that:

> [H]ouseholds cannot meet basic needs for survival. They are chronically hungry, unable to access health care, lack the amenities of safe drinking water

and sanitation, cannot afford education for some or all of the children, and perhaps lack rudimentary shelter . . . and basic articles of clothing such as shoes.

(2005: 20)

Thus, under these circumstances, there will be virtually no poverty in contemporary Britain, at least among citizens and legal immigrants, and, indeed, Sachs is emphatic that such extreme levels of poverty occur only in developing countries.

There is a huge debate over how to define absolute poverty. One perspective is from the OECD: 'a level of minimum need, below which people are regarded as poor, for the purpose of social and government concern, and which does not change over time' (Gordon, 2000: 51). The World Summit on Social Development took a different view, not saying that absolute poverty is constant over time or invariant between societies. They describe absolute poverty as a condition characterised by: 'severe deprivation of basic human needs, including food, safe drinking water, sanitation facilities, health, shelter, education and information' (UN, 1995, para 19, cited in Lister, 2004: 32). But they diluted the absolute status of their delineation even further by requesting that each country should separately develop a precise definition and assessment of absolute poverty rather than collectively agree a universal definition.

Gordon (2000) reports that in 1996 a UN expert group working on behalf of the World Summit came up with the following operational definition of absolute poverty: an acute shortfall of income or assets and a lack of access to certain basic services including health, housing and education. As well as 'an acute shortfall in income' being vague and apparently relativistic, Gordon wryly notes that: 'In developing countries and especially in those with the lowest per capita income, such deficiencies are usually defined in absolute [*sic*] terms in relation to the threshold of basic needs' (2000: 54). By implication, then, in countries except for those with the lowest incomes, absolute poverty is not measured in absolute terms at all. This is consistent with Townsend's critique of Sen's absolutist approach which refers to an irreducible core of absolute deprivation which is an absolute inability to pursue certain valuable functionings (Townsend, 1985; Alkire, 2002b: 156). Gordon (2000) claims that even an absolutist core has to be societally relative, if in nothing else, then in terms of nutritional requirements, shelter and avoidable disease.

Thus, this leaves absolutist approaches as 'absolutist' in name only. Indeed, Townsend and Gordon (1991) argue that unless 'absolute' is measured in a way that is constant over time or invariant between societies then operationally it become virtually indistinguishable from relative poverty. However, there is still room for a rigorous approach to objectively defined poverty that is at least in principle comparable between societies. The original World Summit formulation did attempt to do this. Similarly Gough (1997: 86) links his conceptualisation of poverty squarely with Doyal and Gough's theory of human needs as set out in Chapter 3: 'In short I contend *poverty* refers to deprivation in any of the basic and intermediate needs' (ibid.: 83–4).

Broadly speaking, then, there are two conceptually distinct conceptualisations of absolute poverty which according to some commentators but not others, can be seen to shade into each other and overlap once any meaningful attempt is made to operationalise them in practice. The bottom line in absolutist definitions is physical survival: a person who is dying of starvation must be seen as being in absolute poverty, whatever the definition. Similarly, a person who suffers from hunger so regularly that their physical efficiency is impaired and their life expectancy is substantively reduced (that is, by years rather than by days or months) probably has to be seen as being in absolute poverty and this applies with particular emphasis to children. But here the slippery slope begins; as will be noted in Chapter 7 there are substantial income differences in average mortality rates and life expectancies, even among industrialised countries. Therefore, the life expectancy of significant proportions of the populations of many rich developed countries *is* being seriously circumscribed. Moving away from averages, a sizeable proportion of the poorest groups living in the lowest income areas in developed nations with high levels of income inequality are on extremely low incomes, even by developing country standards, and have correspondingly high death rates. This is particularly true in the USA (Wilkinson, 1996). This is discussed in more detail in Chapter 7 in the context of health-related quality of life in different societies.

Does this provide evidence that there is significant absolute poverty in developed countries with lower than average life expectancy, or among the poorest groups in highly unequal developed nations – even if they have high average life expectancy and if none of their citizens can be seen as starving or as regularly going hungry? The answer seems to be 'yes' if poverty is to be anything other than a synonym for imminent starvation. In order for this to be unequivocally the case, both the World Summit and Gough definitions need to be tightened up in one important sense: the notion of 'actual substantive damage to' *life expectancy* (or 'substantive reduction in' or similar formulation) must be incorporated. Therefore, the World Summit definition has to be changed to 'severe deprivation in basic needs *leading to a substantive reduction in life expectancy*'. Gough's approach is very wide-ranging and needs to be narrowed down as well as tightened up. This can be done by going back to one of the two basic prerequisites of the Doyal and Gough theory of human needs: that of avoiding serious harm. His definition can then be reformulated as: 'poverty refers to deprivation in any of the basic and intermediate needs *to such an extent as to cause serious harm to life expectancy*'. It needs to be noted that this foregrounds the basic need of physical health and the intermediate needs of adequate nutritional food and water, adequate protective housing and appropriate health care; the other needs being more open-ended or less specifically related to physical efficiency.

It is noted above that to be absolute in all its dimensions a definition must be constant over time and between societies. Given the rapid change in medical technology and the increase in life expectancy in industrialised countries over the past two centuries, then the constancy over time requirement seems too restrictive: average life expectancy in Britain is now around twice what it was in 1841 (Douglass, 2002) so it would be perverse to claim that a person with a life expectancy of less than forty years is not suffering serious harm. Instead, the 'absolute' in absolute poverty is taken here to be absolute between societies: in other words absolute poverty is taken to mean the same throughout the world. This of course means absolute in outcome rather than input, for example, food and shelter requirements differ in relation to climate, etc.

Relative approaches to poverty

Given the above definition of absolute poverty being the same across the world, then relative poverty can appropriately be seen to be country-specific. A person in relative poverty in a rich society may well not be in absolute poverty whereas a person in relative poverty in a poor country is sure to be in absolute poverty too. There are several different approaches to relative poverty, three of which are discussed here. These are: (1) citizenship obligation; (2) socially defined needs; and (3) unacceptable levels of inequality.

Strangely enough, that icon of market liberalism, Adam Smith is often cited as the initiator (or populariser) of the citizenship obligation approach to poverty in that he stated that a person needs to have socially acceptable clothing (a linen shirt and leather shoes in his case) in order to be able to be seen in public: in other words a person has a duty to be minimally sartorially respectable (Smith, 1812: 351–2). In this context it is interesting to note that Sen includes 'the ability to go about without shame' as an example of *absolute* poverty (Alkire, 2002b: 185). Townsend's (1979) influential formulation, while including respectable clothing, also includes, for example, the ability to purchase small gifts for relatives' birthdays. This sort of approach to relative poverty is based upon the social duties of citizenship: a person is in poverty if they do not have the wherewithal to perform their social obligations as citizens.

A second, and potentially rather less stringent approach to relative poverty relates to social *needs* rather than citizenship obligations. The World Summit definition of 'overall' as opposed to 'absolute' poverty, includes functionings (Sen's notions of *doing* and *being*) as well as material resources:

> Overall poverty is not having those things that society thinks are basic necessities and, in addition, not being able to do things that most people take for granted either because they cannot afford to participate in usual activities or because they are discriminated against in other ways. What constitutes overall poverty will vary between different societies and at different points of time.
>
> (Gordon, 2000: 52)

What is crucial here is the ability to do things that most people take for granted within a society. This interestingly provides a cross-over between subjective and objective approaches: it is clear that the subsistence-based physiological efficiency approach is based on, or at least gains its legitimacy from, objective 'scientific' constructs and data. Citizenship-based approaches rely less on 'hard science' but their legitimacy is derived from well-established social norms and expectations, some passed down over many generations. What 'most people take for granted', however, changes rapidly over time and differs dramatically from society to society, even among developed, rich nations.

The definitive research on this topic in Britain is the Poverty and Social Exclusion Survey identified by Gordon (2000: 52) as 'the most comprehensive and scientifically rigorous survey of its kind ever undertaken'. Respondents were asked which items they saw as *a necessity*. Items seen as a necessity by more than 90 per cent of respondents were as follows: beds and bedding; heating for living areas of accommodation; a damp-free home; two meals a day; all medicines prescribed by a doctor. Between 80 and 90 per cent considered the following to be necessities: fridge; fresh fruit and vegetables daily; a warm waterproof coat; visits to friends/family; visiting friends/family in hospital; attending funerals and weddings; enough money to keep home in a decent state of decoration; being able to celebrate special occasions (Gordon, 2000: 66–8).

It is interesting to note here that the threshold accepted by 90 per cent plus of the population is very similar to basic needs and to the World Summit absolute approach and takes health and longevity into account through access to necessary medicines. (Given the free access to the NHS in Britain, the issue of medical services themselves did not arise but should still be included as a need.) The 80 per cent threshold takes on board social needs, as well as material needs.

One of the most striking things about this list is its parsimoniousness. Less than 80 per cent of members of the general public thought it was necessary to have meat/fish/vegetables every other day, or a hobby or a telephone; less than 70 per cent thought it was necessary to be able to afford to have family or friends round for a snack or to have carpets in living rooms. Perhaps the most astonishing results concerns some of the items which less than 60 per cent thought were essential: a small amount of money to spend on oneself; presents for family or friends once a year; replacing worn furniture; a holiday away from home; and a TV.

Now, all of these items *were* considered as necessities by more than half the respondents, who can be assumed to be representative of the population as a whole. So it can be assumed that the average citizen would consider all the above items as meeting material or social needs. But it is a matter of some surprise that more than four in ten people consider that a person who cannot afford to buy a present once a year, to have a television or some pocket money is *not* in a state of poverty. Under these circumstances it seems to be clear that many members of the general public, as well as politicians, hold to a rigorous definition of poverty that is both consistent with the English Poor Law tradition and sympathetic to an absolutist approach based on nutrition, warmth, shelter and maintenance of health.

A third approach is the most flexible of all: as it is based on a *proportion of average income*, it can be as generous or as frugal as desired. Here, a person is deemed to be in poverty if their income is below a set proportion of average earnings. This set proportion is the operational definition of what is seen as being an unacceptably low income and of course can only be identified relatively in relation to what is seen as an *acceptable* income. Some commentators, such as

Barry (1998) set a *range* of acceptable incomes with a bottom end below which no-one should be allowed to fall and a top end which he believes no-one should be allowed to exceed. Barry's limits are 50 per cent at the bottom end and 300 per cent at the top end of average earnings. Some other commentators also used a threshold of 50 per cent of average earnings but this is often seen as being rather parsimonious and many other commentators, as well as the UK Government and the EU use 60 per cent of average earnings as the poverty level (Palmer *et al.*, 2002: 13).

The common EU approach adds a slight quirk to the absolute/relative debate in that this unequivocally *relative* formulation (relative in that the poverty line will be different in absolute terms in EU nations with differing average incomes) is absolutely consistent in its definition and operationalisation among EU countries. So at least the income-based approach is entirely commensurate throughout the EU, unlike the citizenship-based and social needs-based approaches which will differ definitionally from country to country. It is for this reason that the income-based approach is the most commonly used. It has to be noted, though, that this is the most pragmatic and least specifically theoretically grounded of the three relativistic approaches in that the actual threshold is set at a somewhat arbitrary level whereas the items in both the other approaches, although by no means fixed, can be justified in relation to empirically testable norms.

Moving from specific to more abstract and general theoretical orientations, it is clear that the income-based approach to poverty has close links with the concept of social inequality. Its relationship to various notions of quality of life is complex and is mediated by both the level at which the poverty threshold is set and the extent of material inequality within the society. Also its relationship to subjective well-being is particularly problematic given the long-standing apparent anomaly of the relatively high proportion of people who can be classified as 'the happy poor'.

The Poverty and Social Exclusion survey, mentioned above, throws important light on people's subjective perceptions of poverty and quality of life and puts the 'happy poor' syndrome in perspective. It also set out to provide a conceptual link between the 'expert definitions' of absolute and overall poverty and subjective-based definitions, linking all these to the level of income necessary to meet these thresholds, thereby strengthening the substantive rationale for an income-based approach. In the study, respondents were asked how much money a household such as theirs would need to avoid absolute and overall poverty and what their own household income actually was. Gordon (2000) reported the results as 'startling': 9 per cent of respondents reported that their disposable household income was 'a lot below' the amount necessary to keep a household like theirs out of *absolute* poverty and a further 8 per cent judged that their household income was 'a little below' the absolute poverty threshold. Gordon comments:

> Therefore 17 per cent of respondents in a representative survey of the British population perceived their incomes to be less than the absolute poverty line as defined by the World Summit on Social Development . . . this is a significant finding as the UN definition of absolute poverty was thought by many experts to only be applicable to conditions in developing countries. Almost no absolute

poverty was thought to exist in advanced countries with welfare states. If absolute poverty was thought to exist in European countries, it was imagined to be only among very small excluded groups, such as the homeless. However, the general population's views on the amounts of absolute poverty in Britain are very different to those of 'experts'.

(2000: 55)

Two questions immediately arise here. The first concerns the notion of the 'happy poor'. These findings do not directly address this question in that it is possible for people to be both in extreme poverty and to be content with their lot. However, it is clear from the above findings that this is in general unlikely to be the case because there is a very clear and sharp perception of the nature and extent of poverty among the British population, certainly sharper than among poverty 'experts'.

The second question is of fundamental importance: it concerns the extent to which subjective perceptions match 'objective' measures of poverty. Gordon is unequivocal here. Using a 'scientific' measurement of poverty as having both a low income and suffering from multiple deprivation, he states that:

79 per cent of those who said their income was 'a lot below' that needed to avoid absolute poverty . . . were scientifically measured to be poor. Moreover, *all* of them 'lacked, on average, more than six necessities of life *because they could not afford them*'.

(2000: 56; italics in original)

Therefore, even according to 'scientific' definitions, around 7 per cent of the population (that is, 79 per cent of the 9 per cent who *said* they were well below the absolute poverty line) are both subjectively a lot below the absolute poverty line and are scientifically and objectively poor. Whether their scientific status is 'absolute' or 'overall' poverty is a moot point but what is of fundamental importance here is a high consonance, and correlation between hard 'scientific' definitions of poverty based on income levels and lacking necessities of life and self-reported subjective assessments of poverty.

It is also important to note that a higher proportion of the population considered that they were in poverty than would have been anticipated from the 'scientific' definitions. There are several possible reasons for this, including the possibility that social needs have been developing faster than average incomes. A more prosaic possibility is a technical problem regarding the issue of taking full account of housing costs which in many areas of the country are higher than allowed for in scientific calculations (Gordon, 2000). It is important to note that this is not just an issue in Britain. Layte and Whelan (2003) in their ground-breaking study of the dynamics of poverty across the EU show that the experience of poverty is far wider than would be anticipated from cross-sectional data, Gallie *et al.* (2003) found similar patterns in their EU-wide study of the relationship between poverty, unemployment, social isolation and social exclusion.

Poverty: strengths and weaknesses

It is clear from the above discussion that poverty is an ideologically highly contested concept and that there are at least two varying approaches to its 'objective' definition, with rather a slippery slope between them. Also, at least in Britain, there is a strong relationship between subjective and objective definitions of poverty, even though the subjective definition has a wider scope. In spite of the contestations and disagreements, poverty is a relatively straightforward concept: it is about unmet needs, both material and social, and it can be measured, either in relation to inputs, that is income, or outputs, whether people can afford certain purchases. In one of its theoretical manifestations – a 'strict' absolute conceptualisation – it is, at least in principle, a universal construct amenable to cross-country comparisons (although it is not easy to see how this can be done in practice). In one of its operational manifestations – as a fixed proportion of average incomes – cross-country comparisons can be made rather straightforwardly (though the theoretical base for this is rather shaky and the resulting metrics are a measure more of relative income inequality between countries than strict comparisons of poverty).

Having said this, there are some conceptual problems with poverty that do reduce its effectiveness as a social or societal construct of quality of life. Vobruba (2000) sums up the main issue by depicting poverty as being 'one-dimensional' in that it is not synonymous with vulnerability or deprivation in broad terms but only in relation to their material manifestation. He claims it is useful for description but not so good at explanation. Layte and Whelan (2003: 188) reiterate this point. They emphasise issues of cultural specificity in cross-national studies of poverty and highlight the different roles played by welfare regimes, country institutions, market incomes and structured inequalities within individual countries. Similarly, de Haan (1999) criticises an over-concentration on problems associated with poverty leading to one-sided policy priorities being set on economic growth rather than on social integration. Gough (1997: 82) brings several of these themes together. He criticises poverty for being conceptually too narrow and as being socially, historically and culturally specific. He claims that it lacks a clear basis in a universalistic ethics and is open to charges of cultural specificity. His main case is that poverty is just not conceptually strong enough in explanatory power and that it is anyway outdated in relation to late modern cosmopolitan culturally plural societies.

All the above criticisms in effect see poverty, whatever its strengths, as being too narrow in its conceptualisation, too culturally specific, too materialistic, too much based on either need or utility and thus not taking societal perspectives into account, and too unidimensional to have effective explanatory power in relation to social vulnerability and deprivation in late modernity. An alternative construct has been put forward to try to overcome these difficulties: that of social exclusion. This is now introduced to see if it can, indeed, provide a better societal perspective on quality of life.

Social exclusion

Social exclusion and poverty

Poverty is to do with not having enough *resources* to meet basic material and social needs. Social exclusion, on the other hand, is about *detachment* from the mainstream of society, *dissociation* from social milieux, social *polarisation*, lack of *social rights* and, of course, as its name implies, *exclusion* (Giddens, 1998; Berghman, 1995; Barry, 1998; Abrahamson, 1997; Room, 1995b respectively). Importantly, it is both a noun and a verb: social exclusion, the noun, is about outcomes, what happens to people; to socially exclude, the verb, is about processes, social structures and systems that operate to include and exclude. There are many areas of overlap between the two constructs of poverty and social exclusion, indeed, it is probable that in most societies the majority of socially excluded people are poor and that a significant proportion of poor people are socially excluded.

The two constructs, however, are largely conceptually distinct. For example, in many societies a high proportion of people who are poor may still be socially included. This happens in highly unequal but socially integrated societies. Perhaps this is best exemplified by quoting from the edition of *Hymns Ancient and Modern*, the standard Church of England hymn book from the 1860s to the present. A favourite children's hymn (sung nearly every week in the Sunday School I attended), 'All Things Bright and Beautiful', had the following verses:

> All things bright and beautiful,
> All creatures great and small
> All thing wise and wonderful
> The Lord God made them all.
> . . .
> The rich man at his castle
> The poor man at his gate
> God made them high and lowly
> And ordered their estate.
> (Monk, 1862)

Here is the epitome of a tightly integrated, well-ordered society where everyone has a place; and where everyone who *knows* their place and behaves appropriately is included, albeit within a highly inegalitarian form of social inclusion. Here the poor man has a low social status but is included within – albeit at the bottom of – the hierarchical social order.

Similarly, in some societies people who are not poor can still be socially excluded against their will. This has happened with horrific consequences in, for example, Nazi Germany, Stalinist Soviet Union, the former Yugoslavia and Rwanda. At a less extreme level, South Asians in Uganda and Kenya in the 1960s and the 1970s were socially excluded, indeed, physically removed to the UK.

So what are the main differences between poverty and social exclusion? The first, and perhaps the most important, relates to breadth of vision. Poverty starts off with a lack of *material resources* so in essence its basis is economic and material. Certainly, the implications of this lack spread out into many facets of everyday life, particularly with regard to social stigma, so it is too simplistic to say that poverty has no relevance outside the material world. Nevertheless its initial focus is always on access to resources to meet need. The primary focus of social exclusion, on the other hand, is *social*: a lack of access to social participation, social status and, perhaps most importantly, social rights. For da Costa (1997: 7) the relationship between social rights and social membership is central to social exclusion: 'Social exclusion can be analysed in terms of the denial (or non-realisation) of these social rights: in other words, in terms of the extent to which the individual is bound into membership of this moral or political community.' In this sense, then, poverty is predicated on a material conception of quality of life and social exclusion is predicated on a social conception of quality of life.

A second distinction is that poverty can be seen as distributional and social exclusion as relational: poverty, and particularly a relative approach to poverty, is to do with the distribution of resources within society. The income-based definition of poverty is operationalised precisely on the basis of the income distribution within a society. Thus, in this context, poverty can be seen as a static construct in that it refers to what happens at a certain point in time. Social exclusion, on the other hand, can be seen as both static and dynamic: static in its orientation towards relational exclusionary outcomes; and dynamic in its orientation to societal exclusionary processes such as the factors that trigger entry into and exit from poverty, and in understanding how the duration of disadvantage shapes how it is experienced and affects its consequences (Room, 1999).

Dimensionality is another difference. It is noted above that the core of poverty relates to material resources. Social exclusion is essentially multi-dimensional: it includes economic resources in that there are links between financial poverty and poor housing, educational failure and lack of skills in the job market, and deprived childhood and patterns of health and sickness, but it also covers other economic activity as well as social, political, cultural, legal and socio-demographic dimensions.

These socio-demographic dimensions point to another set of differences between poverty and social exclusion, related to the level of analysis and measurement. The unit of measurement for poverty is virtually always the individual, family or household. These units are then aggregated in order to ascertain which are the poorest types of households, age groups, localities, etc., but the central focus is upon individuals and households. Social exclusion, too, *can* focus on individuals and households but its main orientation is towards groups and communities; for example it was Jews, people with learning disabilities, homosexuals and gypsies who were chosen for exclusion – and extermination – by the Nazis. Social exclusion is a particularly powerful analytical tool when studying excluded communities or *area deprivation*. Here the dynamic and multi-dimensional nature of social exclusion provides insights which are not available from an analysis based on poverty. This is discussed in more detail later.

There is also a difference in 'moral narratives' between the two constructs. British poverty discourses in the late nineteenth century focused strongly on the moral status of the poor person, whether 'deserving' or 'undeserving'; indeed, a cultural industry was established around this issue with the establishment of the Charity Organisation Society (COS) with the specific purpose of discriminating – in both senses – between the deserving and undeserving. The COS established the professional discipline of 'casework' later incorporated into mainstream social work practice to identify whether a person claiming charitable assistance should be given help, for example, loaning a mangle to a widow of known good character so she could take in washing to pay for her rent and children's food, or whether they should be denied help and directed towards the workhouse, for example, if an unemployed man was known to consume alcohol or otherwise to be of 'bad character'. These moral investigations led to the COS being given the sobriquet of 'Cringe Or Starve' in popular culture (Sainsbury, 1977).

The discourses on social exclusion are no less moralistic, but are on a grander scale: in extreme cases whole groups are *detached from the moral order* even to the extent in the most horrific examples of being classified a 'sub-human' and therefore not accorded even the most basic human rights to life (see Chapter 1 for contemporary examples in relation to people with learning disabilities). Less dramatically, but nonetheless regrettably, increasingly commonly in the UK, groups are being denied citizenship rights, rights of abode or even permission to stay in a country because of their status as illegal immigrants or failed asylum seekers. Again, the notion of desert is crucial here, not necessarily because of any attribute relating to person's *individual* moral worth but because of the lack of moral worth attributable to their legal or national status. Another, again highly regrettable form of moral discourse in social exclusion relates to ethnic or religious group status; for example, Pakistanis, Bangladeshis, African-Caribbean, Irish, Muslims, have all faced exclusionary discrimination just because of the 'moral status' of their group membership.

Finally, most importantly and related to all the above, is the difference in attribution of causality. Given its dependence on material resources, it is not surprising that causal arguments about poverty are related to economic factors, particularly regarding the availability of income from paid work. In general, people are seen to be poor either because they or other members of their household do not work or have not worked in the past and do not have access to other financial resources, or else do work or have worked but have not been paid enough to make ends meet. In some cases the reasons for this are seen to be personal, either through fecklessness or misfortune, or else social structural because of high levels of unemployment, underemployment or underpaid employment.

Material deprivation and unemployment are factors too in causality of social exclusion, as seen later in respect of the insights provided on social exclusion discourses by Ruth Levitas. However, given its multi-dimensional nature, it is no surprise that there is a wide span of potential causes of social exclusion. These range from, at the more moralistic end, sub-cultural explanations based on deviant behaviour, via local economic misfortune, through to large-scale institutionalised societal process of discrimination.

With all these differences, and with social exclusion seeming to be so important, the question arises of whether it is a new phenomenon, perhaps relating to the unprecedented circumstances of late modernity with its emerging cosmopolitan, multicultural, globalised, network-oriented society involving shifting national boundaries, social connections and collective identities (Abrahamson, 1997). Alternatively, more prosaically, and perhaps more cynically, is it just another way of identifying and labelling a condition or set of conditions that is not new at all?

Is social exclusion a new phenomenon?

The term 'social exclusion' is very recent (at least in the English-speaking academic world). Indeed, it was hardly heard of before 1990 when it first appeared in the *Social Science Citation Index* of articles in scholarly journals. There were less than 30 articles in total on the topic up till 1995 but by the late 1990s there were over 50 articles per year, rising to around 100 per year after 2000. The number of books and reports available through the British university library system has followed a similar pattern, again with no publications before 1990, a trickle up to the mid-1990s, rising to between 150 and 300 a year (mostly government reports) in the late 1990s and early 2000s.

Social exclusion has caught the imagination of politicians and policy-makers as well as academics, to such an extent that the British Government has set up a high profile *Social Exclusion Unit* directly answerable to the Deputy Prime Minister and the Cabinet Office. Combating social exclusion has been even more deeply embedded as a basis of social policy in the EU since the early 1990s (Washington and Paylor, 1998; Berman and Phillips, 2000). Social exclusion is also seen as a serious contemporary threat to the fabric of society. For example, Silver (1994) claims that it threatens society as a whole with the loss of collective values and the destruction of the social fabric while Barry (1998) asserts that social exclusion is a violation of the demands of social justice in that it conflicts with equality of opportunity.

The high profile recently given to social exclusion adds urgency to the question of its antecedents and salience. Before addressing these issues, though, a prior question needs to be addressed, that of whether social exclusion is a phenomenon, or scientific construct, *at all*, or whether it is merely a fashionable label to attach to a wide range of disparate social ills. Graham Room, who has produced one of the most perceptive analyses of definitional issues on social exclusion, comes to a pessimistic conclusion: 'it remains too incoherent and confused to serve as a reference point for policy and research, despite various attempts at clarification' (Room, 1999: 166–7). Also, Saraceno makes a telling point about the inverse relationship between consensus on its usage and its meaning:

> I would venture to argue that social exclusion remains a concept on which conceptual consensus is lacking to a degree which is proportionally inverse to the consensus on its usage. Further, this shared usage is possible precisely because it remains an 'open', not rigorously defined, concept pointing to different dimensions and directions.
>
> (1997: 160)

Ratcliffe (1999) goes even further and argues that the term is positively harmful and should be banished from theoretical discussion altogether because of the danger that it may constitute an oppressive, victim-blaming discourse – similar to that around the notion of an 'underclass' – that diverts attention from the important task of analysing inequality and social divisions.

Ratcliffe's, Room's and Saraceno's warnings need to be heeded, but they do not have to be taken as counsels of doom. Their doubts as to the utility of the term can be overcome if it is possible to provide clear and precise definitions of the *different* meanings and usages applied to 'social exclusion'. Perhaps it is asking too much at the present stage of theorising and conceptualising social exclusion to have consensus on a universal meaning, but the term can have analytical power if its different usages can be effectively demarcated and delineated. Thus, the broad answer given here to the prior question of whether social exclusion is indeed a construct is: it is possible that the term is being used as a label for a number of distinct (but probably overlapping) concepts.

One of the major strands in much thinking about social exclusion is primarily concerned with *processes*. For example, Barry (1998) identifies as central to social exclusion the processes by which individuals and their communities become polarised, socially differentiated and unequal. Similarly, for Berghman (1995), social exclusion is a breakdown or malfunctioning of the major social systems that should guarantee full citizenship, including: the democratic and legal system which provides civic integration; the labour market which provides economic integration; the welfare system, providing social integration; and the family and community system, providing interpersonal integration.

A general theme of these approaches to social exclusion is to do with social exclusionary processes that lead to isolation, exclusion and detachment from society and its institutions. This is not to say that social exclusion is concerned only with processes, it also includes outcomes – and often process and outcome are inextricably intertwined in discussions of the nature of social exclusion. Process and outcome can also be treated separately. For example, Berghman (1995) and Berger-Schmitt (2000), following Gore and Figueirdo (1997), argue that social exclusion can be regarded both as a property of societies (largely process-oriented) and as an attribute of individuals, groups and communities (largely outcome-oriented). In the latter context, social exclusion can be defined as a low level of welfare and an inability to participate in social life.

The notions of participation and of access to resources necessary for participation are central to many definitions (Klasen, 2001). Steinert (2003: 5), perhaps expresses this most tellingly in terms of: 'exclusion from full participation in the social, including material as well as symbolic, resources produced, supplied and exploited in a society for making a living, organising a life and taking part in the development of a (hopefully better) future'.

One strand in empirical research on social exclusion is firmly rooted in discussion of outcomes as its primary aspect – in some cases even its *sole* aspect. Writers in this area address issues which can loosely be classified as 'multiple deprivation'. Several empirical studies have used outcome-oriented approaches to social exclusions, with the outcomes classified into different dimensions. Burchardt *et al.* (1999) identify five 'activities': consumption; savings; production; political; and social. These were subsequently reduced to four, with the exclusion of the political area (Richardson and Le Grand, 2002). McCrystal *et al.* (2001) identify the following outcomes: unemployment; deficiencies in local government services, community resources, housing and public transport; and levels of crime, ill health, debt and poor educational achievement. These exclusionary outcomes are each cumulative over time and they also interact with each other cumulatively. Thus, in this formulation, social exclusion is seen as resulting from the interaction of different exclusionary spheres, leading to multiple deprivation that is not too dissimilar from the more holistic, multiple social needs-oriented approaches to poverty noted above, particularly those developed by Townsend and Gordon (Burchardt *et al.*, 1999; Gordon and Townsend, 2000).

To return to the questions posed above on the status and integrity of the notion of social exclusion, some tentative answers can now be given. The approaches concentrating on social and societal *processes* of differentiation and detachment do provide a new focus. The phenomena addressed in these approaches are not themselves new, indeed they have always been central to the sociological endeavour, but bringing them together within the ambit of social exclusion provides a fresh and more holistic perspective that is consonant with changes in late-modern societies where early-modern concerns with *material subsistence* have been superseded by issues of *social integration* (Abrahamson, 1997). This focus enables exciting conceptual developments to be undertaken, relating processes and systems of social exclusion to societal normative value systems and social structures, particularly in relation to constructs such as social capital and social cohesion. This provides an opportunity to explore the societal preconditions for, constraints upon and parameters of both individual and societal quality of life. These societal issues are discussed in more detail in Chapter 5.

Returning to the facet of social exclusion more directly related to individuals, groups and communities, that is, outcome-oriented approaches concentrating on multiple deprivation, it can be seen that social exclusion is not *in itself* a new phenomenon, rather, it can be seen as a combination or a compound of two well-established phenomena. The first is an extension of the most wide-ranging, relational, dynamic and interactive approaches to poverty in the Townsend/Gordon tradition. The second is what had previously been known as 'area deprivation' or 'deprived areas'. An outcome-oriented notion of social exclusion incorporates these into one all-encompassing construct covering both individual and collective deprivation. This does not necessarily provide any theoretical innovation in our understanding of the ways in which society works but it does provide a new analytical framework for empirical study which can provide additional insights into quality of life of groups and communities as well as individuals.

The nature of social exclusion

So what does social exclusion as an outcome actually entail? In Steinert's participation-oriented formulation, exclusion may be continuous, relatively indivisible and gradual, ranging from a status of being fully included through to that of being completely excluded. According to Steinert (2003: 4) 'the "normal" model of being excluded is the dynamic, contested, episodic threat of exclusion that the person can fight against and often compensate'. He identifies political, economic, social and cultural exclusion as arising, respectively, from deficiencies in citizenship, lack of resources, isolation and deficits in education. He claims that these dimensions are often independent and it can be possible to counteract them through mobilising resources in other dimensions. Burchardt *et al*. (1999) similarly claim that social exclusion may be discontinuous and divisible, reflecting some individual dimensions of exclusion rather than all of them simultaneously.

Wessels and Miedema (2002: 73) produce a more formal typology of social exclusion moving on a continuum from mild to severe, thus:

1 *Alternative exclusion*: actors seek alternative lifestyles outside mainstream society. Here to some extent the exclusion is voluntary, although it can be precipitated by negative experiences in everyday life. A good example of this might be where people are subject to employment discrimination because of their ethnicity or religion, set up their own businesses and live in tightly knit communities, not interacting socially with 'outsiders'. The Jewish community in the East End of London at the beginning of the twentieth century is a good example of this alternative exclusion (Phillips, 2002).

2 *Preliminary exclusion*: actors face minor disruption but are still able to participate in social, political and cultural life. This is the beginning of 'real' social exclusion and it could be relatively trivial (for example, there are still some restrictions upon Catholics, such as not being able to marry the heir to the British throne). Alternatively, it might be part of a dynamic of exclusion, the first stage of a slippery slope where initial discrimination is a precursor to more draconian exclusion.

3 *Intermediate exclusion*: actors are excluded from some specific institutional forms and arrangements but they are generally still involved in mainstream institutional frameworks. Exclusion on the basis of gender is an interesting example here, particularly in the light of recent sex discrimination cases among business managers and high-paid City bankers and stockbrokers. The issues of women priests in the Catholic Church and women bishops in Church of England are highly specific examples of intermediate exclusion.

4 *Advanced exclusion*: actors are outside many mainstream and institutional forms of inclusion, via a combination of social and economic factors and are faced with considerable barriers to becoming included. This is the central type of exclusion in Wessels and Miedema's (2002) formulation in that it permeates many different dimensions of social life and is cumulative and multidimensional. Taken together, Wessels and Miedema's *intermediate*

and *advanced* exclusion appears to be similar in scope and nature to Steinert's notion of 'normal' exclusion.

5   *Severe exclusion*: actors exist largely in their own world: they are mostly isolated from common social formal and informal institutions and forms of inclusion. Steinert (2003: 4) identifies such 'overall exclusion' as an extreme and limiting case.

The 'severe' category identified by Wessels and Miedema is in fact a special case in that it approximates to notions of social exclusion as permanent and decisive detachment from society rather than on a continuum of disengagement or segregation. Room, in fact, uses this formulation as a final stage in differentiating between poverty and social exclusion where poverty is seen as a continuum of inequality whereas social exclusion is seen as 'catastrophic rupture' where participation in wider society is curtailed:

> In short, then, to use the notion of social exclusion carries the implication that we are speaking of people who are suffering such a degree of multi-dimensional disadvantage of such duration, and reinforced by such material and cultural degradation of the neighbourhoods in which they live, that their relational links with the wider society are ruptured to a degree which is in some considerable degree irreversible.
>
> (Room, 1999: 171)

This notion of an all-encompassing and decisive exclusion is reminiscent of the underclass discourse where Murray (2002), in particular, claims to have identified a modern form of *lumpenproletariat* living on its wits – and on state welfare provisions – outside the bounds of contemporary society. In a somewhat different and far less moralistic tone, Giddens (1998) claims 'exclusion is not about gradations in inequality, but about mechanisms that act to detach groups of people from the social mainstream'. Saraceno, too, sees social exclusion as 'an expression of social dis-integration and individual detachment from the social order' (1997: 159).

Wessels and Miedema's notion of severe exclusion, Steinert's overall exclusion and Room's catastrophic rupture can be seen as absolute forms of social exclusion in that it is both a *complete* and *irreversible* detachment from society and the social order.

Causes of social exclusion

The proximate causes of poverty are not hard to find, even if the underlying causes are more complex: poverty is a result of not having enough money to be able to meet one's needs. The causes of social exclusion, even proximate causes, are not so easy to pin down. There are at least two different sets of causes of social exclusion, those relating to processes and to outcomes. Wessels and Miedema (2002) identify the notion of *belonging* as being central to processes and access to *relevant resource structures* as central to outcomes. Interestingly, they identify a third set of causes around the notion of *trust* which links social exclusion to the social cohesion construct that is the subject of Chapter 5 of this book. Implicit in this approach is the proposition that social exclusion itself has a third *normative* dimension as well as that of process and outcome. According to Wessels and Miedema (ibid.: 62), if there is a substantive deficiency in either belonging, trust or access to relevant resource structures, then social exclusion will result.

Wessels and Miedema not only postulate three causal dimensions to social exclusion, they also identify three levels of analysis for each of these dimensions, starting first at the individual or biographical level, then moving to the neighbourhood, group or network, which they label the 'social' or 'life world' and finally, the societal or structural level. These levels are similar to the micro-, meso- and macro-levels in the ecological quality of life models discussed in Chapter 2. The identification of different levels, and of the interactions between them, provides a major step forward in operationalising the notion of social exclusion in terms of both processes and outcomes (and trust) pervading all societal levels. Wessels and Miedema (ibid.: 65) give examples at all three levels covering all three dimensions of factors causing social exclusion, as follows:

1 *Societal or structural level*: here lack of belonging is manifested in terms of social fragmentation, anomie, antagonism and retreatism. Similarly, there is lack of trust in institutions and authorities. A lack of access to resources is manifested in problems of subsistence and an increasing dichotomy between the haves and have-nots. At a structural level therefore, Wessels and Miedema see fragmented, alienated, mistrustful groups and communities not having a full national identity or sense of citizenship, as they are mistrusted by the rest of society and perhaps seen as engaging in free-rider activities, using illegal opportunity structures and being antagonistic to mainstream society. Stereo-types that immediately come to mind here include asylum seekers, illegal immigrants, ethnic minorities, and so on.

2 *Lifeworld level – neighbourhood, group, network*: lack of belonging is evidenced by local segregation and disengagement. Lack of co-operation, negative attitudes and stigmatisation all arise from lack of trust. Low quality local infrastructures and public facilities, including health services, schools, housing are all examples of a lack of lifeworld resource availability. Socially excluded communities, according to this formulation, are places suffering from a poor physical and social environment with high levels of crime and low opportunities for social advancement, whose residents are profoundly stigmatised and shunned by other communities, The classic stereotype of the socially excluded community here is the 'sink council estate' or the locality 'on the wrong side of the tracks'.

3 *Biographical, individual level*: here loneliness, isolation, low self-esteem are signs of lack of belonging; there is mistrust of figures in authority and fear of others in general; and resource deprivation is manifested through unemploy-ment and lack of life chances. Thus, socially excluded individuals are seen as

having low self-esteem, as being brought up in disrupted, 'problem' families, being disengaged from social, political and (legal) economic activity and not having the opportunity to engage in a 'normal' social life. Homeless people, 'drug addicts', 'problem families' all represent stereotypes of the individual manifestation of social exclusion.

The incorporation by Wessels and Miedema of items relating to trust, in addition to belonging and access to resources, adds a dimension not normally included in operationalisations of social exclusion, yet the examples they give often replicate indicators of social exclusion used in empirical studies (Burchardt *et al.*, 1999). It is probably fair to say that the jury is still out on whether trust is a mainstream domain of social exclusion *per se* but there is no doubt that Wessels and Miedema have made a strong case for trust – or more properly, lack of trust – as a major causal factor for social exclusion.

The different levels of analysis allow for the integration of different explanatory levels into identifying causes and tracking the extent of social exclusion. For example, the structural and life-world sets of explanations dealing with, for example, social segregation and stigmatisation, can be exemplified at the biographical level directly in relation to primary social exclusion from resource accessibility. Some of the reasons, for example, why many British Muslims of South Asian descent are unemployed, are disengaged from mainstream politics and mistrustful of the police and of other authority figures can be traced to the exclusionary factors at work, relating to belonging, resources and trust, both in their localities, where they live in social excluded communities, and nationally where they suffer from stigmatisation and normative discrimination (particularly with increased Islamophobia since 9/11). Thus, for Wessels and Miedema, the causes of the three levels of social exclusion interact and are cumulative: for an individual, social exclusion is a personal tragedy; for a local geographical community, it is a major social problem; for a whole national community or ethnos grouping, it is a sign of a deeply fractured society.

Another commentator, Levitas (2000: 359–60) has identified three causal pathways for social exclusion. Hers are rather different, though, in that she identifies separate *discourses* on exclusion, each epitomising a distinct ideological tradition. These she identifies, perhaps somewhat tongue-in-cheek, as follows:

- RED – the redistributive discourse. From this largely socialist perspective, social exclusion is caused by poverty and can be dealt with by increasing public expenditure, paid for by redistributive taxation. Social exclusion is seen as dynamic, processual, multidimensional and relational. It is emphatically to do with inequality and the distribution of resources within society. The slogan of the RED discourse is '*the poor have no money*'.
- SID – the social integration discourse. People who are socially excluded are workless, or in danger of being so. The SID solution to social exclusion is to ensure that everyone can work to earn enough money to avoid being socially excluded. This approach is predicated on a broadly social democratic

integrationist paradigm such as the one that underpins the Blair Government's 'New Deal'. The SID slogan is '*the poor have no work*'.

• MUD – the moral underclass discourse. Here, the causality of social exclusion is emphatically moral and cultural and is reinforced by 'the dependency culture'. The single mother – particularly the 'never-married mother' – is the typical socially excluded person in the broadly New Right MUD discourse. Its slogan is '*the poor have no morals*'.

Now, these *are* caricatures of three differing views on the causality of social exclusion and, being caricatures, there is a danger of each of them being belittled and not taken seriously. It has to be stressed, though, that each does have some explanatory power in relation to the causation of some facets of social exclusion as it affects some individuals and groups (Lister, 2004: 76–80). RED has much explanatory power in relation to people in receipt of state benefits and no other means of support, for example, pensioners. Their inability to participate effectively in society would be dramatically ameliorated if they had a decent income. Similarly, people living in areas of high unemployment who are desperate for a job so they can earn money and look after themselves and their families *do* need access to the jobs paying a decent wage as proposed in SID. Also, there *are* some people whose social exclusion may be to some extent either chosen as a rational alternative to inclusion or a result of lack of drive and initiative who would benefit from training and resocialisation – although exactly how many is a highly contested issue.

It is interesting to note that the RED solution would certainly cure *poverty* if it was applied universally and at an adequate level, so it would be a major step along the way to solving the problem of social exclusion in its manifestation of multiple deprivation. It would not, however, deal with issues of prejudice or institutionalised discrimination. Similarly, the SID solution of full employment and a decent minimum wage would alleviate the problems associated with poverty, at least for those of working age and in reasonable health, but would not have any impact on social exclusion as process.

The effect of the MUD solution on social exclusion is far less easy to fathom. It is too easy to say that MUD is merely victim-blaming and therefore its solution would be at best counter-productive – though it is certainly true that this is the case in relation to some of its more extreme and vociferous protagonists. It certainly is the case that many individuals – particularly those with disabilities and health problems and those who have been unemployed for a long time – may need counselling, assistance, advice and training in order to able to make use of employment and other inclusion opportunities. But the main task is to make sure these opportunities are equitably available in the first place.

What is missing from all of these discourses is an engagement with the relational, normative and process-oriented aspects of social exclusion. Levitas reminds us that there is a danger of seeing social exclusion, particularly in its most extreme and florid forms, as something only affecting people on the margins of society and implying that all is well among the vast majority of 'included' people within society. This analysis brings us back to the results of Burchardt *et al.*'s study and the formulations of Steinert's 'normal' exclusion and Wessels and Miedema's 'intermediate' and 'advanced' exclusion, all of which are multidimensionally gradated rather than being a catastrophic rupture, that is, on a continuum rather than being binary. Thus, Levitas, echoing Byrne (1999), draws our attention to the importance of the structure of inequalities *throughout* society, rather than the extremes of polarisation and detachment in her critique of discourses on social exclusion.

Social exclusion and social inclusion

So far, only social *exclusion* has been addressed, not social *inclusion*. This would be entirely straightforward if there were consensus in the literature that inclusion and exclusion were two ends of a continuum or, more starkly, the two sides of a binary attribute. Indeed, much of the literature tacitly assumes this, However, not all commentators agree. Steinert (2003: 6), for example, distinguishes between *integration* and *participation* as potential opposites to exclusion. He rejects integration (presumably synonymous with 'inclusion') as being potentially too passive and potentially stultifying, requiring conformity to social norms and demands. This has resonances with Barry's (1998) comment that highly socially integrated societies can be marked by large inequalities of power and status: indeed, Barry concludes that income differentials need to be restricted in order to counter social exclusion, with an acceptable range being between 50 per cent and 300 per cent of median income. Steinert characterises participation as *active engagement*, which is similar to Doyal and Gough's (1991) notion of critical participation in the context of their theory of human need. Klasen (2001), while not directly contrasting social exclusion with any other construct, takes a rights-based approach to counteracting social exclusion which has a strong affinity with Sen's (1993) capabilities approach and, like Barry, his perspective requires provision of rights for the most disadvantaged in society.

Walker and Wigfield insist that social inclusion is not simply the opposite of social exclusion. They compare inclusion and exclusion as follows:

> If social exclusion is the denial (or non-realisation) of different dimensions of citizenship then the other side of the coin, social inclusion, is the degree to which such citizenship is realised. Formally we might define social inclusion as the degree to which people are and feel integrated in the different relationships, organisations, sub-systems and structures that constitute everyday life.
> (2003: 9)

There are important insights here: in this context social inclusion is not *simply* the opposite of exclusion; it is more than that. It provides, in effect, a starting point for positive citizenship. From this perspective there is seen to be a continuum between exclusion and inclusion where high quality of inclusion requires a high level of critical participation and fulfilment of capabilities, not merely integration within an inegalitarian and rigidly hierarchical society.

Unfortunately, the situation is rather more complex than this in the real world. Some very unequal and highly socially differentiated countries, such as the USA, have high levels of geographical segregation with at one extreme, 'ghetto' communities of socially excluded, poor and disempowered groups and, at the other extreme, a mirror-image of 'gated' communities of the very rich who choose to segregate and insulate themselves from the mass of society within communities reminiscent of medieval walled cities, patrolled by guards and with high-tech surveillance systems. In contexts such as this, social exclusion and inclusion appear to be neither a binary divide nor a continuum but a discontinuous aggregation from involuntarily ultra-excluded at one end through to voluntary ultra-exclusionary at the other extreme, with different degrees of spatial and social segregation in-between.

Therefore, not only does social exclusion have at least two significantly different substantive connotations of process and outcome, and three levels of operation relating to biographical, life-world and societal milieux, it also has at least three potential interactions with its antithesis of social inclusion. The first, and most dramatic, is of binary divide between a small completely detached minority and a large, included and highly socially integrated majority as is the situation with asylum seekers or illegal immigrants in a tight-knit society: Denmark might be an appropriate example here. The second is a smoother continuum of inclusion–exclusion, similar to the gradations of income in the relative definition of poverty where exclusion is by degrees rather than by decisive detachment. This appears to be the situation in Britain – at least for its full citizens – according to the findings of Burchardt *et al*. (1999). The third, a discontinuous, or stepped aggregation, relates to highly segregated and differentiated societies such as the USA (Barry, 1998).

In this context it is also important to note that the antonym of poverty is not completely straightforward either: its *opposite* is wealth or riches whereas its *obverse* is 'non-poor'. Thus, two societies could have the same proportion of people in poverty but one may have a small, very wealthy elite whereas the other might have a relatively flat income distribution with no-one having, say, more than double average income. These societies would have equal poverty, highly unequal wealth, and radically different income distributions and opportunity structures.

A possible synthesis between poverty and social exclusion

Before drawing together the strands of the debates about poverty and social exclusion as separate entities, it is worth noting that attempts have been made to incorporate and integrate them. One of the earliest attempts was made by Gore and Figueirdo (1997) who make a rather neat claim for a symbiotic interaction between the two with social exclusion being *both* potentially subsumed by *and* subsuming poverty, with poverty being a bit like the filling in the middle of a sandwich. They state first that social exclusion can be *narrowly* defined as a component of poverty where a person is so poor as to be unable to participate in society: in other words, a person who falls below the citizenship definition of poverty will automatically suffer from social exclusion because they will, by definition, be unable to participate in social activities because they are too poor. They will therefore automatically be socially excluded entirely and completely because they are poor. Second, social exclusion can be *broadly* defined as subsuming poverty by becoming in effect a multi-dimensional version of poverty: 'material poverty can be seen as a particular form of social exclusion in that social exclusion refers to processes of impoverishment' (ibid.: 12).

A somewhat similar approach is taken by da Costa (1997) who sees merit in both constructs, but only so far as they are defined as being complementary. He defines poverty as being 'a situation of deprivation due to lack of resources'. Such a level of deprivation because of lack of resources, as in Gore and Figueirdo's analysis, leads inexorably to exclusion from basic societal, economic, financial and cultural systems. It may lead to exclusion from neighbourhood and family social networks, and in extreme cases the poverty may be so great as to lead to loss of identity, self-esteem and personal autonomy. These three levels of potential exclusion caused by poverty closely match Wessels and Miedema's three levels of exclusion. Da Costa (1997:114) does not argue that all exclusion is caused by poverty but claims that 'social exclusion includes poverty . . . as well as other forms of exclusion that are not related to resources'.

Both of these approaches identify two facets of social exclusion: a narrow facet, caused by poverty, and a broader one which both subsumes poverty and also includes forms of exclusion which are not related to poverty. From one perspective this is attractive because it incorporates the two constructs. From another perspective, though, it seems to create more ambiguity, with 'broad social exclusion' causing poverty which causes 'narrow social exclusion'. This would be non-problematic if the 'broad' form were entirely to do with processes and the narrow form related exclusively to outcomes: if this were the case, then a major conceptual step forward would have been taken. It is probable that the narrow form *is* mostly, if not entirely, to do with outcomes but that elements of the broad form not connected with poverty have to include outcomes as well as processes. Overall, this approach may be a fruitful avenue for further development but in its present state of conceptualisation has yet to add clarity to the debate about the relationship between poverty and social exclusion.

Poverty, social exclusion and quality of life

In this concluding section, relationships between poverty, social exclusion and quality of life are briefly presented from two perspectives. The first is general and identifies three areas where social exclusion as a concept enables further insights to be gained about quality of life in addition to those available from a poverty analysis. Second, the approaches to quality of life discussed in Chapter 3 are revisited and their relationship with both poverty and quality of life is briefly sketched out.

The first general insight on quality of life provided by the social exclusion construct as compared to poverty is that it replaces a static with a dynamic analysis and focuses attention on the impact of social processes as well as individual outcomes. This requires a quality of life analysis which addresses macro, systemic features of society relating both to the distribution of resources and opportunities and to the discriminatory processes that differentiate, polarise, isolate and eventually detach people from their social milieu.

The second provides additional levels of analysis, moving beyond individuals and families to groups, communities and regions – not just as aggregations but as entities in their own right. Here, exclusion can be because of factors such as discrimination, language barriers or geographical isolation, and affects people as collectivities rather than, or as well as, individuals. The resulting quality of life issues need to be dealt with at a collective group or community level.

The third broadens the analysis from material deprivation to include social and cultural resources. Apart from introducing aspects of quality of life relating to social and cultural capital, this dimension accounts for the apparent anomaly of some non-poor sectors of some societies being socially excluded. So social exclusion allows for the possibility of some people with high incomes having low quality of life. In this context an advantage of social exclusion over poverty is that it can focus on issues such as discrimination and political alienation.

To summarise this general perspective, it can be noted that poverty is an important and relatively straightforward attribute in relation to quality of life, and its main strength lies in its clear connection with material factors and its ease of measurement and international comparison (at least in relation to its operationalisation in terms of a percentage of median national income). But poverty as a construct has less analytical or descriptive power when moving from material to multiple deprivation and here the outcome-oriented formulation of social exclusion can provide a more holistic and fruitful approach. Social exclusion in its process formulation is perhaps even more theoretically important and potentially fruitful in analytical and explanatory terms in relation to quality of life, but needs further work particularly with regard to its operationalisation; and this is even more true for causal formulations of social exclusion. These issues are revisited in the next two chapters

Returning to the constructs discussed in Chapter 3, it can be seen that they interact differently with the constructs of poverty and social exclusion. First, utilitarianism has little substantively to contribute here but it has clear links with poverty in terms of measurement units, i.e. price and income. Poverty is measured in terms both of income and expenditure. Basic needs and the human development index do have clear substantive links with poverty, as does the basic capabilities approach, all in terms of nutrition, shelter, access to basic medical services, etc. Basic education, up to literacy standards, a common feature in all of these approaches, probably has as strong links with social inclusion as with poverty in that lack of literacy is clearly exclusionary.

The other approaches discussed in Chapter 3 – Doyal and Gough's theory of human need (THN), prudential values and both Sen's and Nussbaum's capability approaches – all encompass both poverty and social exclusion, but in rather different ways. Given the THN's grounding in basic needs, it has a clear relationship to poverty, particularly in relation to its primary need of physical health as a means of avoiding serious harm and to the six associated intermediate needs. The THN also has a strong relationship to social exclusion in relation to its second primary need for autonomy of agency in pursuit of minimally disabled social participation and its associated intermediate needs. It should also be noted that these needs are links also to poverty, particularly in its citizenship and social needs formulations. Even more crucially, the 'additional' primary need of critical autonomy in THN has no obvious connection with poverty and is centrally relevant to the strongest form of genuine social inclusion where there is a societal requirement to facilitate genuinely empowered participation.

It was noted in Chapter 3 that there are many substantive similarities among the lists associated with THN, prudential values and Nussbaum's version of capabilities so the links with both poverty and social exclusion arising from these commonalities are the same. There are some intriguing differences too. The most central one is that there are prudential values and capabilities which relate directly neither to poverty nor to social exclusion. The one common one, which is also shared with utilitarianism and with Sen's version of capabilities, relates to enjoyment, pleasure, fun and play. This area of human life is not included in either the poverty or social exclusion discourse but is of course absolutely central to any subjective approach to quality of life, and it is argued here that it ought to be central to any rounded holistic approach to quality of life too. Other attributes mentioned in these approaches which have a claim to being on any holistic quality of life list include such heavyweight values as self-respect, accomplishment, friendship, love, appreciation of beauty, and – more controversially – respect for the world of nature and other species. It will be shown in Chapter 6 that all these are components of one or another of the societal quality of life frameworks.

5   Communities and quality of life

Social capital and social cohesion

In most of the discussion on poverty and social exclusion in Chapter 4 the unit of analysis was the individual, group or community: it deals with their *actual* quality of life in terms of material hardship, inability to participate in everyday social, cultural, economic or political life. In part of the discussion of social exclusion, however, the analysis does not refer directly to outcomes as they affect members of society but instead refers to society itself and to the social processes that influence or determine people's quality of life; those processes which alienate, stigmatise, discriminate against and devalue both individuals and whole groups, categories and communities. This chapter develops this analysis and focuses entirely on quality of life at a collective level, dealing with features of communities and societies which affect the quality of life of their citizens, with both their objective and subjective well-being (Szreter and Woolcock, 2004: 651). These features are social capital and social cohesion which are linked to process-oriented approaches to social exclusion, as can be seen later in the chapter. Broadly speaking, social capital comprises the social resources available within society and how they are distributed and used, and social cohesion refers to the institutions and norms that keep society together.

There is a direct relationship between social exclusion as outcome, social exclusion as process, social capital and social cohesion, so it is clear that the quality of life of individuals is deeply embedded in these societal institutions of quality of life. Indeed, these institutions, along with others that are discussed in Chapter 6, are often referred to as 'quality of societies' (Veenhoven, 1996). In Chapter 4 it is noted that poverty and social exclusion are generally perceived to have negative consequences and that it is in everyone's interests to try to minimise them both as far as possible, with the caveat from economic liberals who approve of inequality and wish to define poverty in absolute terms. Social capital and social cohesion are not quite as straightforward. Social capital can have negative as well as positive consequences for quality of life, and having too much social cohesion in a society can be as harmful as having too little. So instead of being *maximised* – that is getting as much of them as possible – social capital and social cohesion need to be *optimised*, that is getting just the right amount. As can be seen below, this is a major challenge in striving to organise societies so that they achieve the highest levels of quality of life.

Social capital and social cohesion – overview

Most of this chapter is given over to a detailed discussion of the different and sometimes competing definitions and operationalisations of the two constructs. In order to set the scene, a very broad and general overview of social capital and social cohesion is given here.

Like social exclusion, social capital is a relatively recent construct in the social sciences and was hardly ever discussed in the academic literature before the 1990s. It is similar too in its multidimensionality: indeed, it is multi-disciplinary in nature. Its most famous proponent, Robert Putnam, is a political scientist, and it is regularly used in economic sociology, mainstream sociology, development studies, social geography, social policy, and urban planning. According to most commentators, social capital does not belong to individuals but is a collective entity comprising trust, reciprocity and other integrative norms and values accruing to social networks. Some commentators treat it either metaphorically (Portes, 1998) or even literally (Bourdieu, 1986) as a form of capital, like physical or financial capital, in other words, as a *social resource*. Others use 'social capital' more as a label than a description and see these networks and associated integrative norms either as a sort of 'social glue', holding groups, communities and eventually society together, or else as a sort of lubricant – metaphorically oiling the wheels of society – making sure that people can interact with each other smoothly and without too much friction. Two types of social capital are often identified: 'bonding' social capital which bonds group members tightly to each other; and 'bridging' social capital which forms linkages between groups and networks (Narayan, 1999).

Social cohesion, on the other hand, is a long-established and venerable sociological construct, and is more or less directly descended from Tönnies' (1957) notions of *Gemeinschaft* where cohesion is maintained by the family and peer group and *Gesellschaft* where formal authority provides structures for keeping society together. Emile Durkheim developed this further in terms of mechanistic and organic solidarity. In mechanistic solidarity, mostly in pre-industrial societies, common values, beliefs and experiences enable people to co-operate successfully. For organic solidarity, on the other hand, mostly in industrialised societies, cohesion depends on shared moral experiences and expectations embodied in the law and market and maintained through the interdependence necessitated by high levels of functional differentiation: economic and social roles are so fragmented that people cannot survive in isolation. A third central strand comes from the work of Talcott Parsons in the 1950s on 'normative integration' (Gough, 1999). Here, the highly complex, differentiated modern social system is kept together by people's internalisation of, and attachment to, abstract common normative values. So, in the transition from a traditional rural society to a modern industrial society, face-to-face solidarity was replaced by more abstract and impersonal expectations and norms of behaviour.

Vertovec (1999) gives a less abstract summary of different contemporary versions of social cohesion from different ideological perspectives as follows. For Marxists, social cohesion is a collective consciousness, produced by the division of labour in society, in other words, it is class consciousness. From T. H. Marshall's social citizenship perspective (which has affinities with social democracy and Fabianism), social cohesion was created by the provision of a baseline of political, legal and social equality which also was used to legitimise economic inequality. From a liberal perspective, social cohesion flows from the rights and mutual respect of people interacting in pursuit of their own individual ends in interaction with each other. From the more right-wing neo-liberal perspective, social cohesion is provided by buyers and sellers coming together in the market. Finally, for communitarians, social cohesion is provided by the neighbourhood community (perhaps with the wheel coming back full circle to Tönnies' *Gemeinschaft* and Durkheim's mechanistic solidarity). It can be seen that some of these conceptualisations of social cohesion go beyond the descriptive and analytical and are ideological in nature. There are strong ideological strands in many approaches to social cohesion, some of which are highly nationalistic and even xenophobic in nature, and others which have radical egalitarian goals.

It can be seen that there are some broad similarities between social capital and social cohesion, but they operate at different societal levels. Social capital, with its emphasis on norms derived from networks, has its foundations in face-to-face groups and localities, though it spreads outwards from there. Social cohesion, on the other hand, usually refers to cohesion at a societal level, which in turn is normally taken to be at the level of a nation–state (although there is considerable discussion in EU literature of social cohesion at a *European* level). This national societal cohesion relates primarily to the interactions between society-as-a-whole and sub-societal communities.

Both constructs have importance beyond their value as conceptual and explanatory devices in sociological analysis: they have implications for development policy and social policy and in the realm of politics. Social capital is at the forefront of the World Bank's development strategy; optimising social capital in developing countries, it is argued, enhances economic growth and political stability (World Bank, 1998: i). Social capital, qua *capital*, is seen as a major component of a nation's wealth (Fukuyama, 1999: 16; Berger-Schmitt, 2000: 6). More specifically Putnam's (1993a) research indicates that social capital is a precondition for both economic growth and effective government, and Knack and Keefer (1997) identify a strong correlation between two elements of social capital (trust and civic co-operation) and economic performance.

Even stronger claims have been made for the benefits of the most radical conceptualisation of social cohesion. In a multicultural context, it is claimed that high levels of egalitarian social cohesion minimise inter-communal tensions and maximise national identity (Jenson, 1998). Wilkinson (1996: 1) maintains that countries with high levels of egalitarian social cohesion have lower mortality rates than countries with similar economic resources but lower levels of social cohesion. This claim has led to a lively debate which is discussed in detail in Chapter 7.

In political terms it will come as no surprise that the most radical conceptual-isation of social cohesion, with its emphasis on equality, welfare and social justice, is associated with a left-wing, egalitarian political perspective (Jenson, 1998;

Bernard, 1999; Beck *et al.*, 2001). However, a narrower conceptual perspective of social cohesion has also been espoused by more conservative commentators as a component, along with civil society, of a well-functioning free-market society (Pahl, 1991; Broadbent, 2001). Jenson (1998) even suggests that social cohesion 'is sometimes deployed in right-wing and populist politics by those who long for the "good old days"'.

There is common agreement that both concepts have been used in a bewildering variety of ways and are in danger of losing their meanings. Woolcock (1998: 155) complains that social capital 'risks trying to explain too much with too little'. In the World Bank's Environmentally and Socially Sustainable Development Network report it is stated that there is not yet 'an integrated and generally accepted conceptual and analytical framework' (World Bank, 1998: 7). If anything, social cohesion is more problematic (Jenson, 1998), and Bernard (1999: 2) even calls it a 'quasi-concept'.

The scene is now set for a more detailed discussion of the two constructs, starting with social capital. Once this has been done, the similarities, overlaps and interactions between the two constructs are teased out within a conceptual framework of a 'stepped aggregation'.

Social capital

So what *is* social capital? Broadly, there are two different approaches, although they shade into one another and are sometimes difficult to disentangle. They can be labelled as 'social capital as *capital*' and '*social* capital as *social glue*'. For the sake of simplicity, the versions of each approach presented here are rather stereotypical and over-simplified in order to give as clear a distinction as possible, prior to giving a fuller and more detailed exemplification in the following section. The first approach is very specific and tangible. Social capital is exactly what it says it is – a form of capital, along with all the other forms of capital. Examples of other forms are: financial capital (money); economic capital more generally (for example, property or stocks and shares); or human capital such as educational qualifications. In all these formulations the capital is an actual resource. Perhaps property is the most tangible of these resources; it is real, permanent and solid. Money, on the other hand, is the most usable and 'liquid' form of capital in that it is instantly convertible into goods, services, property, etc. Money is also portable.

Human capital, on the other hand, is rather less tangible. Educational qualifications and credentials, such as a qualification in accountancy, are certainly resources which in some circumstances can be utilised to gain employment or access to other resources, but they are not transferable from one person to another in the same way that money is, so a person's human capital inheres in that person and is of primary benefit to that individual only. Interestingly, it can also be of great indirect or secondary benefit to the individual's family, particularly their children (Sampson *et al.*, 1999), and it can permeate through to their kinship, friendship and neighbourhood networks (Gradstein and Justman, 2000). In the example given above, having a neighbour with an accountancy qualification can be a bonus to someone who has to fill out their tax return if they are on good enough terms with their neighbour to ask for their advice.

All these other kinds of capital can belong to an *individual*. Social capital is different in that it belongs only to a *collectivity*. 'Social' here is taken very literally in that it *cannot* be individual. It makes no sense to think of a person on a desert island having any social capital, whereas property, in the form of a boat, or human capital, in the form of botanical knowledge of which plants are poisonous, would be very useful. In parenthesis, it is interesting to note that money would be useless too because money's usefulness is as a means of exchange or stored value; in *itself*, in the form of coins or notes it has no practical use if it cannot be exchanged for goods and services.

Even though it does not *belong* to any individual, though, social capital can be of immense use to individuals in a similar way to which human capital can be useful to those who do not themselves possess it. Being a member of a network with high levels of mutual support, trust and norms of reciprocity gives access to a range of social resources which facilitate the fulfilment of individual social and economic goals. A person wanting to buy or sell a car, for example, will benefit, both in terms of information and confidence that they will not be cheated in the transaction, if they operate via a network with high social capital – even if they have never met the other actor in the transaction before – rather than dealing with a complete stranger via an impersonal medium. Some commentators, particularly Bourdieu, believe that social capital is *fungible*, that is that it can be converted into other sorts of capital. For example, a person might be able to utilise the social capital inhering in the networks they belong to in order to gain privileged access to education or training that results in them getting credentials which enhance their human capital.

However, the main impact of social capital is on the collectivity rather than the individual. Here, the stock of interlocking networks, trust and reciprocity is seen as a resource as important to a nation as its stock of raw materials, land and labour. In other words, in this economic sociology formulation of social capital, it is a factor of production and a prerequisite for economic development. This is the reason why the World Bank is so keen on fostering social capital in developing countries.

The second approach is to look on social capital not as 'capital' in an economic sense at all – which is a label that arguably got attached by an historical accident – and to see social capital as 'social glue' which sticks communities and societies together. Social capital in this context comprises generalised trust and other attributes of networks, with some writers focusing mostly on the effects of varying kinds and degrees of embeddedness and density of social networks. The distinctive feature of this formulation is what it *is not* rather than what it is. Here, social capital is *not* capital in the sense of its exchange value or fungibility. Unlike the economic sociology interpretation, here it does not make sense to talk about an individual 'cashing in' their social capital because in this formulation it just cannot be disaggregated to an individual level or even be utilised in any specific way by an individual.

The 'social glue' proponents now have a question to answer: if social capital cannot be disaggregated, then what happens when a person uses their access to networks, for example, to buy or sell a car? Their answer lies in the field of social network analysis: they agree that people use networks and that networks with a high level of trust are useful but that this sort of activity is using attributes of networks that pertain to the *individual* rather than to the *social*. So it is an individual's *membership* of the network that is crucial to facilitating transactions. Group membership, along with its very specific benefit of increased interpersonal trust, certainly is a tangible resource, but is not, according to the 'social glue' proponents, a direct attribute of social capital. In their formulation, social capital is more to do with features such as civic norms and features of social structure that, by their very nature, exist irrespective of the identity of the individuals who comprise the group.

The next question is 'What does social capital actually *do*?' The glue analogy is a good one in that it is seen to make society – or, more properly, communities – stick together. It is a collective entity, inhering in social structure rather than in individuals. Social capital in a community is comprised of the collectivity of networks and associations – the more the better, and the more interactions between them the better – and of the extent of trust that community members have in each other and in the community and its institutions. So the social capital of a community is measurable, and it is also possible to assess how it is distributed: in any community some people will be members of more networks and will have more access to trust and reciprocity than others and some communities will have more social capital than others. So there is a rich and complex web of interlocking and overlapping sites for social capital. and again – in this rather over-simplified world – the more social capital the better. Thus, some communities (and individuals) who do not have adequate access to social capital can be deprived of social capital and therefore suffer from 'social capital poverty'.

But all is not a bed of roses in the social capital garden. Social capital is not necessarily always a good thing. The classic example here is the Mafia, very high on associational networks and with an absolute emphasis on trust – with ultimate sanctions against breach of trust. Here, to use Svendsen and Svendsen's metaphor, the bonding social capital has become more like 'superglue', stiffening and constraining communities rather than cohering them. Less dramatically, but more importantly in the sociological study of multi-cultural societies, is the extent of social capital that inheres in minority groups, often of migrant origin with different language and culture from the majority group and often instantly distinguishable because of skin colour and/or distinctive clothing. Often high levels of social capital within disadvantaged minority communities, while supporting cultural identity and group cohesion and providing vital socio-economic support systems, also have detrimental effects of isolating the community from wider social resources. Narayan gives a telling example here:

> Powerful networks can restrict access to opportunities, for example, the caste system in India with its rigid boundaries. social capital restricts individual freedom (women in purdah in Northern India), and can lead to excessive claims on successful group members – so excessive that successful individuals

are sometimes driven to break off ties with the larger ethnic group . . . And sometimes the negative impacts of social capital are manifested in powerful, tightly knit social groups that are not accountable to citizens at large, and practice corruption and cronyism . . . Thus societies can be rich in social capital within social groups, and yet experience debilitating poverty, corruption and conflict.

(1999: 8)

Therefore, it is vitally important that communities, groups and networks that have strong internal, bonding social capital also have access to external, bridging social capital too. In a famous paper called 'The strength of weak ties', written before the notion of social capital came into common currency, Mark Granovetter (1973: 1376) claimed that 'the more local bridges in a community and the greater their degree, the more cohesive the community and the more capable of acting in concert'. This important issue of the relationship between bonding and bridging social capital is discussed in detail later in the chapter.

The time has now come to try to be very specific about social capital and to give some definitions. The obvious place to start is with the doyen of the 'social capital as capital' thesis, Pierre Bourdieu. Bourdieu differentiates between three forms of capital – economic, cultural and social – and claims that they are fungible, that they can be converted into each other. In Bourdieu's larger thesis this conversion forms the basis for strategies for the reproduction of capital in all its forms. According to Bourdieu, social capital is:

The aggregate of the actual or potential resources which are linked to possession of a durable network of more or less institutionalised relationships of mutual acquaintance and recognition – or in other words, to membership of a group – which provides each of its members with the backing of the collectively-owned capital . . . The volume of the social capital possessed by a given agent thus depends on the size of the network of connections he [*sic*] can effectively mobilise and on the volume of the capital . . . possessed in his own right by each of those to whom he is connected.

(1986: 249)

Bourdieu here is absolutely clear that not only do group members have the *backing* of the group's capital, they also in a real sense actually *possess* this capital as individuals rather than, or as well as, the group itself as a collectivity possessing capital. This is a highly controversial formulation of social capital and is not shared by many other commentators. Less contentiously, he identifies group size and the volume of the social capital as crucial to the strength of social capital. Bourdieu implicitly only includes internal ties in his definition, which is focused on *a* group, *a* durable network. Most other commentators either explicitly mention bridging ties between groups (Woolcock, 1998; Narayan, 1999) or else give wide-ranging definitions that implicitly include multiplex network membership. A good example of the latter is Grootaert (1997: 78): 'Social capital generally refers to the set of norms, networks and organisations through which people gain access to power and resources.'

The World Bank (1998: i) is one of the most forthright exponents of the social glue approach to social capital: 'Social capital is the glue that holds societies together and without which there can be no economic growth or human well-being.' The World Bank definition of social capital is neat and clear, although it is perhaps one of the widest and most all-inclusive that is in use. It is defined as: 'the size and density of social networks and institutions, and the nature of interpersonal interactions'. The breadth of this definition can be seen from the subsequent exposition that 'It includes the shared values and rules for social conduct expressed in personal relationships, trust and a common sense of "civic" responsibility, that makes society more than a collection of individuals.' Now, the inclusion of civic responsibility under the rubric of social capital is unusual in that it implies societal institutions as well as social networks. As can be seen from the next few paragraphs, the World Bank perspective on social capital in fact strays beyond the conventional dividing line and is very close indeed to many definitions of social cohesion.

Social cohesion

Thus, definitions of social capital range from the ultra-specific, stipulating bonding in just one group, through to bridging among several groups and ending up as including societal institutions. This latter position is the starting place for social cohesion. If social capital can be seen as 'social glue', then social cohesion can be seen as 'societal glue'. Indeed, Breton *et al.* (1980: 4–5) made a plea for a name change from social to societal cohesion in order to keep a clear distinction between societal cohesiveness and cohesion among other groups in society.

Unlike social capital, there are no highly specific definitions for social cohesion: they are all very abstract. Durkheim's shared moral experience and Parsons' normative integration have already been mentioned. Durkheim also famously talked about the 'collective conscience' as epitomising social cohesion. Many commentators are pessimistic about arriving at a tight definition. Lockwood (1999: 82) expressed his surprise at this lack of clarity, given that over a hundred years have passed since Durkheim's original work on this area and his proposition that the study of social solidarity was the central task of sociology. Jenson (1998: 4) agrees:

> Despite lively conversations about social cohesion in policy circles, there is surprisingly little effort to say what it is. Any survey of the literature immediately reveals that there is no consensus about whether the definition of social cohesion or its links to a whole family of concepts often used when discussing it.

Vertovec (1999: xi) does not offer a definition but suggests rather that a variety of concepts, issues, perspectives and understandings be explored in order to arrive at a general sense of the term. He does, however, give as a starting point for a definition: 'the presence of basic patterns of co-operative social interaction and core sets of collective values'. This is a useful start but in effect it does not go any further than the World Bank definition of social capital noted above.

Berger (1998) takes a wide and holistic view of social cohesion as comprising norms, values and institutions, all mediated by the institutions of civil society. His mention here of the institutions of civil society is an important one in terms of the context of which he was writing, that is, a Club of Rome report on social cohesion in Europe, but it is a culturally specific definition. Many Eastern European countries, along with Russia and other ex-Soviet states, have very limited and underdeveloped civil society institutions, and a strong case can be made that the People's Republic of China has virtually no civil society, yet in many of these countries there is a degree of social cohesion – however defined – that is stronger than, for example, Belgium, which has long-standing and strong civil society institutions. Berger is sensitive to this issue of the potential weakness of institutions and, ultimately, plumps for integrative norms as being central:

> A human society is held together by a variety of forces – common interests, sheer habit, the absence of alternatives, reasonable levels of affluence, common historical experience, shared notions of adversities – and these are all fortified through institutions . . . But one does not have to be an orthodox Durkheimian sociologist to agree that a society will sooner or later be in serious trouble if it is not also held together by common normative orientations.
>
> (1998: xvi)

He does raise the issue of whether a modern society can function without normative unity and poses the possibility that a democratic political and legal system might be enough, that is, 'agreement on a set of procedures by which conflicting interests and ideologies can be adjudicated' (ibid.: 353). This is a central theme in the study of social cohesion and is, of course, of immense political, as well as social, significance. The demise of former Yugoslavia, and its descent into mayhem and genocide, appear to give the lie to the hope that political, social and civil society institutions, on their own and without some form of normative integration, can ensure the continued survival of a nation comprising disparate and mutually antagonistic groups. This situation is all the more alarming because Yugoslavia *did* survive for four decades as an amalgam of apparently mutually tolerant, if not socially integrated, different ethnic and religious groups. This issue is of tremendous importance for the future of multi-cultural societies. A central debating point here is whether multi-culturalists like Kymlicka (1995) are realistic in their hopes for pluralist and multi-cultural social cohesion in societies with separate communities, each with a strong individual identity, culture and even language or whether 'monoculturalists' such as Fukuyama (1999) are correct in their pessimistic prognosis that societies need to share the same language, norms and moral values to avoid disintegration. It is of tremendous importance in countries such as Canada, Belgium, Northern Ireland, Cyprus, not to mention the Balkan states, whether an effective pluralistic social cohesion is possible or whether society needs to be culturally homogeneous to survive. Fukuyama's insistence that state education must be in only one language has ramifications even in the principality of Wales and his emphasis that all immigrants must be fluent in the language of their country of settlement has important consequences for newly arrived South Asian spouses in England.

Phillips and Berman (2003: 346), after reviewing much of the relevant literature, come to a composite definition which stresses norms of generosity as well as solidarity: 'Social cohesion concerns the processes and infrastructures that create and underpin social networks, including social norms of solidarity and generosity among community members.' It is related to both social capital (World Bank, 1998) and social integration (Klitgaarde and Fedderke, 1995). Jenson (1998) also stresses processes and even goes as far as to say that social cohesion is used in the Canadian definitions to describe a process rather than a condition or an end state. It involves a sense of commitment, and desire or capacity to live together in some harmony. The Canadian situation is particularly pertinent here in that Canada has both a disadvantaged indigenous population and two dominant immigrant communities, Francophone and Anglophone, with a history of social tensions and high profile separatist movements. Perhaps because of this, Canadian academics such as Jean Jenson and Judith Maxwell are passionate advocates of an inclusive form of social cohesion and Canada also has a leading multi-culturalist in Will Kymlicka.

Berger-Schmitt usefully links social cohesion into both individual quality of life and Veenhoven's (1996) notion of quality of nations:

> Social cohesion can be conceived as a societal quality which is experienced by individuals in their daily lives . . . This perspective considers elements of the social cohesion of a society to form an integral part of the quality of life of the individuals belonging to that society.
>
> (Berger-Schmitt, 2000: 7)

Berger-Schmitt's approach is a useful point at which to finish this broad survey of social cohesion because she is the only commentator to embed social cohesion explicitly in a discussion of quality of life. It is intriguing also to note that she makes an explicit connection between social cohesion and social exclusion: this is a topic which is revisited at the end of the chapter. She also formally conceptualises social capital as being a component of social cohesion. The relationship between these two constructs is now investigated.

From social capital to social cohesion: a stepped aggregation

Considerable strides have been made recently in codifying and clarifying definitions of social capital and social cohesion, the most thorough being by Feldman and Assaf (1999) and Berger-Schmitt (2000) respectively. The intention here is not to replicate or summarise this work but to build on it and to explore the different formulations of both constructs and their interrelationships. This is done in three stages. The first is to identify the building blocks or elements of social cohesion which are contained in the different versions of social capital, starting with the simplest and moving on to the most wide-ranging. Then the interface between wide-ranging definitions of social capital and the more straightforward non-ideological constructions of social cohesion is explored. Finally, ideological conceptualisations of social cohesion are introduced.

From social capital to social cohesion

Perhaps the easiest way to look at the relationship between social capital and social cohesion is to see it as an aggregation, with three staging posts or steps, with each step building on the one that came before. The first step comprises 'pure' social capital of trust and horizontal networks. Then, at the second step, vertical networks and elements of social structure are added. In the third step these elements are expanded and others are added until a wide definition of social capital starts to merge with the more tightly focused non-ideological definitions of social cohesion.

Step one: pure social capital – trust and horizontal networks

The two elements of trust and associational networks are included in all social capital constructs, somewhere or other, to a greater or lesser extent. There is a lot of disagreement, though, as to their relationships with each other and with social capital itself. Most commentators classify them as either inseparable and conjoint manifestations of a unitary notion of social capital (Brehn and Rahn, 1997); or as two separate elements of social capital (Feldman and Assaf, 1999). These are the approaches discussed in detail below, but it needs to be mentioned that there are other versions too.

Woolcock (1998), for example, identifies them as two different aspects of a unitary social capital (associations being the cause and trust the outcome). Knack and Keefer (1997), on the other hand, see them as manifestations of two different kinds of social capital, whereas Hall (1999) sees them as two entirely different social capitals. Finally, Falk and Kilpatrick (2000) in true postmodern mode, postulate that they may both be multiple constructs that can be disaggregated into smaller components, each of which may interact differently with overall social capital.

Most 'pure' social capital definitions give relatively equal weight to trust and associational networks but some prioritise one over the other:

1   *Trust predominates*. The most influential presentation of 'social capital as trust' is by Fukuyama who defines social capital as 'a set of informal values or norms shared among members of a group that permits co-operation between them' (1999: 16). The most important of these values is trust: 'the expectation that arises within a community of regular, honest and co-operative behaviour, based on commonly shared norms' (Fukuyama, 1995: 25). Svendsen and Svendsen (2004: 25) define trust as: 'the mutual confidence that no party to an exchange will exploit another's vulnerabilities, that is that no party will cheat or free-ride even if there is an economic net gain from doing so'. Here trust is seen as 'a

lubricant that makes the running of any group more efficient' (Fukuyama, 1999: 16). For Fukuyama, a central theme is the 'radius of trust': the further it expands beyond the family, the more likely it is to be based on 'moral resources' and ethical behaviours (Fukuyama, 2001).

2   *Horizontal associational networks predominate.* There are two strands to the approach in which networks predominate over trust and its related values and norms. The first is presented cogently by Woolcock (1998: 155) who argues that, irrespective of its manifestations, which undoubtedly include trust, *definitions* of social capital should focus primarily on its sources rather than its consequences. 'Trust and norms of reciprocity . . . do not exist independently of social relationships.' Therefore, according to this analysis, social capital should be defined only in terms of these relationships.

The second strand acknowledges that resources such as trust are indeed a defining characteristic of social capital but nevertheless places primary emphasis upon the networks which nourish these resources. This is an appropriate approach for commentators who conceptualise social capital explicitly as a form of *capital* such as Bourdieu (1986).

3   *Trust plus horizontal networks.* Most mainstream definitions of social capital include both trust and associational networks. The approach used by Putnam in his classic study of Italy is unusual in excluding vertical networks, that is, networks with differential power. His definition of social capital here is: 'horizontal associations between people, i.e. social networks (networks of civic engagement) and associated norms that have an impact on the community' (Putnam, 1993b: 36–7). Putnam's approach has been highly influential and has been used by many researchers in studying social capital in small groups, particularly in relation to micro-credit unions in developing nations (Buckland, 1998). Very few other researchers, however, have taken a similarly restrictive line in relation to vertical associations (Greeley, 1997). Indeed, Putnam himself later used a more expansive definition similar to that used by Woolcock and Narayan, discussed below (Putnam, 2000, 2004).

*Step two: civic social capital – the incorporation of vertical networks
and social structure*

1   *Trust plus horizontal and vertical networks.* Definitions of social capital most commonly include both horizontal and vertical associational networks (World Bank, 1998; Feldman and Assaf, 1999). Woolcock (1998: 153) gives a neat general definition of this type of middle-range conceptualisation of social capital as: 'the information, trust, and norms of reciprocity inhering in one's social networks'. Crucial to this definition is that the norms and values are attached to specific relationships rather than being at a more abstract level. In other words, in this level of social capital there is no place for 'generalised trust', only for 'specific trust'. Arguably, generalised trust can be seen as a necessary requirement for social cohesion. Further, it can be argued that the reliance here on reciprocity inhering only in social networks requires that trust

associated with this level is restricted to face-to-face (or similarly close) relationships. in other words, the trust associated with this level of social capital does not cover members of the same association, group, church, etc. who are not personally known to each other.

2   *Social capital and social structure.* Coleman (1988) adds 'non face-to-face' relationships into the equation and provides for trust and other norms to be spread across communities of interest that transcend an individual's networks. For Coleman, social capital is 'a variety of different entities, with two elements in common: they all consist of some aspect of social structure, and they facilitate certain actions of actors – whether personal or corporate actors – within the structure' (1988: s98). Coleman's approach, while normally interpreted as middle-ranging, does leave open the possibility of a wider interpretation including more abstract and generalised social norms.

Step three: social capital meets social cohesion: trust and networks plus civic and societal institutions

This leads on to the more wide-ranging conceptualisations of social capital, including such generalised social norms as civic responsibility. Here, the precise link between specific networks and specific sets of norms is transcended. These conceptualisations of social capital, opening the door to social cohesion, all share an allegiance to generalised rather than context-specific trust.

1   *Trust, networks, other-regarding behaviour and societal institutions.* Brehn and Rahn (1997: 1001) take an approach consistent with Coleman's definition but which moves beyond network-specific norms in that it introduces a civic dimension: 'Our specific operationalisation of the social capital mechanism represents the concepts as a tight reciprocal relationship between civic engagement and interpersonal trust.' This approach links in to Simmel's notion of 'reciprocity transactions', which is one of four contextualising factors for a broad conceptualisation of social capital as noted by Woolcock (1998: 161).

Lockwood (1999) and Hall (1999) both refer to altruism and 'other-regarding' behaviour as central to the development of social capital towards being positively useful as a 'social glue' enabling society to operate effectively. Other-regarding behaviour, trust and civic responsibility are all ingredients not only of broad definitions of social capital but also of all definitions of social cohesion.

2   *Norms, values, institutions and social coherence.* Perhaps the broadest approach to social capital is taken by one of the most significant policy players in a global sense: the World Bank's (1998: i) review identifies social capital as referring to 'the internal social and cultural coherence of society, the norms and values that govern interactions among people and the institutions in which they are embedded'. Central to this approach is a commonly agreed sense of 'civic responsibility' and common identification with forms of government, cultural norms and social rules.

Non-ideological approaches to social cohesion

Many non-ideological approaches to social cohesion are not dissimilar to these broad definitions of social capital, although mostly at a wider, societal level. Vertovec (1997: 1.1.2.1), for example, claims that it implies the presence of basic patterns of co-operative social interaction and core sets of collective values: 'a cohesion indicated by the cultivation of mutual loyalties or "we-feeling", trust, successful prediction of behaviour and the ability of people to engage in co-operative action'. Percy-Smith (2000) uses Geddes' (1998: 20) definition: reconciliation of a system of organisation based on market forces, freedom of opportunity and enterprise with a commitment to the values of internal solidarity and mutual support which ensures open access to benefit and protection for all members of society. Stanley (1999) calls it the bonding effect within a society that arises spontaneously from the unforced willingness of individual citizens to enter into relationships with one another in their efforts to survive and prosper. Pahl (1991) sees it as a binding normative framework.

In a major report on social cohesion in Europe, it is concluded that it is not possible for a society to operate only on the basis of a state's legal and political systems, without recourse to any form of normative unity (Berger, 1998: 353). This approach, with its emphasis on common normative orientations, is derived from a Durkheimian perspective, as is Gough and Olofsson's (1999) approach, which stresses organic solidarity, grounded in moral experience. Gough and Olofsson link this to Parsons' work on normative integration which they conclude 'can be seen as an argument for the integration of a society based on a consensus about fundamental civil, political and social rights' (Gough and Olofsson, 1999: 2).

Woolcock's and Narayan's approaches

Most of these approaches have strong affinities with Woolcock's (1998) approach to social capital which fits in with category (1) on p. 143 above, right on the interface between social capital and social cohesion. Woolcock's analysis covers the micro-, meso- and macro-levels and it emphasises the importance of the interaction between bottom-up and top-down activities and channels of communication. Narayan (1999) takes a similar approach and clarifies and develops Woolcock's formulation, particularly at the macro-level (see also Woolcock and Narayan, 2000).

MICRO-LEVEL

At the micro-level both Woolcock and Narayan stress the importance of intra-community ties (identifying them respectively as 'integration' and 'bonding') and of extra-community ties (identifying them respectively as 'linkage' and 'bridging'). Woolcock (1998) brings these together, identifying four possible outcomes. The most negative outcome, of low integration and low linkage, is identified as *amoral individualism*. This could equally appropriately be labelled as complete social breakdown or anarchy at the micro-level. Here the outlook for individual quality of life is grim for most individuals unless they have access to power, possibly through gang leadership. The most positive outcome – high integration and high linkage – is identified as *social opportunity*. This can be seen as a precondition for high social cohesion and as providing a framework for achieving individual quality of life, although there can often be a tension – and possibly even a contradiction – in simultaneously achieving both (Leonard, 2004).

One of the other outcomes – high integration and low linkage – produces the not uncommon outcome of a community with a high level of internal social capital but high social isolation and poor links with other communities and with society in general. In other words, these are socially excluded communities. Many such communities are often labelled as ghettos or 'sink estates'. In this sort of situation an increase in internal social capital via 'enclave associations' will often be counter-productive and lead to the community becoming more isolated and excluded. Hall (1999) puts this rather more formally by stating that social capital is a 'club' good as well as a 'public good'. Woolley (2001) identifies the *type* of associational membership as being crucial in relation to social cohesion, the most appropriate being based on 'giving participation' rather than 'instrumental participation', particularly in relation to bridging ties.

Narayan (1999: 13) pays particular attention to the potential for these less powerful or socially excluded groups to benefit as collectivities from bridging, or 'cross-cutting' ties whereas it is only the individual members who benefit from primary groups without these bridging ties. Narayan points out too that these bridging ties also build social cohesion, which requires dense, though not necessarily strong, cross-cutting ties among groups:

> Cohesive family, clan or tribal groups lay the foundation for social and economic well-being, but it is only when these groups develop ties (both weak and dense) with other social groups that societies can build cohesive webs of cross-cutting social relations at all levels . . . In the Netherlands, for example, adoption of consociational forms of democracy has been given credit for achieving the social cohesion necessary for economic development.
>
> (1999: 35)

Woolcock calls his remaining outcome – low integration and high linkage – *anomie*. This is perhaps not appropriate if the high level of linkage is associated with a strong sense of civic responsibility (indeed, Woolcock in a footnote associates linkage with civic engagement). This might be better called 'independent citizenship' or 'unattached citizenship' where a person has no strong interpersonal bonding links with a tightly knit family or group of friends but plays a meaningful civic role via the weak ties identified by Granovetter (1973) as being vital to social cohesion, particularly bridging vertical ties. Indeed, this might be seen as a template for effective social cohesion in late-modern or postmodern society where individuals form shifting allegiances within a pluralistic overall framework for social cohesion.

MESO- AND MACRO-LEVELS

Woolcock's original conceptualisation of social capital focused on micro- and macro-systems but did not pay much attention to their interaction or to the meso-level. This has been rectified in a recent publication: in addition to bonding and bridging social capital, Szreter and Woolcock (2004: 655) identify *linking* social capital which refers to norms of respect and networks of trusting relationships between people who interact across explicit, formal or institutionalised power or authority gradients in society. In effect, this can be seen as a special case of bridging social capital, specifically linking individuals and groups with social institutions.

At the macro-level Woolcock's and Narayan's approaches vary. Narayan identifies only the efficiency or inefficiency of formal institutions of the state, whereas Woolcock identifies two factors: synergy and integrity. Synergy relates to state–society relationships and integrity relates to institutional capacity and credibility. Synergy is defined as 'ties that connect citizens and public officials across the public–private divide' (Woolcock, 1998: 169) and depends upon the extent to which these connections are *embedded* in social relationships, cultural practices and political contexts. Integrity is to do with institutional capacity and credibility as well as in the literal meaning of 'integrity' itself: honesty, trust-worthiness, moral strength and soundness. So institutional integrity incorporates Narayan's efficiency, along with capacity to undertake all its roles effectively, credibly and honestly. Synergy without integrity can be seen as corruption and integrity without synergy can be seen as a distant bureaucracy.

Bringing together the micro- and macro-levels Narayan concludes that state institutions need to be run efficiently to give an opportunity for any outcome of well-being, but this will only occur if there are effective bonding and bridging ties, otherwise social exclusion will occur. On the other hand, effective social cohesion is impossible if state institutions are not run efficiently.

Woolcock identifies the combination of high levels of integration, linkage, synergy and integrity as *beneficent autonomy*; and conversely identifies low integration, linkage, synergy and integrity as *anarchic individualism*. Given that Woolcock's conceptualisation of social capital overlaps with non-ideological approaches to social cohesion, the 'ideal' state of beneficent autonomy could be characterised as comprising high social cohesion, and anarchic individualism could be characterised as comprising low social cohesion. But beneficent autonomy only characterises high *non-ideological* social cohesion: from a normative perspective on social cohesion, beneficent autonomy would only equate with high levels of social cohesion if it also met the criteria for a socially just society.

Woolcock provides a pathway from social capital to ideological social cohesion when discussing social structural factors that interfere with the effectiveness of social capital in promoting economic development. These, among others are as follows: widespread class, sex and ethnic disparities; endemic and unchecked poverty; lack of a shared stake in common outcomes between dominant and subordinate groups; and discrimination against minority groups (Woolcock, 1998: 182). This analysis opens the way for an ideological approach to social cohesion:

if poverty and inequality are bad for social capital and social cohesion then they need to be included in any equation which attempts to measure these attributes (Wakefield and Poland, 2005).

Lockwood – system integration and social integration

An important theoretical development in relation to social cohesion occurred with the (1999) publication of *Capitalism and Social Cohesion* (edited by Gough and Olofsson). The book's aim is to link the themes of social integration and social exclusion across sociological and social policy debate within the context of integration/differentiation theory.

A central theme of the book is Lockwood's distinction between social integration (relationships between *actors*) and system integration (relationships between the parts) in a social system. System integration here has much in common with Woolcock's notion of institutional integrity at the macro-level but it also relates to Coleman's important contribution to definitions of social capital in his stress on the role of elements of *social structure*. System integration is also consonant with the element of the World Bank definition relating to institutions in which integrative norms and values are embedded.

Social integration is decomposed by Lockwood into *civic integration*, the integrity of the core institutional order of citizenship at the macro-social level, and *social cohesion*, the strength of primary and secondary networks at the micro- and meso-social levels. The antonyms of these are *civic corruption* and *social dissolution* respectively (Lockwood, 1999). Confusingly, Lockwood's use of 'social cohesion' in this context is not consistent with usage by other authors cited in this chapter – Lockwood's usage is very similar to the Putnam or Coleman usage of *social capital*. So, Lockwood's overall model of system integration and social integration comprises what virtually all other commentators would call 'social cohesion', or even 'societal cohesion' and what he calls social cohesion would be identified by others as 'social capital'.

Civic integration/corruption is manifested through three different channels: political; economic; and social welfare (Lockwood, 1999: 69). High levels of political integration are expressed through support for democracy, including high levels of voting and political party membership, whereas political corruption is manifested by support for political extremism such as anti-democratic movements and terrorism. Economic integration is expressed through high levels of employment and other economic activity such as saving and investment whereas economic corruption is manifested through high levels of economic crime (such as tax evasion), non-legal employment, and involvement in the parallel economy. High levels of social welfare integration are expressed through universalism in social rights and the widespread provision of state welfare whereas lack of social welfare integration is manifested by low provision, high levels of poverty and deprivation. Manifestations of social cohesion/(capital) and social dissolution relate to voluntary associations, the extent of traditional crime and of family disorganisation.

For Lockwood, civic integration and social cohesion/(capital) are distinct both analytically and empirically but high levels of civic corruption have a negative effect on social cohesion/(capital) and vice versa. The boundary between civic integration and social cohesion/(capital) is bridged by secondary associations inter-mediating between the individual and the state. These secondary associations are those bodies, organisations and individuals which comprise what other authors refer to as civil society. Lockwood makes a distinction between actors at the macro-level (political parties, trade unions, the church, etc.) and associations at the meso- or micro-level (Lockwood, 1999: 76). So, for Lockwood, the actors involved in civic integration are largely *collective* actors which represent or act on behalf of groups of individuals.

In relation to system integration, Lockwood (ibid.: 64) warns that the extent to which system legitimacy is grounded in principles that are *procedural* – that is, impersonal, universalistic, 'rules of the game' – should not be underestimated. In this he takes a somewhat different view to Berger (1998) who privileges integrative norms. Gough and Olofsson (1999: 4) also stress that modern types of solidarity 'cannot rest at the level of mere consciousness, but must be institutionalised as rights and duties, if anomie and other types of pathological consequences are to be avoided'.

Lockwood's distinction between civic integration and what others would call social capital is most helpful in that it introduces a meso-level of intermediary networks and institutions between the micro-levels of groups of individual actors and the macro-level of systems. This overcomes an apparent weakness in Woolcock's and Narayan's conceptualisations which otherwise have much in common with Lockwood's approach. This topic reappears in Chapter 6 when discussing the social quality construct which both utilises and modifies Lockwood's construct.

Ideological approaches to social cohesion

The differences between the ideological and the non-ideological conceptualisations of social cohesion relate to the substantive nature of the integrative norms and values that are central to cohesion itself. In the non-ideological approaches above, social cohesion is seen as being positive because it enables a society – whatever its political persuasion – to function efficiently and smoothly. The ideological approaches discussed here go beyond efficiency within society and address the substantive ideological nature of the society itself: social cohesion here is seen as 'good' because it is an attribute only of a certain *type* of society, a society not only with shared values in general but with shared *egalitarian* values. From this perspective, an efficient and highly cohesive inegalitarian society is seen as having less (or worse) social cohesion than an egalitarian one.

At this point it is worth noting that no non-egalitarian ideological approaches to social cohesion are being presented. This is largely because there do not seem to be any in contemporary sociological – or other social science – literature. In the past there have been some very influential manifestos for non-egalitarian social cohesion, but these have often been based upon highly nationalistic and often xenophobic and racist visions of a cohesive societies: for example, the Fascist and Nazi views of society were highly cohesive. In contemporary intellectual social science discourse there are no such extreme formulations. Perhaps the closest approach to non-egalitarian ideological social cohesion is the conservative vision presented by Frances Fukuyama (1999), but this lies closer to the non-ideological than ideological approaches. Views on social cohesion among liberal and New Right social scientists and commentators are firmly in the non-ideological camp and are indeed minimalist in relation to macro-societal cohesion, a construct which the New Right at least deeply distrusts, as can be recalled from Margaret Thatcher's famous denial or rebuttal of society in her assertion that 'there is no society'.

Social cohesion as equality of opportunity

Perhaps the most modest of the ideological approaches to social cohesion is that adopted by Dahrendorf (1995). Its bottom line is that no members of society should be deprived of opportunity:

> Social cohesion comes in to describe a society which offers opportunities to all its members within a framework of accepted values and institutions. Such a society is therefore one of inclusion. People belong: they are not allowed to be excluded.
>
> (cited in Berger-Schmitt and Noll, 2000: 14)

Percy-Smith (2000a: 20) uses a somewhat more forceful definition requiring 'reconciliation of a system based on market forces, freedom of opportunity and enterprise with a commitment to the values of internal solidarity and mutual support which ensures open access to benefit and protection for all members of society'.

It is worth noting that, modest in scope though they are, both these approaches are strongly socially inclusionary and require protection against social exclusion. Neither of them, however, are committed to full *equality* of opportunity. The Canadian Government's definition does make this commitment and requires an 'ongoing process of developing a community of shared values, shared challenges and equal opportunities . . . based on a sense of trust, hope and reciprocity' (Jenson, 1998: 4). Nevertheless, as Jenson points out, this equality is of *opportunity* only and it is seen as just one value among several. This definition of social cohesion does not strive 'to achieve social justice via the active promotion of equitable outcomes' (ibid.).

Social cohesion as mitigation of inequalities

The ideological element in defining social cohesion becomes more prominent in the following approaches. Berger-Schmitt (2000: 7) argues that elements of a society's social cohesion form an integral part of the quality of life experienced by individuals – including perceived inequalities in the workplace, school or neighbourhood – and that 'quality of life represents the common overarching policy goal with social cohesion as an important component to be addressed'.

The Council of Europe's definition introduces the notion of human dignity: 'Because it makes respect for human dignity and personal integrity paramount and enables the social link between the individual and society to be restored, the best response to the tragedy of exclusion . . . is to strengthen social cohesion' (Council of Europe, 1998: 15). The link explicitly made here between social cohesion and social exclusion raises an issue that is revisited later in this chapter.

In Canada, social cohesion is a major issue among policy-makers as well as social scientists. While many of the former use the Canadian Government definition given above, many academics use the more radical definition given by Judith Maxwell:

> Social cohesion involves building shared values and communities of inter-pretation, reducing disparities in wealth and income, and generally enabling people to have a sense that they are engaged in a common enterprise, facing shared challenges, and that they are members of the same community.
>
> (1996: 13)

Egalitarian social cohesion: aspiring towards equity and social justice

Finally, we arrive at the most strongly ideological approaches. These take one of two forms in the literature. The first is to link a non- (or minimally) ideological approach to social cohesion to other social goals in the pursuit of higher aspirations. Gough (1999: 104) does this in striving towards Lockwood's aspiration of maximising both system integration and social integration by pursuing solidarity and social cohesion along with minimising inequality, poverty and exclusion. For Uslaner (2002) and Rothstein and Uslaner (2005), generalised trust – a constituent of social cohesion and central to a thriving democracy and economy, to lower crime and corruption – is causally related to structural equality and thus governments must enact egalitarian social policies in pursuit of the dual goals of social cohesion and social justice.

The second approach provides an ideological definition of social cohesion linked to the larger overarching social construct of *social quality*: 'the extent to which citizens are able to participate in the social and economic life of their communities under conditions which enhance their well-being and individual potential' (Beck *et al.*, 2001b: 7). Within this framework a high level of social cohesion maximises solidarity and shared identity and enables people 'to exist as real human subjects, as social beings' (Beck *et al.*, 1997c: 284). On the other hand, anomie – the opposite to social cohesion within the social quality construct – is fostered by regional disparities, the suppression of minorities, unequal access to public goods and services and an unequal sharing of economic burdens. The role of social cohesion in relation to the social quality construct is discussed in Chapter 6, in the light of conclusions drawn from discussion of other theoretical and conceptual frameworks.

Bringing social cohesion and social exclusion together

The time has now come to explore the relationship between social cohesion and social exclusion in more depth. As noted above, this is a largely unexplored area.

Blokland (2000: 56), though she argues that 'cohesion is gradually fused with social exclusion', complains that present theoretical frameworks are inadequate for studying either construct. Indeed, only three overarching models of quality of life which incorporate both constructs have been found in the academic literature and even in these there is only very limited discussion of the relationship between the constructs, where a more detailed analysis would be expected (but see Kay and Bernard, forthcoming). These models all deal with other constructs as well as social cohesion and social exclusion and are explored in detail in Chapter 6 but a brief preview of their stance with regard to these two constructs is given here.

In Bernard's (1999) democratic dialectic, social exclusion is conceptualised within the framework of social cohesion and is seen as a failure in cohesion. Berger-Schmitt and Noll's (2000) overarching quality of life model perhaps has the clearest exposition of the relationship: here social cohesion has two parts, one is a social capital dimension and the other is an inequalities dimension, an integral part of which is the outcome-oriented manifestation of social exclusion. So for Berger-Schmitt and Noll, social exclusion and social capital are two, conceptually separate, elements of social cohesion. In the third model, social quality (Beck *et al.*, 1997b; Beck *et al.*, 2001a) the relationship between the two constructs is different; instead of social exclusion being incorporated within social cohesion, the two are conceptualised as being distinct dimensions with neither having priority or dominion over the other.

In relation to social quality, Walker and Wigfield (2003: 7) identify a link between the two constructs via the notion of *social relations*: social cohesion concerns the structure or construction of social relations whereas social inclusion focuses on access to and level of integration in those relations. As will be seen later, the role of relations, networks and ties is pivotal in the relationship between social cohesion and the process-oriented definitions of social exclusion. In the overarching quality of life context, Berger-Schmitt links the causes and processes of social exclusion to an impairment of social cohesion through the way in which societal institutions regulate and constrain access to goods, services, activities and resources normally associated with citizenship rights (Berger-Schmitt, 2000: 5). She claims that such deficiencies in social cohesion include: social exclusion from the labour market, weak social ties and feelings of solidarity within private networks, and a low level of civic engagement in voluntary work (Berger-Schmitt, 2002: 405).

Given that all the commentators cited in this chapter present social cohesion as a good and positive thing and social exclusion as a bad or negative thing, then, in principle, and other things being equal, the nature of their interrelationship and interaction should be straightforward. *If* the two constructs are causally related in any way, then it is clear that this should be an inverse relationship: an increase in social cohesion ought to lead to a decrease in social exclusion, or at least that high levels of social cohesion imply low levels of social exclusion.

But, in contradiction to this, it is also arguable that high levels of social cohesion imply *high* levels of social exclusion too. This is the argument forcefully made in a somewhat different context by Jordan who claims that exclusion – or excluding – is a defining characteristic of all groups: 'In emphasising the demands of active citizenship, theorists are (usually unintentionally) strengthening the case for various kinds of exclusion. Conversely, those who focus on principles of inclusion weaken the case for grounding rights and duties in membership' (1996: 262). Jordan makes his case in the context of social exclusion and citizenship, not social cohesion, but the argument still holds. Strong ideological social cohesion can be substituted here for strong citizenship: the greater the amount of social justice and resource redistribution, the more important become issues of entry, exit, inclusion and exclusion. Peled (1992) and Shafir and Peled (1998) make a similar point about strong versus weak communities: strong communities (including those with high ideological levels of social cohesion) have high levels of social inclusion, are harder to join and have higher costs of exclusion than weak communities where criteria for inclusion are less rigorous and therefore fewer members run the risk of exclusion.

A paradox appears to be emerging here in the potential simultaneous correlation between social cohesion and *both* social inclusion *and* social exclusion. Alternatively, a third, hitherto hidden, factor might have come into play: the bifurcation of social inclusion and social exclusion into two strands, that of *quality* and *quantity*. Perhaps the implication of Jordan's and Shafir and Peled's insights is that high quality social cohesion and high quality social inclusion may be entirely compatible with – or even causally related to – high *quantity* social exclusion, i.e. high *levels* of inclusion among the included and large *numbers* of socially excluded people (extreme examples of this would be highly cohesive societies with apartheid or slavery or even genocide).

This issue is particularly pertinent to tightly knit, homogeneous societies: the stronger the bonds of membership, the harder it is to meet these requirements and the larger the number of people potentially excluded. This also has implications for the different conceptions of social cohesion; is the ideological, egalitarian version *better* because it implies a lack of hierarchy and disparities of wealth and other resources within the 'in-group' or is it *worse* because egalitarianism is hard to achieve and therefore raises the stakes, making membership more exclusive and thus potentially condemning a larger number of people to be excluded?

It does seem that a loosely socially structured, heterogeneous or pluralistic society will have lower levels, or a lower threshold, of exclusion than a tightly socially structured, homogeneous mono-cultural society. The crucial issue is whether it will *necessarily* have lower or worse social cohesion. This raises the difficult question of whether social cohesion is a condition to be maximised or optimised: in other words, is *more* social cohesion always *better* social cohesion or can a society have too much of this good thing? Indeed, is there a necessary trade-off between cohesion and exclusion where a balance between the two maximises quality of life, quality of society or social quality? If not, and if it is possible to maximise both inclusion and cohesion, then what attributes would a totally inclusive and cohesive society have?; what would such a society look like? And would there be any barriers to entry into this utopia?

Put more formally, the above questions could be expressed as follows: with regards to any formulation of social exclusion and social cohesion: (1) are they independent of each other?; (2) are they causally related but distinct constructs –

and, if so, then what is the nature of the relationship between them?; and (3) is one of them contained wholly within the meaning of the other or are they two inter-related aspects of a wider analytical construct? In answering these questions, the issue needs to be addressed of whether different sets of answers come from different combinations of the range of definitions of each construct.

First, though, specimen definitions of the different approaches to social cohesion and social exclusion need to be presented. This is more straightforward with regard to social cohesion than social exclusion where there is less consensus, but it is still not unproblematic for either construct. The social cohesion definitions given here are largely generic whereas the social exclusion definitions are either derived from individual sources or are an amalgam of commonly used definitions. This is not intended to imply that the definitions given are intended to be seen as final, rather, they are intended to be representative of contemporary discussion of these topics. The definitions are as follows:

Social cohesion

- *Non-ideological social cohesion*: interlocking networks; high levels of trust; other-regarding behaviour; plus social coherence, i.e. civic institutions embedded in social structure (rule of law, civil and political liberties).
- *Ideological social cohesion*: this is on a sliding scale, starting with non-ideological social cohesion plus, cumulatively: mitigating inequalities of opportunity; equality of opportunity; reduction of disparities in income and wealth; and minimising inequality and poverty and social exclusion. NB: in the strongest ideological definitions, it is part of the meaning of social cohesion that social exclusion should be minimised (although whether this is the *level* of social exclusion among members of society or the *number* of people actually excluded from society is not specified).

Social exclusion

- *Outcome-based social exclusion*: a person is socially excluded if he or she is geographically resident in a society but is excluded from full participation in the normal activities of making a living and organising a life (an amalgam of Steinert and Pilgrim (2003) and Burchardt *et al.* (1999)). Outcome-based social exclusion can be a discontinuous or gradual exclusion from one or more individual dimensions, or alternatively and more rarely, a catastrophic rupture from participation in wider society.
- *Process-based social exclusion*: the failure of one or more of the democratic and legal system; labour market; welfare state system; communication network and bridging relationship systems; family and community system (drawn mainly from Berghman (1995), augmented by insights gained from Room (1999)).
- *Causal-based social exclusion*: denial or unavailability of belonging; trust; and access to relevant resource structures required by social actors in order to possess positive self-concepts (Wessels and Miedema, 2002).

Are social exclusion and social cohesion independent of each other?

For two of the definitions of social exclusion it is immediately apparent that they cannot be independent of social cohesion. Causally-oriented definitions of social exclusion are necessarily linked through trust, and implicitly through access to resources, to both ideological and non-ideological approaches to social cohesion. Similarly, process-based social exclusion, defined in terms of the failure of systems, is necessarily related to the systems central to both sets of social cohesion definitions. For example, interlocking networks and civic institutions are common to both sets of definitions.

On the other hand, there does not have to be a necessary link between the outcome-based definition of social exclusion and social cohesion. One of the strengths of the outcome-based definition in analytical terms is that it makes no inferences about the causes of an individual's exclusion: in principle, these might be either not related at all to issues of social cohesion or else heavily dependent upon them. Such a definition of social exclusion can be operationalised so as to be used to empirically test the relative importance of various aspects of social cohesion, or other factors in the different dimensions of the exclusion of different groups in society.

Are social exclusion and social cohesion causally related but distinct constructs – and, if so, then what is the nature of the relationship between them?

It is clear from the discussion above that outcome-oriented definitions of social exclusion are not necessarily causally related at all so here the emphasis will be on the other two approaches to social exclusion. The key to their relationship lies in the issue of the quality versus quantity of inclusion and exclusion discussed above. This topic is perhaps best approached using the distinction between the two constructs adopted by Walker and Wigfield (2003) who suggest that social cohesion concerns the structure or construction of social relations whereas social inclusion focuses on the access to and level of integration in those relations.

Taking non-ideological social cohesion, first; here a highly cohesive society would be well organised, fair, socially integrated and with high levels of trust, but it would not necessarily be an egalitarian society. Indeed it is – at least according to conservative commentators – entirely compatible with a minimal-state, free market society with high levels of economic inequality (Fukuyama, 1995, 1999, 2001). Under such circumstances, as in a free economic market, the costs to society of ensuring that all residents are socially included are low. So unless there are distortions in the fabric of social cohesion (for example, high levels of institutional and relational racism), it is unlikely that there will be large numbers of people totally excluded from such a society. So here the key feature would be the extent to which the relational and institutional systems are well structured and provide equitable access. Both the process-based and causal-based approaches are, in principle, relevant here. In practice, an approach based on the causes of social exclusion is probably the easiest to use because a helpful starting point for just such an investigation is provided by Wessels and Miedema's matrix, presented in Chapter 4. Interestingly, the extent to which individuals in such a society are socially excluded could be measured by an outcome-based instrument too.

There is a lot more at stake in relation to ideological than non-ideological approaches to social cohesion, and this has considerable consequences for its interaction with social exclusion. Ideological social cohesion of the kind espoused by Bernard, Berger-Schmitt and Noll, and the social quality promulgators requires major state intervention in the pursuit of social justice and tackling inequalities of income, wealth and life chances. This is an important policy issue in Canada, for example, with both an egalitarian conception of cohesion and dramatic inequalities between Anglophones and Francophones, on the one hand, and the indigenous population, on the other.

Any society which is striving towards strong social justice and minimising material and non-material inequalities will also strive towards maximising access to and integration into cohesive social relations and institutions. In other words, high levels of social cohesion *entail* high levels of social inclusion. As noted above, though, there is a membership-inclusion issue here. This can perhaps best be explored in relation to the position of immigrant members of a society. Returning to Peled's (1992) point about strong communities having tough entry requirements, there is a danger of refugees, asylum seekers and economic migrants suffering from the extreme form of outcome-oriented social exclusion – catastrophic rupture – in societies with high levels of ideological social cohesion (Uslaner and Conley, 2003). This is also a problem in relation, for example, to elderly dependants of recently naturalised immigrant citizens who may be barred from entry to such societies. As with non-ideological approaches to social cohesion, there is much to be gained by using a causally-based approach to social exclusion in analysing the interactions between structure of and access to the relations and systems that are central to ideological social cohesion.

A further tension emerges in relation to societies with strongly ideological approaches to social cohesion: this relates to issues of diversity, homogeneity and heterogeneity. This is a profoundly problematic issue in culturally diverse societies and is returned to briefly in Chapter 6.

Is one of them contained wholly within the meaning of the other or are they two inter-related aspects of a wider analytical construct?

There is no agreement in the literature on this topic. For Bernard, social exclusion is contained wholly in the meaning of social cohesion. For Berger-Schmitt, the extent of social exclusion in society is central to commonly accepted definitions of social cohesion and indeed, social exclusion is an essential part of one of the two dimensions of social cohesion. In spite of this, and as noted above, Berger-Schmitt clearly states that social exclusion and social capital 'must be viewed as independent of each other to a degree' (2002: 406). This is entirely consistent with her use of an outcome-based approach to defining social exclusion in this context. So within the overarching quality of life construct, social exclusion (as well as other aspects of the inequality dimension) is contained wholly within the social cohesion construct but social exclusion and social capital are (at least largely) independent of each other.

In relation to social quality, its original formulation assigned each of the four components to separate cells in a quadrant formed by the intersection of axes relating to biographical and societal processes, on the one hand, and systems, institutions, organisations and communities, configurations, and groups, on the other. Therefore, social exclusion and social cohesion were presented as discrete entities. Contemporary theorising on social quality presents all four components in the context of the manifestation of 'the social' through the dialectical interaction between individual self-realisation and the creating of collective identities, so in this context social exclusion and social cohesion can be identified as inter-related aspects of the wider analytical social quality construct.

In all three constructs, social cohesion is presented within an ideological context. In Bernard's operationalisation, it is most likely (though never specifically stated) that a process-oriented definition of social exclusion is used. Berger-Schmitt uses an outcome-oriented definition in relation to the overarching quality of life construct. The definition used in relation to social quality is likewise outcome-oriented but the construct is used in a context, interactively with the other three social quality components, where a causal-based approach would not be inappropriate. It is these three constructs which form the subject matter of Chapter 6.

6 Societal quality of life constructs

In Chapters 4 and 5 two major themes in quality of life were introduced. The first is social exclusion which operates both in relation to individuals, groups and communities and, more abstractly, at societal level in terms of social processes. The second relates to social capital and social cohesion, which are collective attributes based on associations and networks but referring more to quality of life at community and societal, rather than at an individual level. This chapter discusses overarching quality of life constructs which incorporate process and outcome, individual and collective, and in some cases also, subjective and objective aspects of quality of life. The three major constructs discussed here, Bernard's *democratic dialectic*, Berger-Schmitt and Noll's *overarching quality of life* and Beck, van der Maesen and Walker's *social quality* were all briefly introduced in Chapter 5. The chapter finishes with a brief discussion of applying the social quality construct to quality of life in ethnic minority and socially excluded communities.

Before introducing these main themes, though, some other overarching quality of life constructs are briefly introduced.

Overarching quality of life constructs

There are two distinguishing features of an *overarching* quality of life construct. The first is that the construct deals with a full and not a partial conception of quality of life, including all the areas that can be considered as relevant for enhancing quality of life. The second is that the construct has a societal or collective focus. The needs-based approaches to quality of life discussed in Chapter 3 do not meet the first requirement in that they specifically exclude values and life circumstances that are relevant to quality of life but go beyond a normal conception of needs. Thus Doyal and Gough's theory of human needs, although unquestionably a fundamentally important contribution to our understanding of quality of life and overtly societal in focus, does not go far enough in its conception of quality of life to meet the first criterion. This does not mean that it will be cast aside: it is revisited in the final chapter of the book as one of the bases for constructing a full account of quality of life. Similarly, the hedonic and eudaimonic approaches to quality of life encountered in Chapter 1 are not included here because they are individualistic rather than societal in focus. There is another group of societally oriented quality of life models which are not discussed here but appear in Chapter 7. These are the health-related and public health overarching models and these are excluded here because they focus on health rather than on quality of life in the round (although it has to be admitted that some of the definitions of health used are so wide as to make them contenders for a 'full' conception of quality of life).

Broadly speaking, there are three traditions of synoptic and overarching approaches to quality of life, conceptual, empirical and what can be referred to as 'rampant empiricist'. This third tradition involves collecting masses of data in a way that sometimes seems to be higgledy-piggledy, and regrettably such 'statistics mountains' have done a disservice to the goal of enhancing the study of quality of life (Rapley, 2003). Examples of this third tradition will not be discussed here.

Conceptual approaches

One of the first systematic conceptual overarching quality of life frameworks emerged from Canada in the early 1990s (Rioux and Hay, 1993: 5) and focuses on well-being within a societal context. One of its basic assumptions is that well-being transcends the notion of needs in relating to both processes and outcomes of self-determination and individual fulfilment. It is also based on the premise that true well-being cannot be conceptualised independently of social inter-relationships and mutual interdependence within a context of distributional justice which guarantees personal and economic security, protection of citizenship and human rights, Here well-being is defined as 'the pursuit and fulfilment of personal aspirations and the development and exercise of human capabilities, within a context of mutual recognition, equality and interdependence' (ibid.: 5).

The conceptual framework comprises a matrix of three elements of well-being (self-determination; mutual recognition and interdependence; and equality) and three contributors to well-being (security; citizenship; and democratisation). Here, elements are the fundamental characteristics of well-being and contributors are those factors which are essential for the realisation of the elements of well-being – in other words, what subsequent commentators have called 'domains'. As with many other Canadian approaches (Maxwell, 1996; Jenson, 1998; Bernard, 1999), equality is central to this formulation of well-being, particularly in relation to issues of ethnicity. Rioux and Hay (1993) also take gender equality as a consistent theme throughout their exposition. This framework was innovative in linking individual well-being with social justice and equality and can be seen as a point of departure towards later more sophisticated theoretical developments in this area, particularly in Bernard's democratic dialectic discussed later in this chapter.

At around the same time Dasgupta and Weale (1992), in an article discussing indicators and measures of quality of life in a development context, made a distinction between the constituents and determinants of quality of life. These two sets of constructs are more clearly articulated and tangible than Rioux and Hay's (1993) 'elements' and 'contributors' to well-being. Dasgupta and Weale's constituents of quality of life are health, welfare, freedom of choice and basic liberties; and their determinants of quality of life are availability of food, clothing, shelter, potable water, legal aid, educational facilities, health care, resources for national security, and income in general (1992: 119).

Following this, Veenhoven (1996) made an important contribution to conceptualising overarching quality of life in his distinction between quality *in* societies and quality *of* societies, which has resonances with the classifications made by Rioux and Hay (1993) and Dasgupta and Weale (1992). Quality in societies relates to the quality of life of individuals within society whereas quality of societies refers to the societies themselves as holistic entities. Veenhoven identifies four aspects of quality of societies: system stability; productivity; expression of ideals; and liveability. System stability, comprising order, predictability and continuity, has strong links with both Lockwood's system integration and the theoretical base of the social quality construct, discussed below. Productivity, according to Veenhoven, covers cultural as well as financial resources and refers to a holistic notion of societal growth and development. Ideal-expression refers to tolerance and pluralism in relation to both universal goals such as human rights and to a range of moral systems found within a pluralistic society, including honour, religious devotion, filial piety, and humanism.

Liveability is the link between quality of societies and quality in societies. It is defined as the degree to which a nation's provisions and requirements fit with the needs and capacities of its citizens (Veenhoven, 1996: 7). Veenhoven's happy life expectancy (HLE) construct, discussed in Chapter 1, is designed as an indicator of liveability and so therefore is a measure of one aspect of quality of societies. HLE has not been widely used and Veenhoven's notion of liveability has been criticised by Berger-Schmitt and Noll (2000) and Fahey *et al.* (2002) as not adding substantively to the notion of quality of life. However, when located within his wider quality of society construct, along with system stability, productivity and ideal-expression, it does provide a well-rounded, multidimensional framework for conceptualising and appraising quality of life at societal level. It also has a transparent and conceptually clear measure of one of the four elements of the quality of society construct.

Empirical traditions

Moving on to the empirically-oriented studies, there is a wide range to choose from. All except the most recent important studies have been summarised and evaluated in the exhaustive review undertaken by Hagerty *et al.* (2001). Virtually all these studies have focused either largely or entirely at the individual level and do not effectively address quality of life at a collective level. A few recent empirically-oriented studies, though, do address collective, macro-level issues.

The Australian Bureau of Statistics (2003) has developed a social statistics system incorporating both individual and social aspects of well-being and addressing relevant 'social issues' such as poverty, unemployment, crime, and homelessness. This combination of approaches in effect provides a bridge between issues relating to social exclusion and social cohesion, with the former coming under the 'social issues' heading and the latter being incorporated into the social factors relevant to well-being, along with social capital, transactions, social change and economic conditions. It is interesting to note that 'life transitions' is included among the individual factors affecting individual well-being, along with the other factors normally in such lists, such as health, education, income, etc.

Perhaps the best developed of the empirically-oriented approaches is that of the Dublin-based European Foundation for the Improvement of Living and Working Conditions (Fahey *et al.*, 2002) which has a framework covering both 'living conditions' and quality of life, which includes both objective and subjective conditions and focuses on resources and opportunities, including those provided collectively. This approach draws heavily on Sen's capabilities model in that it takes account, not only of the actual choices that people make but also the opportunities they have to make choices.

Fahey *et al.* (2002: summary, p. 2) emphasise the cultural relativity of quality of life and they insist that relevant indicators 'derive their meaning and legitimacy ultimately from consensus among the general public'. Their approach is multi-dimensional and strongly emphasises causal and interactive social processes. In particular, they stress the critical role played by the dynamics of socio-economic circumstances and social relations. Their framework moves firmly into the 'overarching' category in its aim to 'seek to capture aspects of societal well-being going beyond the individuals' capacity to pursue their own ends' (Fahey *et al.*, 2002: 85).

Bernard's democratic dialectic

This is the most uncomplicated of the three major overarching quality of life models. This is largely because it deals explicitly only with collective issues of societal quality of life rather than the quality of life of individuals which is covered only implicitly. This is both a weakness and a strength. Its lack of attention to individuals reduces its usefulness as a synoptic construct but the incisiveness of its dissection and analysis of three major societal constructs are of considerable benefit in assessing societal quality of life in heterogeneous, pluralistic and multicultural societies. It is also a useful starting place because Bernard's model begins with a discussion of the *problematique* of social cohesion, which he construes as being only a quasi-concept, a hybrid that requires deconstructing in order to make it more than just a 'useful conceptual focus point'.

The framework he uses is based on a noble pedigree; the watchwords of the French Revolution, with one textual amendment – liberty, equality and now 'solidarity', in place of fraternity. Bernard represents these diagrammatically as a triangle, as can be seen from the Figure 6.1. His thesis is that all three are necessary for democracy and that their interaction, and the tensions between them, provide the space within which the 'democratic dialectic' takes place. Only when all three are in a positive equilibrium will the prerequisites for societal quality of life be in place.

Bernard identifies strengths and weaknesses, problems and distortions both in relation to individual points on the triangle and to the three sets of pairings between

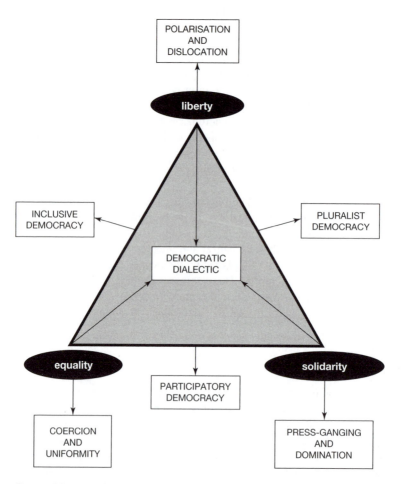

Figure 6.1 Bernard's democratic dialectic (Bernard, 1999: 6)

them. In relation to the individual attributes, first, it is clear that a society without liberty is in danger of coercion, enslavement and servitude but that excessive freedom or libertarianism can lead to polarisation, dislocation and social fragmentation – and ultimately, to a complete disregard of one's fellow citizens. Second, equality before the law, equality of access and equality of opportunity are non-controversial in any democratic society, as are combating inequalities of condition so gross that serious material poverty would result. However, reducing disparities of wealth and income and striving for equality of outcome or condition can lead to coercion and uniformity, as well as being in conflict with liberty. Solidarity, the essence of cohesion, is of course necessary for any group, community or society to survive. But a sense of togetherness and mutual obligation can result in reductions in freedom by 'press-ganging and domination' (Bernard, 1999: 6).

So all three individual goals in Bernard's formulation are conditions to be optimised rather than maximised: too much of any one of them can lead to, indeed will and must lead to, damage to the fabric of democratic society. Bernard argues that these goals cannot be optimised in isolation from each other. Liberty needs to be leavened by a sense of community and respect for the needs of other individuals. Any solidarity which is essentially inegalitarian is exploitative, and solidarity without freedom, like equality without freedom, does not respect individual human rights. Finally, respect for equality that takes no account of solidarity, while utopian in an individualistic sense – reminiscent of the nineteenth-century land reform movement's demand for 'three acres and a cow' for everyone, provides an alienating vision of a land populated by 'atomised' individuals but with no *society* to speak of.

Bernard next looks at the democratic possibilities of pairings of these elements. He gives the label of 'participatory democracy' to the pairing of equality and solidarity and uses Scandinavian social democracy as an example, where state intervention promotes equality. This is perhaps the least strong of his bipolar conceptualisations, because it might be considered that liberty, too, is a major component of democracy in Scandinavia, unless the necessity of paying high taxes to finance egalitarian state welfare is seen as coercive and anti-libertarian. This is certainly a position that is taken by many neo-liberal commentators (e.g. Hayek, 1944) so Bernard is not being inconsistent here. Nevertheless, the 'democratic centralism' of Soviet and Eastern European state-socialist nations, particularly in the 1960s and 1970s might be a better example here of strongly solidaristic and egalitarian states which did not prioritise individual liberty. Indeed, *democratic centralism* might be a better label here than *participatory democracy*.

Bernard is on firmer ground for the other two pairings, which, to be fair to him, are the ones he pays most attention to and which are most central to his democratic dialectic thesis. Equality and liberty are paired under the label of 'inclusive democracy'. Here Bernard follows Marshall's (1972) notion of 'hyphenated citizenship'. Following on from his seminal thesis of social citizenship depending upon legal, political and social rights providing a threshold of social equality – equality of status as citizens – which legitimates economic inequalities, Marshall developed the notion of democratic-welfare-capitalism where the political, the social and the economic interact. A person has political rights as a citizen and has social rights to welfare benefits to avoid poverty but has to make their own way in the economic system where unequal material outcomes are the rewards for ability, hard work and entrepreneurial skills. Thus, Marshall envisaged a trade-off between, on the one hand, equality of status, along with social security and, on the other, personal liberty, along with economic inequality.

Bernard identifies a 'fragile bipolar equilibrium between liberty and equality in the traditional western welfare state'. Rather controversially, he claims that solidarity is missing from this model, whereas many other commentators would claim that the welfare state was the epitome of social solidarity, particularly in the immediate post-war period (Fraser, 2003). Bernard defends this claim as follows:

When the rich want unimpeded access to the medical care that their money allows them to purchase, how can one object except by saying that our common fate as mortals imposes on us all a compassion without exclusion? When they quit the public school system, what can we say except that they are weakening one of the most basic institutions of their own society?

(Bernard, 1999: 12)

Here the tension identified by Marshall and Bernard is clear: there *is* social equality of a sort, in that everyone has equal access to state-run health, welfare and education services, but the economic inequality fostered by individual liberty, enables the rich to get 'better than equal' provision. And it is the call to solidarity that provides the moral resolution to this tension without falling prey to coercion – or at least without falling prey to *explicit* coercion. In order for this to happen, of course, the call to solidarity here has to be answered by the rich from their own free will. Bernard is here entering the difficult territory identified by Barry (1998) when discussing acceptable and unacceptable degrees of inequality as parameters to a socially inclusive society.

The bipolar equilibrium is even more fragile in relation to the interaction between liberty and solidarity, the dynamic of which 'is intended to soften the hardships brought about by the free play of the economy' (Bernard, 1999: 13). His complaint here is that the state is enjoined to promote consensus on values rather than to resolve conflicts of interests. Liberty and solidarity combined can, according to Bernard, certainly lead to an integrated society but it can also be a highly unequal one: in the words of the hymn cited in Chapter 4, with the 'rich man in his castle and the poor man at his gate' having consensual values about how 'God ordered their estate'. Where does this lead social cohesion? Bernard is unequivocal:

It is here as well that the concept of social cohesion most clearly reveals its nature as a quasi-concept: it is difficult to suggest circumscribing the effects of neoliberalism without alluding to the inequalities that it engenders, just as any appeal to the solidarity of all members of society cannot avoid all reference to elementary principles of equality. From whence comes the pussyfooting about the concept of social cohesion: it most often remains undefined, and when it is, the definition does not always include equality, unless it appears in the attenuated form of equality of opportunity.

(ibid.: 13)

So for Bernard, social cohesion is about much more than just solidarity, or even solidarity plus liberty: it *has* to include equality as well. So his version of egalitarian social cohesion is at the centre of the democratic dialectic. This version of social cohesion transcends its status as a quasi-concept and it becomes a full-blooded macro-construct of quality of life in its own right. Bernard then fleshes out the democratic dialectic of social cohesion in the light of the guiding principles of liberty, equality and solidarity, by identifying six dimensions (following Jenson, 1998) which he classifies as relating to three spheres of activity – economic, political

Table 6.1 Bernard's typology of the dimensions of the democratic dialectic of social cohesion

	Formal	*Substantive*
Economic	insertion/exclusion	equality/inequality (or social justice/injustice)
Political	legitimacy/illegitimacy	participation/passivity
Socio-cultural	recognition/rejection	belonging/isolation

and socio-cultural – and as being either formal or substantive. Bernard's delineation of formal and substantive has similarities to the 'process' and 'outcome' orientations noted in the discussion of social exclusion in Chapter 4. His typology is as shown in Table 6.1 (Bernard, 1999: 20).

Bernard's formal economic dimension contrasts exclusion with insertion rather than with inclusion. His primary focus here is on formal access to the labour market so that there is equality of access to jobs. His substantive economic dimension is equality versus inequality or, alternatively, justice versus injustice – and it is noteworthy that he equates equality with justice here. Within the political sphere, legitimacy refers to maintenance of public and private institutions that mediate conflicts on the basis of equitable treatment of all citizens, and participation in the management of public affairs is necessary to avoid political disenchantment. However, Bernard warns of the dangers of narrow activism and stipulates that those not involved in activism must not be deprived of their citizenship rights. In the socio-cultural sphere, recognition requires that differences be tolerated while belonging means being a part of the same community and 'corresponds to involvement in the construction of a community, to a sharing of values – which is not unanimity, but acceptance of an active dialogue about these values' (ibid.: 22).

It can be seen that Bernard's model is squarely in the 'quality of societies' category, with his vision of a high-quality society encompassing the notions of belonging, participation, social justice/equality, recognition, legitimacy and insertion. It is interesting to note too that while liberty, equality and solidarity are all elements to be optimised rather than maximised in order to achieve a high quality society, these six dimensions are all, more or less, amenable to maximisation, particularly if social justice is substituted for equality. The only question mark is over participation: although increasing political participation is in general a good thing, coerced participation can be oppressive. However, Bernard has already entered a caveat on this, that lack of participation should not be a bar to the benefits of citizenship.

Bernard does see a possible tension between the formal and substantive, particularly in the socio-cultural fields, between recognition of difference and belonging to the same community:

> On the socio-cultural level, we must steer a course between, on the one hand, a pluralism that is so distended that it no longer conveys to individuals a sense

of a community or destiny, and on the other hand, a burdensome communion of values. The construction, for example, of a common and open Quebec culture in which all citizens within its boundaries participate is a legitimate goal, but it must not become an instrument of exclusion.

(ibid.: 22)

The reference to Quebec is salutary here. It is important to remember that Canadian commentators write in the shadow of a Francophone political separatist movement as well as in the knowledge of a deeply excluded and impoverished indigenous population. It is in this context that Bernard labels the solidarity–liberty axis of the democratic dialectic as 'pluralistic democracy'. This does not seem to be any intrinsic reason for this label but Bernard does justify it extrinsically in relation to plural or heterogeneous societies such as Canada: 'Social cohesion can take the form of the cohesion of some in opposition to others, who are excluded' (ibid.: 12). So, for Bernard the search for a common denominator is important and any appeal to solidarity must take account of societal diversity. Here is where social justice and equality become important goals, particularly in relation to members of the indigenous population:

Exalting solidarity while focusing on respect for difference and failing to call on the State to implement social rights, common to all citizens, can only lead in one direction: that the responsibility for each community's welfare be taken on by its members and their relations. This is often what lies, hidden or not, behind appeals to community, accompanied by usually inadequate offers of support.

(ibid.: 14)

According to Bernard, it is equality, and the state's role in promoting it that are central to social cohesion rather than attempting to achieve commonality through striving for common substantive values in an increasingly diversified society where group solidarity is often turned inwards to ethnic and similar affiliations rather than outwards towards a sense of national solidarity: 'In contrast, equality and its main instrument, the State, unite us in common and equivalent citizenship' (ibid.: 16–17).

Berger-Schmitt and Noll's overarching quality of life construct

Regina Berger-Schmitt and Heinz-Herbert Noll took a major step forward in creating their overarching quality of life construct (Berger-Schmitt, 2000, 2002; Berger-Schmitt and Noll, 2000; Noll, 2000, 2002). In so doing they brought together several important and previously unconnected strands including: the American 'subjective well-being' tradition of quality of life; the Scandinavian 'objective well-being' quality of life tradition; the European Union's societal goals and welfare policy; and social science theorising about sustainability, social exclusion, social capital and social cohesion. They put these together within a well-argued and coherent conceptual framework based on the notion of quality of life augmented to include societal as well as individual qualities, such as equality, equity, freedom, security and solidarity. They operationalised this framework into a detailed set of dimensions, sub-dimensions and indicators into what Noll has called a *European System of Social Indicators* (Noll, 2002).

Their ultimate aim is to be able to measure and analyse changes in the welfare of European citizens as follows:

> As a result of our research, the scientific community, policy makers as well as other potential users shall be provided with a theoretically as well as methodologically well-grounded selection of measurement dimensions and indicators which can be used as an instrument to continually observe and analyse the development of welfare and quality of life as well as changes in the social structure of European societies and the European Union.
>
> (Berger-Schmitt and Noll, 2000: 6)

Overview and rationale

In this manifesto, Berger-Schmitt and Noll closely link together the notions of quality of life and welfare. In so doing they explicitly structure their framework as being primarily a tool for social policy. They choose 'quality of life' rather than, for example, social cohesion, social capital, social exclusion or even social quality, because they claim, 'among the welfare concepts considered here, the concept of quality of life is probably the most widely recognised and the most frequently used framework for analysing the welfare development of a society' (ibid.: 8). Interestingly, they claim that quality of life as a construct has fewer deficiencies in empirical operationalisation and theoretical elaboration and clarification than the other above-mentioned constructs. The empirical aspect of this claim is probably uncontroversial but its theoretical judgement is, as seen below, hotly contested by the social quality protagonists (Baers *et al.*, 2005).

Two of the most important contributions made by Berger-Schmitt and Noll are in relation to bringing together subjective and objective aspects of individual quality of life *and* individual and societal quality of life. At the individual level they further distinguish between cognitive and affective aspects of subjective well-being and, in relation to objective well-being, between means (resources and capabilities) and ends or outcomes (living conditions). At the societal level they introduce two main quality of life constructs: social cohesion and sustainability (Berger-Schmitt and Noll, 2000: 11). Here social cohesion is seen as having two elements: reduction of disparities and inequalities; and strengthening social connections and ties. Thus, their approach is very similar to Bernard's in that it is both egalitarian and solidaristic in relation to strengthening social ties as well as values. Their notion of sustainability is defined in terms of preserving societal capital for future generations and, in this context, societal capital can be decomposed into human capital, social capital and natural capital.

There is one somewhat confusing aspect of their construct in that quality of life is used twice, with rather different meanings. At the overall level 'overarching quality of life' is the label for the whole model, comprising all three constructs, whereas 'individual quality of life' is itself one of these three constructs. In order to minimise confusion, they will be referred to in the same nomenclature as that given above in the following discussion.

It would be interesting to speculate on the theoretical and conceptual rationale for using social cohesion and sustainability as the two macro-aspects of the model. In fact, though, their inclusion in the model is largely determined by a social policy imperative in that one of Berger-Schmitt and Noll's aims is to provide a framework for assessing the European Union's social policy objectives and welfare goals, as set out in the Treaties of Rome (1957), Maastricht (1992) and Amsterdam (1997), plus various White Papers, Action Programmes and Communications. Noll (2002: 64) summarises these EU policies under three heads:

1   *Improvement of living conditions and quality of life*, including: employment; education; standard of living; health; social protection and security; public safety and crime; transport; and environment.
2   *Strengthening of economic and social cohesion*, including: (a) reduction of economic and social disparities between regions and social groups: reducing backwardness of less-favoured regions; equal opportunities for women and disabled people; and struggling against social exclusion; and (b) strengthening the connections between people and regions: improving transport; strengthening solidarity between peoples; encouraging European cohesion; reinforcing a common European identity; encouraging cultural, educational and employment exchanges.
3   *Sustainability*, including: promoting more efficient use of energy and resources; supporting 'clean' technologies; increasing the share of renewable energy sources' and promoting the concept of sustainable mobility.

These, of course, are virtually identical to the three arms of the overarching conceptual framework, so the overall justification for their inclusion can be seen to be policy-driven and therefore pragmatic as well as being grounded in a review of major conceptualisations of, and discourses on, welfare: 'The conceptual framework will set forth the goal dimensions of the welfare development of Europe which will determine the selection of measurement dimensions and indicators' (Berger-Schmitt and Noll, 2000: 37).

Definitions and structures

Berger-Schmitt and Noll operationalise their model by first identifying conceptually-oriented goal dimensions for each of their constructs. Then indicators are created for each of these via empirically-oriented measurement dimensions in relation to individual life domains largely derived from the EU policy objectives identified above.

They define individual quality of life straightforwardly as the combination of subjective well-being and objective living conditions, the latter including all aspects of the living situation which are relevant to the individual welfare (Berger-Schmitt and Noll, 2000: 37). The individual quality of life goal dimensions are:

1 Enhancement of subjective well-being, including affective and cognitive components, and positive and negative components.
2 Improvement of objective living conditions, including outcomes, resources and capabilities, and external circumstances.

Intriguingly, Berger-Schmitt and Noll never actually define social cohesion – possibly a wise move on their part given the complexities and pitfalls in this area. They do, however, identify social cohesion goal dimensions as follows:

1 Reduction of disparities, inequalities and social exclusion.
2 Strengthening social relations, interactions and ties, or in other words, *social capital*.

It was noted above that their operationalisation of social cohesion is very similar to that of Bernard. This is equally true in relation to social exclusion which is similarly seen as coming under the auspices of social cohesion. They explicitly state that they do not wish to operationalise the process aspects of social exclusion and that 'it is decided to refer to a perspective which views social exclusion as an outcome, a deficient state concerning the economic, social or political situation of individuals' (Berger-Schmitt and Noll, 2000: 39).

In the second social cohesion goal dimension, their conceptualisation of social capital is very wide indeed. It includes informal relations, intermediary associations and macro-institutions and its components are: enhancement of personal relations, networks and associational membership; promotion of social and political activities and voluntary engagements in networks and associations; the formation and strengthening of social relations between population groups; and the improvement of the quality of relations via shared values, common identity, trust or solidarity' (ibid.: 39).

Bringing all this together, an apt shorthand exposition of their operationalisation of social cohesion might be 'social capital plus social justice', given the emphasis here on combating inequalities. Thus, their overarching quality of life model has at least one component, social cohesion, which is radical in its espousal of goals consistent with a collectivist version of social justice.

Indeed, Berger-Schmitt, in a paper dealing with the operationalisation of the social cohesion component of the overarching quality of life model, gives a definition of social cohesion which is consistent with this interpretation:

> Social cohesion can be conceived as a societal quality which is experienced by individuals in their daily lives, for example in the form of the perceived inequality of the social climate . . . This perspective considers elements of the

social cohesion of a society to form an integral part of the quality of life of the individuals belonging to that society . . . In this sense, quality of life represents the common overarching policy goal with social cohesion as an important component to be addressed.

(Berger-Schmitt, 2000: 7)

For the third construct of sustainability they use the World Bank's 'four capital approach' to societal capital, namely, human, social, natural and physical capital (although they do not provide goal or measurement dimensions for physical capital given the social orientation of the model). The two goal dimensions are as follows:

1   Enhancement/preservation of the societal capital for current and future generations.
2   Equal opportunities within and across generations.

Two things are worth noting here. The first is that the sustainability construct is not so well developed as the other two. Indeed, its 'equal opportunities within and across generations' goal dimension is not clearly delineated and the inclusion of social capital, which is also an element of the social cohesion component also leads to lack of clarity. Second, and much more positively, sustainability is an extremely important facet of quality of life which has not been effectively addressed in the social policy literature and it is to their credit that Berger-Schmitt and Noll have included it at all, even in its present rather rudimentary conceptual formulation.

The final piece of the overarching quality of life structure relates to the life domains, which cover the following areas: population; households and families; housing; transport; leisure, media and culture; social and political participation and integration; education and vocational training; labour market and working conditions; income, standard of living and consumption patterns; health; environment; social security; public safety and crime; and finally 'total life situation'. The final holistic category is used to provide a cross-domain perspective and to cover issues which are not related to a specific life domain (Noll, personal correspondence).

Operationalisation

Now that all the components are in place, the time has come to see the model in operation. Noll sums it up as follows:

The European System of Social Indicators covers 14 life domains. Within each life domain up to six dimensions of welfare . . . are being distinguished. At a third level there are dimensions of measurement and at a fourth level subdimensions, which are going to be operationalised by one or more indicators each.

(2002: 76)

First, though, it is important to point out some complexities and overlaps which might lead to problems in utilising the model. Perhaps the most important complexity – and this is one shared by all non-unitary models – is how the components relate to each other. Bernard identifies this issue as a 'dialectic' and does directly address it. However, no indication is given in the overarching quality of life model of the relative weighting or the interaction between the three parts. It is particularly important to know whether the idea is just to aggregate them to provide an overall score or whether any thresholds need to be met. This is crucial in relation to sustainability because there can be a trade-off between quality of life – both individual and overarching – today and tomorrow.

Berger-Schmitt in a later paper specifically exploring the social cohesion construct, does start to address this issue:

> How are the concepts of social cohesion and quality of life related to each other? At an empirical level, positive associations have been observed. The results of several studies point towards favourable effects of various aspects of social cohesion on macroeconomic performance . . . [and] individual health and well-being. Despite these empirical efforts there still is a need for future research in this field.
>
> (Berger-Schmitt, 2000: 15)

Another issue which has already been alluded to is that of potential overlap. Social capital, for example, is addressed in both the sustainability and the social cohesion component of the model. Berger-Schmitt and Noll note that:

> An unequivocal assignment of measurement dimensions to goal dimensions will not be feasible in all cases. The reasons are the substantial overlaps between the welfare concepts at the level of goal dimensions as well as at the level of measurement dimensions . . . The goal dimensions of the concept of social cohesion are partially related to the notions of quality of life as well as sustainability.
>
> (Berger-Schmitt and Noll, 2000: 40)

There is, in fact, no overlap between sustainability and individual quality of life (except perhaps in relation to the 'equal opportunities within generations' goal dimension of the latter) but the goal dimension of social cohesion referring to reduction of disparities, inequalities and social exclusion relates to both individual quality of life and sustainability as well as social cohesion. Now, in one sense, overlap is not necessarily a problem in that sustainability, social cohesion and individual quality of life can each add a different dimension to, for example, social exclusion, or to reduction of disparities. But in order for this to take place in a way which is productive and helpful, there must be different nuances of interpretation, or even of definition from each of the three larger constructs.

Thus, for social exclusion, the combination of an outcome-oriented definition related to individual quality of life with a process-oriented definition related to social cohesion and perhaps even a causal-oriented definition related to sustainability would have the potential to add depth and real insight to our understanding of how social exclusion operates. Unfortunately this cannot happen because the only type of definition used is the outcome-oriented one which is not so amenable to interpretation in terms of social cohesion or sustainability as it is to individual quality of life.

A second form of overlap takes place between the goal dimensions and the measurement dimensions (which provide the gateway to the indicators). Given that the goal dimensions are mediators between the measurement dimensions and the three constructs that comprise the overarching model, it is not clear how the indicators are aggregated. The issues involved here can be seen in relation to the operationalisation of the measurement dimensions for each relevant life domain. An example of the complexity involved is given below just using the measurement dimensions of the two social cohesion goal domains. For each goal dimension the relevant measurement dimensions are given (underlined) followed by each relevant life domain. Further details on the sort of indicator are provided where this is not obvious. Some goal dimensions have more bullet points than others because not all life dimensions are relevant to each goal dimension.

Measurement dimensions for social cohesion

These dimensions are taken from Berger-Schmitt and Noll (2000: 46–57), augmented by Berger-Schmitt (2000: *passim*).

1 Reduction of disparities, inequalities and social exclusion within a society

Objective and subjective evaluations of inequality of income levels and standard of living.

Regional disparities in:
- housing conditions
- access to and quality of transport
- leisure, media and culture, availability of facilities and goods
- access to and investment in education and vocational training
- labour market and working conditions; employment opportunities and risks
- income level and standard of living
- health-care facilities
- state of the environment
- public safety and crime: crime rates
- total life situation: 'quality of life index' (not specified).

Equal opportunities (subdivided by gender; generations; social strata; disability; citizenship groups)
- households and families: housework, child care, existence of family relations

- housing conditions
- access to transport
- access to leisure time and to leisure, media and culture facilities
- social and political participation and integration: social and political activities and engagement, availability of social relations and social support
- education and vocational training: educational enrolment and qualifications
- labour market and working conditions: employment opportunities and risks
- income levels and standard of living
- health status
- social security social insurance coverage, benefits
- public safety and crime, becoming a victim of crime
- total life situation: 'quality of life index' and overall subjective well-being.

Social exclusion
- housing: homelessness, poor housing conditions
- lack of access to public and private transport
- social and political participation and integration: social isolation, social discrimination
- lack of completed education and vocational training
- labour market and working conditions: long-term unemployment
- income levels and standard of living: poverty
- permanent health impairments
- total life situation: multiple deprivation.

2 Strengthening the social capital of a society

Availability of social relations
- households and families: existence and intensity of family relations, care for old-age household members, quality of relations between household members
- leisure, media and culture: membership of leisure associations, activities in leisure organisations
- social and political participation and integration: existence of personal relations, membership of political and social organisations
- social and political activities and engagement: frequency of contacts, support in informal networks, volunteering, political engagements.

Social and political participation and integration
- frequency of personal contacts, support in informal networks, civil engagement in the public realm
- labour market and working conditions: participation in the area of working life.

Quality of social relations (for example, shared values, conflict, solidarity)
- households and families: quality of relations between household members
- social and political participation and integration: extent of trust, feelings of

belonging, shared values, solidarity, conflicts, attitudes towards population groups, loneliness
• labour market and working conditions: quality of relations in the workplace.

Quality of societal institutions
• social and political participation and integration: political, religious and social institutions
• trust in:
    • education and vocational training institutions
    • labour market and working conditions: trade unions, labour offices, labour courts
    • health-care systems
    • social security institutions
    • public safety and crime: legal system.

European-specific concerns: aspects of social cohesion between individual countries (e.g. European identity)
• quality of transport connections and frequency of journeys between European countries
• leisure, media and culture: dissemination of cultural products
• social and political participation and integration: European identity; social relations and attitudes to nationals from European countries; similarities in basic values and attitudes; social and political activities at the European level
• education and vocational training: exchange of pupils, students, apprentices; teaching and dissemination of European languages
• labour market and working conditions: connections between European countries in working life.

There are forty-seven nodes of measurement dimensions/life domains for social cohesion and there is scope for many different indicators at each node, and there are many more nodes for the other two constructs, so it is clear that operationalising this European System of Social Indicators is a major logistical endeavour. Aggregating and collating them, even within each measurement dimension will be a huge task and there are no published data sets at present covering all these dimensions. Considerable progress has, however, been made. Indicators and time series data are now available for between twenty and thirty countries covering seven of the proposed domains (GESIS, 2005).

Regina Berger-Schmitt has also undertaken a pilot study in relation to social cohesion which has produced some interesting and important illustrative material, including indicators on gender inequality in earnings, the quality of social relations, and on European identification (Berger-Schmitt, 2000, 2002). She concludes:

> Empirical results show considerable deficiencies in social cohesion, both within and between European countries. There is also some empirical evidence that social cohesion improves other aspects of quality of life in a society, although

the details and mechanisms of this relationship have still to be clarified further. This underlines the importance of developing indicators of social cohesion and analysing their impact on quality of life. Maybe it will turn out that policies aiming at strengthening the social cohesion of a society will also promote individual quality of life.

(Berger-Schmitt, 2002: 423)

There are some hopeful signs here but it is also clear that the empirical relationship between the elements of the overarching quality of life construct are not at all clear and that there is no unambiguous theoretical pathway either among them or between them and the overall model.

It is too early to come to a balanced judgement on how this construct can work in practice and on its empirical usefulness. In both conceptual and operational terms it is a construct still in a prototype stage, open to alternative and perhaps conflicting interpretations. Noll concludes:

Having developed the conceptual framework and the main elements of the architecture of the European System of Social Indicators, the scientific community as well as policy makers are supposed to examine and discuss the suggestions made. This process of reviewing and critical perception and reaction will be of crucial importance to validate and improve this new tool of social monitoring and reporting.

(2002: 81)

Given its foundation in EU policy promulgation, the overarching quality of life construct will always have a pragmatic orientation, but it needs to be remembered that it has a very strong and unequivocally ideologically radical foundation based upon an egalitarian conception of social cohesion, a commitment to combat social exclusion and a forceful emphasis on sustainability. The final construct discussed in this chapter, social quality, has a similarly radical ideological orientation, but differs in its unremitting emphasis on the importance of theory in articulating and justifying the construct.

Social quality

There are many similarities between the overarching quality of life approach and social quality. Perhaps the most important is that they both come from the same European tradition based upon the EU goals of enhancing social cohesion and combating social exclusion. In this context they are both overtly normative in their approaches to social cohesion: they both espouse an egalitarian formulation and see the reduction of disparities as central to their vision of 'quality'. They both have a strong social policy focus in striving to achieve social justice through Europe-wide social policies. Their genesis is somewhat different; overarching quality of life is firmly embedded within the rubric of EU goals as set out by treaties, laws and White Papers, whereas social quality emerged from a critique of, and as a counterbalance to, an *economic* rather than a *social* conceptualisation of quality of life within the EU. Social quality is seen very much as a humanistic antidote to the highly utilitarian and ubiquitous practice of equating quality of life with income or wealth. So one major impetus for the construction of social quality has been to produce an alternative measure to GDP for assessing the quality of societies.

One other major difference – *the* major difference according to the promulgators of social quality – between social quality and overarching quality of life is that the ultimate justification of social quality is as a coherent theoretical edifice. So, in other words, social quality is to be judged, not just as a conceptually consistent, transparent and usable policy tool in the furtherance of social justice but also and more importantly as a comprehensive, consistent and rational theoretical structure; a construct that encapsulates and explains societal quality of life or, more precisely *social quality*. The theoretical underpinning is discussed below. Before that, the inception and development of the construct are sketched out, along with a brief 'anatomy' of social quality.

In June 1997, a group of academics launched the *Amsterdam Declaration on the Social Quality of Europe*, timed to coincide with a meeting of the EU heads of state under the auspices of the then Dutch Presidency of the EU. The preamble to the declaration is as follows:

> Respect for the fundamental dignity of all citizens requires us to declare that we do not want to see growing numbers of beggars, tramps and homeless in the cities of Europe. Nor can we countenance Europe with large numbers of unemployed, growing numbers of poor people and those who have only limited access to health care and social services. These and many other indicators demonstrate the current inadequacy of Europe to provide social quality for all its citizens.
>
> (Walker, 1998: 109–10)

Social quality is defined as: 'the extent to which citizens are able to participate in the social and economic life of their communities under conditions which enhance their well-being and individual potential' (Beck *et al.*, 1997a: 3).

The social quality of a collectivity is not just the accumulation of the life quality of each of its individual members: it incorporates collective as well as individual attributes and is holistic in its orientation. A society with high social quality is envisaged by its promulgators as one where 'citizens must have access to an acceptable level of economic security and of social inclusion, live in cohesive communities, and be empowered to develop their full potential' (Walker, 1998: 109).

The influence of social quality in both academic and policy circles has grown rapidly. The 1997 *Amsterdam Declaration* was signed by seventy-four academics from the fields of social policy, sociology, political science, law and economics. By the end of 1999 it had been signed by 1,000 European social science academics, and the European Union has now actively embraced the concept and has incorporated it into its social reporting. The primary European Union annual social statistical report, *The Social Situation of the European Union 2001*, is themed around social quality. In addition, the European Commission's Directorate General for Employment and Social Affairs chose social quality as one of its three priority area for action in 2000. Two books have been devoted to the exposition and theoretical development of social quality (Beck *et al.*, 1997b, 2001b) with a third book in the pipeline, and an international journal devoted to the topic – the *European Journal of Social Quality* was inaugurated in 1999. Social quality is now probably the most thoroughly theorised and operationalised societal quality of life construct.

The anatomy of social quality

Social quality is intended to be comprehensive and to encompass both objective and subjective interpretations. Central themes are resources and social relations. Its theoretical foundation is predicated upon the 'realisation of the social' as follows: 'the subject matter of "the social" refers to the outcomes of the dialectic between processes of self-realisation of individual people as social beings and processes resulting in the formation of collective identities' (Baers *et al.*, 2005). The theoretical power of this formulation has been graphically illustrated by Ferge's (1997) analysis of the 'individualisation of the social' in contemporary Eastern Europe where this dialectic has resulted in highly individualistic individual self-realisation as a response to the previous predominance of collective identities in the Soviet era.

Social quality has four 'conditional factors' – socio-economic security; social inclusion; social cohesion; social empowerment – which can be defined and delineated as follows:

• *Socio-economic security is the extent to which people have sufficient resources over time*. It concerns the outcomes of the provision of protection by collective entities (communities as well as systems and institutions) as conditions for processes of self-realisation. Socio-economic security has two aspects: (1) all welfare provisions which guarantee the primary existential security of citizens (income, social protection, health), basic security of daily life (food safety, environmental issues, safety at work) and internal freedom, security and justice; and (2) enhancing people's life chances: 'Its mission is to enlarge the realm of options between which people can choose' (Beck *et al.*, 2001c: 341). Its domains are:
   • financial resources
   • housing and environment
   • health and care
   • work
   • education.
• *Social inclusion is the extent to which people have access to institutions and social relations*. It refers to participation and to processes of being included in collective identities and the realities that determine self-realisation. Social inclusion is connected with the principles of equality and equity and their structural causes. Its subject matter is citizenship, which 'refers to the possibility of participation in economic, political, social and cultural systems

and institutions' (Beck *et al.*, 2001c: 346). This participation has three dimensions: material – articulating and defending special interests; procedural – guaranteeing citizens' public and private autonomy; and personal – voluntary participation. Its domains are:

- citizenship rights
- labour market
- public and private services
- social networks.

- *Social cohesion is the nature of social relations based on shared identities, values and norms.* Social cohesion refers to solidarity as the basis for collective identities and concerns the processes that create, defend or demolish social networks and the social infrastructures underpinning these networks. An adequate level of social cohesion is one which enables citizens 'to exist as real human subjects, as social beings' (Beck *et al.*, 1997c: 284). In effect, this conceptualisation of social cohesion is equivalent to Lockwood's concept of social integration, encompassing civic integration as well as Lockwood's micro-version of social cohesion. Its domains are:
  - trust
  - other integrative norms and values
  - social networks
  - identity.

- *Social empowerment is the extent to which the personal capabilities of individual people and their ability to act are enhanced by social relations.* Social empowerment is the realisation of human competencies and capabilities, in order to fully participate in social, economic, political and cultural processes. It refers to being enabled to engage in collective identities as essential preconditions for self-realisation and primarily concerns enabling people, as citizens, to develop their full potential. Three types of empowerment are identified: (1) personal: knowledge, skills and experiences that lead to self-respect and self-development; (2) social: interpersonal, intermediary and formalised relationships; and (3) political: access to processes of decision-making, information and resources. Its domains are:
  - knowledge base
  - labour market
  - supportiveness of institutions
  - public space
  - personal relations.

There is a strong normative and ideological content to social quality both overall in terms of its emphasis on enhancing the well-being and potential of individuals through participating socially and economically and in relation to each of its conditional factors. Its socio-economic security element relates to a fairer distribution of wealth and to social justice; social inclusion refers to enhancing citizens' rights; social cohesion implies an interdependent moral contract and solidarity; and empowerment refers to equity in life chances (Beck *et al.*, 2001c: 314).

Its theoretical basis is linked to its normative orientation through the emphasis on *the social* with regard to the links between individual self-realisation and the development of collective identities. 'The social' is realised with regard to the four conditional factors in terms of 'the social quality quadrangle of the conditional factors' (see Figure 6.2). This quadrangle is central to the epistemology of the social quality construct and is continuing to undergo theoretical development (ibid.: 323–52; Baers *et al.*, 2005).

The quadrangle lies at the intersection of two dimensions or continua. One – displayed horizontally – ranges from systems, institutions and organisations on the one side, through to communities, configurations and groups, on the other. This continuum is conceptually similar to Lockwood's model of system integration and social integration, discussed in Chapter 5. The other dimension ranges vertically from 'biographical processes' at the bottom to 'societal processes' at the top. Here, biographical and societal processes can be seen as approximating to the micro and macro level respectively, these distinctions being not dissimilar to the micro–macro framework used by Woolcock (1998) and Narayan (1999). Each of the dimensions bridges the interaction between the individual and the social: the horizontal dimension in terms of actors and the vertical dimension in terms of processes.

The intersection of these two axes results in four sectors, in each of which Beck *et al.* (2001c) have located one of the social quality elements. Social empowerment is positioned in the bottom right-hand sector where communities, configurations and groups interact with biographical processes. This appears to be entirely apt given that empowerment is specifically about individuals and groups being enabled to act – to engage in biographical processes – in realisation of their collective identities. There is some interaction with the other sectors of the quadrangle in that social institutions and societal processes are involved in enabling process but this can be seen as a secondary rather than a primary aspect of social empowerment.

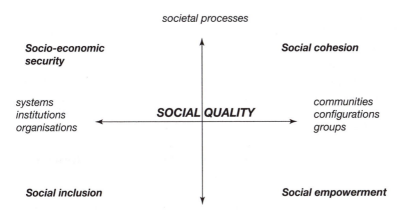

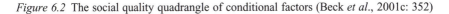

Figure 6.2 The social quality quadrangle of conditional factors (Beck *et al.*, 2001c: 352)

Socio-economic security is in the top left-hand sector, where systems, institutions and organisations meet societal processes. Viewing socio-economic security from the perspective of the provision of resources by collective entities, this can be seen as an appropriate 'anchor', although its influence permeates the other three parts of the quadrangle. It particularly affects the bottom right sector in that it directly affects individual actors in their daily lives. Beck *et al.*, however, do not have universal support for this approach. Svetlik (1999), for example, situates socio-economic security unequivocally in the *bottom* left-hand sector given that it refers both to institutions and biographical processes.

The rationale for the positioning of the other two conditional factors is rather more opaque. Baers *et al.* (2005) places social cohesion in the top right-hand sector and social inclusion in the bottom left-hand sector, but this does not take into account the interaction between these two elements identified by Berger-Schmitt (2000) and Wessels and Miedema (2002). Phillips and Berman (2001b) suggest that social cohesion is as relevant to systems, institutions and organisations as it is to communities, configurations and groups because it is dependent upon the societal systems and institutions that regulate access to public goods and services. Their perspective is consistent with Lockwood's formulation of civic integration and Coleman's insistence that social capital, a foundation for social cohesion, is social structural in orientation. From this alternative perspective, social cohesion can be seen as being anchored to the whole of the upper half of the quadrangle. Similarly, although undeniably relevant at the societal level, issues of social cohesion are arguably pertinent at the biographical or micro-level too because of social cohesion's associational content. Therefore, rather than just occupying one discrete point, social cohesion is placed by Phillips and Berman (2001b) in a zone that maps on to all four areas of the social quality quadrangle as well.

Similarly, Berman and Phillips (2000) argue that social inclusion, while depending upon infrastructures which prevent or minimise exclusion, particularly in its process-oriented manifestation, is also primarily concerned with communities, groups and citizens (particularly in its outcome-orientation) and therefore perhaps should be situated across the whole of the horizontal continuum. Similarly, exclusionary processes operate throughout the whole of the vertical continuum. Therefore, they classify social inclusion as pervading all four parts of the social quality quadrangle. In this context, it is noted above that Berger-Schmitt (2000) identifies a complex relationship between social exclusion and social cohesion, and situates outcome-oriented social exclusion *within* the ambit of social cohesion, which Beck *et al.* placed in the top right-hand sector, rather than as a separate and discreet entity. In this context there are considerable similarities between Berger-Schmitt's approach to social cohesion and Wessels and Miedema's (2002) discussion of social exclusion, as noted in Chapter 3.

This raises an important theoretical issue of whether the four conditional factors of social quality are entirely independent of one another, each occupying a discrete sector of the quadrangle with no overlap between them, thus implying that the two axes demarcate inviolable and uncrossable borders providing the conceptual delineation between the components of social quality, or whether the conditional factors are, instead, four *facets* of an indivisible whole, with these facets merging into each other and providing overlapping and complementary insights into the holistic and indivisible entity that is social quality.

In other words, the question is whether the social quality quadrangle is largely a heuristic device to enhance understanding and conceptualisation of the social quality construct or whether it is conceived primarily as an analytical tool for differentiating between the conditional factors. If the former then, the axes of the quadrangle can be seen as being indicative continua; if the latter, then they are closer to dichotomies. If they are dichotomies, then each of the cells is definitionally discrete and there is no possibility of overlap between them. If, on the other hand, they are continua and are only represented as a quadrangle for presentational purposes then, following Phillips and Berman (2001b), the quadrangle can be treated topographically, with each component occupying a zone that may encompass more than one cell.

Svetlik (1999: 76) insists that the four components need to be mutually exclusive and exhaustive in order to achieve the operational definitions necessary for research and policy-making: 'one might otherwise encounter certain problems and criticisms pointing towards the overlapping of particular components and the neglect of significant cases'. On the other hand, Berman and Phillips (2000) see complementarity and overlap as both necessary and appropriate.

Beck *et al.* (2001c) agree that the relationship between the four social quality elements is not linear or strictly causal. They identify an analytic technique whereby, in principle, the effects of each element on each of the others should be simultaneously taken into account. Baers *et al.* (2005: 13–14) accept that 'in the context of the social quality theory the four conditional factors are . . . intrinsically connected with each other. Social cohesion, for example, is not defined as such as an entity *sui generis*.' Phillips and Berman (2001b) come to a similar conclusion, but they reach it from a somewhat different perspective. They argue that their proposal of moving away from discrete classification within separate sectors of the social quality quadrangle more accurately represents the dynamics of the relationship between the four social quality factors. Part of the resulting untidiness in representation of the components of social quality on the quadrangle can be explained by what they claim to be the appropriate and necessary complementarity and overlap between the factors.

This complementarity is evident from the domains for each factor. For example, the labour market is a domain in two of the factors and work is a domain in a third. Similarly, there are social network domains in two of the factors. In a similar context, Berger-Schmitt and Noll (2000: 40) mention that there are substantial overlaps of indicators between the goal dimensions in their overarching quality of life construct because an unequivocal assignment of measures to discrete dimensions is not always feasible. Therefore, in practical terms, there is consonance between the outcomes of Beck *et al.*'s formulation and Phillips and Berman's topographical approach to operationalising the social quality construct (and this matches the conclusions drawn from the exponents of the cognate overarching quality of life construct).

Social quality and theory

With the social quality quadrangle becoming more of a heuristic device than a theoretical foundation, there appears to be a theoretical gap between the definition of social quality as 'the extent to which citizens are able to participate in the social and economic life of their communities under conditions which enhance their well-being and individual potential' (Beck *et al.*, 1997a: 3) and its operationalisation in terms of the four conditional factors of socio-economic security, social inclusion, social cohesion and social empowerment. Baers *et al.* (2005) attempt to fill this gap through the presentation of five theses.

The first thesis, 'constitutive interdependency', is the foundational social quality statement that the subject matter of 'the social' refers to the outcomes of the dialectic between processes of self-realisation of individual people as social beings and processes resulting in the formation of collective identities.

The second thesis is that this constitutive interdependency is determined by the four conditional factors of socio-economic security, social inclusion, social cohesion and social empowerment. These four factors are chosen because:

> First, people must have the possibilities for self-realisation as well as the capability to interact (social empowerment). The institutional and structural conditions must be accessible to them for the effectuation of their empowerment (social inclusion). People have to dispose of the necessary material and immaterial resources that facilitate their self-realisation, these interactions and the meant effectuation (socio-economic security). Finally, there should be the necessary collectively accepted values and norms that enable community building as sources for the development of self-realisation, actions and interactions (i.e. social cohesion).
>
> (Baers *et al.*, 2005: 4)

The third thesis states that people are constituted into conscious social actors through the outcome of the interaction between constitutive dependency and the dynamics of the tension between societal processes and biographical processes.

The fourth thesis identifies four 'points of gravitation' or 'constitutional factors' derived from the dynamics of the third thesis. These are: participation; responsiveness; social justice; and social recognition. The constitutional factors relate to the dynamics of the third thesis in a way that can be represented by another quadrangle: 'the quadrangle of the constitutional factors of social quality competence' (see Figure 6.3). It is important to note that, as with the social quality quadrangle, here too 'the four constitution factors are not restricted to the four parts but they will cross the axes' (Baers *et al.*, 2005: 7). The fifth thesis, mirroring the third thesis, states that the tensions between the axes 'function as sources for dynamics which influence the nature of the self-realisation of the individual and the formation of collective identities' (ibid.: 8).

It can be seen that two different 'quadrangles' arise from these five theses, each quadrangle leading in a somewhat different direction. The conditional factors lead

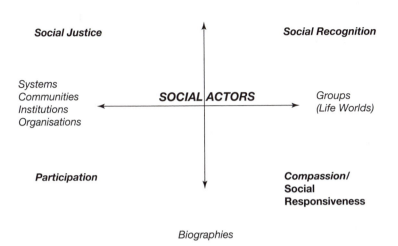

Figure 6.3 The quality competence quadrangle of the constitutional factors of social quality competence

to sets of domains and indicators, mostly based on objective data, that have been identified and tested and are being piloted in thirteen EU nations. The constitutional factors are in the early stages of development and have yet to be theoretically fleshed out. Eventually they will lead to sets of more subjectively-oriented 'profiles' of social quality which will complement and add depth to the more objective indicators derived from the conditional factors.

The theoretical ambitions for social quality are thus huge in scope and they are at present in their early stages. Focusing on the four conditional factors, it can be seen that their theoretical justification, as presented in the second thesis, is plausible and – as far as it goes – probably non-controversial. Each of the factors can be justified as an operationalisation of 'the social' and as an aspect of social quality. But there are other contenders too and many of these have not been discussed. Even those that have been discussed have been rather cursorily dismissed, for example, whether the inclusion of needs would be relevant for countries as developed as those of the EU (Baers *et al.*, 2005). This dismissal might be apt for basic needs but certainly is not in relation to, for example, Doyal and Gough's theory of human need which deserves critical attention in relation to social quality.

Similarly, the capabilities perspective deserves consideration here, as does social integration as an alternative to social cohesion and/or social inclusion. Indeed, the notion of capabilities has considerable resonance with the definition of social quality itself in that both focus strongly on enhancing individual well-being through enhancing human potential and capabilities and having the ability to participate. Also, as seen above, Berger-Schmitt and Noll made a compelling case for the inclusion of a social dimension of sustainability in their construct: there appears to be no *prima facie* reason why sustainability should be seen as not being relevant to the creation of collective identities through processes of individual self-realisation that is the foundation of social quality. It may well be the case that the four conditional factors chosen are the best but this has yet to be demonstrated. Also, given the non-necessity of exact and discrete matching on the quadrangle, there is no *theoretical* reason why there should be exactly *four* factors – there could equally be more or less.

Therefore, considerable theoretical work still needs to be done on both of the social quality quadrangles, both as separate theoretical entities and in their inter-actions with each other. It is not clear, for example, where the role of the family and of civil society fit in to the social quality theoretical structure (Fairweather *et al.*, 2002). The family seems central to at least three of the conditional factors (socio-economic security, social inclusion and social empowerment) and at least one of the constitutional factors (participation). Similarly, civil society is deeply enmeshed in issues of the conditional factor of social cohesion and to all four of the constitutional factors.

Social quality in action

Social quality, then, is not fully theoretically developed and still faces major conceptual challenges. This is no reason, however, for discarding it. It has no less theoretical justification than any of the other overarching quality of life approaches and it has the great advantage of verisimilitude. Even leaving aside all the dense and complex theoretical justifications, the bringing together of socio-economic security, social inclusion, social cohesion and empowerment as steps in enabling citizens to participate under conditions which enhance their well-being and individual potential has an intuitive ring of truth in relation to common-sense understandings of quality of life for both individuals and communities.

There are two tangible examples of the real-world application of social quality: one, the *European Network on Indicators of Social Quality*, is indicator-based, contemporary, international and quantitative; and the other, *Community Social Quality*, is conceptually-based, relating to socially-excluded ethnos communities including examples from an historical case study of Jewish migrants to Britain.

European Network on Indicators of Social Quality (ENIQ)

This is an EU-funded three-year project aimed at identifying and collecting indicators of each of the conditional factors of social quality for thirteen EU and accession countries. As with all other EU projects, it has an acronym: ENIQ. One of the most intriguing issues that has arisen when trying to identify domains, sub-domains and indicators for social quality is that there can be major differences between countries over even the most basic issues, such as whether a high score on some specific indicators is good or bad. Over most indicators, for example, crime, there has been complete unanimity, but cultural differences have emerged over others. For example, are high levels of state-funded residential provisions for frail elderly people a sign of high or low social quality? From a northern European, particularly Nordic, perspective this can be seen as an indicator of high social quality because it demonstrates high levels of collective solidarity, inclusion and socio-economic security, ensuring that no-one is forced to live on their own in poverty. From a more Mediterranean perspective, it can be seen as a sign of low social quality with the state being forced to intervene to replace the role of the family in caring for its own members as a result of a low level of family solidarity and a breakdown in informal social inclusion networks.

These issues have been discussed at length among network members and the conclusions are distilled in the ENIQ final report (van der Maesen *et al.*, 2005) and reported on in relation to the individual countries in volume five of the *European Journal of Social Quality* (Gordon, 2004).The full list of domains, sub-domains and indicators constructed by the ENIQ group are provided in the Appendix at the end of this book.

Community social quality

The potential of the social quality construct in relation to community studies and community development has been identified by Yitzhak Berman and David Phillips (Berman and Phillips, 2000; Phillips and Berman, 2001a, 2001b, 2003; Phillips, 2001). In this context, a community is distinguished from a society by using Delanty's (1998) formulation of *ethnos* and *demos*. For Delanty, demos is at a macro-level and includes whole societies, countries or nation–states whereas ethnos is a 'cultural community' which derives its identity from ethnic, religious, cultural, regional or linguistic bonds. At its most all-inclusive, an ethnos community can comprise an indigenous ethnic group with its own language, religion and territory in a country dominated by descendants of migrants, such as native Canadians and Americans, Australian aborigines or New Zealand Maoris. Other examples of ethnos communities include Roma throughout Europe, South Asian communities in Britain, Algerians in France and Turks in Germany. Perhaps the weakest form of ethnos community is a town or city district with enough cultural commonality to have a sense of community identity.

Many ethnos communities are among the most disadvantaged and socially excluded in society and typically suffer from multiple deprivations including low levels of socio-economic security and social empowerment. The notion of community social quality is a helpful analytical tool here in that a community's social quality depends on both its own strength as a collective entity and on its relationship, both culturally and in policy terms, to the society in which it resides. For example, a relatively autonomous and self-sufficient ethnos community will thrive in a culturally pluralistic society which has decentralised national government policies empowering local communities but will suffer in a culturally homogeneous, xenophobic society with strong central government control.

Belgium is a good example of a country with decentralised government policies enabling the two ethnos communities, French-speaking and Flemish-speaking, to have virtual self-government across the whole range of health, education and local government services. At the other extreme, France has strong French language requirements for all its immigrant citizens and has a highly centralised system of government that, for example, allows no leeway for cultural difference in its education system (Limage, 2000). The United Kingdom lies between the two, having no language requirements for immigrants and allowing limited self-determination in the educational sphere for ethnos communities by allowing in some circumstances the establishment of quasi-independent but state-funded religious denominational schools.

It can be seen, then, that a community's social quality depends on factors both within and outside the community itself. Both sets of factors need to be positive in order to result in strong community social quality.

Internal community social quality depends upon the interaction of the four conditional factors within the community. Of these, community socio-economic security is to some extent independent of the other three and is, in general, straightforward: the higher the level of community socio-economic security, then the higher the level of community social quality. This is not always the case: as has been seen in Chapter 4, relatively affluent communities can suffer extreme social exclusion. Nevertheless, achieving a high level of community social quality requires a level of socio-economic security that enables its members to have incomes above the 'citizenship threshold' poverty level. Also, other things being equal, any increase in community socio-economic security should lead to an increase in community social quality.

The other three factors are interrelated: strong communities have high levels of empowerment, cohesion and inclusion. It is not just the amount or quantity of these factors that change as a community gets stronger; they change qualitatively too (Phillips, 2002). Strong communities have a powerful sense of identity and are more 'exclusive' than weaker communities in that it is harder to join them (indeed membership is often ascribed and cannot be chosen) and the costs of exclusion are great (Peled, 1992). They also have dense and mutually reciprocal bonds of community cohesion which generally reinforce the community's social quality.

A word of caution is needed here, though, in that some inclusive and powerful communities become inward-looking and valorise internal (and often hierarchical) bonding ties at the expense of external bridging ties and therefore limit the possibilities for integrating more closely within the wider society (Purdue, 2001; Leonard, 2004). Under such circumstances an increase in one aspect of a community's *internal* social quality (cohesion) might reduce its overall social quality by increasing the community's *external* social exclusion.

With regard to external aspects of community social quality, three conditional factors of societal social quality are essential to the development of community social quality: empowerment, cohesion and inclusion. As with the internal factors relevant to community social cohesion, these interact with each other.

The extent to which any ethnos community can have a high level of social quality as a collective entity in its own right depends on the extent it is allowed or encouraged to do so by the socio-political structures and dynamics of the wider society. This refers to the external social empowerment of the community. A community whose leadership and institutions have strong connections with or are embedded in the societal power structure will have greater community empowerment than one which does not. As noted below, the British Jewish community in the last quarter of the nineteenth century was deeply embedded in the higher echelons of British society, with strong links to royalty and the government. This enabled it to optimise its community social quality over a period of mass immigration of destitute, non-English-speaking East European Jews. On the other hand, the British Roma or Gypsy community has never had any involvement with the British socio-political elite and has seen its community social quality diminish with the passage of laws restricting the traditional Roma way of life (Hawes, 1996).

In order for external community empowerment to occur, both the right sort and the right level of societal social cohesion need to be in place. Broadly speaking, societal cohesion, like community cohesion, can be bonding and homogeneous, or bridging and pluralistic. Societies with strongly homogeneous cohesion are monocultural in nature, do not encourage diversity and dissent and can tend towards totalitarianism (Kershaw, 2000). Such societies are not amenable to strong community empowerment or community social quality. Pluralistically cohesive societies are multicultural in nature, respect difference and – up to a point – tolerate dissent. These are the societies in which community empowerment and community social quality are most likely to flourish. The centralised French and federalised Belgian policies on education, noted above, are good examples of homogeneous and pluralistic social cohesion respectively.

The relative strength or weakness of societal cohesion is also relevant. At first sight, it would appear that low societal cohesion is consistent with high levels of community social quality, such as in Belgium with a federal state and strong ethnos communities. However, the traumatic disintegration of the former Yugoslavia, with catastrophic consequences for the social quality of some of its ethos communities, shows that the situation is more complex than this. Following Phillips and Berman (2003) it is perhaps safest to conclude that there might be no 'best model' for societal cohesion: 'for some countries, relatively high levels of homogeneity consistent with tolerance and liberal democracy may be the most appropriate formula; whereas for others, wide-ranging pluralism coupled with enough cohesion to avoid social disintegration may be best' (Phillips and Berman, 2003: 348). The British response to the Jewish immigrants, discussed below, is an example of the former whereas the Canadian approach to its Anglophone and Francophone communities reflects the latter approach.

The third societal conditional, social quality factor – inclusion – can perhaps be best approached in relation to individual community members. The overall social inclusion of community members will be enhanced if the community itself is strongly included in society in its own right. Conversely, even a strong community with high levels of internal social inclusion will have a low overall social inclusion and social quality level if the community is not fully included in society. In addition, its members will have low levels of social inclusion within society as a whole. For example, in most European countries Gypsy communities find themselves in this position; they have high levels of community inclusion and cohesion but are prey to discrimination and social exclusion (ibid.: 351). Here, until the community's inclusion in society is enhanced, there is often a trade-off between societal and community inclusion: for an individual to be included in wider society it may be necessary to hide or deny membership of the ethnos Gypsy community (Hawes, 1996).

The British Jewish and Muslim communities provide interesting case studies of the ups and downs of community social inclusion. For over 150 years the Jewish community has had a special status in British society, initially through government recognition of the role of the Chief Rabbi and the Jewish Board of Deputies in community governance (including civil and marital law) and subsequently in relation to education (Phillips, 2002). The level of its inclusion in society can be gauged by the fact that the community is often referred to as *Anglo-Jewry*.

Anglo-Jewry went through a difficult time at the turn of the twentieth century when Britain had to cope with 150,000 East European Jewish refugees. But, the community itself policed the immigrants, repatriated those who were not able to become financially self-sufficient, provided financial support for those who needed it, and provided education through the Jews Free School which at its height had over 3,000 pupils at any one time (Black, 1988; Godley, 1996). Its success in coping with this crisis further strengthened the community's inclusion in British society (Feldman, 1994).

The Anglo-Jewish community had all the ingredients of community social quality which enabled it to cope with the huge influx of immigrants. It had high levels of socio-economic security through its wealthy families, including some of the richest merchant bankers in the country. It had extremely high levels of internal social inclusion and cohesion through its religious and cultural rituals and traditions; and even though it was subject to religious discrimination, it was otherwise extensively empowered. Its societal inclusion was very strong through its links with the Royal Family and politicians, including a Prime Minister, Disraeli, of Jewish descent (Lipman, 1954). Its initially strong community inclusion was stretched to the limits by the influx of non-English-speaking immigrants unused to British social mores. In response Anglo-Jewish community leaders endeavoured to reduce the risks of anti-Semitism and to 'Anglicise' the immigrants by strongly encouraging them to learn the English language and English customs; stringent public health enforcement; ensuring that no Jews were in receipt of government social assistance; and implementing civil law through *Beth Din* courts (Gartner, 1960).

The British Government encouraged Anglo-Jewry to look after its own community and enabled it to take responsibility for a range of functions normally undertaken by national or local government bodies, including, immigration control, social security, education, civil law, and public health. Thus, the Anglo-Jewish community took charge of many areas of citizenship rights and responsibilities.

The British Muslim community, on the other hand, has never achieved such a high level of inclusion in society. The primary reason for this is that the community itself has not achieved similar levels of either internal cohesion or inclusion to that of the Anglo-Jewish community; and this in turn has led to the Muslim community having a relatively weak collective identity. In particular, it does not have an individual or collective leadership that is unambiguously recognised either at national level or by the community itself.

Compared to Anglo-Jewry, the British Muslim community has been severely disadvantaged on two counts (Dwyer, 1993). First, it is not so well established: large-scale Muslim immigration, initially from Pakistan, only started in the 1960s and there was no well-established, societally included, Anglo-Muslim community to welcome them or to act as role models for Anglicisation. This had implications for both community and individual social inclusion. Lack of community inclusion has precluded access to high levels of governmental decision-making that enabled Anglo-Jewry to lobby and negotiate on behalf of its interests. Lack of individual inclusion – exacerbated by the Salman Rushdie affair and the aftermath of September 11th 2001 – has had double-edged consequences: (1) among the majority community there has been an increase in Islamophobia and racist attacks on Muslims (Parekh, 1995); and (2) there has been a rise in quasi-separatist self-determination among Muslim communities, particularly with regard to education, that is, the antithesis of community inclusion. Thus instead of the community taking responsibilities on itself as a distinct element of its members' national citizenship rights – i.e. via Anglicisation striving to be *more* British – it does so to insulate itself from mainstream society, i.e. striving for an identity that is not unequivocally British (Joppke and Lukes, 1999; Vasta, 2000; Schuster and Solomos, 2001).

Second, most Muslim immigrants from the Indian sub-continent come from rural backgrounds and do not have the high levels of human capital of the earlier urban East European Jewish immigrants (Shaw, 1988). This means, among other things, that the level of community socio-economic-security has always been much lower among British Muslims than in the Anglo-Jewish community (Werbner, 1990).

Putting the above elements together, it can be seen that there are both internal and external aspects to a community's social quality. Internally, community social quality depends upon socio-economic security and the interaction between community cohesion, inclusion, and empowerment. Externally the situation is rather more complex. It is essential for a community to achieve a high level of inclusion in society and to be societally empowered in order to have influence at the national level. Also the nature of societal social cohesion constrains the extent to which any community can reach out and be responsible for aspects of its members' social quality that would otherwise be under the control of national or societal institutions.

Conclusion

All three of the societal quality of life constructs discussed here show a strong commitment to high levels of social cohesion based on egalitarianism and social justice. This basis is of course, ideologically controversial: from some ideological perspectives egalitarianism is not necessarily a suitable goal, except for equality before the law, equality of access and equality of opportunity. As Bernard points out, solidarity and equality do not necessarily have to go together. Many highly solidaristic ideologies are not egalitarian, the most notable examples in twentieth-century Europe perhaps being Fascism and Nazism.

Two other questions about solidarity and equality arise. The first, global, issue is the extent of inequality that is acceptable and whether there is an inequality threshold or a formula related to average incomes as in Barry's (1998) approach and in the EU poverty line. None of the three models give a direct answer to this question. The closest Bernard gets to specificity is to equate equality with social justice; Berger-Schmitt and Noll lump together reduction of disparities, inequalities and social exclusion but do not say how *much* reduction should take place; and social quality addresses issues of sufficiency of resources in relation to socio-economic security, which seems to imply a threshold, but does not elaborate on what 'sufficiency' means in this context.

The second issue is about the relationship between pursuing equality, particularly in relation to universal human rights, and simultaneously respecting difference. This issue is addressed directly by Bernard in his quest for a genuinely 'pluralistic democracy' and the discussion above of community social quality shows that the social quality construct is an appropriate vehicle for addressing this issue. Similarly, Berger-Schmitt's (2000, 2002) comparative analysis of the status of women from a social cohesion perspective gives an indication that the overarching quality of life construct can be used in this context. These are all positive signs but none of the proponents of these three models have addressed the substantive trade-offs between universalistic egalitarianism and respect for difference.

The three societal constructs discussed here have all foregrounded social cohesion and egalitarianism – in one form or another – as central ideological attributes of a society with high societal quality of life. In the next chapter these attributes are explored further in the context of a radical and controversial thesis that not only are these attributes ideologically worthwhile and incremental to quality of life in general but they are also causal factors in societies achieving high *quantity* of life too – in other words that it is not in the richest but in the most socially cohesive and egalitarian societies that people live longer and healthier lives.

7   Healthy societies
Quality and quantity of life

One of the premises of the macro-societal models of quality of life is that a society with high quality of life is a better society in which to live than a society with a low quality of life. Perhaps the most certain measure of what makes one society better than another is whether its citizens live longer, healthier and more fulfilled lives. A substantial part of this chapter is taken up with discussing Richard Wilkinson's thesis that – for developed countries at least – it is the social fabric of a society, measured in terms of its income equality and social cohesion, which is the prime determinant of the longevity of its citizens and not the commonly accepted view that it is the country's wealth which is most important.

The chapter begins with a societal quality of life model that could have been appropriately included with the macro-societal models in Chapter 6 but it has been held over to this chapter because it primarily has a health-oriented focus. This is followed by a case study of healthy communities incorporating a health pathways model which again has resonances with Chapter 6 in its emphasis on trust, reciprocity and civic engagement. Finally, Wilkinson's important thesis is explored in depth, along with the contributions from its supporters, critics and detractors.

Hancock's public health model

Hancock (1993) developed a dynamic and interactive holistic and wide-ranging health-related quality of life model. This differentiates between three systems – economic, environmental and community – and portrays all of them as operating from the micro through to the macro-level. This model is explicitly health-related, and focuses particularly on public health. Hancock's approach, in incorporating equity and sustainability, explicitly takes a social justice perspective, embracing what he calls 'ecological sanity'.

The model is based upon first-order relationships within the three systems. It is predicated upon an adequately prosperous economy, a viable environment and a convivial community. Here the notion of an *adequately* prosperous economy depends upon the goal of maximising human rather than economic development. Thus, an adequately prosperous economy is one which fully meets citizens' basic needs, enhances the social system and strengthens a community's social resources.

An environment is seen as viable from a human rather than a biocentric perspective. (Hancock makes the wry point that the most viable environment from the latter perspective might be one with no humans in it at all to disrupt the workings of nature.) From a human perspective, a viable environment is one which sustains life in general and effectively supports human life and well-being in particular.

Finally, according to Hancock, a convivial community 'needs to have support networks, its members need to live harmoniously together and participate fully in the life of their community' (1993: 44). The notion of a convivial community is an important link between two strands of conceptualising quality of life at a collective level, those of public health and social cohesion, which come together in Wilkinson's thesis on equality, social cohesion and healthy societies that is discussed in the next section of this chapter. Hancock (2001) further develops this idea into the notion of 'community capital' whereby the stock of all forms of resources, or 'capital' within a community is increased by harmonious participation.

Each of these systems interacts with each of the others both separately and collectively. The separate interactions take the form of three pairs. First, the viable environment and the convivial community come together to achieve *liveability* which can be defined as being suitable for habitation. A community environment with a high degree of liveability will be one where the built environment of the urban structure is designed in such a way as to support conviviality and to produce a viable human environment. Examples of liveable communities are those with: safe play areas for children; defensible space; effective segregation of pedestrians and traffic with priority given to pedestrian access to social and communal facilities; easily accessible local shops, social venues and municipal facilities; housing designed to provide an effective combination of opportunities for privacy and for neighbourliness, etc. (Raphael *et al.*, 2001).

Second, the viable environment and the adequately prosperous economy need to interact to achieve *sustainability*. For the economy to be environmentally sustainable, economic activity must not deplete renewable resources by using them beyond a sustained yield basis, must keep levels of pollution and other physical by-products of economic activity (e.g. carbon dioxide production) low enough to avoid irredeemable damage to the ecosystem, and must use non-renewable resources sparingly. Following Berger-Schmitt and Noll's (2000) formulation presented in Chapter 6, sustainability in this context entails ensuring that the world will be fit for our children and grandchildren to live in. Hancock identifies the essence of sustainability as residing in 'the need for a system of economic activity that enhances human development while being environmentally and socially sustainable' (1993: 43). This in principle is unproblematic, but the undignified squabbling between nations over the Kyoto Protocol shows that there are serious practical and political problems in attaining sustainability (Brown, 2005).

Third, the convivial community and the adequately prosperous economy are linked together *equitably*. Equity is seen here as the essence of the social sustainability referred to above. This approach is, for Hancock, based on a non-negotiable ethical position:

A key concept here is equity. The earth's resources and the wealth generated by economic activity must be so distributed that everyone's basic needs are met. The prevailing ethical principle is that of equity; people in a fair and just society will have an equal opportunity to achieve health and maximise their own human potential.

(1993: 43)

Hancock's exposition of equity has resonances with the theories met with in Chapter 3. Like prudential values, basic needs, capabilities and Doyal and Gough's theory of human needs, it is predicated on a notion that meeting needs, or at least meeting the most basic and fundamental needs, is an inalienable human right and central to social justice. Hancock is fully aware that this is a controversial position. He clearly states that 'the radical and subversive nature of an ecological approach needs to be recognised' (ibid.: 41).

It can be seen that, in this model, the economy both underpins and should be subservient to health, the convivial community and a viable environment. In addition, the notion of health – public health or community health – is seen as depending upon liveability, equity and sustainability. Hancock's vision here is to develop a holistic approach to public health policy that informs both the development of existing communities and the creation of new communities by addressing their social, environmental, economic, land use, health and human development needs in an integrated manner. His notion of health and of a healthy community is even wider than the WHO definition, in that it incorporates additional dimensions of place and time, the former in relation to the environment and community and the latter in relation to the long-term consequences of sustainability. Indeed, this formulation might have been appropriately discussed in Chapter 6 on macro-visions of quality of life in that its applicability at societal level has considerable similarities to Berger-Schmitt and Noll's overarching quality of life and Beck *et al.*'s social quality constructs.

Healthy communities – a case study

The previous section concentrated on policies to encourage community-based health-related quality of life. Interpersonal relationships, networks, and conviviality were seen to be central features of a healthy community along with Hancock's idea of 'community capital' being enhanced by harmonious participation. This harmonious participation is also central to Wilkinson's thesis on 'healthy societies' which is discussed below. But before jumping to the societal level it is worthwhile to explore a little further the factors associated with harmonious participation that might enhance health in a community.

As noted in Chapter 5, social capital relates to, or even entirely comprises, trust and networks and can be seen as an exemplification of harmonious participation. In an exploration of the extent to which social capital affects the health of communities, a study undertaken in Luton in 1997 compared two relatively deprived areas with approximately equal income levels but different levels of health

(Campbell, 1999). Some of Campbell's findings were unsurprising, for example, that the healthier area had higher levels of trust and of confidence in activist social networks. Other findings were more unexpected, for example, that the less healthy area had higher levels of local identity, more well-established face-to-face networks and more community-oriented lives including extensive street-based peer networks of young people. Again contrary to what might have been expected, the less healthy area had more local amenities and facilities than the healthier area.

The two areas had very different identities and the extent and nature of what can be referred to as their 'community cohesion' were very different. The less healthy area fitted the stereotype of the traditional working-class community described in the classic community studies in the 1950s and 1960s such as Young and Willmott's study of Bethnal Green (Young and Willmott, 1986). Thus, it was a lively community with high levels of visible street activity where residents had strong local, place-based identities and there were vibrant street-based women's networks, mostly small in size and largely centred around children. Also, large groups of youths, sometimes up to forty in number, regularly congregated on street corners, outside off-licences, take-aways, post offices and supermarkets.

Residents in the healthier area, on the other hand, lived more private lives, indeed, the researchers noted that the locality was virtually deserted during the daytime. Their long-term networks were radically different too; instead of 'public place-based' they focused either narrowly on the household or else widely, extending beyond the locality boundaries, reflecting findings in a Canadian community of links between health status and work-based but not locality-based socialisation (Veenstra, 2000) and exemplifying Granovetter's (1973) emphasis on the importance of weak links. There were also short-term, activist networks in this area, which Campbell identified as the most effective feature in distinguishing between the two localities.

> The presence of these often very small-scale successful activist networks and groupings in the community generated an amorphous sense of what we shall call 'perceived citizen power' – a belief in the power of ordinary people to influence local community life – which our pilot study suggests was the most important dimension of health-enhancing social capital in our high-health ward.
>
> (1999: 135)

This leads her to conclude that high levels of civic engagement along with high levels of perceived citizen power are important aspects of health-enhancing social capital (ibid.: 152). More formally, she suggests:

> The civic community is a social network which delivers particular forms of social support to people in health-enhancing ways. Membership of such a social network puts one in the position of giving and receiving a range of forms of health-related emotional, material and instrumental support, with their associated health benefits.
>
> (ibid.: 24)

Unfortunately, it is not entirely clear how this abstract conceptualisation maps onto the specific rather sparse pattern of networks in the more healthy of the two localities studied.

This definition links in with a model of the pathways between social capital and health where macro-social relations interact with levels of social capital in a community and together impact on psycho-social mediators, behavioural pathways, physiological pathways through to health outcomes (ibid.: 28). This is expressed diagrammatically in Figure 7.1.

It can be seen that Campbell's model is very similar to the one presented by Berkman and Glass (2000) except that it foregrounds social capital as a *collective* construct rather than the more individualistic network-based orientation of Berkman and Glass.

Campbell's study is interesting and important; it provides a unique insight in comparing the social capital status of two socio-economically similar areas with different health outcomes. However, although its results show a correlation between different types of social capital and health outcomes, this in itself does not prove

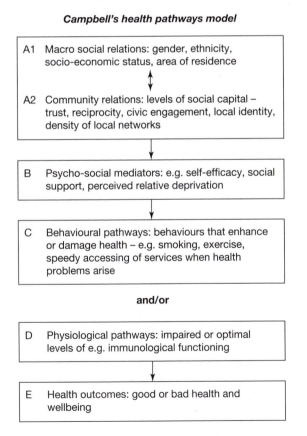

Figure 7.1 Campbell's health pathways model

that there is a *causal* link. There are at least two alternative explanations. The first is that the correlation might be spurious anyway and that there might be other pairs of localities with similar income levels where there is an inverse correlation. The second and, from our perspective, much more important possibility is that another factor, or set of factors, might account for the differences in *both* social capital and health; this factor might, for example, be related to demographic differences in age structure, educational attainment or occupation. If this confounding factor were related to income inequalities within the areas, this could have ominous consequences for protagonists who believe that social capital and/or social cohesion have a major independent impact on health.

This possibility is discussed in more detail below in relation to Wilkinson's thesis, but for the present it can be summarised as follows: if the less healthy area has a wider range of income inequality than the more healthy area, then this might be entirely explained by the income distribution itself. In other words, it is quite possible that individuals in both areas have *exactly the same* income-related morbidity and mortality rates but that the higher proportion of poorer people in one area will lead to lower health rates than in the other area with the same average income but less inequality.

Why are some societies healthier than others?

If two localities can have the same level of income but differing health levels, then the same is also true for nations. There has been a huge amount of research and an extensive debate about what makes one country healthier than another. Among poorer countries there is a strong and obvious association between income and health: a country with not enough money to provide food and basic medical services for all its population will have lower levels of health than one whose citizens are all well-fed and have their basic medical needs met. But there is a heated debate over whether this association also holds among richer countries that have undergone an epidemiological transition into industrialisation and economic development (Lynch *et al.*, 2000; Wilkinson, 2000). Whether or not there is a direct association between national income and health among richer countries, it certainly is the case that some countries with very similar incomes have very different health outcomes.

Wilkinson's thesis: equality, social cohesion and health

Richard Wilkinson, in his seminal book *Unhealthy Societies* and subsequent publications (Wilkinson, 1996, 1999, 2000, 2005), claims that among developed and industrialised countries with roughly the same national incomes, other things being equal, the most egalitarian countries are the most healthy and the most unequal countries are the least healthy – in other words that for two countries with the same GDP, the one with the narrower spread of income (and therefore fewer poor and fewer rich people) would have higher life expectancy than the one with the wider spread of incomes (and more poor and more rich people). This in itself is rather controversial but can be tested empirically (Judge and Paterson, 2001). Wilkinson also claims that some countries such as Greece, Japan, Iceland and Italy, have lower income but higher life expectancies than richer countries such as the USA and Germany (Wilkinson, 1996: 1).

Wilkinson's basic hypothesis is that the higher the level of income inequality, the greater the amount of health inequality. Wilkinson argues that what is important is not absolute income but relative income and the effect of income inequality on the psycho-social conditions of people's lives. In other words, it is the effects of relative deprivation that are crucial.

From this he posits that these differences in health are not caused by the material consequences of the absolute income differences in these countries. Instead, they are caused by the psycho-social consequences of the differences in relative incomes. In other words, Wilkinson believes that, at least in wealthy developed countries, the poverty experienced by an unequal society's poorer members disadvantages them not so much in terms of material deprivation such as poor food, housing, etc. but more in terms of the non-material social environment and their response to it. He claims that it is the social cohesion of more egalitarian societies that makes them healthier and the lack of cohesiveness coupled with the stress and damage to self-esteem suffered by poorest people in unequal societies that makes them more unhealthy.

Wilkinson is somewhat imprecise in his use of the term 'social cohesion' and in *Unhealthy Societies* never pins it down precisely. In Chapter 5 it was noted that the meaning and definition of social cohesion are hotly contested. In this context, Kawachi and Berkman (2000: 175) helpfully summarise Wilkinson's usage of social cohesion as referring to two intertwined features of society: '(1) the absence of latent social conflict – whether in the form of income/wealth inequality; racial/ethnic tensions; disparities in political participation; or other forms of polarisation; and (2) the presence of strong social bonds'. They characterise these strong social bonds as including social capital, civil society, and a responsive democracy. According to Hawe and Shiell (2000: 875), Wilkinson's work also links social capital to social cohesion through the influence that inequality exerts through psycho-social and cognitive mechanisms. They claim that, for Wilkinson, inequality of social status as well as income has a fundamental influence on the content of social relationships and interactions and that this social and status inequality affects not only the health of individuals but also the integrity of the fabric of society itself.

According to Wilkinson, egalitarian societies are more socially cohesive and more trusting; they have a stronger sense of social morality and community life and are highly supportive of their members. In these societies, public space remains a social space and becomes a source of supportive and health-promoting social networks rather than a source of stress, conflict and ill-health. The lower the income differences in a society, the more supportive the environment, the less stressed its citizens and the higher the levels of health they experience. Egalitarian societies suffer fewer of the corrosive social effects of inequality. On the other hand, according to Wilkinson, social inequality damages the social fabric, it increases crime rates and violence, undermines the likelihood of densely overlapping horizontal social networks which characterise egalitarian societies, and it imposes a psychological burden on poorer individuals. In addition, its individualistic values undermine any sense of social solidarity among the rich who isolate themselves from the rest of society in gated communities and use segregated private schools and private health-care services which in turn further reduces the well-being of the whole society.

Wilkinson (1996) produces some persuasive evidence on the major differences in death rates between rich and poor localities and countries. For example, a 1994 study of 678 electoral wards in the northern region of England found that death rates were four times as high in the poorest 10 per cent than the richest 10 per cent of wards (Wilkinson, 1996: 53); and a 1990 study in New York found that death rates in Harlem were higher than in rural Bangladesh (ibid.: 53, 158). In this context he reports that life expectancy for the whole of China in 1990 was virtually the same as in the USA in 1970 even though China, according to the World Bank, had average incomes scarcely 2 per cent of those in the USA (ibid.: 128). This is perhaps the ultimate demonstration of the health-related benefits of egalitarianism, even for a country in an economic phase prior to the epidemiological transition. It is interesting to note, however, that Wilkinson did not speculate whether it was social cohesion or some more tangible reason that led to China having such outstandingly high life expectancy given its extremely modest income levels.

In this context, even Kennelly *et al.* (2003), who strongly dispute Wilkinson's thesis, agree that there is:

> convincing evidence that, within countries, lower income means poorer health and higher mortality . . . all of the studies that have investigated the relationship between income and health over time find that income is significantly related to health outcomes, with income loss having a much stronger effect on health than increases in income.
>
> (ibid.: 2367–8)

Although all the above findings strengthen the case for the relationship between income inequality and health, they do not throw any light upon the role of social cohesion that is so central to Wilkinson's thesis. To rectify this, Wilkinson provides five examples of high levels of equality and cohesiveness: Britain in wartime; Roseto, Pennsylvania; the regions of Italy; Eastern Europe in the 1970s and 1980s; and contemporary Japan:

- *Britain in wartime.* World wars are not events normally associated with reductions in death rates but in Britain during and after both the First and Second World War there was a substantial increase in life expectancy among civilians. In the two decades including the wars, increases in life expectancy more than doubled compared to the average of all other decades between 1901 and 1991 and were over 50 per cent higher than in the next highest decades: by over 6 additional years of life expectancy for both men and women compared with a range from 0.9 to 4.1 in all other decades. Both wars saw a dramatic narrowing of income differentials and a return to full employment. From Wilkinson's perspective, however, it was the camaraderie, sense of common purpose and social cohesion that were central to creating a more healthy society. As noted at the beginning of Chapter 2, the Beveridge Report, looking forward to a more just and equal society can be seen as emblematic of the cohesive and solidaristic British experience of the Second World War.

- *Roseto, Pennsylvania*. This is probably the epitome of Wilkinson's ideal egalitarian, socially cohesive community. Roseto is a small town, close to being a large village, of around 1,600 people, which came to attention in the mid-1930s as having very low death rates, particularly from heart attacks which were around 40 per cent lower than in neighbouring towns. The population was descended from migrants who had arrived in the USA from the Italian town of the same name in the 1880s. It was a very closely knit and egalitarian small town where overtly materialistic and ostentatious behaviour was frowned upon. Researchers were unable to distinguish richer from poorer residents from their dress or their living arrangements. The community was strongly family-based with high levels of neighbourliness characterised by 'unconditional interpersonal support' (Wilkinson, 1996: 117). By the 1960s this ethos had become diluted and consequently, it is argued, not only did the town become more inegalitarian but its death rates increased and by the mid-1970s its health advantage had disappeared entirely.

- *Italy, eastern Europe and Japan*. These three examples are less striking than the other two and are perhaps less robust so they are summarised more briefly here. The Italian example is derived from Putnam's famous 1993 study of differences between northern and southern Italy that did so much to bring the notion of social capital to international attention. Putnam and colleagues found that northern Italy had both more social capital and less income inequality than southern Italy and that there was a correlation between areas of high social capital or civic community and low infant mortality rates. The Eastern Europe example is more complicated but in Sen's careful study of improvements in life expectancy in the 1960s and 1970s found that Eastern European countries had made dramatic advances (with the notable exception of Hungary which had undergone a failed uprising in 1956 with subsequent brutal repression). These findings led Sen to remark that his findings showed that communism is good for poverty removal. Wilkinson argues that it was a strong sense of social cohesion in these years that enhanced life expectancy and that disillusionment with communism in the 1980s led to a loss of advantage even though material conditions improved. Finally, Wilkinson presents contemporary Japan as a classic example of a country where life expectancy is increasing – indeed, it is the highest in the world – at the same time as its income differentials are narrowing and also having a considerably lower GDP than other, less healthy, countries such as the USA.

In drawing together the strands from these examples Wilkinson disarmingly admits that he is not entirely clear about the *direction* of causation between reduction in income differentials and increase in social cohesion: 'Although a narrower income distribution leads to a more egalitarian social ethic, it also looks as if exogenous factors which create a more egalitarian ethic tend also to lead to narrowing income differentials (Wilkinson, 1996: 134). Other researchers have been similarly cautious in attributing causal links. For example, Kennedy (1998) reports that in post-communist Russia there was a dramatic increase in death rates and a similarly large decrease in levels of social capital. He was initially inclined to assume that the decline in social capital had caused the increase in mortality rates but instead found that 'some at least of the observed relationship could be due to the influence of high mortality on social cohesion rather than the reverse' (ibid.: 2308). Similarly, Putnam (2004: 670) takes Wilkinson to task on this issue and speculates that in Sweden, for example, egalitarian policies might well be the *result* rather than the *cause* of 'high levels of connectedness and mutual solidarity'.

So far, Wilkinson has had little to say on the actual mechanisms which enhance health in socially cohesive societies and which adversely affect health in those unequal societies where the social fabric is badly damaged. At the macro-level, social cohesion, incorporating notions of civil society and civic community, comprises high levels of altruism and reciprocity mediated via dense (but not necessarily strong), mostly face-to-face, horizontal associational networks and highly integrated vertical networks between citizens, municipal and national agencies, all characterised by high levels of both specific and generalised trust. According to Wilkinson, citizens in a socially cohesive society will feel safe, secure and unstressed.

However, even this presentation does not give an intuitively clear picture of how individuals' health is enhanced and how their life expectancy is increased. Perhaps a clearer view can be gained from Wilkinson's portrayal of the adverse consequences of an unequal society deficient in social capital and social cohesion:

> To feel depressed, cheated, bitter, desperate, vulnerable, frightened, angry, worried about debts or job and housing insecurity; to feel devalued, useless, helpless, uncared for, hopeless, isolated, anxious and a failure; these feelings can dominate people's whole experience of life, colouring their experiences of everything else. It is the chronic stress arising from feelings like these which does the damage . . . In terms of the quality of life, which is ultimately a matter of people's subjective sense of well-being, the psychological processes around inequality, social cohesion and its effect on health, are overwhelmingly important.
>
> (Wilkinson, 1996: 215)

A crucial concept in the above quote is 'chronic stress'. Wilkinson devotes considerable space in his book to studies of the effects of stress. Starting from relatively inconsequential but clinically proven results, he identifies a strong relationship between stress and vulnerability to minor infectious illnesses such as the common cold (ibid.: 179). It is interesting to note here that students' immunity levels are lower when undertaking examinations. More substantively he refers to evidence that marital breakdown affects the immune system and he cites Rosegreen *et al.*'s (1993) findings that death rates (particularly from cancers and heart disease) were over three and a half times higher among people who had recently experienced major stressful life events (Wilkinson, 1996: 180). Using the example of a specific tragedy in Aberfan, Wales, when a slag heap collapsed and engulfed a local school in 1966, in the following year relatives of the 166 children and 28 adults who died had death rates seven times higher than members of a matched control group (ibid.: 180). These examples led Wilkinson to conclude, perhaps rather surprisingly: 'It is clear that the psycho-social burden we have identified is now *the most important* limitation on the quality of life in modern societies' (ibid.: 230; italics added). Macinko and Starfield (2001: 412) encapsulate the core of Wilkinson's position as proposing that 'perceptions of social inequality lead to stress and poorer health outcomes'.

A vivid example of the potential relationship between inequality and death rates comes not from ill-health *per se* but from a more dramatic cause of mortality – that of murder – where research indicates that the extent of income inequality accounts for over a third of international differences in homicide rates in a study of thirty-nine countries (Wilkinson, 1996: 156). Similarly Kennelly *et al.* (2003) claim that poverty and income are powerful predictors of homicide and violent crime. They hypothesise that the growing gap between rich and poor is mediated through an undermining of social cohesion or social capital, and that decreased social capital is in turn associated with increased firearm homicide and violent crime. They provide evidence that there are strong associations between all three.

In a later study, Wilkinson *et al.* (1998) claim that homicide shows an even closer relationship to income inequality than does mortality from all other causes combined. Their data indicate that not just homicide but also other violent crimes are closely related to income inequality and to levels of social trust. They explore psycho-social processes linking inequality, violence, social cohesion and mortality and conclude:

> What we can take away from this discussion is that the most pressing aspect of relative deprivation and low relative income is less the shortage of the material goods which others have, as the low social status and the desperate lack of sources of self-esteem which usually goes with it. If social cohesion matters to health then perhaps the component of it which matters most is that people have positions and roles in society which accord them dignity and respect.
>
> (ibid.: 594)

It is interesting to note that support from this perspective comes from an unexpected source. An OECD research review, where one might expect to see a defence of the levels of income inequality which derive from capitalist economies, concludes that, controlling for other factors, it is anonymity and limited acquaintance among residents, unsupervised teenage peer groups and low levels of civic participation that predispose communities to high levels of crime in western capitalist nations (OECD, 2001: 53–5).

Development and clarification of Wilkinson's thesis

It is noteworthy that perhaps the clearest exemplification of Wilkinson's thesis on healthy societies arises from mortality associated with crime rather than with 'health' itself. This might be because the social causal pathways seem much clearer for murder than for, say, cancer. Another reason might be more to do with an ambiguity in Wilkinson's (1996) book about the relationship between the societal notions of social fabric and social cohesion, on the one hand, and the health of individual citizens on the other. As noted above, Wilkinson links these via psychological processes related to stress but is less easy to pin down outside the area of violent crime.

In his most recent book *The Impact of Inequality: How to Make Sick Societies Healthier*, Wilkinson focuses less on social cohesion or social capital *per se* and more on the broader notion of social relations (Wilkinson, 2005: 285) and he identifies three specific psychosocial risk factors: low social status; poor social affiliations; and stress associated with early childhood experiences (ibid.: 25). For Wilkinson the scale of income inequality impacts upon these three psychosocial factors via the social relations associated with both social status differentials and relative income differentials: 'The pathway runs from inequality, through its effects on social relations and the problems of low social status and family functionings, to its impact on stress and health' (ibid.: 26).

Kawachi, a strong supporter of the Wilkinson thesis, accepts that the processes by which relative inequality affects health are not well understood, but points to the strong empirical evidence that unequal societies are much less healthy than more egalitarian societies with similar average income levels (Kawachi, 2000: 91). Similarly, Kawachi *et al.* (2004), reviewing recent research, claim that most ecological studies have found a positive association between social capital and population health. In an earlier paper Kawachi hypothesises that increased income inequality leads to increased mortality via a reduction in social cohesion caused by disinvestment in social capital (Kawachi and Kennedy, 1997: 1491).

Kawachi and Berkman (2000) clarify and develop Wilkinson's thesis by making an important distinction between the compositional and contextual effects of social capital. In so doing they link social capital both to collective societal constructs such as social cohesion (which cannot be decomposed to the individual level) and to the support and resources available to individuals through their membership of social networks (which in their collective manifestation help to create the levels of trust, altruism and reciprocity that strengthen social cohesion).

In its collective sense, social capital, derived from social networks, and contributing to social cohesion, has *contextual* effects on people's lives through, for example, facilitating the provision of high quality health facilities in localities with high levels of social capital (Campbell, 1999). This social capital is likewise *composed* of networks providing resources to individuals and thus its compositional facet has a direct and specific effect on the health of individuals. This can be seen most clearly in cases where people are socially isolated and therefore cannot gain from the compositional effects of social capital.

There has been a huge amount of research showing that the health status of socially isolated people is, on average, much lower than that of people who have close networks of family and/or friends (Kawachi and Kennedy, 1997; OECD, 2001; Bolin *et al.*, 2003). Putnam (2000) suggests two reasons for this: first, social networks provide tangible assistance with care which reduces psychic and physical stress; and second, high levels of access to social capital might trigger individuals' immune systems.

Kawachi and Berkman (2000) note that a high number of socially isolated people live in areas of low social capital and that there are, in general, strong links between social isolation and poor health outcomes; this being a compositional effect of individuals having access to only low levels of social capital. However, they also claim that socially isolated people living in areas of *high* social capital do not share this negative fate (ibid.: 185). If this can be unambiguously demonstrated to be the case, then it looks as if compositional social capital cannot be the cause of the enhanced life chances of isolated people living in high social capital areas – because they do not have direct access to the social resources emanating from these networks to which they do not belong. Indeed, it could be argued that they might be prone to *higher* levels of ill-health by their high level of relative inequality in terms of social contacts compared to their well-networked neighbours. Therefore, they receive their health benefit either from the contextual effects of living in areas with high social capital, or else they benefit from other factors, some of which may be correlated with, but not attributable to, social capital.

But what *are* these contextual effects of social capital? According to Kawachi and Berkman (2000), there are at least three plausible pathways at the neighbourhood level by which social capital could affect individual health:

1 By influencing health-related behaviours: for example, by promoting more rapid diffusion of health information or promoting healthy activities; exerting social control over deviant behaviour.
2 By influencing access to services and amenities: this is mostly through local collective action to initiate and then to safeguard local facilities and amenities. Campbell's Luton case study discussed above gives an example of this sort of collective action in the 'healthier' area – action which benefited activists and non-activists, the socially engaged and the socially isolated alike in the locality.
3 By affecting psycho-social processes: including self-esteem and mutual respect, thus trusting social environments beget trustworthy citizens in a virtuous circle – 'Children growing up in a social capital rich neighbourhood quickly learn that people must take a modicum of responsibility for each other even if they have no ties to each other' (Kawachi and Berkman, 2000: 185).

One of the problems in measuring contextual effects is that they are difficult to identify and quantify. Compositional effects are much easier to identify because they can be measured in terms of the nature and extent of people's social contacts and engagement in local activities (Wilkinson, 1996: 5). However, there are two sets of problems here. The first is in distinguishing the more collectively oriented social capital effects of networks and their associated norms from the individual social support consequences of network membership. In practice, this is rather a muddy area (Caughy *et al.*, 2003; Veenstra *et al.* 2005). Here it is worth bearing in mind Kawachi and Berkman's enjoinder to remember that 'social cohesion and social capital are both collective, or ecological, dimensions of society, to be distinguished from the concepts of social networks and social support, which are characteristically measured at the level of the individual' (2000: 175).

The waters get even more muddied when trying to disentangle the effects of human capital from those of social capital. In his post-communist study of Russia, Rose (2000) claims that human capital and social capital together account for a notable amount of variance in health. When they are separated out, he identifies a substantial cumulative effect of social capital on physical health, derived from 'positive involvement in some networks, for example having someone to rely on when ill, control over what happens to oneself, access to market networks, and being plugged into impersonal rather than informal sources of information' (ibid.: 1432). It is worth noting that none of these examples (with the last being a possible exception) meet Kawachi and Berkman's criterion for social capital noted above – that it is *collective* in nature – and perhaps actually relate instead to the individualised notion of social support.

Critiques of – and alternatives to – Wilkinson's thesis

From the above discussion it is clear that Wilkinson's thesis can be separated into two parts: the first is an empirically testable proposition that, other things being equal, egalitarian societies are healthier than inegalitarian societies; and the second is a set of explanatory hypotheses to explain this phenomenon. Broadly, these hypotheses are as follows: first, egalitarian societies have higher levels of social cohesion than unequal societies; second, social cohesion is positively associated with health; third, this positive association is caused by psycho-social pathways whereby high levels of social cohesion reduce levels of disease-promoting individual stress and enhance levels of health-promoting self-esteem; and, finally, that these social pathways are the major cause of enhanced health and are not merely correlated with or caused by other factors which themselves are the major causes of enhanced health.

Both parts of Wilkinson's thesis are examined in this section. The first to be explored is the apparently simple task of testing the extent to which people living in egalitarian societies are healthier than those in inegalitarian societies, controlling for income. The results are not as clear-cut as might be hoped and do not provide the unambiguous across-the-board support for the first part of Wilkinson's thesis. Testing the second part of the thesis is even more complex. The primary task here is to provide clear and unambiguous definitions and measures of social cohesion and social capital. This is followed by an assessment of the methodological rigour of the empirical studies supporting the thesis. Then the strengths of the causal links are assessed in comparison with alternative theoretical approaches. Finally, empirical evidence on the strengths and weaknesses of the alternative approaches is assessed.

Are egalitarian societies more healthy than inegalitarian countries?

This proposition can be expressed in several ways. Wilkinson (2000) presents two different sets of data. The first is a comparison between levels of health (measured by life expectancy) and national income (measured by GDP) among the twenty richest countries. He finds no positive correlation at all between the wealth and health of these countries; indeed, there is a modest negative correlation in that the richer countries in this group have health levels a little below the less rich countries. On the other hand, Lynch *et al.* (2000: 405), in a study of the thirty-three countries with GDP over $10,000, find a strong *positive* correlation between the wealth and health of these countries (r 0.51: p 0.003). Using aggregate data therefore it seems that the cut-off point is crucial. Wilkinson (2000, 2005) criticises Lynch *et al.* for using a wider range of countries than he does. In particular, he objects to the inclusion of the lower-income ex-communist Eastern European countries whose health levels dramatically deteriorated in the 1990s.

Instead of using aggregate statistics with possibly arbitrary cut-off points, an alternative approach is to undertake a country-by-country comparison. One way of doing this is to compare extreme cases: comparing the health status of the wealthiest countries with the wealth status of the healthiest countries. Another, and more systematic, approach is by either comparing the health status of countries with the same average income but different income distributions or comparing the incomes and income distribution of countries with similar health levels. As seen above, Wilkinson has produced examples supporting his thesis using all these approaches. But he has not done so in a comprehensive or even systematic way: there are examples he could have chosen which are not so supportive of his thesis.

Several commentators have reviewed a range of systematic country-by-country and aggregate approaches. Deaton (2001) is the most uncompromising: he concludes both that there is no direct link between income inequality and ill-health and that individuals living in unequal societies are no more likely to be sick or to die than those living in egalitarian societies. Judge and Paterson (2001) are a little more cautious:

> We conclude that the relative effect of income inequality per se as a determinant of population health has been greatly exaggerated. . . . although we cannot dismiss the possibility that income inequality may also act as a marker for other characteristics that influence health.

> (ibid.: 1)

Kennelly *et al.* (2003) interpret the literature up to 2001 as providing only modest support for the view that income inequality is associated with variations in national health and they give examples of four more recent studies providing only little support for a relationship between income inequality and mortality or health.

What is social cohesion and can it be measured?

This topic in general has already been discussed in Chapter 5 so it need not be covered in too much detail here. Suffice it to say that many commentators point out that social cohesion and social capital are often used in the health literature with even less clarity and rigour than in sociological literature (Macinko and Starfield, 2001), and indeed are often used interchangeably. It is noted above that Wilkinson is rather vague in using social cohesion and social capital although he is clear that the former has a major moral dimension and that social capital begets social cohesion (Wilkinson, 1996: 4). Muntaner and Lynch (1999) note that social cohesion, as with many other psycho-social constructs, is intuitively appealing but difficult to define. They strongly criticise Wilkinson's imprecision: 'it is unfortunate that he does not attempt a more rigorous definition of the construct of social cohesion, and settles for "the social nature of public life"' (ibid.: 67–8).

Macinko and Starfield (2001) have undertaken an extensive – and at the time of its publication probably definitive – review of conceptualisations, definitions, operationalisations and indicators of social cohesion as it affects health. They note that virtually all relevant empirical studies opt to measure social capital and do not try to measure social cohesion directly. They conclude that there does not appear to be consensus on the nature of social capital, its appropriate level of analysis, or the appropriate means of measuring it. Further, they state that there is even less clarity on how it might be related to inequalities in health outcomes (Macinko and Starfield, 2001: 410).

In spite of this rather pessimistic conclusion, they are unwilling to abandon the search for links between health and social capital. Even if it is not the only or even the most important explanation, they think that the idea of income inequalities disrupting social relations, norms and trust has a wide intuitive appeal and that it offers an intriguing explanation for one of the pathways linking income inequalities and health status (ibid.: 414). However, they remind us that the causal link can go the other way too and that social and health inequalities may well be the *cause* rather than the result of problems with social cohesion or 'the social fabric'. Kawachi *et al.* (2004) provide an update on Macinko and Starfield's review, identifying a further thirty empirical studies, again with a wide range of diverse indicators of social capital.

Importantly from a quality of life perspective, Macinko and Starfield (2001) remind us that whatever the outcome of the debate on the Wilkinson thesis, it is certain that it is not just medical and physiological factors that cause ill-health: social networks, social support, social class and social hierarchies are all centre-stage in accounting for health outcomes at both national and individual level.

Methodological issues

So there seems to be a consensus that social factors are relevant when trying to understand health inequalities, even if there is at best only limited agreement on how to conceptualise or measure them. Therefore it seems important to undertake empirical studies to try to tease out causality among social variables. Unfortunately, all the major reviews of the literature point not only to conceptual and measurement difficulties but also to methodological problems in many studies (Baum, 2000; Kennelly *et al.*, 2003). Indeed, Judge and Paterson (2001) produce a most pessimistic overview which seems to show that *most* of the studies are too flawed to provide helpful evidence one way or the other. Macinko and Starfield (2001) concur with this judgement and are sceptical about interpreting the results of *any* studies that use only one approach without testing alternatives. For them, the consequences of these methodological problems strike to the very heart of Wilkinson's thesis:

> Moreover, the apparent lack of sufficient empirical justification for the validity and reliability of the different social capital measures casts further doubts on the generalisability of proposed explanatory pathways linking income inequality with health and other social outcomes.
>
> (ibid.: 411)

This fundamental methodological criticism is mirrored by Judge and Paterson who claim that *no* existing studies have found a satisfactory way of identifying clear distinct pathways even relating to more straightforward constructs such as incomes, educational attainment and employment status among individuals. The major problem here is that although these characteristics are conceptually distinct, they are very closely inter-related and difficult to disentangle in practice (Judge and Paterson, 2001: 21).

Other possible explanations

It was seen above that any relationship between health and income inequality at national level is less clear-cut than claimed by Wilkinson. If it *is* to be accepted, however, that there is a link between income inequality and ill-health, Wilkinson's social cohesion thesis is not the only possible explanation for this. So it is necessary to evaluate the alternatives as well.

Three major alternatives are presented in the literature (Kawachi *et al.*, 1999; Baum, 2000; Hawe and Shiell, 2000; Kennelly *et al.*, 2003). These are:

- *individual psychological pathways* – feelings of hopelessness, lack of control and loss of respect. connected to stress through perception of placement in social hierarchy related to access to income (Wilkinson *et al.*, 1998).
- *a neo-materialist approach* – systematic under-investment in human, physical, health and social infrastructure that reduces the resources available to individuals and undermines medical care systems; as the rich get richer they buy their way out of problem areas and become more and more reluctant to support public spending that benefits the whole of society (Muntaner and Lynch, 1999). Baum (2000) augments this approach by focusing on issues of *power*.
- *an 'absolute income approach'* – perhaps the most devastating alternative to the Wilkinson thesis – which postulates that, other thing being equal, egalitarian

nations are *certain* to have slightly higher life expectancy than inegalitarian societies with the same average income, *even if the actual income-related death rates are exactly the same*. In other words the absolute income thesis maintains that any differential death rates are entirely a statistical artefact and have no substantive causes whatsoever (Gravelle,1998; Deaton, 2001; Judge and Paterson, 2001; Kennelly *et al.*, 2003).

Each of these is now dealt with in turn.

First, it might seem odd to be identifying individual psychological pathways as a separate explanation when they are so central to Wilkinson's thesis, particularly in relation to what can be called 'the four S's': stress, self-esteem, social support and social isolation. Wilkinson certainly does place them at the heart of his thesis. However, they do not necessarily have to be related to his central strand of social cohesion. Indeed, there is a major dispute about the dividing line between the individual and the collective here (Wilkinson, 1996; Berkman and Glass, 2000). Whereas Wilkinson (1996) asserts that health problems associated with the four S's are manifestations of a breakdown in social cohesion, Berkman and Glass (2000: 140) insist that the four S's are more to do with the structure of social networks at an interpersonal level than with social cohesion at a societal level. They do not claim that social cohesion is totally irrelevant but instead that it is only one of many important factors.

Judge and Paterson (2001: 21) make a similar point, arguing that although psychological pathways are important for health, they cannot adequately explain it in isolation from other factors. They go even further in agreeing that 'the four S's' are influenced by individuals' perception of their relative position in the social hierarchy but they insist that 'greater attention must be paid to the multiple factors that determine the location of individuals within the social strata in the first place'. These include direct material effects – such as absolute income, state welfare and social security provision, employment opportunities and access to public and private health care – which they claim have a greater impact on the health of those with the lowest relative incomes than their psychological responses to being in this position. In other words, for Judge and Paterson (2001), psycho-social explanations are fine so long as they are seen in the context of, and as being to a large extent, a *consequence* of what Lynch *et al.* (2000) call 'real world living conditions'. It is these which form the basis of the neo-materialist perspective.

Second, a neo-materialist perspective starts from the proposition that improving social cohesion in itself is just not good enough in isolation to attack the material manifestations of inequality. Indeed, there is a suspicion among many neo-materialists that an approach based on social cohesion can be seen as a diversionary tactic to draw attention away from the real issue of structural inequality in conditions and resources and thus, in effect, attempt to shift the responsibility onto the victims of inequality themselves. For example, Hawe and Shiell (2000: 879) criticise Putnam's perspective on social capital, which they see as being 'romantic' and essentially middle class. They even suggest that social capital 'may perhaps even act to dilute social health initiatives already in place' (ibid.: 880). In this context they assert that psychological empowerment is not the same as *real* empowerment.

Similarly, Muntaner and Lynch (1999) criticise Wilkinson's model for implying that social cohesion rather than political change is the major determinant of health. They are concerned that an emphasis on social cohesion can be used for victim-blaming and transferring responsibility for health to communities. In response, Wilkinson (1999: 539) defends the link with social cohesion as a way of 'helping to put greater equality back on the political agenda by making it more attractive'.

Muntaner *et al.* (2001) are unconvinced by Wilkinson's defence and they maintain that the use of social capital and social cohesion is often a 'third-way' ploy to shift the emphasis away from structural inequalities and neo-materialist determinants of health towards a romanticised view of an idealised community and represents a move towards a reduced role for the state and the privatisation of health and social services. Similarly, Coburn (2000) stresses the political aspect of the debate and puts forward the case that the causes of both income inequality *and* of lowered social cohesion can be attributed to the political philosophy of neo-liberalism. He claims that this has led to a massive reduction both in working-class power and the ability of the working classes to defend public services. It is clear, therefore, that one strand of the neo-material perspective is to do with political power. Rather than the lack of social cohesion, it is the lack of power (and thus of material resources) which, it is claimed, adds to the stress and pressure that are so bad for the health of poorer members of unequal societies. This approach is consonant with Doyal and Gough's theory of human need, which in itself can be seen as being closer to a neo-materialist than a psycho-social approach.

Interestingly, though, this emphasis on power does not necessarily mean that social capital has to be totally disregarded. Both Hawe and Shiell (2000) and Baum (2000) make the point that power, which is central to neo-materialism is also central to social capital in at least one of its manifestations: that presented by Bourdieu. Baum indeed reminds us that Bourdieu analyses both power and social capital from a neo-Marxist perspective, which also underpins most neo-materialist analyses of health inequalities which are predicated on inequalities of class. The material environment and material resources form the basis of a neo-materialist perspective, including inequalities in investment in health and social infrastructures, material standards of living and absolute income.

Similarly, Macinko and Starfield (2001: 412) categorise a neo-materialist position in terms of differences in material conditions themselves operating to cause health inequalities. Lynch *et al.* (2000) take a broader view of neo-materialism to include, healthy diet, exercise, and avoidance of pollutants, toxics and firearms, as well as more obvious dimensions such as decent housing and access to medical care. Baum (2000: 409) summarises the differences between Wilkinson's thesis and a neo-materialist perspective by saying that it is not the lack of social capital but the lack of objective economic resources, beginning with decent jobs, that is central to the plight of the poorest and least healthy groups in society.

Finally, the absolute income explanation is in one sense very close to the neo-materialist perspective in that it fully accepts a strong inverse relationship between material circumstances (i.e. income) and health. The main difference between the two is that a neo-materialist accepts that a person with a low income in a highly unequal society will probably be less healthy than a person with an identical income in a more equal society. The basic starting point from the absolute income perspective, though, is that two people with similar incomes living in different countries, other things being equal, will probably have *exactly the same* health status and life expectancy, irrespective of whether they live in egalitarian or inegalitarian or richer or poorer societies (so long as they are societies which have been through the epidemiological transition).

It was noted above when discussing Campbell's case study of two different localities with the same average income but different health statuses, that their health differences might possibly not reflect any substantive difference in mortality or morbidity rates between the localities but might merely be an artefact. A similar 'artefactual' argument can be used in relation to the Wilkinson hypothesis. This was first made in an elegant article by Gravelle (1998) who demonstrates that *actual* differences in mortality and morbidity between two countries with similar average incomes but different income distributions are highly likely to occur even where the underlying income-related mortality rates of the two countries are, in fact, identical.

The Wilkinsonian relative income hypothesis can be stated simply as follows: 'someone with a given income would have worse health if he or she lived in a society with greater inequality of income than in a society in which income is more equally distributed' (Gravelle, 1998: 382). But Gravelle claims that most findings that are consistent with the relative income hypothesis can, in fact, be explained much more simply by a straightforward *absolute* income hypothesis where relative differences in income are completely irrelevant.

He demonstrates this by presenting a simple model of two hypothetical countries with equal average incomes and exactly the same income-related mortality risk (see Figure 7.2). This mortality risk is entirely dependent on income and decreases as income increases. In other words, rich people live longer than poor people. The decrease in mortality associated with increases in income is assumed to slow down as income increases. This is intuitively appealing in that a small addition of income for people close to starvation will lead to a much bigger increase in longevity than for people who are well fed. Thus, every increase in income brings a gain in longevity, but these gains get smaller as income levels increase.

In this model, one country happens to have a wider income range than the other. For the sake of simplicity, Gravelle assumes that half the population in each country has the minimum income and the other half has the maximum income – but the results are the same (if less easy to demonstrate diagrammatically) for more realistic assumptions of income distribution.

Under these circumstances the population mortality in the more unequal country is *certain* to be higher in the more equal country even though the income-related mortality rates are identical. This is because of the diminishing returns at the upper end in the income distribution:

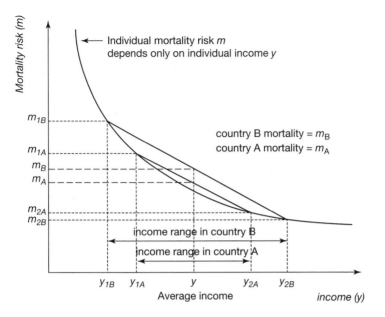

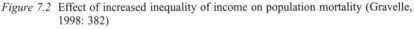

Figure 7.2 Effect of increased inequality of income on population mortality (Gravelle, 1998: 382)

> The spurious or artefactual correlation at population level between population mortality and income dispersion will always occur if the effect of individual income on the individual risk of mortality is smaller at higher incomes than at lower incomes. This will be so even if there is no underlying relation between the distribution of income and the risk of mortality at the level of the individual.
>
> (ibid.: 383)

So the secret behind this phenomenon is simply the requirement in the model that health gains of an increase in income are higher for people on low incomes than on high incomes. If this is the case, then in a universe where everyone has the same income-related life expectancy, then for two countries with the same average income, the more unequal country will *always* have the higher death rate. So population mortality increases when inequality increases and decreases when population inequality decreases.

It is important to note that Gravelle does not entirely throw out the relative income hypothesis:

> I do not suggest that an individual's health is not affected by the overall distribution of income as well as by their own income. The point I am making is that correlations between population level measures of mortality and inequality provide biased estimates of the importance of any relative income effect.
>
> (ibid.: 385)

. Thus, in the strongest version of Gravelle's absolute income thesis, there is no room for the relative income effect, and unequal death rates can be entirely explained by the absolute income effect, whereas in its less thoroughgoing version these unequal death rates act to exaggerate the relative income effect (Lynch *et al.*, 2004). This latter approach is recognised as having some merit by Wilkinson who accepts that it might explain up to a third of differential death rates (Wilkinson 2005: 134–6).

Gravelle's approach is further developed by Deaton (2001) who presents a model of mortality and income that integrates the phenomenon of the gradient of a negative relationship between income and mortality with the basic proposition in the Wilkinson hypothesis that income inequality, in itself, poses a risk to health. He starts with the proposition, also central to Wilkinson's hypothesis, that within a reference group, which can be as large as a whole population, individual health and mortality are independent of average income but are negatively affected by relative deprivation. Deaton (2001) goes further than Gravelle in that he sets out to test these hypotheses. His findings are reported below.

* * *

So, altogether there are now four different theses to compare. One, the absolute income hypothesis, in its most thoroughgoing form, predicts that the Wilkinson thesis is substantively incorrect. It accepts that there may be an observed difference in life expectancy, mortality and morbidity between two developed countries with the same average income but different income distributions. However, according to the absolute income hypothesis, it is highly likely that this is merely a statistical artefact and it is probable that all members of both societies in fact have the same income-related death rate. In other words, relative income is, from this perspective, completely irrelevant to health.

The other three theses all accept that, to greater or lesser extents, relative income or the extent of inequality in a society, in itself, does have an impact on health. The neo-materialist thesis claims that most of this effect results from access to and power over material resources, including health and social services. The individual psycho-social pathways explanation downplays the relevance of material resources and instead focuses on individuals' differential access to stress, self-esteem, social support and social isolation. The social cohesion approach incorporates aspects of the psycho-social pathways approach but identifies them as consequences of collective societal attributes linked with integrative social norms and values, trust, reciprocity and altruism that together comprise social cohesion which itself thrives in egalitarian societies.

Empirical findings

The time has now come to assess the empirical evidence for these theses, starting with the absolute income hypothesis. The only study that has been found which creates a rigorous absolute income model and then tests it in comparison with Wilkinson's thesis is Deaton's (2001) study. He reports that Wilkinson's relative income thesis provides a good account of the mortality gradient within US states but not between states. Thus, the intra-state findings support the findings of Kawachi *et al.* (1997) but the inter-state findings do not. Unfortunately for Wilkinson, Deaton's analysis also shows that the effects of income inequality are not robust when controlled for other variables, particularly the proportion of African-Americans and Hispanics in the population of individual US states. So there is evidence of a relative income effect within – but not between – states of the USA but even this disappears when other socio-demographic variables are introduced into the analysis.

Similarly, Judge and Paterson (2001: 38–9) find that where non-flawed studies appear to provide evidence in support of the income inequality hypothesis, it tends to disappear when other influences on health are controlled for; and that any correlation between life expectancy and income inequality is almost certainly due to something that is correlated with income inequality but is not income inequality itself. They conclude from their overview of relevant studies that any relative inequality effect is the by-product of two factors: first, absolute income, its non-linear relationship with health adversely affecting people on low incomes: second, other area characteristics such as ethnicity or social welfare infrastructure, for which income inequality acts as a marker. Lynch *et al.* update Judge and Paterson (2001) by reviewing ninety-eight recent aggregate and multilevel studies. They conclude: 'The evidence suggests that income inequality is not associated with population health differences – at least not as a general phenomenon – among wealthy nations' (Lynch *et al.*, 2004: 81).

On the other hand, in the most rigorous recent study – conducted subsequent to both Deaton's study and Judge and Paterson's overview and regrettably not included in the Lynch *et al.* (2004) review – Kennelly *et al.* (2003) found that at national level poorer citizens are less healthy than richer citizens, and this is exacerbated in highly unequal societies. This latter finding is consistent with the relative income hypothesis and with Wilkinson's (2000) findings. Like Wilkinson, Kennelly *et al.* used a small number of rich nations in their data set (nineteen compared to Wilkinson's twenty) unlike Lynch *et al.* (2000) who used a larger number of countries in their study which came to different conclusions from those of Wilkinson.

At the local level, Lynch *et al.* (2000) produce some strong evidence in favour of the absolute but against the relative income hypothesis. They point out that the poorest 10 per cent of people living in the five richest metropolitan areas of the USA have average incomes of $12,000 per annum (well above the national epidemiological transition threshold) whereas the poorest 10 per cent of people living in the five poorest areas of the USA have average incomes of only $4,000 per annum (a long way below the national epidemiological transition threshold). This is a massive absolute difference and must be important for health independent of the fact that these two deciles are identically disadvantaged in *relative* terms. Lynch *et al.* also remind us that millions of children in the USA still do not get enough to eat.

Moving on to the three relative income hypotheses, there is very little rigorous empirical evidence to support the social cohesion approach. Lynch *et al.* did find some significant correlates of indicators of social capital (including trust and organisational membership) but unfortunately for Wilkinson these indicators were more strongly related to GNP than to inequality. This goes in the opposite direction to that anticipated by the Wilkinson thesis which predicts that social cohesion is stronger in egalitarian societies than non-egalitarian societies instead of richer than poorer societies.

The most definitive contemporary study is a multivariate econometric study using panel data covering three different time periods in nineteen OECD countries, undertaken by Kennelly *et al.* (2003). Their findings provide no support at all for the theory that the level of social cohesion or social capital has an effect on health. Kennelly *et al.* (ibid.: 2374) found that the coefficients for social capital were insignificant for the vast majority of the regressions which they undertook and they conclude that their paper 'casts doubt on the widely accepted hypothesis that social capital has a positive effect on health' (ibid.: 2367).

Kennelly *et al.* concede that there is still a possibility that social capital *might* be important: if so, then either the indicators which they used did not measure it properly or else perhaps it might only operate at an interpersonal psycho-social level not amenable to national scrutiny. In their literature review, Kennelly *et al.* do note that there seems to be evidence for the Wilkinson hypothesis at the individual level where a large number of studies have found significant association between health status and various psycho-social factors such as trust, quality of interpersonal relations, civic association, etc.

Overwhelmingly, though, Kennelly *et al.*'s findings lend support to the neo-materialist explanations:

> Our results are consistent with the neo-material theory of health. We find that, on average, higher levels of per capita GDP are associated with better health outcomes. In addition, we find that the share of health expenditure that is financed by the government is generally associated with longer life expectancy and lower mortality.
>
> (ibid.: 2374)

The policy implications from this range of studies seem to be clear-cut: that it is essential to concentrate health-related resources, income maintenance and social security on the poorest members in unequal societies. Judge and Paterson (2001: 40) express this pithily as follows: 'If poverty is properly addressed as a determinant of health, then income inequality per se should not be a concern for health policy makers.' Similarly, both Hawe and Shiell (2000) and Kennelly *et al.* (2003) caution against devoting too much attention to social capital and social cohesion when the main objectives of health promotion policy should be to improve the living standards of poor and impoverished communities, improving access to services and encouraging macro-economic and cultural change.

Given the importance of their study, perhaps it is best to give the last word on this to Kennelly *et al.*:

> The message for policy makers is not that the psycho-social environment is unimportant – individual level studies show that the social fabric of society

is important for health – but that material and structural factors play a major role in explaining the variation in health across developed countries.

(ibid.: 2375)

Implications for Wilkinson's thesis

Wilkinson's thesis can be divided into three parts: first, that among developed societies it is the most equal which are the healthiest and not the richest; second, that social cohesion is higher in equal societies and has a major causal effect on health; and, third, low levels of social cohesion associated with relative deprivation in unequal societies cause adverse health consequences via psycho-social pathways associated with stress, self-esteem, social support and social isolation. There are mixed responses to the first part, depending on the cut-off point chosen for what is a developed society. In general a high cut-off point, including only the nineteen or twenty richest countries, lends some support to Wilkinson, whereas a lower cut-off point, including the ex-communist countries in the thirty-three richest countries provides strong evidence against Wilkinson. Similarly, a study of the states in the USA shows some initial support but this evaporates when other demographic variables are factored in.

The verdicts on the second theme are even less encouraging. No systematic evidence has been found which supports the contention that equality *causes* social cohesion which *causes* good health, although there is much anecdotal evidence that there are some associations operating here. Indeed, the most persuasive evidence is that social cohesion is higher in richer rather than more egalitarian societies. In relation to the third part, there is no doubt that stress and the other psycho-social pathways have a major effect on health, and it is likely that they are related in some way to levels of trust and other integrative norms associated with social cohesion, but there is no evidence of a link with relative (as opposed to absolute) deprivation in itself.

Taken together, the best that can be said about Wilkinson's thesis in its above formulation is that it has not actually been disproved but that there is very little positive evidence in favour of it, particularly in relation to the role of social cohesion. On the other hand, Wilkinson's emphasis on the relative benefits of increasing equality for health have been given considerable support, particularly from the neo-materialist perspective, as seen above. All in all, according to a neo-materialist perspective, the poor are sicker than the rich because they have less money, less job security, worse neighbourhood environments and amenities, poorer quality housing and food, and worse access to high quality health and social care facilities than the rich. These factors may be less psycho-social in nature than Wilkinson's – but they are also more amenable to public policy intervention.

But even the absolute income perspective, while pouring cold water on Wilkinson's proposition that it is *only* relative deprivation that is important, has similar policy consequences to his approach on two counts. The first is that it is always cost effective to raise the income of the poor rather than the rich because they will benefit more; second, and more radically, even if there is no extra money to go round, the health of the population as a whole can be increased by taking money from the rich and giving it to the poor. In other words, transferring income from the rich to the poor – i.e. making a country more equal – will reduce its mortality rate *even without the relative income hypothesis*. This will always be the case so long as the effect on individual income on the individual risk of mortality is smaller at higher than lower incomes.

Although the absolute income thesis is highly damaging to the social cohesion aspect of Wilkinson's position, nevertheless, it still gives very strong support to Wilkinson's policy goal of increasing equality within societies. Indeed, from an absolute income perspective, it can be done much more easily: there is no need to find a way to enhance the elusive and abstract nature of social cohesion to make a society healthier – all that is needed is a cash transfer, perhaps through progressive taxation.

8 Conclusion

The findings in Chapter 7 relating to health and quality of life are wide-ranging and thought-provoking. Some are clear-cut, for example that objective well-being, in terms of absolute levels of income and access to health-care services is strongly related to life expectancy. Also, although less well documented, it is clear that stress and other psycho-social pathways have an important impact on health and it seems likely that these are to some degree related to trust and other integrative norms associated with social capital and social cohesion. It is also true that a more equal society will generally have a healthier population than a less equal society with the same average income. All these findings have important consequences for both social policy and for the study of quality of life. It is unfortunate for Wilkinson that his major proposition – increased social cohesion both being caused by greater equality and itself causing society to be more healthy – is at best unproven. Indeed, on the contrary, some of the evidence seems to show that there is more social cohesion in unequal than in equal societies (Kennelly et al., 2003).

So social cohesion seems to be the Achilles' heel of Wilkinson's thesis. Yet, along with its closely related construct of social capital, social cohesion is also central to other models of quality of life and health (Campbell, 1999; Kawachi and Berkman, 2000) and to the major overarching quality of life constructs (Hancock, 1993; Bernard, 1999; Berger-Schmitt and Noll, 2000; Beck et al., 2001a). There is no doubt therefore that it is seen as highly important to conceptualising quality of life. As has been noted in passing throughout the book, though, social capital and social cohesion are not at all straightforward in relation to quality of life. One of the tasks in this chapter is to try to disentangle those aspects of these concepts which are generally positive in relation to quality of life.

Overall, the aims of the chapter are: to draw together the threads running through the book relating to the strengths and weaknesses of different approaches to quality of life; to investigate the contradictions – both apparent and real – between some of them; and, finally, to identify some principles which can act as firm foundations for making progress in furthering our understanding of quality of life. To facilitate this, the chapter starts with a résumé.

Résumé and identification of cross-cutting themes

The rationale for the ordering of material in the book has been straightforward: to move from the individual to the collective. This starts with the most elemental building blocks of quality of life for each individual and then moves upwards to more rounded, holistic and other-regarding subjective approaches, through to objective and normative judgements on individual well-being, including health-related quality of life. Individual well-being is then situated in a social context, starting with ecological models and then, via a critique of utilitarianism, introducing prudential values, basic needs, the human development approach, Doyal and Gough's theory of human need, and both Sen's and Nussbaum's interpretations of the capabilities perspective. Then, the socially-oriented concepts of poverty and social exclusion are discussed prior to introducing the collective constructs of social capital and social cohesion. These four concepts are important elements in the societal quality of life models which are then presented; the interactions between social cohesion and social exclusion being central to Bernard's democratic dialectic, Berger-Schmitt and Noll's overarching quality of life construct and Beck *et al.*'s notion of social quality. Also, interactions between social capital, social cohesion and health are central to the three final societal models introduced: Hancock's public health model; Campbell's health pathways model; and Wilkinson's thesis which itself also hinges on issues of relative and absolute poverty and income inequality.

Moving incrementally from the individual to the collective in this way is rational and orderly but there are important connections and themes which do not fit into this tidy pattern. Some of these are discussed now before returning to the original ordering to draw some conclusions from the individual, social and collective constructs. Here the focus moves between the different levels in identifying themes relevant to the further study of quality of life. These themes fit into three broad categories: (1) pathways linking the individual, social and collective; (2) thresholds and measurements; and (3) tensions and contradictions surrounding core ideological values and epistemological foundations.

Pathways

The pathways discussed here can all be fitted into the ecological model of quality of life discussed in Chapter 2. The first set of pathways are the ones introduced by Wilkinson and Campbell in Chapter 7. The conduit for these pathways is situated in the collective social fabric whereas the second set of pathways discussed here, linked to Sen's capabilities approach, has its focal point at a more individualistic level and is concerned with freedom to choose between beings and doings. The third set of pathways is concerned with the relationship between material well-being, needs-based approaches, poverty and issues regarding quality of life and inequality.

*Pathway one: from subjective well-being and stress to health
outcomes*

Wilkinson's thesis is discussed at length above but for present purposes the pathway
he postulates can be described very simply. In its positive form it is societal equality
leads to enhanced social cohesion which makes people feel good about themselves
which consequently makes them healthier. And in its negative form, societal
inequality damages the social fabric which in turn increases social conflict and
perceptions of inequality, reduces social solidarity and thus leads to psychological
damage among deprived members of society, ultimately resulting in excessive
levels of stress which are highly detrimental to health. For Wilkinson, low social
status and low self-esteem are the issues: people need dignity and self-respect which
they can only achieve in egalitarian societies (Wilkinson *et al.*, 1998).

Virtually all commentators would agree that very high levels of stress have a
deleterious effect upon health, although whether the effect is of a small or large
magnitude is open to dispute, and it is noted in Chapter 1 that happy people live
significantly longer than unhappy people – and, related to this, they have lower
blood pressure, stronger hearts, fewer illnesses and stronger immune systems
(Argyle, 1996; Berkman and Glass, 2000; Blanchflower and Oswald, 2004a). This
anchors one end of this psychosocial pathway in place. The crucial question is,
what causes stress and creates happiness? The findings reported in Chapter 1 about
the causes of happiness and SWB more generally are clear-cut and unequivocal:
apart from genetic predisposition, the main causal factors include being in a
loving relationship, being employed, and having financial security and success.
The proximate causes of stress are also not in serious dispute: among them are
financial insecurity, unemployment, relationship breakdown, and death of a close
family member. So the pathway is still in place. However, it is when the ultimate
rather than the proximate causes of SWB and stress are postulated that it splits into
different directions.

For Wilkinson the major ultimate causes of the high levels of stress in unequal
societies lie in the symbiotic interrelationship between perceptions of social
inequality and damaged social cohesion. Leaving aside for the present whether
stress levels are in fact higher in unequal societies and whether *psycho-socially*
induced stress is a significant factor in increased death rates, the primary questions
here are: first, whether there *is* a clear link between the generally agreed proximate
causes of stress and perceptions of social inequality; and, second, whether *inequality*
necessarily damages social cohesion. It is clear from Chapter 7 that the empirical
evidence for both links is at best slight but one possible explanation is that there
might in fact be a strong causal link which is difficult to measure or else is masked
by some other confounding factor. The purpose here is to explore the case that can
be made for there being a conceptual link.

Dealing first with perceptions of inequality, some of the proximate causes of
stress noted above, such as death of a loved one, are less obviously connected in
any way with possible perceptions of inequality than others, such as financial
insecurity. And even the stressors with the most obvious potential causal links to
psychological perceptions of inequality all have equally if not greater potential

causal links with material or neo-material consequences of being poorer. In other words as good a case can be made for the physical consequences of absolute deprivation as for the psychological consequences of relative deprivation in relation to stress pathways associated with relative inequality.

But an even stronger case can be made against Wilkinson's thesis here: even on the assumption that a psychological perception may have more deleterious causal power over life expectancy than physical deprivation, it can be argued that it is not the perception of *inequality* that is the crucial factor, but instead the perception of *injustice*. Now, in some circumstances these will be the same; that is, in a situation where society is seen to be unfairly unequal. However, inequality of condition is not necessarily equivalent to injustice. A society with inequality of condition but full equality of opportunity for all its citizens, as in the stereotypical American Dream, could be seen as being fair and just, and thus perceptions of inequality would not then result in the sorts of stress that Wilkinson imputes. Indeed, a just but unequal society is likely to result in the apparently paradoxical phenomenon of the happy poor, as noted in Chapter 1.

Now, in such a society there *may* be high levels of stress associated with perceptions of injustice resulting from, for example, racial discrimination, sexism, restrictive practices, cartels, etc., and it is entirely plausible that these stress levels may adversely affect health but if this possibility is accepted – and if what Wilkinson identifies as 'inequality' stressors fall within the same set of psycho-social pathways as these 'injustice' stressors then Wilkinson's thesis needs to be amended. Here, then, the pathway splits, with Wilkinson's notion of perception of relative deprivation and inequality on one branch and a perception of unfairness and injustice taking another branch: sometimes these branches will go in different directions, that is where an unequal society is seen as being fair; and sometimes these branches will go in the same direction, where a society is seen as being both unequal and unfair.

Wilkinson has a similar problem with social cohesion. If an unequal society is seen as not unjust but fair – as in the hymn about the rich man in his castle and the poor man at his gate, quoted in Chapter 4 – then there is no reason to expect the social fabric or social cohesion to be damaged and thus the whole of Wilkinson's thesis about the relationship between inequality *per se* and social cohesion becomes untenable.

Returning to the psycho-social pathways, there can be seen to be relatively clear connections between health status, stress, happiness, perceptions of injustice and levels of social support – although the *strength* of these links is open to question. From the perspective of even a modified Wilkinsonian approach, however, it is not easy to jump from the individual to the collective, from the compositional to the contextual aspects of social cohesion.

One of the characteristics of Wilkinson's pathway, in its broad sweep from the individual through to the fabric of society, is its apparent top-down determinism with an associated lack of consideration given to issues of agency and choice among individuals. Another, of course is Wilkinson's de-emphasising of the potential impact of material as opposed to psycho-social factors. The next two pathways, both concerned with quality of life in general rather than health in particular and both relating to Sen's capability construct, deal with these issues in turn.

Pathway two: subjective well-being, capabilities, needs, utilitarianism and quality of life

In one sense Sen's approach to quality of life, based as it is on individuals' freedom to flourish by doing valuable acts or reaching valuable states of well-being – doings and beings – seems a long way removed from Wilkinson's emphasis on structural inequality, social cohesion and life expectancy. And it is certainly true that their ideological stances appear to be radically different: Wilkinson is explicitly egalitarian whereas Sen strongly emphasises the importance of freedoms. But their ultimate quality of life goals, that is, the end points of both their pathways, are identical. They both want all people to be able to live long, healthy fulfilled lives in convivial and supportive communities.

Sen's work is important in this context because it acts as a bridge between the individualism and experientialism of a utilitarian perspective, on the one hand, and the collectivism and emphasis on social and economic resources of the needs-based and the macro societal quality of life constructs on the other. It is also worth noting here that Sen's capabilities approach has a close affinity with the more empirically-oriented self-defined approach to identifying individual quality of life pioneered by Bowling (1995a) discussed in Chapter 1. The rationale for both constructs is embedded in respect for the freedom of individuals to define what is important in their lives.

In Chapter 3 the foundational actual-desire basis of utilitarianism is contrasted with the informed-desire basis of prudential values which in turn is compared with needs-based approaches culminating with Doyal and Gough's extensive theory of human needs (THN) prior to introducing Sen's notion of capabilities. Here an important link is made between the THN and capabilities in terms of Gough's recognition that it would be appropriate to use capabilities to operationalise the THN and that this would also leave the THN less open to charges of paternalism (Gough, 2003: 16). Thus, the freedom to choose whether or not to pursue the universal goals of THN becomes part of an individual's capability set.

And it is this freedom to choose between alternative valuable beings and doings that provides the link with utilitarianism with its emphasis upon reaching the valuable mental state of happiness through experienced utility, in other words through the meeting of actual desires. This in turn provides a link, albeit indirect and tenuous, between desires-based and needs based approaches. The needs-based approach in effect insists that everyone should have the wherewithal to be able to meet their needs if they so desire, and the capabilities perspective gives them the freedom to choose whether or not so to do. Issues of autonomy are central here and these are revisited later. This pathway has an anchor point fixed firmly on the rights associated with individual freedoms and leads to opportunities to exercise choice over the extent to which – and the ways in which – universal needs-oriented goals are pursued.

Pathway three: material well-being, basic capabilities, poverty and quality of life

One of the most important policy-related aspects of Sen's capabilities approach is *basic capabilities* which covers the same substantive area as basic needs, that of providing for a minimally decent life. Sen describes basic capabilities as the 'ability to satisfy certain crucially important functionings up to certain minimally adequate levels' (1993: 40). So although Sen still stresses the importance of freedoms, and thus does not prioritise public over private provision of relevant services as does the basic needs approach, nevertheless these basic capabilities all relate to commonly agreed standards of well-being and the avoidance of at least a subsistence-oriented version of absolute poverty, as discussed in Chapter 4.

Here the basis of the pathway is the necessity to preserve life through the provision of objectively defined necessities to ward off absolute poverty. It is important here to include the reference to absolute poverty, partly because it is anyway an essential anchor point for quality of life, partly because it regrettably is still of major practical significance in addressing the actual quality of life of a high proportion of the world's population and partly because of its potential relevance to the Wilkinson thesis, given the strong case to be made for the relevance of absolute income levels to life expectancy and health, even in developed nations where people on low incomes still die prematurely compared to people on high incomes. In this latter context the threshold of what can be considered as poverty is, of course, of central importance, and the whole issue of thresholds is discussed below.

There is an important link here between capabilities and both the 'social needs' based and subjective definitions of poverty discussed in Chapter 4 (Gordon, 2000). In the social needs approach, members of the general public are asked what is a necessity in order to be able to do things which most people take for granted within a society, or in capabilities language, which functionings most people take for granted, and then these are costed and aggregated into an income which is enough to be able (that is providing the capability) to do all these things. The rationale for, and operationalisation of, this approach are in essence very similar to Bowling's self-defined approach to quality of life. It also follows a pattern very similar to that in the consensus-based normative approaches to operationalising health-related quality of life. The subjective definitions of poverty take the social needs approach as their starting point but then instead of the costing and aggregations being undertaken by professionals, people on low incomes themselves are asked to identify what income levels would be necessary to meet these social needs. This again resonates strongly with Sen's insistence upon the sovereignty of the individual in making decisions about resources and valuable functioning in their lives.

The upshot of moving from basic needs through basic capabilities to social needs and subjective approaches to material well-being is that the pathway can be seen to divide between absolute and relative, objective and subjective and to fan out into several, often cross-cutting, minor paths. Some paths, however, are better defined than others. Among these, perhaps the most important in a development context is a combination of basic needs, basic capabilities and absolute poverty. Another is the somewhat wider path denoted by the combination of the notion of overall poverty and Doyal and Gough's theory of human need, as augmented to include capabilities. A third, even less precisely delineated, but nevertheless extremely important path encompasses the meeting point between capabilities in their wide sense of living a flourishing life (including the subjective well-being that derives from achieving what is valuable in one's life) and subjective and socially defined criteria for being able to do things which most people take for granted within a society.

Thresholds and measurements

In one sense, any discussion of thresholds and measurements is by its nature technical and concerns the details of operationalising a model or construct. This sense is not, however, the major focus here: the main question to be addressed regarding thresholds concerns their relationship with the nature of the construct itself, and the measurement question is simply whether some of the constructs discussed are in fact amenable to measurement *at all* without further conceptual and theoretical development.

Thresholds

Poverty is the obvious and indeed the classic example of the centrality of the positioning of the threshold to the integrity of the concept itself. This has been discussed at length and it is noted there that, except for the most brutally parsimonious definitions of starvation-avoidance, all definitions of absolute as well as overall poverty are relative and thus the threshold has to be defined and operationalised empirically and inductively rather than deductively on an *a priori* basis. So not only will the threshold vary between societies but it will also change over time within any individual society and will probably be ideologically and politically contested within most societies at any given time.

Therefore, for some constructs, such as 'absolute', overall or social needs-based definitions of poverty, even if there is agreement on the theoretical or conceptual basis of the definition of the term and therefore on what in principle should constitute the threshold, this does not necessarily mean that it can be unambiguously operationalised because of potential disagreement about what the term means in practice. This problem is perhaps even more serious for specific needs-based constructs such as basic needs, basic capabilities and the THN because they include basic health services and education as well as poverty. Health is particularly difficult to pin down in terms of thresholds because there is no absolute criterion for minimum health beyond survival and because of the different medical requirements for people with different health statuses (this perhaps being even more of a problem for basic capabilities than for the other constructs). More importantly in conceptual terms there are three thresholds to be met, thus introducing issues of pluralism not only in terms of the number but also the relative weighting to be given to each threshold and whether this weighting should be constant even in societies in different stages of development.

The problems associated with plural thresholds are discussed in Chapter 3 with particular reference to prudential values where Qizilbash identifies not only component and weight pluralism but what he calls 'good life' pluralism where individuals can have conflicting visions of what constitutes high quality of life. At the risk of delving into technicalities, it is worth mentioning that Qizilbash utilises Borda scores and Pareto rankings in order to try to overcome these problems and does move towards constructing an overall index of prudential values on this basis (Qizilbash, 1997b: 2013).

Pluralism of thresholds is an issue in any quality of life construct which comprises a list or lists where at least some items are irreducible in nature. Nussbaum, for example, is very specific about this in relation to her interpretation of capabilities and insists that a lack in *any* of the items on her list leads to a shortfall in the goal for a good human life (Nussbaum, 2000: 75). The THN does not suffer from this problem to the same extent as either Nussbaum's approach or prudential values because its hierarchical nature leads to less irreducibility in that all eleven of the THN intermediate needs are subordinate to the primary needs of physical health and autonomy of agency, thus facilitating the operationalisation of the THN (Gough, 2000b: 129).

There is another sense in which there is a plurality of thresholds in that there is a variety of threshold types, each having a different epistemological status. Two have been met already. The first is the absolutist definition, unambiguously measurable without dissent which really only exists as an ideal type or extreme case. The second is derived from theory and is *conceptually* clear, objective and unambiguous, but its operationalisation is contingent upon empirical interpretation and may thus be open to contestation. A third type is normative rather than positivistic in nature, where the actual threshold is based upon social and cultural conventions rather than being deductively derived from the theoretical edifice. Fourth, and related to normative approaches, are consensual thresholds. Examples here are the social needs approach to poverty and some of the health-related quality of life measures discussed in Chapter 2 where the thresholds are derived by empirical survey of the views of the population. The four types of absolute, theoretically derived, normative and consensual are distinct in principle and have differing epistemological statuses and operational consequences but in practice many actual thresholds are compounds, incorporating elements from more than one type.

Metric and hybrid measures

Quality of life constructs that are measured metrically rather than by thresholds are, in general, much more straightforward. Happiness and subjective well-being (SWB) are ascertained via numeric scales by survey questionnaire. Utility is, of course, ubiquitously measured in money terms, often by per capita GNP. The most straightforward of the macro quality of life instruments, Veenhoven's (1996) *Happy Life Expectancy*, is an index constructed by multiplying the two quality of life metrics in its title. None of these instruments is without its problems, but they all have the advantage of transparency (if not necessarily accuracy or validity) and of being interval measures. Currency units, years of life expectancy and even 'units' or degrees of happiness are all intuitively clear, unlike the operational definitions of most of the thresholds.

Hybrid measures or aggregate indices share the advantage with metric measures of being interval measures but they also have transparency problems similar to those of thresholds. The best-established international hybrid construct is the human development index (HDI). This aims to give an indication of well-being in terms of leading a long and healthy life, being educated and enjoying a decent standard of living. The HDI is a combination of life expectancy, literacy and years of schooling, and per capita GNP. This gives an overall 'well-being' ranking of all countries but there is no clear indication of what an individual score *means*, except that high scoring countries do better than low scoring countries.

Other, more complex, hybrids include some of the outcome-oriented definitions of social exclusion discussed in Chapter 4 (Burchardt *et al.*, 1999; McCrystal *et al.*, 2001). It is interesting to note in this context that the instrument used by Burchardt *et al.*, which included a combination of theoretically derived and normative thresholds, has been modified after consultation with residents from deprived areas, resulting in an instrument incorporating a strong consensual element (Richardson and Le Grand, 2002).

Constructs where measurement is problematic

There are at least two sets of issues involved here. The first relates to constructs which are *intrinsically* problematic and the second to constructs which have yet to be fully developed and where there might or might not be intrinsic problems.

To deal with the intrinsically problematic first, it will not come as a surprise to find both social capital and social cohesion in this category. The problems in operationalising these constructs are not discussed here except to echo Macinko and Starfield's (2001: 410) conclusion that, at least in the health field, there appear to be no adequate measures of social cohesion at all and that there is no consensus either on an appropriate level of analysis or means of measuring social capital. This does not mean that these constructs are therefore of no use, rather that they are not yet conceptualised precisely enough for their effective mensuration to be undertaken. Some of their elements, such as network membership, generalised trust, and trust in institutions, of strangers, can be measured but as yet there is no commonly accepted and clearly theorised protocol for providing an overall measure of either construct.

Moving on to constructs which have yet to be fully developed, it can be seen from Chapter 7 that the two most substantial of these, Berger-Schmitt and Noll's overarching quality of life construct and Beck *et al.*'s social quality construct both incorporate versions of social cohesion so they both are liable to suffer from the intrinsic problems noted above. However, they deal with social cohesion in different ways which leads to differing consequences. Berger-Schmitt and Noll (2000) define social cohesion in terms of reducing disparities, inequalities and social exclusion;

and of strengthening social relations, interactions and ties. They then identify forty-seven nodes of measurement dimensions and life domains for measuring what they have defined as social cohesion.

They therefore sidestep the conceptual issues in operationalising social cohesion by providing a long list of items to measure, all of which relate to some or other aspect of different definitions of social cohesion. However, they give no indication of how these measures can be put together to arrive at an overall index. It needs to be noted here too that there are two other strands to the overarching quality of life construct: quality of life *per se*; and sustainability. Berger-Schmitt and Noll have undertaken a great deal of work in identifying measurement dimensions for these strands too, but again there is no indication yet of how these will all be put together to give a measure, – or, more accurately, an indicator – of overarching quality of life.

The social quality construct, although subjected to more theoretical exposition than the overarching quality of life construct, is not yet as fully developed in terms of operationalisation or measurement. Here social cohesion is defined as the nature of social relations based on shared identities, values and norms, and its domains are trust, other integrative norms and values, social networks, and identity (Baers *et al.*, 2005). This conceptualisation is probably more coherent than that in the overarching quality of life construct, and the indicators which have been constructed for each domain are all pertinent, but again there is no protocol for aggregating them into an overall index. And again as with the overarching quality of life construct, social cohesion is only one part of social quality. Here there are three other elements – socio-economic security, social inclusion and empowerment – and as yet there is no indication of how they fit together to constitute social quality.

Constructs with no measures

It may seem perverse to have quality of life constructs that are not operationalised or fully specified in practical terms. However, one of the most important and influential quality of life constructs has been deliberately and explicitly left incomplete: this, of course is Sen's notion of capabilities. It is not easy to pin down Sen's position – because of his insistence on freedoms and choices, he never provides a list of capabilities. There is perhaps another reason for this too. Capabilities have been universally accepted as a foundation for human development largely because there is nothing specific about them for anyone to criticise. For example, his lack of specificity leaves open the fundamental question of Aristotelian universality, as espoused by Martha Nussbaum, versus cultural relativity, which allows for different capability priorities in different cultures, thus leading to, for example, differential roles, statuses and capability sets for women (Alkire, 2002b).

The upshot of this is that capabilities have been accepted by both feminists and egalitarians on the one hand and traditionalists on the other and by both sides in the passionate debate on fertility control. This is no mean feat and, although it has the inevitable consequence of the force of the construct being diluted, it also ensures both widespread acceptance of the importance of quality of life and a common conceptual framework within which to discuss it.

The final category here comprises what can be termed as heuristic devices or utopian visions. Bernard's democratic dialectic and Hancock's public health models fit into both of these categories with Bernard's perhaps placing more emphasis on illuminating the dynamics and the complexity of the notion of social cohesion, as well as unequivocally critiquing it for being what he calls a 'quasi-concept'. A strength of Bernard's approach, where he in effect takes a position diametrically opposed to Sen's, is that he lays bare the tensions pertaining to the dynamic between liberty and equality and to their potentially contradictory natures. Hancock perhaps is more interested in sketching out the framework for the 'good society' and he has no compunction about identifying precisely where his ideological preferences lie. Neither of these models are designed to be operationalised in terms of domains or indicators but they both serve a useful purpose in consciousness raising and in setting out ultimate criteria for quality of life.

Core values – tensions and contradictions

As with pathways and thresholds, there are some interrelated discourses and disputes about core values which are common themes throughout the book. Perhaps the most important of these are the interrelated tensions between liberty and equality and between individualism and collectivism, along with their ideological, ethical and epistemological offshoots: these are thus discussed first. The second discourse is about the nature of pleasure, joy or hedonism, whether it is only an individual-level phenomenon or if it also exists collectively and, if so, whether it has consequences for social cohesion and if it has overall beneficial or detrimental societal effects. The third concerns the tensions between individual freedom and autonomy, on the one hand, and the mutual interdependence associated with even moderate levels of socials cohesion, on the other. The fourth relates to an unexpected commonality across all conceptual frameworks: the avoidance of pain or serious harm.

Individualism and libertarianism versus collectivism and egalitarianism

As noted above, Hancock's unequivocal espousal of a collectivist paradigm firmly rooted in social justice and equity, lays down a marker for one set of core values which, following Bernard, can loosely be identified as being collective and egalitarian. The other set identified by Bernard, those relating to liberty, are more individualistic in nature and lie at the heart of hedonic approaches to subjective well-being and reach their theoretical apogee in utilitarianism. In terms of macro quality of life constructs, Veenhoven's Happy Life Expectancy is perhaps the one closest to an individualistic perspective.

Collectivist perspectives are less easy to specify because they range from the highly ideologically egalitarian through to the ideologically neutral. Hancock's model is strongly egalitarian as is Bernard's, with his vision of the 'good society' achieving maximum levels of inclusion, equality and social justice, legitimacy, participation, recognition and belonging. Wilkinson too espouses egalitarian social cohesion. The needs-based approaches also have a strong ideological basis, in their requirement for collective obligations to meet needs as a social right. This is expressed most forcefully in Doyal and Gough's theory of human need (THN). The UN Human Development approach has similar aims to the THN but takes a narrower focus whereas the basic needs approach lowers its sights to ensure minimum standards of decently acceptable life for all. Nussbaum's approach has an ideological requirement for no-one to fall below the threshold in any of the 'core' capabilities and for everyone to have equal opportunities to achieve a 'good' life.

Two other sets of perspectives can be introduced here: the first is 'middle range', occupying ground between the individual and the collective. The prudential values approach is on the borderline between the collective and the middle range: it goes beyond the purely individual because of its basis on shared values and it does aim for all human life to go better (although it does not entail any ideological require-ment for so doing). Thus, it has similar goals – and similar lists – to Nussbaum and to Doyal and Gough. However, its epistemological basis is embedded in being 'characteristically human' and having common values rather than in anything specifically collective or intrinsically social such as being 'other regarding', so there is a case for saying that it falls just outside the collective. Sen's capabilities approach unequivocally falls outside the collective because of its overriding emphasis on valuable freedoms and individual capabilities. Thus, it differs from prudential values because of its emphasis on *actual* freedoms rather than informed desires, that is what people *would* desire if they were fully informed. In its emphasis upon development goals via the notion of basic capabilities it also differs from the hedonistically oriented individualistic perspectives, as discussed in the context of the second pathway above.

The second set is interconnecting rather than middle range in that it incorporates both individual and collective paradigms. The most far-reaching examples of these are Berger-Schmitt and Noll's overarching quality of life model and Beck *et al.*'s social quality construct. In the former, subjective well-being is one of the two parts of the quality of life component of the overall model which in itself is solidaristic and egalitarian (Berger-Schmitt, 2000: 11, 37), and the latter has elements incor-porating both citizen empowerment and social cohesion and has an overall aim including increased equity, equality, rights and solidarity (Beck *et al.*, 2001c: 314). Berger-Schmitt and Noll do not make any explicit theoretical connections between the individual and the collective but on the other hand one of the main strengths of Beck *et al.*'s approach is their theoretical grounding of this dynamic, which they pithily express as *the dialectic between individual self realisation and the formation of collective identities* (Baers *et al.*, 2005). Less wide-ranging and generally non-ideological approaches incorporating the individual and the collective include Campbell's (1999) and Berkman and Glass's (2000) health pathways models, Lindstrom's (1992) model and the other ecologically based approaches.

Hedonism: a collective as well as individual attribute?

Hedonism has already received considerable attention in Chapters 1 and 3. However, one aspect of the construct has received little attention: the extent of its applicability at collective levels. So far, discussions about pleasure or enjoyment, the hedonic aspects of quality of life, have taken place at an individual level, either in relation to individuals by themselves or in aggregates or averages, and not in relation to collectivities, either communities or societies. This means that the debates, or at least the academic debates, about the good life which include discussion of pleasure or joy have tended to be at the individual rather than the collective level. Thus there is considerable academic literature on 'the good society' – indeed, much socialist writing for example is on this topic – and much on collectivist public health, but there is little on notions of hedonic, happy or pleasure-full societies. The only genres which do seem to pay much attention to collective happiness are religious and utopian writing – with William Morris's *News from Nowhere* (Morris, 1970) being a delightful example of the latter.

Now, there is an obvious reason for this omission, that, in general, pleasure and joy are thought of as individual and not collective attributes. This is not because they cannot be conceived of collectively – a happy family, for example, can be seen as being more than just a collection of happy people who happen to be related to each other. This omission is more because the social philosophers and other social scientists who most commonly use hedonic constructs in general have individualistic epistemological frameworks. Additionally, many academics whose epistemological stock-in-trade is at the collective level do not take much of an intellectual interest in pleasure or joy but are interested instead in what they would claim to be more serious values and constructs. This is emphatically and necessarily the case in relation to needs-based theorists for whom any hint of hedonism would dilute the obligatory societal rights-based meeting of needs. Perhaps more surprisingly, there is no direct mention of joy in the major overarching quality of life constructs discussed in Chapter 6, except to the extent that it is inherent in the subjective quality of life of individuals in Berger-Schmitt and Noll's model.

Similarly, pleasure and joy are missing from the collective societal constructs of social capital and social cohesion which, broadly speaking, comprise interlocking networks, social bonds, trust, other-regarding behaviour, reciprocity, altruism and civic and social responsibility. In extensive literature reviews of social capital and cohesion, these hedonic attributes are not even mentioned (see, for example, Feldman and Assaf, 1999, and Macinko and Starfield, 2001). There are three possibly good reasons for this. The first is that collective happiness might not be relevant to social cohesion, in other words, that whether a society is happy or not putatively does not affect its cohesiveness. This appears rather implausible: intuitively at least generalised trust, reciprocity and altruism would appear to be positively rather than negatively correlated with generalised happiness. Anyway, this is an empirical question which can be answered relatively easily.

A second reason is that happiness might indeed be correlated with social capital and social cohesion but only as a consequence, and, more telling, perhaps as only a consequence of a certain kind of positive social bonding. Such causal links are not easy to test empirically. However, even if plausible evidence were to be produced in favour of this proposition, then, in this context, collective happiness would then have the same status as generalised trust, which although contested in terms of its causality, is accepted as being central to social capital (see, for example, the different views taken by Keefer, 1997; Woolcock, 1998; Knack and Hall, 1999; Falk and Kilpatrick, 2000, all discussed in Chapter 5).

The third possibly good reason would be an assertion that, contrary to what is stated above in relation to families, it might not, after all, be appropriate to see hedonism as a collective as well as an individual attribute and instead that happiness resides only in individuals. This is the most potentially damaging proposition. To use Veenhoven's phraseology: happiness might only be seen as being to do with quality of life *in* societies rather than quality of life *of* societies, the latter being what he would call *liveability*. This whole ontological issue is revisited in the final section of the chapter but for the present it is worth mentioning that at least one commentator, Hancock (1993), does place collective happiness centrally in his macro quality of life and public health construct: for him, a convivial community is essential to liveability and public health.

It is claimed above that the question as to whether happiness can be seen as a collective construct is important to the conceptual and theoretical development of the notion of quality of life. At first sight this may not be fully apparent: indeed, given the criticism of hedonism as being potentially shallow in terms of its meeting of desires for pleasurable sensation, then the notion of collective hedonism may carry connotations (as from the Old Testament in relation to the Cities of the Plains) which are not appropriate for any wholesome and well-rounded perspective on collective quality of life. Nevertheless, leaving aside this extreme-case example of licentiousness, there is a lot to be said for collective pleasure. Other things being equal, a joyful community with societal norms of pursuing valuable doing and beings, will have a higher quality of life than a similar but less joyful society. Also, a strong case can be made that part of the implicit criticism of individual hedonism (in terms of the social comparison relative judgement models discussed in Chapter 1) is neutralised if there are *societal* rather than just *individual* norms of happiness – hedonism is arguably not so conceptually problematic if *everyone* is happy. Admittedly this is a contentious proposition on which further research is needed.

Freedom and autonomy and social cohesion

Freedom and the pursuit of happiness often go together in opposition to, or at least with a differing emphasis to, equality and collectivism. But the relationship between freedom and social cohesion might be rather different to that between happiness and social cohesion. It is argued above that, contrary to conventional wisdom – or at least to virtual universal silence on the topic – there might well be a positive relationship between happiness and social cohesion. However, freedom, or more precisely, *liberty* might not be so compatible with social cohesion. This is particularly pertinent when considering freedom in relation to both utilitarianism and Sen's notion of capabilities. The tension in the relationship between freedom and cohesion is theoretically implicit in the social quality formulation of the dialectic between individual self-realisation and the formation of collective identities where there has to be a trade-off between the individual and the collective in terms of identity.

Arguably there is the same need for a trade-off between individual liberty and social cohesion given that the latter refers to the norms and institutions which keep society together, including collective values of other-regarding behaviour, reciprocity, altruism and civic and social responsibility. When social cohesion is at its most highly integrative, it will form a binding normative framework incorporating high levels of mutual interdependence. The potential trade-off is anticipated in Bernard's *Democratic Dialectic* where he identifies a specific tension not only between liberty and equality but also between liberty and solidarity. This interaction is potentially an important factor in conceptually developing the notion of quality of life because it is not immediately clear to what extent, and under what circumstances, it is possible simultaneously to increase both liberty and social cohesion and to what extent and when they are mutually incompatible.

It is clear that a high level of integrative or homogeneous social cohesion can be accompanied by a highly collectivist ethos characterised by egalitarianism. In situations such as this, there is a high likelihood that liberty, as understood by Sen or in utilitarianism, will be constrained but that the same might not be true for autonomy in Doyal and Gough's or possibly a prudential values interpretation. Alternatively, it may be the case that liberty might not be so constrained in societies with high levels of social cohesion which is of a pluralistic rather than an integrative nature.

The avoidance of pain

Moving away from the collective and back to the individual, it is gratifying to note that this is one area, perhaps indeed the only area, where there is complete agreement among all the different perspectives. Whereas there is deep controversy about the importance or otherwise of pleasure, there is virtual unanimity on the importance of avoiding pain and/or serious harm. It is noted in Chapter 1 that negative affect and absence of positive emotion are central to both Diener and Lucas's (1999) and Argyle's (1996) definitions of subjective well-being and in Chapter 3 that avoidance of pain or serious harm is a core value in prudential values, central to the whole of Doyal and Gough's theory of human need and indeed to all the needs-based approaches and to Nussbaum's capabilities approach, and implicitly in Sen's approach via basic capabilities. Similarly, avoiding harm is integral to the macro societal quality of life constructs. Utilitarianism too, in seeking to maximise utility through meeting actual desires will avoid pain. Most utilitarian theories emphasise maximising utility though the greatest happiness of the greatest number but *negative utilitarianism*, using the same starting point seeks to minimise harm or preventing the greatest amount of harm to the greatest number.

Major themes: from the individual to the societal

It is now time to return from the cross-cutting and multi-level themes back to the original structure of the book and to focus on each level in turn, following a pattern similar to that in ecological approaches to quality of life, starting with the quality of life of the individual and finishing with societal quality of life.

Individual quality of life

At the individual level a person's quality of life can broadly be seen as having two facets: subjective and objective. Subjective quality of life, in its most pure experiential form is comprised of mental states derived from sensations of positive affect, of pleasure or, in utilitarian language, experienced utility. This is the basis for hedonic, happiness-oriented, approaches to subjective well-being (SWB). But SWB in its normal usage comprises more than just a calculus of pleasure; it also includes notions of satisfaction with life, which can be seen as widening the horizons of quality of life so that it potentially includes autonomy, personal growth and self-realisation. This vision of a 'flourishing' human being moves away from a hedonic to a eudaimonic tradition and introduces the first of many tensions and potential disagreements in conceptualising quality of life. From a hedonistic perspective, individuals' judgements about their own quality of life are paramount and must be fully respected. On the other hand, a eudaimonic perspective foregrounds personal growth and the actualisation of human potential as being more worthwhile than 'mere' pleasure and it therefore interposes external judgements into the notion of SWB, leaving itself open to charges of paternalism.

In an ideal society where everyone lives worthwhile, flourishing lives according to the tenets of Aristotelian reason, there would be no tension between the two approaches because citizens would maximise their SWB by achieving a modicum of happiness from pleasurable activities and would gain appropriate levels of satisfaction through activities furthering their personal growth.

The problem in actual societies is that there are downsides to both hedonic and eudaimonic approaches. The dangers of paternalism in eudaimonia have already been noted, and in this context there was a strong libertarian backlash against the 'nanny state' in the 1980s and early 1990s in Britain when government was seen as intervening too much in individuals' lives. Conversely, respecting individuals' own assessments leads to situations such as the 'happy poor' where there is no impetus to ameliorate social hardship where the sufferers have adapted to their lot and do not complain. This phenomenon is perhaps at its most vivid and damaging in relation to health-related quality of life (HRQOL) where there is a strong tendency for sick and disabled people to be their own worst enemies by putting a brave face on their circumstances and reporting higher levels of HRQOL than would be derived from normative, consensus or 'objective' approaches.

In these circumstances, then, it makes sense to pay serious attention to objective approaches to quality of life, irrespective of what individuals themselves think. This can be justified in terms of what is noted above as the universally agreed requirement to avoid serious harm, or in Kahneman's (1999) terms to increase good experiences even if they do not add to SWB. Briefly, objective well-being at individual level is most commonly taken primarily to comprise material well-being, along with civil, political and social rights. The primary accounts of objective material well-being relate to poverty and needs-based approaches, both of which have as their foundations avoiding serious harm. The most parsimonious of the needs-based accounts, including basic needs and basic capabilities, have a threshold of leading a minimally decent life; and absolute poverty can be identified as having a deprivation in basic needs so severe as to risk serious harm to life expectancy. These two together can be used as an 'absolutist' baseline in the terms used in the thresholds and measurements section above.

Leaving aside this extreme case of parsimoniousness, material well-being is in the real world normally conceived of either in terms of the social duties of citizenship or else of social needs (having the resources to be able to do what most people take for granted), including the requirement to be able to dress decently and the need to be able to give small gifts to close relatives at times of celebration. There is no doubt that these activities enhance quality of life but the borderline between what is and is not a genuine need is ideologically hotly contested. This contestation lies at the centre of the relationship between quality of life and policy because needs-based approaches are predicated upon the normative requirement for societies to meet genuine needs among their members. The rationale for this requirement, so elegantly presented by Gough (1998) in relation to the THN is summarised in Chapter 3.

Social perspectives

The societal obligation to meet needs moves quality of life from the individual to the social arena. The THN is the most fully developed objective needs-oriented theory and forms an important element of the foundations for any thoroughgoing development of the quality of life construct. Another important approach is the one that underpins both the social needs version of poverty and the normative and consensual approaches to HRQOL: this is the notion of 'social acceptability' or of commonly agreed thresholds. They are not too easy to pin down ontologically because in one sense they are neither subjective, in that they do not relate specifically to a person's judgement of their own quality of life, and – in their consensual manifestation at least – are not objective, rather, they are collectively subjective in that the norms they specify result from the aggregation of a population's subjective judgements. This methodology of arriving at a quality of life threshold is inductive and pragmatic as opposed to the hierarchically deductive outcome of the THN.

It is worth noting that the social needs approach to poverty is couched in terms not of provision of goods and services, as in basic needs, but of the ability to do things, in other words, in terms of capabilities. The importance of Sen's work on capabilities is noted above in pathways two and three and need not be reiterated here. The other major capabilities-based framework, advanced by Nussbaum (2000), results in a list of central human functional capabilities which has many similarities with the needs list in the THN. Both these lists have similarities too, with the lists of prudential values produced by Griffin (1986, 1996) and Qizilbash (1997a, 1998). The similarities in the lists is noteworthy given that the three approaches have radically different theoretical foundations. It is particularly noteworthy that virtually all the needs in the THN approach are mostly explicitly (but in all cases implicitly) matched in Nussbaum's and the prudential values lists. These, at least from a consensual approach, and probably theoretically too, can form a practical foundation for future quality of life lists.

However, it has to be noted that there are some differences as well as similarities in the lists. One is Nussbaum's inclusion of other species – being able to live with concern for and in relation to animals, plants and the world of nature (Nussbaum, 2000: 78–80) – which Gough (2003: 14) sees as an oddity but which can appropriately be aligned with the sustainability domains of Berger-Schmitt and Noll's (2000) and Hancock's (1993) models. The other difference, which is much more far-reaching in its implications, is the omission from the THN list of any facet of enjoyment or pleasure, whether it be hedonic or more aesthetic and eudaimonic in nature. Both facets are central to the prudential values and Nussbaum lists, and pleasure is central too of course to utilitarianism and in Sen's version of capabilities. It is re-introduced in the final section of the chapter as an essential part of quality of life.

Moving back to more sombre aspects of quality of life, the above discussion covers the differing approaches to poverty but social exclusion has yet to be mentioned. This is because many facets of social exclusion go beyond referring only to the individual within their social context and instead relate more to collective aspects of quality of life, particularly its processual and causally oriented formulations. However, the outcome-oriented manifestations of social exclusion, particularly those related to multiple deprivation, are relevant here. In passing, it is also worth repeating the point made above in the section on hybrid measures, that the operational definition of social exclusion used by Richardson and Le Grand (2002) incorporates a consensual element. Social exclusion, or more aptly, social inclusion, as an outcome is of central relevance too to the THN in that one of its two universal needs-based goals is minimally disabled social participation and the goal in its liberation facet is critical participation. In this context, inability to participate is a form of social exclusion.

Collective constructs relevant to quality of life

Whereas the outcome-oriented aspects of social exclusion relate directly to the lives of individuals and communities within a social setting, its processual and causal aspects are firmly situated in the collective realm and link closely with social capital and social cohesion. The processes of social exclusion are systemic features of society relating to the distribution of resources and opportunities and to discriminatory processes which operate to detach people from society either individually or more commonly as collectivities. The causal aspects of social exclusion are linked to denial of, or restriction in access to, resource structures necessary for social belonging, including non-material resources such as trust and the interpersonal respect needed for self-esteem, both individually and collectively. In all its manifestations social exclusion is of central importance to quality of life.

Social capital and social cohesion also have a central role here in providing the collective social environment within which people lead their lives. The amount and extent of trust, reciprocity, social bonds, etc. have profound consequences for all but the hermit, and indeed even the extent of, and the propensity for, social isolation are directly causally linked to the nature of social capital and social cohesion. These are heavily researched constructs but their nature is still enigmatic and their relationship with quality of life has not been fully worked out. Put bluntly, it is possible to have too much as well as too little of them, and different types or aspects of these constructs can be both benign and malign in quality of life terms: thus, social capital with high levels of bonding – and low levels of bridging – social networks can lead to gang culture; and highly integrative and homogeneous social cohesion can lead to racism, xenophobia, and even to genocide. Thus, unlike poverty and social exclusion which can be seen as linear continua (being inversely related to collective quality of life), social capital and social cohesion are complex multi-faceted entities which need to be optimised rather than maximised in order to enhance quality of life.

One potentially fruitful way forward is to focus research on ascertaining the impact on quality of life of each of their elements rather than to try to take a holistic approach (Hero, 2003). For example, mapping the distribution of integrative norms (such as the radius of trust) among and in relations to different groups, communities and social divisions would provide valuable information both on the nature and extent of this element of cohesiveness within society and on the distribution of one aspect of social exclusion (Uslaner, 2002, 2004). Also, a similar exploration of the extent and interconnectedness of networks comprising weak links, seen consistently in the literature as a positive aspect of social capital, would yield complementary results. This would not only identify the magnitude of these elements but also map their discontinuities, identifying which groups do not trust and/or have no linkages with each other.

Even an exercise mapping just these two elements would provide important insights into the extent of homogeneous versus pluralistic social cohesion. For example, a society with high levels of generalised trust but distinct discontinuities in networks of weak links between, for example, several ethnic communities, can be seen as having positive pluralistic social cohesion whereas a society with a similar pattern of weak links but a corresponding discontinuity in generalised trust would have less positive pluralistic social cohesion. Similarly, a society with both high levels of generalised trust and highly pervasive networks of weak links could be seen as having positive homogeneous or integrative social cohesion.

But even an approach as specific and grounded as this will not be able to address a fundamental issue about the nature of social cohesion, which is the extent to which it has ideological connotations. In Chapter 5 a distinction is made between non-ideological and ideological social cohesion with the former comprising interlocking networks, trust, other-regarding behaviour and social coherence (via civic institutions) and the latter additionally including elements of social justice and egalitarianism. Such ideological social cohesion entails high levels of reciprocity, along with the social transfers and redistribution necessary in an egalitarian and collectivist society.

There are two (possibly interrelated) sets of issues in such highly cohesive societies, both of which can be effectively viewed through the lens of social inclusion and exclusion. The first relates to treatment of *difference* among citizens and the second relates to membership – who is allowed to become a citizen. First, with regard to difference, in a society comprising different ethnos or cultural communities, all with their own traditions and individual community identities and with a sense of collective national or demos identity, there will be a trade-off between ethnos and demos (Phillips and Berman, 2001a, 2003). With a strong homogeneous societal social cohesion, this could lead to weaker ethnos communities facing social exclusion in terms of discrimination or even physical exclusion. In a society with weaker or more pluralistic social cohesion, on the other hand, there is a danger of loss of national identity or of secession, often mentioned in Canadian literature (Jenson, 1998; Leibfried, 1998) or even of disintegration of federal states, as happened in the former Yugoslavia.

Second, the issue of who is or is not allowed even to enter a country or have the right of abode or citizenship rights is not only a pressing political problem in the EU and its member and candidate states but also strikes at the heart of the relationship between inclusion, exclusion and cohesion. Societies with high levels of strong, egalitarian and homogeneous social cohesion will have both high levels of, and a high quality of social inclusion. But they will also probably be highly exclusive or exclusionary in that the homogeneity, feelings of belonging, generous social support, mutual interdependence, reciprocity, trust and altruism will be predicated upon a strong sense of identity, togetherness and recognition that comes from being in a tightly knit, bonding society. Also, and perhaps more to the point, if incomers are poor, do not speak the host language and/or have social needs, then they will be much more of a burden on a collectivist, highly egalitarian society with ideological social cohesion than on an individualist non-egalitarian society with non-ideological social cohesion.

To paraphrase and at the risk of over-simplification, countries with non-ideological social cohesion can offer 'low quality' social inclusion to a high quantity of incomers and therefore will have a low *quantity* of social excluded people. Countries with ideological social cohesion will have high quality social inclusion, therefore may be likely to have a high *quantity* of social exclusion. One vision of a high level of societal quality of life is where social exclusion is low and ideological social cohesion is high. It is not clear from the present state of research and conceptualisation on social cohesion and social exclusion how this can be achieved.

Overarching and holistic quality of life constructs

This lack of clarity in the relationship between social cohesion and social exclusion becomes very apparent when examining the three quality of life constructs which deal with this relationship. For Bernard (1999), social inclusion is integral to the notion of social cohesion and the existence of social exclusion represents a failure in social cohesion. In the social quality construct, social exclusion and social cohesion are seen as separate but they interact within the overall social quality theoretical framework (Beck *et al.*, 2001a; Baers *et al.*, 2005). Berger-Schmitt and Noll (2000) classify social exclusion as being distinct from social capital but consider them both to be elements of social cohesion.

Berger-Schmitt and Noll's approach to conceptualising the relationship between social exclusion, social capital and social cohesion, while it may not necessarily be the only or even the best way, is of both theoretical and practical importance to developments in understanding quality of life. There are two other elements of their approach which are similarly important. The first is their notion of sustainability which is unquestionably vital for quality of life. Second, they mirror the value stance taken in this book of insisting on explicitly including both objective and subjective well-being of individuals within their framework.

The major contribution made by proponents of the social quality construct lies in their bold attempt at developing a theoretical justification for their vision: for citizens to participate in their communities under conditions which enhance their potential and their well-being. This can be summarised in terms of the dialectic between the processes of self-realisation of individuals as social beings and the processes resulting in the formation of collective social identities. This performs two important functions for the present purpose: the first is that it unambiguously identifies a eudaimonic approach to individual quality of life through the notion of self-realisation; and, second, it links the individual to the collective through the formation of social identities. These two functions pave the way to the operationalisation of at least three of the four conditional social quality factors, the first leading to social empowerment and the second to social cohesion and, perhaps more implicitly, to social inclusion. The fourth factor, socio-economic security is perhaps less clearly embedded in the individual-social dialectic, but it is of course of central importance to individual and collective quality of life, being strongly related to the needs-based approaches.

Turning from the overarching to the holistic perspectives, Bernard's vision of the 'good society', achieving maximum levels of inclusion, social justice, legitimacy, participation, recognition and belonging, while salutary, is perhaps over-optimistic – here *optimisation* seems a much more realistic goal than maximisation. If social justice were to be left out, this list would probably be an acceptable starting place for the non-ideological versions of social cohesion. In this context Bernard's framework can be seen as a model for a *collective* version of quality of life.

Hancock's public health model has affinities with all three of the models discussed in Chapter 7. Like Bernard's approach, it provides a strong tripartite collective model and like Berger-Schmitt and Noll's overarching quality of life model, it stresses the crucial goals of sustainability and a viable environment. He also introduces the notion of community capital which covers a wider range of resources than social capital and emphasises the importance of the community as a repository for these resources. This is a useful development of the notion of social capital.

Another element introduced by Hancock which is missing from the other macro formulations, is the idea of *conviviality*. This perhaps expresses at a collective level what Nussbaum referred to as 'play, enjoyment, laughter, recreation' in her list of individual capability attributes (Nussbaum, 2000: 78). Conviviality is an important facet of quality of life in groups, communities and societies.

All the societal quality of life constructs discussed here show a strong commitment to high levels of social cohesion based on egalitarianism and social justice. However, none of them address the question of how much inequality would be acceptable, as does Barry (1998) with boundaries of 50 per cent and 300 per cent of average earnings. Similarly, none of the proponents of these three models have addressed the substantive trade-offs between universalistic egalitarianism and respect for difference.

Principles of quality of life

This, the final section of the chapter and of the book, is the place where difficult and complex issues raised earlier are due to be revisited with the hope of bringing them all together to make an overall appraisal of the core attributes of quality of life, to define it and to give an indication of potentially fruitful avenues for further development of the construct. Before beginning to undertake these tasks in exploring what quality of life *is*, it is worthwhile to note its boundaries in terms of what it does not encompass, in other words what it is *not*. The most important boundary post, at least with respect to the way in which quality of life is treated in this book, is at the borderline with ethics or morality.

Quality of life is about the good life, and collectively it is about the good society, in the sense of what is valuable or worthwhile to individuals and societies and of what makes them flourish. Quality of life here is not *being good* in the sense of being moral or behaving with ethical propriety, it is about what makes human lives and societies *go better*, to use Qizilbash's (1998) phrase. There are, of course, areas where issues of quality of life are inextricably intertwined with those of morality or ethics, particularly in relation to issues in health-related quality of life where life and death decisions have to be made and where quality of life is relevant to, or even the primary consideration in, these decisions. Similarly there is a strong moral imperative in relation to meeting basic needs and combating absolute poverty, in addition to the rights-based imperative presented in Chapter 3. Their moral dimension adds weight and purpose to deliberations about these issues but for the purposes of this book the primary focus is not on their moral status as such.

Having noted what quality of life does not refer to in relation to ethics and morality, the rest of this section deals with what the construct *does* comprise. This begins with a brief discussion of the particularities of quality of life at both individual and collective level in order to try to identify its core attributes. These are then explored before attempting – for the first time in the book – to give a definition of quality of life. Then finally some unfinished business, in terms of both unresolved issues and of potentially fruitful avenues for further inquiry, is addressed.

Core attributes of individual quality of life

The obvious foundation for delineating the core attributes of quality of life, at least at the individual level, is undoubtedly the universally agreed goal of avoiding pain and harm. Perhaps the best starting point for this is basic needs. Whether it is expressed in terms of the THN, basic capabilities, or an element of either a prudential values or Nussbaum's (2000) capabilities list – the meeting of basic needs as the minimum threshold standard for a decently acceptable existence for a reasonably acceptable lifespan is the foundation of quality of life. This is uncontroversial when expressed in a free-standing needs-based context but becomes controversial when linked to a rights-based discourse which requires a societal duty to meet all basic needs. Thus, the first core attribute of quality of life for individuals concerns meeting essential needs (arguably as an unconditional universal right).

Once essential needs are met, the opportunity arises to pursue other valuable activities and it is here that Sen's capabilities approach provides a useful volitional framework giving individuals the autonomy to choose between doings and beings that could either further meet their needs, enhance their pleasure, enable them to flourish, or indeed do all of these simultaneously (as would be the case with enjoying reading a worthy book which helps enhance one's literacy). So a second core attribute of quality of life is to do with autonomy of agency, shading into critical autonomy in Doyal and Gough's (1991) formulation. This is not as entirely watertight as the first but no commentator referred to in this book has actually denied the value of autonomy, so long as it is not abused. The next three core attributes are more controversial, not least with regard to their ordering. The choice of the ordering here is a personal one and is as follows: subjective well-being; flourishing in the Aristotelian sense used by Nussbaum; and social inclusion, as defined consensually.

For the third core attribute, subjective well-being, Argyle's (1996) definition is used here. This not only includes satisfaction and presence or absence of positive emotion, but also another, more specifically eudaimonic element including purpose in life and personal growth. Now, placing subjective well-being, even with an eudaimonic element, ahead of heavyweight prudential values of Aristotelian flourishing – in other words placing *actual* desires ahead of *informed* desires – can be characterised as being shallow or frivolous given the heavyweight import of leading a fulfilling life. Its justification, repeated from the conclusion of Chapter 1, lies in the tenet that the primacy of autonomy as a core attribute requires that an individual's own feelings, thoughts and emotions must be taken seriously and that any rounded conceptualisation of quality of life must take account of individuals' judgements about their own lives. This core attribute is fully consistent with utilitarianism and is as such prey to the pitfalls associated with the adaptive behaviour of the 'happy poor' and the 'happy disabled'. Given these potential problems, it is important that the eudaimonic facet of subjective well-being is foregrounded and that its fulfilment is facilitated.

In one sense it has to be accepted that the fourth core attribute, flourishing, is more intrinsically valuable than the third in that it deals with values, capabilities and desires which are by definition worthwhile. It is, indeed, hard to argue against the value of accomplishment, aspiration, self-respect, love, deep personal relations, the exercise of practical reasoning, and particularly –as so delightfully expressed by Griffin (1986:67) – freedom from muddle, ignorance and mistakes. However, the spectre of paternalism hovers over this worthy endeavour. These prudential values, informed desires and Aristotelian capabilities are undoubtedly worth aspiring to but this is done most effectively through individual volition rather than by decree.

The fifth core attribute continues the theme of taking the views of individuals seriously in that it uses a normative approach to social inclusion based on consensual criteria for meeting social needs and social citizenship, as introduced in Chapter 4 in relation to poverty and social exclusion. Put simply, this attribute comprises social inclusion based on commonly accepted minimum levels of active citizenship. In order to be able to achieve this, it is necessary to be able to do things that most people take for granted within a society. The material wherewithal for this is delineated for Britain in the Poverty and Social Exclusion Survey (Gordon, 2000) and its socio-cultural requirements have been identified by Walker and Wigfield (2003: 9) as 'the degree to which people are and feel integrated in the different relationships, organisations, sub-systems and structures that constitute everyday life'.

Core attributes of collective quality of life

The discussion of systems and structures along with citizenship in relation to the individual core attribute of social inclusion provides a bridge to the collective core attributes of quality of life. It is here, however, that the definitional chickens come home to roost in relation to both social capital and social cohesion. If they were both unambiguously 'quality of life enhancing', then they could be simply adnumbered here. Given the serious problems in identifying the nature and extent of what could be identified as 'positive' as opposed to 'negative' social capital and social cohesion, neither of these terms will be used in this list of core collective attributes. This approach differs from that of Berger-Schmitt and Noll's overarching quality of life model and of Beck *et al.*'s social quality construct in omitting them as constructs to be met in their entirety but it is argued here that decomposing social capital and social cohesion and then using only those elements which are unambiguously positive is more useful in the present state of theorising and operationalising of these constructs than trying to use them holistically. Initially only the non-ideological elements of social cohesion are included; their ideological elements are introduced at the end of the list.

The first core attribute of collective quality of life identified here is what Lockwood (1999) calls civic integration – the integrity of the core institutional order of citizenship at the macro-social level – and what the World Bank calls 'civic responsibility and common identification with forms of government, cultural norms and social rules' (World Bank, 1998: i). It also covers Woolcock's (1998) constructs of synergy and integrity and Narayan's (1999) notion of efficiency at macro-societal level. Within this attribute Lockwood includes political integration, including respect for democracy, and economic integration, including high levels of economic activity and employment – which have resonances with Bernard's (1999) democratic dialectic and Hancock's (1993) adequately prosperous economy, respectively.

The second and third collective core attributes are of equal status to each other. The second comprises high levels and a wide-ranging distribution of integrative norms and values, including trust, reciprocity and other-regarding behaviour. The third is a wide range, high level and high density of weak network links and bridging ties throughout society. Together these would indicate both a high degree of social integration and of tolerance and respect for difference, as noted in the sub-section above on collective constructs.

Sustainability, the fourth collective core attribute adds an extra dimension, time, to the analysis. This is because quality of life needs to be safeguarded for the lifetime of this and succeeding generations. It also introduces a global focus in relation to phenomena such as global warming. In Hancock's (1993) holistic public health construct, sustainability is encapsulated through his notion of a viable environment. The only other construct discussed in this book which directly addresses sustainability is Berger-Schmitt and Noll's overarching quality of life model where it is conceptualised in terms of the preservation of *societal capital*, including human and natural capital. This is a helpful presentation of both the social and environmental aspects of sustainability where it is not only the physical but also the social environment which need to be nurtured and looked after.

The final collective core attribute returns to integrative norms and values which are elements of social cohesion – the ideological ones. In one sense this is a continuum of ideological perspectives similar to those discussed in Chapter 5, ranging from fairness, equity and equality of opportunity at its least ideological, through to more full-blooded conceptualisations of equality of outcome at its most ideological. This attribute is at the end of the list because it is, of course, by far the most controversial. It is particularly contentious when coupled with the parenthesised proposition at the end of the first individual core attribute that basic needs should be met as an unconditional universal right.

At their most modest level, ideological norms associated with fairness, such as the golden rule of treating others as you would expect them to treat you, will gain virtually universal acceptance. Also most people would probably countenance the meeting of the most basic of needs of fellow citizens but– recalling Enoch Powell's dictum from Chapter 3 – not necessarily meeting them as a *social right*.

At this point it is worth mentioning that one element of Lockwood's (1999) civic integration construct was not included in discussion of the first core collective attribute above because of its ideological content. This element is social welfare integration. Lockwood states that high levels of social welfare integration are expressed through universalism in social rights and the widespread provision of state welfare whereas lack of social welfare integration is manifested by low provision, high levels of poverty and deprivation. So for him, universal social rights – going some distance down the ideological road – are essential for even basic (putatively non-ideological) civic integration.

It is also worth at this point revisiting the discussions about equality and health. It is interesting to note that all commentators agree that there will be lower death rates in the more equal of two societies with the same average incomes. This will either be because of neo-material factors – worse health services and resources for the poor – or because of the detrimental effect of lower absolute income or of psycho-social factors, or all three. So from the perspectives of all these commentators, moving towards greater equality by transferring health-related resources from the rich to the poor would lead to society becoming more healthy. This again makes a significant link with the first individual core attribute of quality of life.

A definition of quality of life

If the above core attributes are accepted as circumscribing the territory within which quality of life lies, then they can be used as the basis for its definition. A discursive definition based on the above might be as follows:

> Quality of life is both an individual and collective attribute. At the individual level it includes objective and subjective elements. People's objective quality of life requires that their basic needs are met and that they have the material resources necessary to fulfil the social requirements of citizenship. Their subjective quality of life depends on them having the autonomy to make effective choices to (1) 'enjoy' – enhance their subjective well-being, including hedonism, satisfaction, purpose in life and personal growth; (2) 'flourish' in the eudaimonic, other-regarding, Aristotelian sense of fulfilling informed as well as actual desires; and (3) participate in the full range of social activities of citizenship. People's collectively focused quality of life requires global environmental sustainability, both physical and social, and the following social resources within the communities and societies in which they live: civic integration, synergy and integrity; extensive weak network links and bridging ties at all levels of society; wide-ranging integrative norms and values including trust, reciprocity and other-regarding behaviour; and societal norms and values relating at least to fairness and equity and possibly to some degree of social justice and egalitarianism.

And a short version might be:

> Quality of life requires that people's basic and social needs are met and that they have the autonomy to choose to enjoy life, to flourish and to participate as citizens in a society with high levels of civic integration, social connectivity, trust and other integrative norms including at least fairness and equity, all within a physically and socially sustainable global environment.

The definition has been constructed in a way which privileges objective over subjective individual quality of life and which uses a capabilities framework in relation to enjoyment, fulfilment and participation. In order to avoid charges of paternalism, it would have been possible, following Gough (2003: 16), to have included the objective aspects under the capabilities umbrella too, but this was rejected on the grounds of 'importance': the meeting of basic needs is considered here to be so fundamental that it is specified (rather than basic capabilities) as a non-negotiable requirement. However, the longer version, while requiring the meeting of basic needs, does open the door to autonomy in relation to the social requirements of citizenship in requiring only that people have *access* to the material resources necessary to meet them but not specifying that they must be used for that purpose.

The framing of the subjective individual quality of life elements within an 'open' capabilities framework based on autonomy, reflects the tension between utilitarianism and hedonism, on the one hand, and eudaimonics, prudential values and Nussbaum's approach, on the other. In an ideal world the quality of life of all people would be enhanced by them freely choosing to devote a significant proportion of their energies to 'flourishing' – and one of the major pieces of unfinished quality of life business is to find the best way to maximise this – but respect for freedom of choice has to come first here, given the tenet in this book that any rounded theory of quality of life must take account of individuals' own judgements about their own lives. This emphasis on autonomy also, following Bernard (1999), downplays any *obligation* to participate socially as would be required in, for example, a republican formulation of citizenship.

The openness of this framework resonates with Sen's notion of 'principled pluralism', as presented by Alkire (2002b: 102–5). Also, and more pragmatically, it reflects the inherent complexity of the notion of an individual's quality of life: in this context it is worth recalling Gasper's (2004: 24) plea that we should 'accept plurality/complexity and hopefully . . . not drown in it'.

At the collective level, sustainability is in effect the equivalent of basic needs at the individual level and is thus equally important. It is a matter of regret that, up to the present, it has been given so little attention in the quality of life literature (with the honourable exceptions of Berger-Schmitt and Noll, 2000, and Hancock, 1993). Therefore no apology is made for it being so central to this definition.

Collective societal resources are also integral to the definition of quality of life. The omission of the terms 'social capital' and 'social cohesion' has made the definition tighter and more specific but has led to it being more sparse and lacking the warm and comforting emblematic aura surrounding social capital and social cohesion. This is a price worth paying for more precision but it does perhaps leave some unfinished business, particularly in relation to identity, respect for difference, pluralism and cosmopolitanism. The definition might be strengthened if additional elements relating to these could be clearly identified.

Finally, the 'ideological' integrative norms, while an essential part of any definition, are not easy to specify and are impossible to stipulate precisely because they are so hotly contested. It is worth stating, however, that because the meeting of basic needs is central to quality of life and because life expectancy is, as noted above, higher in more equal developed societies at any given income level, then a presumption based on maximising quality of life would be towards at least some degree of egalitarianism or mitigation of inequalities.

Unfinished business

There are at least four different types of unfinished business to be noted here. Two of them could have been remedied in this book with more space and time: the first refers to omissions from the substantive chapters both in terms of material that has been unread or read and unreported, and even whole chapters which could have been in the book but are not; the second refers to operationalising the definition given above – much more could have been done in fleshing it out in terms of dimensions, domains, sub-domains and indicators. The third type relates to conceptual work than can usefully be done in the future to develop our understanding of quality of life. Finally, the fourth type is unfinished business in the real world, comprising a reminder of action that needs to be taken here to enhance quality of life.

Omissions

The area of quality of life with the most extensive literature is undoubtedly that to do with health, illness, disability and ageing. Although health-related quality of life (HRQOL) is discussed in this book to some extent, only a very small proportion of this work has been mentioned here; so this is undeniably the biggest gap in relation to quality of life literature. This omission is not too problematic, though, because much of the HRQOL literature is complementary to the material presented here. Perhaps a more important area with considerable relevant literature where the complementarity is not so obvious relates to altruism, particularly with regard to its socially and societally integrative attributes. It would be valuable to review the social literature on altruism and to incorporate it into a quality of life perspective.

As noted above, the same is true for the literature on sustainability, particularly in relation to its political economy and sociological facets. This immediately links in with the immensely important literature in development studies, much of which is, of course informed by the debates in Chapter 3. In relation to the actual quality of life of individuals in the world, issues of global development are of paramount and immediate importance. The interaction of development and sustainability with the core quality of life requirement for basic needs to be met is one of the most pressing long-term issues the world is facing in the twenty-first century.

One other issue which has only been touched upon here but deserves far more extensive treatment is that relating to gender and family. There is a quality of life literature on this topic with perhaps the most important contributions being made in relation to women and development by Nussbaum (1995, 2000, 2006) and Alkire (2002a, 2002b) but much more needs to be done, particularly in theoretical terms in relation to reviewing the important women's studies literature on patriarchy and the gendered division of quality of life with a view to incorporating it into quality of life theorising.

Operationalising the definition

There are several good reasons why no attempt has been made to operationalise the definition given above. The first, the most important and the best reason is that there is no substantive point in operationalising a definition until it has been scrutinised and exposed to critical appraisal and alternative exposition. At present, the definition is provisional in that it is conditional upon the proposed core attributes of quality of life, which themselves are still tentative and open to scrutiny. In due course, some elements of the definition might be amended or even deleted and some might be added.

Second, and also of vital importance, there is little hope of being able to operationalise a definition effectively if the relative importance of each of its elements has not been ascertained. For example, some elements might be seen as core, as non-negotiable and therefore as prerequisites for quality of life. Here, basic needs might be an example. Others might be seen as highly important and fulfilling a normative expectation without being absolutely essential and these might be thresholds for having a reasonable quality of life, either severally and irreducibly as in Nussbaum's capabilities list, or incrementally and summatively coming together as a 'critical mass'. Yet others might be less central and be seen as aspirations rather than expectations: having some or all of these would point to having a high quality of life. These sorts of issues have already been alluded to in general above when discussing thresholds and measurement.

The experience of the two overarching societal quality of life models discussed in Chapter 6 is instructive here. In Berger-Schmitt's and Noll's model there are forty-seven nodes of measurement dimensions/life domains for social cohesion alone and there is scope for many different indicators at each node. Similarly, there are eighteen domains, fifty sub-domains and ninety indicators of the four conditional factors of social quality. Yet for neither of these is there any indication of how the indicators relating to these node and sub-domains are to be combined to give overall quality of life or social quality ratings. Perhaps one of the reasons for this is that the 'importance' status and relative weights of the various dimensions and domains in these two models have not yet been finalised.

Conceptual developments

It will come as no surprise that the nature, definition and operationalisation of both social capital and social cohesion come high on the list of unfinished quality of life business presented here. The problems with these constructs have already loomed large in this and the previous three chapters, so large indeed that neither social capital nor social cohesion appear in the definition of quality of life given here. Yet, as seen in Chapters 6 and 7, they are central elements in some of the best-developed and important constructs and models relating to quality of life. There is no doubt that as holistic, sensitising constructs, they both have immense heuristic value and that they have facilitated and framed new ways of thinking about social resources, particularly in relation to economic development and social stability. It is necessary to build upon these advances by undertaking a meticulous study of the range and intricacies of the different meanings attributed and ascribed to these terms. A start has been made on this task in Chapter 5 but a great deal of extra work needs to be done on assessing both the positive and negative effects of different types of networks, norms and values and how these vary in different social contexts.

There are three aspects of social cohesion in particular which need teasing out in order to further our understanding of collective aspects of quality of life. One relates to the whole area of conviviality, of what leads to a 'happy society', if such a thing can be said to exist. This is an important area to explore, both in its own right and as a potential bridge between the 'pleasure' aspect of hedonism and the other-regarding aspect of eudaimonic approaches to quality of life because one of the bases of collective happiness has to reside in shared collective norms. The second concerns the relationship between different configurations of social cohesion, both at community or ethnos and at national or demos level, and recognition of difference, pluralism and cosmopolitanism. Following on from this, the third aspect of social cohesion which is central to furthering the conceptual development of quality of life concerns notions of national identity. This relates to the earlier discussion in this chapter and in Chapter 5 about the interaction between social cohesion and social exclusion.

It is important in addressing the issues noted above to make a distinction between undertaking work which clarifies and furthers the conceptual and theoretical clarity of the quality of life construct and identifying topics which are in essence conceptually irresolvable because they are in fact disputes about values and morality and not about the meaning of concepts.

Unfinished practical business

The definition of quality of life chosen here is not as specific as the lists of Griffin, Qizilbash, Nussbaum or Doyal and Gough nor does it have the prescriptive status of the latter two lists, so it does not give a definitive 'recipe' for quality of life. Nor is it as general and incomplete as Sen's capabilities account or as *laissez-faire* as utilitarianism. At the individual level, attention is drawn to two sorts of unfinished business, one to do with a result of the emphasis on autonomy, that is on the indeterminate element of the definition, and the other with a result of that part of the definition which is prescriptive.

It is noted here and in Chapter 1 that, from the perspective of this book at least, in value terms, the primacy of autonomy is a *sine qua non* of quality of life. This has the great practical advantage of avoiding charges of paternalism and is fully consistent with Enlightenment traditions of respect for individual liberty. However, the vision of a better life provided by the informed desires of the prudential values approach and in Nussbaum's version of capabilities is extremely appealing and, again in terms of personal values, is presented here as having a very high priority. The encouragement and facilitation of this Aristotelian flourishing through furthering eudaimonic integrative norms and value will need to be a high priority in order to reach the situation where people as a matter of course choose to pursue personal growth, self-actualisation, practical reason and critical reflection as well as less lofty hedonic goals

The final sort of unfinished business does have a highly prescriptive element globally for all individuals and also has the potential for prescriptiveness societally at the collective level. At the individual level, autonomy is paramount in relation to choice between enjoyment, flourishing and participation and, to some extent, over use of the material resources necessary to fulfil the social requirements of citizenship. But the requirement for meeting basic needs is universal and unconditional and indeed prescriptive. The prescription here does not extend as far as in Doyal and Gough's theory of human needs or Nussbaum's capabilities list. But even so, it is a difficult enough task to achieve if quality of life is to be seen as a universal goal. Thus, the major piece of unfinished quality of life business lies in ensuring that the basic needs of each individual in the world are met.

At the collective level there is considerable scope for ideological prescriptiveness, if the integrative norms relating to fairness and equity are taken to include some degree of at least mitigation of inequalities. This is entirely defensible in the terms of the definition, as follows. The requirement to meet basic needs and to provide the resources to meet the social requirements of citizenship necessarily entails some redistribution from the rich to the poor; provision of health services for the poorest members of society helps meet their basic needs; and the more equal a society is, other things being held constant, then the lower its overall death rates because of the positive gains from redistribution (Gravelle, 1998). Therefore, mitigating inequalities irrefutably adds to quality of life.

If this argument is not accepted on the basis of its ratiocination then – for the first time in the book – moral arguments have to come into play. Zygmunt Bauman (2000: 12) in an article entitled 'Am I my brother's keeper?' claims that

> the human quality of a society ought to be measured by the quality of life of its weaker members . . . Rational arguments will not help . . . Morality has only itself to support it: it is better to care than to wash one's hands.

This is a fitting point on which to end.

Appendix

ENIQ indicators of social quality

Indicators of socio-economic security

Domains	Sub-domains	Indicators
Financial resources	Income sufficiency	1. Part of household income spent on health, clothing, food and housing (in the lower and median household incomes)
	Income security	2. How certain biographical events affect the risk of poverty on household level
		3. Proportion of total population living in households receiving entitlement transfers (means-tested, cash and in-kind transfers) that allow them to live above EU poverty level
Housing and environment	Housing security	4. Proportion of people who have certainty of keeping their home
		5. Proportion of hidden families (i.e. several families within the same household)
	Housing conditions	6. Number of square metres per household member
		7. Proportion of population living in houses with lack of functioning basic amenities (water, sanitation and energy)
	Environmental conditions (social and natural)	8. People affected by criminal offences per 10,000 inhabitants
		9. Proportion living in households that are situated in neighbourhoods with above-average pollution rate (water, air and noise)
Health and care	Security of health provisions	10. Proportion of people covered by compulsory/voluntary health insurance (including qualitative exploration of what is and what is not covered by insurance system)
	Health services	11. Number of medical doctors per 10,000 inhabitants
		12. Average distance to hospital, measure in minutes, not in metres
		13. Average response time of medical ambulance
	Care services	14. Average number of hours spent on care differentiated by paid and unpaid

Work	Employment security	15.	Length of notice before employer can change terms and conditions of labour relation/contract
		16.	Length of notice before termination of labour contract
		17.	Proportion employed workforce with temporary, non-permanent, job contract
		18.	Proportion of workforce that is illegal
	Working conditions	19.	Number of employees that reduce work time because of interruption (parental leave, medical assistance of relative, palliative leave) as a proportion of the employees who are entitled to these kinds of work time reductions
		20.	Number of accidents (fatal/non-fatal) at work per 100,000 employed persons (if possible: per sector)
		21.	Number of hours a full-time employee typically works a week (actual working week)
Education	Security of education	22.	Proportion of pupils leaving education without finishing compulsory education (early school leavers)
		23.	Study fees as proportion of national mean net wage
	Quality of education	24.	Proportion of students who, within a year of leaving school with or without certificate, are able to find employment

Source: Keizer and van der Maesen (2003)

Indicators of social cohesion

Domains	Sub-domains	Indicators	
Trust	Generalised trust	25.	Extent to which 'most people can be trusted'
	Specific trust	26.	Trust in: government; elected representatives; political parties; armed forces; legal system; the media; trade unions, police; religious institutions; civil service; economic transactions
		27.	Number of cases being referred to European Court of Law
		28.	Importance of: family; friends; leisure; politics; respecting parents; parents' duty to children
Other integrative norms and values	Altruism	29.	Volunteering: number of hours per week
		30.	Blood donation
	Tolerance	31.	Views on immigration, pluralism and multiculturalism
		32.	Tolerance of other people's self-identity, beliefs, behaviour and lifestyle preferences
	Social contract	33.	Beliefs on causes of poverty: individual or structural
		34.	Willingness to pay more taxes if you were sure that it would improve the situation of the poor

Domains	Sub-domains	Indicators
		35. Intergenerational: willingness to pay 1 per cent more taxes in order to improve the situation of elderly people in your country
		36. Willingness to actually do something practical for the people in your community/ neighbourhood, like: picking up litter, doing some shopping for elderly/disabled/sick people in your neighbourhood, assisting neighbours/ community members with filling out (tax/ municipal/etc.) forms, cleaning the street/porch/doorway
		37. Division of household tasks between men and women: Do you have an understanding with your husband/spouse about the division of household tasks, raising of the children, and gaining household income?
Social networks	Networks	38. Membership (active or inactive) of political, voluntary, charitable organisations or sport clubs
		39. Support received from family, neighbours and friends
		40. Frequency of contact with friends and colleagues
Identity	National/ European identity	41. Sense of national pride
		42. Identification with national symbols and European symbols
	Regional/ community/ local identity	43. Sense of regional/community/local identity
	Interpersonal identity	44. Sense of belonging to family and kinship network

Source: Berman and Phillips (2004)

Indicators of social inclusion

Domains	Sub-domains	Indicators
Citizenship rights	Constitutional/ political rights	45. Proportion of residents with citizenship
		46. Proportion having right to vote in local elections and proportion exercising it
	Social rights	47. Proportion with right to a public pension (i.e. a pension organised or regulated by the government)
		48. Women's pay as a proportion of men's
	Civil rights	49. Proportion with right to free legal advice
		50. Proportion experiencing discrimination
	Economic and political networks	51. Proportion of ethnic minority groups elected or appointed to parliament, boards of private companies and foundations

		52.	Proportion of women elected or appointed to parliament, boards of private companies and foundations
Labour market	Access to paid employment	53.	Long-term unemployment (12+ months)
		54.	Involuntary part-time or temporary employment
Services	Health services	55.	Proportions with entitlement to and using public primary health care
	Housing	56.	Proportion homeless, sleeping rough
		57.	Average waiting time for social housing
	Education	58.	School participation rates and higher education participation rates
	Social care	59.	Proportion of people in need receiving care services
		60.	Average waiting time for care services (including child care)
	Financial services	61.	Proportion denied credit differentiated by income groups
		62.	Access to financial assistance/advice in case of need
	Transport	63.	Proportion of population who have access to public transport system
		64.	Density of public transport system and road density
	Civic/cultural services	65.	Number of public sport facilities per 10,000 inhabitants
		66.	Number of public and private civic and cultural facilities (e.g. cinema, theatre, concerts) per 10,000 inhabitants
Social networks	Neighbourhood participation	67.	Proportion in regular contact with neighbours
		68.	Proportion in regular contact with friends
	Friendships	69.	Proportion feeling lonely/isolated
	Family life	70.	Duration of contact with relatives (cohabiting and non-cohabiting)
		71.	Informal (non-monetary) assistance received by different types of family

Source: Walker and Wigfield (2003)

Indicators of social empowerment

Domains	Sub-domains	Indicators
Knowledge base	Application of knowledge	72. Extent to which social mobility is knowledge-based (formal qualifications)
	Availability of information	73. Percentage of population literate and numerate
		74. Availability of free media
		75. Access to internet
	User friendliness of information	76. Provision of information in multiple languages on social services
		77. Availability of free advocacy, advice and guidance centres

Domains	Sub-domains	Indicators
Labour market	Control over employment contract	78. Percentage of labour force that is member of a trade union (differentiated to public and private employees)
		79. Percentage of labour force covered by a collective agreement (differentiated by public and private employees)
	Prospects of job mobility	80. Percentage of employed labour force receiving work-based training
		81. Percentage of labour force availing of publicly provided training (not only skills based) (Please outline costs of such training if any)
		82. Percentage of labour force participating in any 'back to work scheme'
	Reconciliation of work and family life (work/life balance)	83. Percentage of organisations operating work life balance policies
		84. Percentage of employed labour force actually making use of work/life balance measures (see indicator above)
Openness and supportive- ness of institutions	Openness and supportiveness of political system	85. Existence of processes of consultation and direct democracy (e.g. referenda)
	Openness of economic system	86. Number of instances of public involvement in major economic decision-making (e.g. public hearings about company relocation, inward investment and plant closure)
	Openness of organisations	87. Percentage of organisations/institutions with work councils
Public space	Support for collective action	88. Percentage of the national and local public budget that is reserved for voluntary, not-for-profit citizenship initiatives
		89. Marches and demonstrations banned in the past 12 months as proportion of total marched and demonstrations (held and banned)
	Cultural enrichment	90. Proportion of local and national budget allocated to all cultural activities
		91. Number of self-organised cultural groups and events
		92. Proportion of people experiencing different forms of personal enrichment on a regular basis
Personal relationships	Provision of services supporting physical and social independence	93. Percentage of national and local budgets devoted to disabled people (physical and mental)
	Personal support services	94. Level of pre and post-school child care
	Support for social interaction	95. Extent of inclusiveness of housing and environmental design (e.g. meeting places, lighting, layout)

Source: Herrmann (2003)

Bibliography

Abel-Smith, B. (1965) *The Poor and the Poorest*, London, Bell.

Abrahamson, P. (1997) Combating poverty and social exclusion in Europe, in Beck, W., van der Maesen, L. and Walker, A. (eds) *The Social Quality of Europe*, The Hague, Kluwer Law International.

Albrecht, G. and Devlieger, P. (1998) The disability paradox: high quality of life against all odds, *Social Science and Medicine*, 48, 977–88.

Albrecht, G. and Devlieger, P. (2000) Disability assumptions, concepts and theory: reply to Tom Koch, *Social Science and Medicine*, 50, 761–2.

Alkire, S. (2002a) Dimensions of Human Development, *World Development*, 30, 181–205.

Alkire, S. (2002b) *Valuing Freedoms: Sen's Capability Approach and Poverty Reduction*, Oxford, Oxford University Press.

Antonovsky, A. (1987) *Unravelling the Mystery of Health*, San Francisco, Jossey-Bass.

Argyle, M. (1996) Subjective well-being, in Offer, A. (ed.) *In Pursuit of the Quality of Life*, Oxford, Oxford University Press.

Argyle, M. (1999) Causes and correlates of happiness, in Kahneman, D., Diener, E. and Schwarz, N. (eds) *Well-Being: The Foundations of Hedonic Psychology*, New York, Sage.

Australian Bureau of Statistics (2003) *Measuring Social Capital*, Canberra, Australian Bureau of Statistics.

Baers, J., Beck, W., van der Maesen, L., Walker, A. and Herriman, P. (2005) *Renewing Aspects of the Social Quality Theory for Developing its Indicators*, Amsterdam, European Foundation on Social Quality.

Bannister, D. and Fransella, F. (1986) *Inquiring Man: The Psychology of Personal Constructs*, London, Croom Helm.

Barnes, C. and Mercer, G. (2004) *Implementing the Social Model of Disability: Theory and Practice*, Leeds, Disability Press.

Barry, B. (1998) *Social Isolation and the Distribution of Income*, London, London School of Economics.

Baum, F. (2000) Social capital, economic capital and power: further issues for a public health agenda, *Journal of Epidemiology and Community Health*, 54, 409–10.

Bauman, Z. (2000) Am I my brother's keeper? *European Journal of Social Work*, 3, 5–11.

Beck, W., van der Maesen, L. and Walker, A. (1997a) Introduction, in Beck, W., van der Maesen, L. and Walker, A. (eds) *The Social Quality of Europe*, The Hague, Kluwer Law International.

Beck, W., van der Maesen, L. and Walker, A. (1997a) *The Social Quality of Europe*, The Hague, Kluwer Law International.

Beck, W., van der Maesen, L. and Walker, A. (1997c) Social quality: from issue to concept, in Beck, W., van der Maesen, L. and Walker, A. (eds) *The Social Quality of Europe*, The Hague, Kluwer Law International.

Beck, W., van der Maesen, L., Thomése, F. and Walker, A. (eds) (2001a) *Social Quality: A Vision for Europe*, The Hague, Kluwer Law International.

Beck, W., van der Maesen, L., Thomése, G. and Walker, A. (2001b) Introduction: who and what is the European Union for? in Beck, W., van der Maesen, L., Thomése, G. and Walker, A. (eds) *Social Quality: A Vision for Europe*, The Hague, Kluwer Law International.

Beck, W., van der Maesen, L. and Walker, A. (2001c) Theorizing social quality: the concept's validity, in Beck, W., van der Maesen, L., Thomése, G. and Walker, A. (eds) *Social Quality: A Vision for Europe*, The Hague, Kluwer Law International.

Becker, G. (1996) *Accounting for Tastes*, Cambridge, MA, Harvard University Press.

Berger, P. (ed.) (1998) *The Limits of Social Cohesion: Conflict and Mediation in Pluralist Societies, A Report of the Bertelsmann Foundation to the Club of Rome*, Boulder, CO, Westview Press.

Berger-Schmitt, R. (2000) Social cohesion as an aspect of the quality of societies: concept and measurement, *Euroreporting Working Paper #14*, Mannheim, Centre for Survey Research and Methodology (ZUMA).

Berger-Schmitt, R. (2002) Considering social cohesion in quality of life assessments: concept and measurements, *Social Indicators Research*, 58, 403–28.

Berger-Schmitt, R. and Noll, H. (2000) Conceptual framework and structure of a European system of social indicators, *Euroreporting Working Paper #9*, Mannheim, Centre for Survey Research and Methodology (ZUMA).

Berghman, J. (1995) Social exclusion in Europe: policy context and analytical framework, in Room, G. (ed.) *Beyond the Threshold: The Measurement and Analysis of Social Exclusion*, Bristol, Polity.

Berkman, L. and Glass, T. (2000) Social integration, social networks, social support and health, in Berkman, L. and Kawachi, I. (eds) *Social Epidemiology*, New York, Oxford University Press.

Berlin, I. (1969) Two concepts of liberty, in Berlin, I. *Four Essays on Liberty*, London, Oxford University Press.

Berman, Y. and Phillips, D. (2000) Indicators of social quality and social exclusion at national and community level, *Social Indicators Research*, 50, 329–50.

Berman, Y. and Phillips, D. (2004) Indicators for Social Cohesion, 5th Draft, *EFSQ Working Paper*, Amsterdam, EFSQ.

Bernard, P. (1999) Social cohesion: a critique, *CPRN Discussion Paper #F09*, Ottawa, Canadian Policy Research Networks.

Beveridge, W. (1942) *Social Insurance and Allied Services*, London, HMSO: Cmnd 6404.

Black, E. (1988) *The Social Politics of Anglo-Jewry 1880–1920*, Oxford, Blackwell.

Blanchflower, D. and Oswald, A. (2004a) Well-being over time in Britain and the USA, *Journal of Public Economics*, 88, 1,359–86.

Blanchflower, D. and Oswald, A. (2004b) Money, sex and happiness: an empirical study, *Scandinavian Journal of Economics*, 106, 393–415.

Blokland, T. (2000) Unravelling three of a kind: cohesion, community and solidarity, *Netherlands Journal of Social Sciences*, 36, 56–70.

Bolin, K., Lindgren, B., Lindstrom, M. and Nystedt, P. (2003) Investments in social capital

– implications of social interactions for the production of health, *Social Science and Medicine*, 56, 2379–90.

Bourdieu, P. (1986) The forms of capital, in Richardson, J. (ed.) *Handbook of Theory and Research for the Sociology of Education*, Westpoint, CT, Greenwood Press.

Bowling, A. (1991) *Measuring Health: A Review of Quality of Life Measurement Scales*, Buckingham, Open University Press.

Bowling, A. (1995a) *Measuring Disease: A Review of Disease-Specific Quality of Life Measurement Scales*, Buckingham, Open University Press.

Bowling, A. (1995b) What things are important in people's lives? A survey of the public's judgements to inform scales of health related quality of life, *Social Science and Medicine*, 41, 1,447–62.

Brehn, J. and Rahn, W. (1997) Individual-level evidence for the causes and consequences of social capital, *American Journal of Political Science*, 41, 999–1,023.

Breton, R., Reitz, J. and Valentine, V. (1980) *Cultural Boundaries and the Cohesion of Canada*, Montreal, Institute for Research on Public Policy.

Brickman, P., Coates, D. and Janoff-Bulman, R. (1978) Lottery winners and accident victims: is happiness relative? *Journal of Personality and Social Psychology*, 36, 917–27.

Broadbent, E. (2001) Ten propositions about equality and democracy, in Broadbent, E. (ed.) *Democratic Equality: What Went Wrong*, Toronto, University of Toronto Press.

Brocks, E. (2006) View from the chair, *Guardian*, 4 March, *http://www.guardian.co.uk/g2/ story/0,,1161436,00.html*

Brown, P. (2005) What is this Kyoto thing all about anyway? *Guardian*, 3 February.

Buckland, J. (1998) Social capital and sustainability of NGO intermediated development projects in Bangladesh, *Community Development Journal*, 33, 236–48.

Bulbolz, M., Eicher, J., Evers, J. and Sontag, S. (1980) A human ecological approach to quality of life: a conceptual framework and results of an empirical study, *Social Indicators Research* 7: 103–36.

Burchardt, T., Le Grand, J. and Piachaud, D. (1999) Social exclusion in Britain 1991–1995, *Social Policy and Administration*, 33, 227–44.

Byrne, D. (1999) *Social Exclusion*, Buckingham, Open University Press.

Campbell, C. (1999) *Social Capital and Health*, London, Health Education Authority.

Campbell, C. (2003) *Letting Them Die*, Oxford, James Currey.

Caughy, M., O'Campo, P. and Muntaner, C. (2003) When being alone might be better: neighbourhood poverty, social capital, and child mental health, *Social Science and Medicine*, 57, 223–37.

Clarke, D. (2003) Concepts and perceptions of human well-being: some evidence from South Africa, *Oxford Development Studies*, 31, 2, 173–96.

Coburn, D. (2000) Income inequality, social cohesion and the health status of populations: the role of neo-liberalism, *Social Science and Medicine*, 51, 135–46.

Coleman, J. (1988) Social capital in the creation of human capital, *American Journal of Sociology*, 94, S95–S120.

Collard, D. (2003) Research on well-being: some advice from Jeremy Bentham, *WeD Working Paper 2*, Bath, ESRC Research Group on Wellbeing in Developing Countries.

Council of Europe (1998) *Fighting Social Exclusion and Strengthening Social Cohesion in Europe*, Brussels, Council of Europe.

Cummins, R. (1996) The domains of life satisfaction: an attempt to order chaos, *Social Indicators Research*, 38, 303–28.

Cummins, R. (1997) *The Comprehensive Quality of Life Scale: Intellectual Disability, Fifth Edition*, Toorak, Deakin University School of Psychology.

Cummins, R., Gullone, E. and Lau, A. (2002) A model of subjective well-being homeo-stasis: the role of personality, in Gullone, E. and Cummins, R. (eds) *The Universality of Subjective Well-Being Indicators*, Dordrecht, Kluwer Academic.

da Costa, A. (1997) Social policy and competitiveness, in Beck, W., van der Maesen, L. and Walker, A. (eds) *The Social Quality of Europe*, The Hague, Kluwer Law International.

Dahrendorf, R. (1995) *Report on Wealth Creation and Social Cohesion in a Free Society*, London, Commission on Wealth Creation.

Dasgupta, P. and Weale, M. (1992) On measuring the quality of life, *World Development*, 20, 119–31.

Deaton, A. (2001) *Relative Deprivation, Income Inequality and Mortality*, Cambridge, MA, National Bureau of Economic Research.

de Haan, A. (1999) Social exclusion: towards a holistic understanding of deprivation, *Deutsche Stiftung für Internationale Entwicklung*, Villa Borsig Workshop Series.

Delanty, G. (1998) Reinventing community and citizenship in the global era: a critique of the communitarian concept of community, in Christodoulidis, E. (ed.) *Communit-arianism and Citizenship*, Aldershot, Avebury.

Deletant, D, (1995) *Ceauşescu and the Securitate: Coercion and Dissent in Romania, 1965–1989*, London, C. Hurst.

Diener, E. and Biswas-Diener, R. (2002) Will money increase subjective well-being? *Social Indicators Research*, 57, 119–69.

Diener, E. and Lucas, R. (1999) Personality and subjective well-being, in Kahneman, D., Diener, E. and Schwarz, N. (eds) *Well-Being: the Foundations of Hedonic Psychology*, New York, Sage.

Diener, E. and Oishi, S. (2000) Money and happiness: income and subjective well-being across nations, in Diener, E. and Suh, E. (eds) *Culture and Subjective Well-Being*, Cambridge, MA, MIT Press.

Diener, E. and Suh, E. (1999) National differences in subjective well-being, in Kahneman, D., Diener, E. and Schwarz, N. (eds) *Well-Being: The Foundations of Hedonic Psychology*, New York, Sage.

Diener, E. and Suh, E. (eds) (2000) *Culture and Subjective Well-Being*, Cambridge, MA, MIT Press.

Donovan, N. and Halpern, D. (2002) *Life Satisfaction: The State of Knowledge and Implications for Government*, London, UK Government Cabinet Office, Strategy Unit.

Douglass, L. (2002) *Health and Hygiene in the Nineteenth Century*, The Victorian Web, accessed April 2005, http://www.victorianweb.org/science/health/health10.html.

Doyal, L. and Gough, I. (1991) *A Theory of Human Need*, Basingstoke, Macmillan.

Dwyer, C. (1993) Construction of Muslim identity and the contesting of power, in Jackson, P. and Penrose, J. (eds) *Constructions of Race, Place and Nation*, London, UCL Press.

Easterlin, R. (2003) Explaining happiness, *Proceedings of the National Academy of Sciences of the United States of America*, 100, 1,176–83.

Fahey, T., Nolan, B. and Whelan, C. (2002) *Monitoring Living Conditions and Quality of Life in Europe: Developing the Conceptual Framework – Final Report*, Dublin, European Foundation for the Improvement of Living and Working Conditions.

Fairweather, A., Roncevic, B., Rydbjerg, M., Valentova, W. and Zajc, M. (2002) Recon-ceptualisation of social quality, *European Journal of Social Quality*, 3, 118–43.

Falk, I. and Kilpatrick, S. (2000) What is social capital? A study of interaction in a rural community, *Sociologica Ruralis*, 40, 87–110.

Fayers, P. and Machin, D. (2000) *Quality of Life: Assessment, Analysis and Interpretation*, Chichester, Wiley.

Feldman, D. (1994) *Englishmen and Jews: Social Relations and Political Culture, 1840–1914*, New Haven, CT, Yale University Press.

Feldman, T. and Assaf, S. (1999) *Social Capital: Conceptual Frameworks and Empirical Evidence – an Annotated Bibliography*, Washington, DC, World Bank.

Ferge, Z. (1997) A central European perspective on the social quality of Europe, in Beck, W., van der Maesen, L. and Walker, A. (eds) *The Social Quality of Europe*, The Hague, Kluwer Law International.

Fitzpatrick, R. (1996) Alternative approaches to the assessment of health-related quality of life, in Offer, A. (ed.) *In Pursuit of the Quality of Life*, Oxford, Oxford University Press.

Fraser, D. (2003) *The Evolution of the British Welfare State: A History of Social Policy Since the Industrial Revolution*, Basingstoke, Palgrave.

Fukuyama, F. (1995) *Trust: The Social Virtues and the Creation of Prosperity*, New York, Free Press.

Fukuyama, F. (1999) *The Great Disruption: Human Nature and the Reconstitution of Social Order*, London, Profile.

Fukuyama, F. (2001) Social capital, civil society and development, *Third World Quarterly*, 22, 7–20.

Gabriel, Z. and Bowling, A. (2004) Quality of life from the perspective of older people, *Ageing and Society*, 24, 675–91.

Gallie, D., Paugam, S. and Jacobs, S. (2003) Unemployment, poverty and social isolation: is there a vicious circle of social exclusion?, *European Societies*, 5, 1–32.

Gasper, D. (1997) Sen's capability approach and Nussbaum's capabilities ethic, *Journal of International Development*, 9, 281–302.

Gasper, D. (2002) Is Sen's capability approach an adequate basis for considering human development? *Review of Political Economy* 14: 435–61.

Gasper, D. (2004) *Subjective and Objective Well-being in Relation to Economic Inputs: Puzzles and Responses*, Bath: ESRC Research Group on Welfare in Developing Countries.

Gartner, L. (1960) *The Jewish Immigrant in England, 1870–1914*, London, Allen and Unwin.

Geddes, M. (1998) *Local Partnership: A Successful Partnership for Social Cohesion?* Luxembourg, Office for Official Publications of the European Communities.

George, V. and Wilding, P. (1976) *Ideology and Social Welfare*, London, Routledge and Kegan Paul.

GESIS (2005) *European System of Social Indicators*, German Social Science Infrastructure Services, accessed 23 May 2005, http://www.gesis.org/en/social_monitoring/social_indicators/data/EUSI/index.htm.

Giddens, A. (1998) *The Third Way*, Cambridge, Polity.

Godley, A. (1996) Jewish soft loan societies in New York and London and immigrant entrepreneurship, 1880–1914, *Business History*, 38, 101–16.

Gordon, D. (2000) *Poverty and Social Exclusion in Britain*, York, Joseph Rowntree Foundation.

Gordon, D. (2004) Editorial, *European Journal of Social Quality*, 5, 1/2.

Gordon, D. and Pantazis, C. (eds) (1997) *Breadline Britain in the 1990s*, Aldershot, Ashgate.

Gordon, D. and Townsend, P. (eds) (2000) *Breadline Europe: the Measurement of Poverty*, Bristol, Policy Press.

Gore, C. and Figueirdo, J. (1997) *Social Exclusion and Anti-Poverty Policy: A Debate*, Geneva, International Labour Office.

Gough, I. (1997) Social aspects of the European model and its economic consequences, in Beck, W., van der Maesen, L. and Walker, A. (eds) *The Social Quality of Europe*, The Hague, Kluwer Law International.

Gough, I. (1998) What are human needs? in Franklin, J. (ed.) *Social Policy and Social Justice*, Cambridge, Polity.

Gough, I. (1999) Social welfare and competitiveness: social versus system integration? in Gough, I. and Olofsson, G. (eds) *Capitalism and Social Cohesion*, Basingstoke, Macmillan.

Gough, I. (2000a) *Global Capital, Human Needs and Social Policies*, Basingstoke, Palgrave.

Gough, I. (2000b) Why do levels of human welfare vary across nations? in Gough, I. (ed.) *Global Capital, Human Needs and Social Policies*, Basingstoke, Palgrave.

Gough, I. (2003) *Lists and Thresholds: Comparing the Doyal-Gough Theory of Human Need with Nussbaum's Capabilities Approach*, WeD Working Paper 1, Bath, ESRC Research Group on Wellbeing in Developing Countries.

Gough, I. (2004a) Welfare regimes in development contexts: a global and regional analysis, in Gough, I. and Wood, G. (eds.) *Insecurity and Welfare Regimes in Asia, Africa and Latin America: Social Policy in Development Contexts*, Cambridge: Cambridge University Press.

Gough, I. (2004b) Human well-being and social structures: relating the universal and the local, *Global Social Policy*, 4, 289–311.

Gough, I. and Olofsson, G. (1999) Introduction: new thinking on exclusion and integration, in Gough, I. and Olofsson, G. (eds) *Capitalism and Social Cohesion*, Basingstoke, Macmillan.

Gough, I. and Thomas, T. (1994) Why do levels of human welfare vary among nations?, *International Journal of Health Services*, 24, 715–48.

Gough, I. and Wood, G. (2004) *Insecurity and Welfare Regimes in Asia, Africa and Latin America: Social Policy in Development Contexts*, Cambridge: Cambridge University Press.

Gradstein, M. and Justman, M. (2000) Human capital, social capital and public schooling, *European Economic Review*, 44, 879–90.

Granovetter, M. (1973) The strength of weak ties, *American Journal of Sociology*, 78, 1,360–80.

Gravelle, H. (1998) How much of the relation between population mortality and unequal distribution of income is a statistical artefact? *British Medical Journal*, 316, 382–5.

Greeley, A. (1997) Coleman revisited: religious structures as a source of social capital, *American Behavioral Scientist*, 40, 587–94.

Griffin, J. (1986) *Well Being: Its Meaning, Measurement and Moral importance*, Oxford, Oxford University Press.

Griffin, J. (1996) *Value Judgement: Improving our Ethical Beliefs*, Oxford, Clarendon Press.

Grootaert, C. (1997) Social capital: the missing link? in *Expanding the Measure of Wealth: Indicators of Environmentally Sustainable Development*, Washington DC, World Bank.

Grundy, E. and Bowling, A. (1999) Enhancing the quality of extended life years. Identification of the oldest old with a very good and very poor quality of life, *Aging and Mental Health*, 3, 199–212.

Guiton, E. (2004) 'Would I trade my life now for the old me? I'd be surprisingly reluctant', *Guardian*, 24 March, *http://www.guardian.co.uk/g2/story/0,,673393,00.html.*

Hagerty, M., Cummins, R., Ferriss, A., Land, K., Michalos, A., Peterson, M., Sharpe, A., Sirgy, J. and Vogel, J. (2001) Quality of life indexes for national policy: review and agenda for research, *Social Indicators Research*, 55, 1–96.

Hall, P. (1999) Social capital in Britain, *British Journal of Political Science*, 29, 417–61.

Hancock, T. (1993) Health, human development and the community ecosystem: three ecological models, *Health Promotion International*, 8, 41–7.

Hancock, T. (2001) People, partnership and human progress: building community capital, *Health Promotion International*, 16, 275–80.

Hancock, T. and Perkins, F. (1985) The Mandala of health: a conceptual model and teaching tool, *Health Promotion*, 24, 8–10.

Hawe, P. and Shiell, A. (2000) Social capital and health promotion: a review, *Social Science and Medicine*, 51, 871–85.

Hawes, D. (1996) *The Gypsies and the State: The Ethnic Cleansing of British Society*, Bristol, Policy Press.

Hayek, F. von (1944) *The Road to Serfdom*, London, Routledge and Kegan Paul.

Hero, R. (2003) Multiple theoretical traditions in American politics and racial policy inequality, *Political Research Quarterly*, 56, 401–8.

Herrmann, R. (2003) *Discussion Paper on the Domain Empowerment*, 3rd Draft, Amsterdam, ENIQ.

Huxley, A (1932) *Brave New World*, London, Heinemann.

Inglehart, R., Basanez, M. and Moreno, A. (1998) *Human Values and Beliefs: A Cross-Cultural Sourcebook*, Ann Arbor, MI, University of Michigan Press.

Inglehart, R. and Klingermann, H. (2000) Genes, culture, democracy and happiness, in Diener, E. and Suh, E. (eds) *Culture and Subjective Well-Being*, Cambridge, MA, MIT Press.

Jenson, J. (1998) *Mapping Social Cohesion: The State of Canadian Research*, Ottowa, Renouf.

Joppke, C. and Lukes, S. (1999) Introduction: multicultural questions, in Joppke, C. and Lukes, S. (eds) *Multicultural Questions*, Oxford, Oxford University Press.

Jordan, B. (1996) *A Theory of Poverty and Social Exclusion*, Cambridge, Polity.

Judge, K. and Paterson, I. (2001) *Poverty, Income Inequality and Health*, Wellington, NZ, New Zealand Government, Treasury Working Paper 01/29.

Kahneman, D. (1999) Objective happiness, in Kahneman, D., Diener, E. and Schwarz, N. (eds) *Well-Being: The Foundations of Hedonic Psychology*, New York, Sage.

Kahneman, D., Wakker, P. and Sarin, R. (1997) Back to Bentham? Explorations of experienced utility, *Quarterly Journal of Economics*, 112, 375–405.

Kawachi, I. (2000) Income inequality and health, in Berkman, L. and Kawachi, I. (eds) *Social Epidemiology*, New York, Oxford University Press.

Kawachi, I. and Berkman, L. (2000) Social cohesion, social capital and health, in Berkman, L. and Kawachi, I. (eds) *Social Epidemiology*, New York, Oxford University Press.

Kawachi, I. and Kennedy, B. (1997) Socioeconomic determinants of health: health and social cohesion: why care about income inequality? *British Medical Journal*, 314, 1,037–40.

Kawachi, I., Kennedy, B., Gupta, V. and Prothrow-Stith, D. (1999) Women's status and the health of women and men: a view from the States, *Social Science and Medicine*, 48, 21–32.

Kawachi, I., Kennedy, B., Lochner, K. and Prothrow-Stith, D. (1997) Social capital, income inequality and mortality, *American Journal of Public Health*, 87, 1,491–8.

Kawachi, I., Kim, D., Coutts, A. and Subramanian, S. (2004) Commentary: reconciling the three accounts of social capital, *International Journal of Epidemiology*, 33, 682–90.

Kay, F. and Bernard, P. (forthcoming) The structure and dynamics of social capital: who wants to stay in if nobody is to be out?, in Kay, F. and Johnston, R. (eds) *Diversity, Social Capital and the Welfare State*, Toronto, University of Toronto Press.

Keizer, M. and van der Maesen, L.J.G. (2003) *Social Quality and the Component of Socio-economic Security*. 3rd draft. Working Paper, Amsterdam, ENIQ.

Kennedy, B. (1998) The role of social capital in the Russian mortality crisis, *World Development*, 26, 2,029–43.

Kennelly, B., O'Shea, E. and Garvey, E. (2003) Social capital, life expectancy and mortality: a cross-national examination, *Social Science and Medicine*, 56, 2,367–77.

Kershaw, I. (2000) *Hitler, 1936–45: Nemesis*, London, Allen Lane.

Klasen, S. (2001) Social exclusion, children and education, *European Societies*, 3, 413–47.

Klitgaarde, R. and Fedderke, J. (1995) Social integration and disintegration: an exploratory analysis of cross-country data, *World Development*, 23, 357–69.

Knack, S. and Keefer, P. (1997) Does social capital have an economic payoff? A cross-country investigation, *Quarterly Journal of Economics*, 112, 1,251–88.

Koch, T. (2000) The illusion of paradox: commentary on Albrecht, G. and Devlieger, P. (1998) The disability paradox: high quality of life against all odds, *Social Science and Medicine* 48, 977–988, *Social Science and Medicine*, 50, 757–9.

Koch, T. (2001) Equality and disability symposium on disability and difference: balancing social and physical constructions, *Journal and Medical Ethics*, 27, 370–6.

Kymlicka, W. (ed.) (1995) *The Rights of Minority Cultures*, Oxford, Oxford University Press.

Layard, R. (2004) *Happiness and Public Policy*, London, LSE Health and Social Care Discussion Paper number 14.

Layard, R. (2005) *Happiness: Lessons from a New Science*, London, Allen Lane.

Layte, R. and Whelan, C. (2003) Moving in and out of poverty: the impact of welfare regimes on poverty dynamics in the EU, *European Societies*, 5, 167–91.

Leibfried, S. (1998) Spins of (dis)integration: what might 'reformers' in Canada learn from the 'social dimension' of the European Union? *Social Policy and Administration*, 32, 365–88.

Leonard, M. (2004) Bonding and bridging social capital: reflections from Belfast, *Sociology*, 38, 927–44.

Levitas, R. (2000) What is social exclusion? in Gordon, D. and Townsend, P. (eds) *Breadline Europe: The Measurement of Poverty*, Bristol, Policy Press.

Limage, L. (2000) Education and Muslim identity: the case of France, *Comparative Education*, 36, 73–94.

Lindstrom, B. (1992) Quality of life: a model for evaluating health for all, *Soz Praventivmed*, 37, 301–6.

Lipman, V. (1954) *Social History of the Jews in England 1850–1950*, London, Watts.

Lister, R. (2004) *Poverty*, Cambridge, Polity.

Lockwood, D. (1999) Civic integration and social cohesion, in Gough, I. and Olofsson, G. (eds) *Capitalism and Social Cohesion*, Basingstoke, Macmillan.

Lynch, J., Davey Smith, G., Harper, S., Hillemeier, M., Ross, N., Kaplan, G., and Wolfson, M. (2004) Is income inequality a determinant of population health? Part 1: a systematic review, *Millbank Quarterly*, 82, 5–99.

Lynch, J., Due, P., Muntaner, C. and Davey Smith, G. (2000) Social capital – is it a good investment strategy for public health? *Journal of Epidemiology and Community Health*, 54, 404–8.

Macinko, J. and Starfield, B. (2001) The utility of social capital in research on health determinants, *Milbank Quarterly*, 79, 387–427.

Marshall, T. H. (1972) Value problems of welfare capitalism, *Journal of Social Policy*, 1, 15–32.

Maxwell, J. (1996) Social dimensions of economic growth: Eric John Hanson memorial lecture, Vol. III, Alberta, University of Alberta.

McCrystal, P., Higgins, K. and Percy, A. (2001) Measuring social exclusion: a lifespan approach, *Radical Statistics*, 76, 3–14.

Monk, W. (1862) *Hymns, Ancient and Modern, for Use in the Services of the Church, with Accompanying Tunes*, London, Novello.

Morreim, H. (1992) The impossibility and the necessity of quality of life research, *Bioethics*, 6, 218–32.

Morris, W. (1970) *News from Nowhere: Or An Epoch of Rest: Being Some Chapters from a Utopian Romance*, London, Routledge and Kegan Paul.

Muntaner, C. and Lynch, J. (1999) Income inequality, social cohesion and class relations: a critique of Wilkinson's neo-Durkheimian research programme, *International Journal of Health Services*, 29, 59–81.

Muntaner, C., Lynch, J. and Smith, G. (2001) Social capital, disorganised communities, and the third way: understanding the retreat from structural inequalities in epidemiology and public health, *International Journal of Health Services*, 31, 213–37.

Murray, C. (2002) The war against poverty, in Pierson, C. and Castles, F. (eds) *The Welfare State Reader*, Cambridge, Polity.

Narayan, D. (1999) *Bonds and Bridges: Social Capital and Poverty*, Washington, DC, World Bank.

Noll, H. (2000) Social Indicators and Social Reporting: the international experience, in Canadian Council on Social Development (ed.) *Symposium on Measuring Well-Being and Social Indicators*, Ottawa.

Noll, H. (2002) Towards a European system of social indicators: theoretical framework and system architecture, *Social Indicators Research*, 58, 47–87.

Nussbaum, M. (1995) Human capabilities, female human beings, in Nussbaum, M. and Glover, J. (eds) *Women, Culture and Development: A Study of Human Capabilities*, Oxford, Oxford University Press.

Nussbaum, M. (2000) *Women and Human Development: The Capabilities Approach*, Cambridge, Cambridge University Press.

Nussbaum, M. (2004) On hearing women's voices: a reply to Susan Okin, *Philosophy and Public Affairs*, 32, 193–205.

Nussbaum, M. (2006) *Frontiers of Justice; Disability, Nationality, Species Membership*, Cambridge, MA, Harvard University Press.

OECD (2001) *The Well-Being of Nations: The Role of Human and Social Capital*, Paris, OECD Centre for Educational Research and Innovation.

Oldfield, A. (1990) *Citizenship and Community: Civic Republicanism and the Modern World*, London, Routledge.

Pahl, R. (1991) The search for social cohesion: from Durkheim to the European Commission, *Archives Européennes de Sociologie*, 32, 345–60.

Palmer, G., Rahman, M. and Kenway, P. (2002) *Monitoring Poverty and Social Exclusion 2002*, York, Joseph Rowntree Foundation.

Parekh, B. (1995) The Rushdie affair: research agenda for political philosophy, in Kymlicka, W. (ed.) *The Rights of Minority Cultures*, Oxford, Oxford University Press.

Peled, Y. (1992) Ethnic democracy and the legal construction of citizenship: Arab citizens of the Jewish state, *American Political Science Review*, 86, 432–43.

Percy-Smith, J. (ed.) (2000) *Policy Responses to Social Exclusion: Social Inclusion?* Buckingham, Open University Press.

Phillips, D. (2001) Social capital, social cohesion and social quality, paper presented at European Sociological Association Conference 2001: Social Policy Network, Helsinki.

Phillips, D. (2002) Community citizenship and community social quality: the British Jewish community at the turn of the twentieth century, *European Journal of Social Quality*, 3, 1/2, 26–47.

Phillips, D. and Berman, Y. (2001a) Social quality and community citizenship, *European Journal of Social Work*, 4, 17–28.

Phillips, D. and Berman, Y. (2001b) Social quality: definitional, conceptual and operational issues, in Beck, W., van der Maesen, L., Thomése, G. and Walker, A. (eds) *Social Quality: A Vision for Europe*, The Hague, Kluwer Law International.

Phillips, D. and Berman, Y. (2003) Social quality and ethnos communities: concepts and indicators, *Community Development Journal*, 38, 344–57.

Portes, A. (1998) Social capital: its origins, and applications in modern sociology, *Annual Review of Sociology*, 24, 1–24.

Purdue, D. (2001) Neighbourhood governance: leadership, trust and social capital, *Urban Studies*, 38, 2,211–24.

Putnam, R. (1993a) *Making Democracy Work: Civic Traditions in Modern Italy*, Princeton, NJ, Princeton University Press.

Putnam, R. (1993b) The prosperous community: social capital and public life, *American Prospect*, 13, 35–42.

Putnam, R. (2000) *Bowling Alone: The Collapse and Revival of American Community*, New York, Touchstone.

Putnam, R. (2004) Commentary: 'Health by association': some comments, *International Journal of Epidemiology*, 33, 667–71.

Qizilbash, M. (1997a) Needs, incommensurability and well-being, *Review of Political Economy*, 9, 261–76.

Qizilbash, M. (1997b) Pluralism and well-being indices, *World Development*, 25, 2,009–26.

Qizilbash, M. (1998) The concept of well-being, *Economics and Philosophy*, 14, 51–73.

Raphael, D., Renwick, R., Brown, I. and Rootman, I. (1996) Quality of life indicators and health: current status and emerging conceptions, *Social Indicators Research*, 39, 65–88.

Raphael, D., Renwick, R., Brown, I. Steinmetz, B., Sehdev, H and Phillips, S. (2001) Making the links between community structure and individual well-being: community quality of life in Riverdale, Toronto, Canada, *Health & Place*, 7, 179–96.

Rapley, M. (2003) *Quality of Life Research: A Critical Introduction*, London, Sage.

Ratcliffe, P. (1999) Housing inequality and 'race': some critical reflections on the concept of 'social exclusion', *Ethnic and Racial Studies*, 22, 1–22.

Rawls, J. (1998) Justice as fairness in the liberal polity, in Shafir, G. (ed.) *The Citizenship Debates: A Reader*, Minneapolis, University of Minnesota Press.

Richardson, L. and Le Grand, J. (2002) Outsider and insider expertise: the response of residents of deprived neighbourhoods to an academic definition of social exclusion, *Social Policy and Administration*, 36, 496–515.

Rioux, M. and Hay, D. (1993) Well-being: a conceptual framework, in *Well-Being: A Conceptual Framework and Three Literature Reviews*, Vancouver, Social Planning and Research Council.

Robeyns, I. (2003) Valuing freedoms: Sen's capability approach and poverty reduction, *Economics and Philosophy*, 19: 371–7.

Rogerson, R. (1995) Environmental and health-related quality of life: conceptual and methodological similarities, *Social Science and Medicine*, 41, 1373–82.

Rogerson, R., Findlay, A., Paddison, R. and Morris, A. (1996) Class, consumption and quality of life, *Progress in Planning*, 45, 1–66.

Room, G. (ed.) (1995a) *Beyond the Threshold: The Measurement and Analysis of Social Exclusion*, Bristol, Policy.

Room, G. (1995b) Poverty and social exclusion: the new European agenda for policy and research, in Room, G. (ed.) *Beyond the Threshold: the Measurement and Analysis of Social Exclusion*, Bristol, Policy.

Room, G. (1999) Social exclusion, solidarity and the challenge of globalisation, *International Journal of Social Welfare*, 9, 103–19.

Rose, R. (2000) How much does social capital add to individual health? A survey study of Russians, *Social Science and Medicine*, 51, 1,421–35.

Rosegreen, A., Orth-Gomer, K., Wedel, H. Wilhelnsen, L. (1993) Stressful life events, social support, and mortality in men born in 1933, *British Medical Journal*, 307, 1,102–5.

Rosenberg, R. (1995) Health-related quality of life between naturalism and hermeneutics, *Social Science and Medicine*, 41, 1,411–15.

Rothstein, B. and Uslaner, E. (2005) *All for All: Equality and Social Trust*, London, LSE.

Runciman, W. (1966) *Relative Deprivation and Social Justice: A Study of Attitudes to Inequality in Twentieth Century England*, London, Routledge and Kegan Paul.

Ryan, R. and Deci, E. (2001) On happiness and human potentials: a review of research on hedonic and eudaimonic well-being, *Annual Review of Psychology*, 52, 141–66.

Ryff, C. and Keyes, C. (1995) The structure of psychological well-being revisited, *Journal of Personality and Social Psychology*, 69, 719–27.

Sachs, J. (2005) *The End of Poverty: How We Can Make it Happen in Our Lifetime*, London, Penguin.

Sainsbury, E. (1977) *The Personal Social Services*, London, Pitman.

Sampson, R., Morenoff, J. and Earls, F. (1999) Beyond social capital: spatial dynamics of collective efficacy for children, *American Sociological Review*, 64, 633–60.

Saraceno, C. (1997) The importance of the concept of social exclusion, in Beck, W., van der Maesen, L. and Walker, A. (eds) *The Social Quality of Europe*, The Hague, Kluwer Law International.

Schuster, L. and Solomos, J. (2001) Introduction: citizenship, multiculturalism, identity, *Patterns of Prejudice*, 35, 3–12.

Scitovsky, T. (1976) *The Joyless Economy*, New York, Oxford University Press.

Sen, A. (1982) *Choice, Welfare and Measurement*, Oxford, Blackwell.

Sen, A. (1993) Capability and well-being, in Nussbaum, M. and Sen, A. (eds) *The Quality of Life*, Oxford, Clarendon Press.

Sen, A. (1995) Gender inequality and theories of justice, in Nussbaum, M. and Glover, J. (eds) *Women, Culture and Development: A Study of Human Capabilities*, Oxford, Oxford University Press.

Shafir, G. and Peled, Y. (1998) Citizenship and stratification in an ethnic democracy, *Ethnic and Racial Studies*, 21, 408–27.

Shaw, A. (1988) *A Pakistani Community in Britain*, Oxford, Blackwell.

Silver, H. (1994) Social exclusion and social solidarity: three paradigms, *International Labour Review*, 133, 531–77.

Smith, A. (1812) *An Inquiry into the Nature and Causes of the Wealth of Nations*, London, Baynes

Stanley, D. (1999) Hearing secret harmonies: towards a dynamic model of social cohesion, paper presented at Fourth International Metropolis Conference, Georgetown University, Washington, DC.

Steinert, H. (2003) Introduction: the culture of welfare and exclusion, in Steinert, H. and Pilgrim, A. (eds) *Welfare Policy from Below: Struggles Against Social Exclusion in Europe*, Aldershot, Ashgate.

Steinert, H. and Pilgrim, A. (2003) *Welfare Policy from Below: Struggles Against Social Exclusion in Europe*, Aldershot, Ashgate.

Stewart, F. (1996) Basic needs, capabilities, and human development, in Offer, A. (ed.) *In Pursuit of the Quality of Life*, Oxford, Oxford University Press.

Svendsen, G.L.H. and Svendsen, G.T. (2004) *The Creation and Destruction of Social Capital: Entrepreneurship, Co-operative Movements and Institutions*, Cheltenham, Edward Elgar.

Svetlik, I. (1999) Some conceptual and operational considerations on the social quality of Europe, *European Journal of Social Quality*, 1, 74–89.

Szreter, S. and Woolcock, M. (2004) Health by association? Social capital, social theory, and the political economy of public health, *International Journal of Epidemiology*, 33, 650–67.

Thatcher, M. (1987) There is no such thing as society, *Woman's Own*.

Titmuss, R. (1963) *Essays on 'the Welfare State'*, London, Allen and Unwin.

Titmuss, R. (1968) *Commitment to Welfare*, London, Allen and Unwin.

Tönnies, F. (1957) *Community and Society (Gemeinschaft und Gesellschaft)*, East Lancing, MI, Michigan State University Press.

Townsend, P. (1967) *Poverty, Socialism and Labour in Power*, London, Fabian Society.

Townsend, P. (1979) *Poverty in the United Kingdom*, Harmondsworth, Penguin.

Townsend, P. (1985) A sociological approach to the measurement of poverty – a rejoinder, *Oxford Economic Papers – New Series*, 37, 659–68.

Townsend, P. and Gordon, D. (1991) What is enough? New evidence on poverty allowing the definition of a minimum benefit, in Alder, M., Bell, C., Clasen, J. and Sinfield, A. (eds) *The Sociology of Social Security*, Edinburgh, Edinburgh University Press.

Townsend, P. and Gordon, D. (2000) Introduction: the measurement of poverty in Europe, in Gordon, D. and Townsend, P. (eds) *Breadline Europe: The Measurement of Poverty*, Bristol, Policy Press.

Townsend, P. and Gordon, D. (eds) (2002) *World Poverty: New Policies to Defeat an Old Enemy*, Bristol, Policy Press.

Uslaner, E. (2002) *The Moral Foundations of Trust*, Cambridge, Cambridge University Press.

Uslaner, E. (2004) Trust and social bonds: faith in others and policy outcomes reconsidered, *Political Research Quarterly*, 57, 501–7.

Uslaner, E. and Conley, R. (2003) Civic engagement and particularised trust – the ties that bind people to their ethnic communities, *American Politics Research*, 31, 331–60.

UNDP (1990) *Human Development Report*, Oxford, Oxford University Press.

van der Maesen, L., Walker, A. and Keizer, M. (2005) *European Network Indicators of Social Quality – ENIQ – 'Social Quality': The Final Report*, Amsterdam, European Foundation on Social Quality.

van der Mass, P., van der Wal, G., Haverkate, I., de Graaff, C. Kester, J. *et al.* (1996) Euthanasia, physician-assisted suicide and other medical practices involving the end of life in the Netherlands, 1990–1995, *New England Journal of Medicine*, 335, 1,699–705.

Vasta, E. (2000) The politics of community, in Vasta, E. (ed.) *Citizenship, Community and Democracy*, New York, St Martin's Press.

Veenhoven, R. (1996) Happy life expectancy: a comprehensive measure of quality-of-life in nations, *Social Indicators Research*, 39, 1–58.

Veenhoven, R. (2003) Hedonism and happiness, *Journal of Happiness Studies*, 4, 437–57.

Veenstra, G. (2000) Social capital, SES and health: an individual-level analysis, *Social Science and Medicine*, 50, 619–29.

Veenstra, G., Luginaah, I., Wakefield, S., Birch, S., Eyles, J. and Elliott, S. (2005) Who you know, where you live: social capital, neighbourhood and health, *Social Science and Medicine*, 60, 2799–818.

Vertovec, S. (1997) Social cohesion and tolerance, paper presented at Second International Metropolis Conference, Copenhagen.

Vertovec, S. (1999) Introduction, in Vertovec, S. (ed.) *Migration and Social Cohesion*, Cheltenham, Edward Elgar.

Vobruba, G. (2000) Actors in processes of inclusion and exclusion: towards a dynamic approach, *Social Policy and Administration*, 34, 601–13.

Vonnegut, K. (1994) *Vonnegut Omnibus: 'Welcome to the Monkey House', 'Palm Sunday'*, London, Vintage.

Wakefield, S. and Poland, B. (2005) Family, friend or foe? Critical reflections on the relevance and role of social capital in health promotion and community development, *Social Science and Medicine*, 60, 2,819–32.

Walker, A. (1998) The Amsterdam declaration on the social quality of Europe, *European Journal of Social Work*, 1, 109–11.

Walker, A. and Wigfield, A. (2003) *The Social Inclusion Component of Social Quality*, Amsterdam, EFSQ.

Warburton, D. (1996) The functions of pleasure, in Warburton, D. and Sherwood, N. (eds) *Pleasure and Quality of Life*, Chichester, Wiley.

Washington, J. and Paylor, I. (1998) Europe, social exclusion and the identity of social work, *European Journal of Social Work*, 1, 327–38.

Waterman, A. (1993) Two concepts of happiness: contrasts of personal expressiveness and hedonic enjoyment, *Journal of Personality and Social Psychology*, 64, 678–91.

Werbner, P. (1990) Manchester Pakistanis: division and unity, in Clarke, C., Peach, C. and Vertovec, S. (eds) *South Asians Overseas*, Cambridge, Cambridge University Press.

Wessels, B. and Miedema, S. (2002) Towards understanding situations of social exclusion, in Steinert, H. and Pilgrim, A. (eds) *Welfare Policy from Below: Struggles Against Social Exclusion in Europe*, Aldershot, Ashgate.

Whitehead, M. (1992) *The Health Divide*, London, Penguin.

WHOQOL Group (1995) The World Health Organisation Quality of Life Assessment (WHOQOL): position paper from the World Health Organisation, *Social Science and Medicine*, 41, 1403–9.

Wiggins, D. (1998) *Need, Values, Truth,* Oxford, Clarendon Press.

Wilkinson, R. (1996) *Unhealthy Societies: The Afflictions of Inequality*, London, Routledge.

Wilkinson, R. (1999) Income inequality, social cohesion and health: clarifying the theory – a reply to Muntaner and Lynch, *International Journal of Health Services*, 29, 525–43.

Wilkinson, R. (2000) Inequality and the social environment: a reply to Lynch *et al.*, *Journal of Epidemiology and Community Health*, 54, 411–13.

Wilkinson, R. (2005) *The Impact of Inequality: How to Make Sick Societies Healthier*, New York, New Press.

Wilkinson, R., Kawachi, I. and Kennedy, B. (1998) Mortality, the social environment, crime and violence, *Sociology of Health and Illness*, 20, 578–97.

Willitts, M., Benzeval, M. and Stansfeld, S. (2004) Partnership history and mental health over time, *Journal of Epidemiology and Community Health*, 58, 53–8.

Wittgenstein, L. (1953) *Philosophical Investigations*, Oxford, Blackwell.

Woodrow, P. (2001) Measuring quality of life, *Journal of Medical Ethics*, 27, 205.

Woolcock, M. (1998) Social capital and economic development: towards a theoretical synthesis and policy framework, *Theory and Society*, 27, 151–208.

Woolcock, M. and Narayan, D. (2000) Social capital: implications for development theory, research and policy, *World Bank Research Observer*, 15, 225–49.

Woolley, F. (2001) Social cohesion and the voluntary sector, in Osberg, L. (ed.) *Teams Work Better: The Economic Implications of Social Cohesion*, Toronto, University of Toronto Press.

World Bank (1998) *The Initiative on Defining, Monitoring and Measuring Social Capital: Overview and Program Description*, New York, World Bank.

Young, M. and Willmott, P. (1986) *Family and Kinship in East London*, Harmondsworth, Penguin.

Index